D1052928

# Brotherhood
# of Arms

# Brotherhood of Arms

*General Dynamics
and the Business
of Defending America*

by Jacob Goodwin

𝕿imes BOOKS

**Library of Congress Cataloging in Publication Data**

Goodwin, Jacob B.
  Brotherhood of arms.

  Includes index.
  1. General Dynamics Corporation.  2. Munitions—
United States.  I. Title.
HD9743.U5G464  1985     338.76234'0973     85-40268
ISBN 0-8129-1151-2

Manufactured in the United States of America
9 8 7 6 5 4 3 2
First Edition

My son, Gabriel, was born and my father, Paul, died while I was completing this book. I dedicate it to both of them, with bright hopes for the future and cherished memories of the past.

# Acknowledgments

I now understand why author acknowledgments are usually so bountiful in their praise. It simply would not be possible for an author to complete a major book without the active encouragement of a large group of friends, family members, and professional associates. I am indeed fortunate to be surrounded by such a group.

I'd like to thank my agent, Raphael Sagalyn, who took an immediate interest in this project and has stood behind it ever since; Jonathan Segal, editor in chief at Times Books, who combines the wisdom of Solomon with the patience of Job; Ruth Fecych, my industrious editor, who cheerfully put up with countless missed deadlines and nevertheless managed to pull this book together; and the rest of the staff at Times Books and Random House, Inc., who copyedited, designed, and marketed this book with great skill and professionalism.

I could not have written this book without the help of two wonderful women, Pat McNees and Chris Herdell. Pat's editorial judgments were firm and authoritative, but at the same time gentle and understanding. Chris was not only a tireless, dedicated typist but also a much needed morale booster.

I spent more days than I care to remember working in libraries throughout the Washington, D.C., area. I am particularly grateful to the courteous, cooperative, and efficient staffs at the Pentagon library, Library of Congress, National Archives, Office of Air Force History, and many local libraries in northern Virginia.

Several people shared with me their special knowledge of the defense industry and reviewed portions of my manuscript. Among them are Rear Admiral Walter M. Locke (USN-Ret.), who knows more than anyone about the development of cruise missiles; David Berteau, a friend from my days in the Office of the Secretary of Defense, who displays a rare understanding of the bureaucratic process in the Pentagon; Richard A. Sauber, a former Justice Department prosecutor, who provided valuable insights into defense contract fraud; Colonel Alan C. Chase (USAF-Ret.), who described his experiences as head of the air-launched cruise missile program and as a congressional staff member; and Fred W. Geldon, an old friend and knowledgeable attorney who led me through the labyrinthine world of government contract claims. Others tutored me on naval ship design and tank procurement and reviewed relevant parts of my manuscript but asked not to be identified.

The General Dynamics Corporation, which consciously attempts to avoid the public spotlight, assisted me in the most minimal way. After turning down my repeated requests for more than a year, the company grudgingly offered me a single one-hour interview with the corporate officer of my choice. I asked to speak with GD's chairman, David S. Lewis, Jr. My conversation with Lewis took place at GD's corporate headquarters in Clayton, Missouri, and ran about three and a half hours.

In the course of my research I interviewed more than 100 people who understand the workings of the weapons business, and I thank them all for their invaluable assistance. I am grateful to each of them, yet lay on none of them responsibility for the accuracy or objectivity of what I've written. That burden is mine.

I want to thank Jean Levin and Beverly Nadel of The Work Place, Stephan Loewentheil, Ron Smith, Colonel Stephen Luster, Michael Gordon, Derek Vander Schaaf, Paul and Katherine Knox, and Debra Barclay.

I'm grateful to my mother, Rhea Goodwin, for the selfless love and unwavering encouragement she has always lavished upon me. And, finally, I want to thank my wife, Catherine Rossbach, a book editor who has held the hand of countless weary authors over the years, for sharing the pain with one more author under her own roof. I couldn't have done it without Catherine, nor would I have wanted to.

# Contents

# Introduction

Forty-seven cents out of every dollar in the Defense Department's budget request for 1986 were earmarked for the development or procurement of weapons and military hardware. Most of that money—about $146 *billion,* or nearly $2,400 for every family in the United States—will find its way into the coffers of the nation's defense contractors. Yet few people in the country understand how this huge sum is spent.

Americans read about outrageous cost overruns for sophisticated aircraft, tanks, missiles, and warships. They see news broadcasts about "superweapons" that refuse to work. They watch contractors charge the military services $600 for an aircraft toilet seat and $155 to board an executive's dog. And they hear about competitive "fly-offs" or "shoot-offs" of prototype weapons to determine which companies should win multibillion-dollar production contracts. But they are rarely exposed to the technical brainstorming, bureaucratic infighting, congressional lobbying, legal maneuvering, and aggressive salesmanship that characterize the world of U.S. weapons makers.

How are weapons conceived? Who decides what arms the Pentagon will buy? When and how do formal negotiations between contractors and the military services take place? Who actually selects the winning contractors? What roles do politicians, consultants, and private contract lawyers play? And why do costs skyrocket so frequently?

The U.S. defense industry is peopled neither by the warmongering arms merchants some cynics suggest nor by the high-minded businessmen some industry apologists would have the public believe. It is a competitive, profit-hungry industry that employs ingenious engineers, skillful marketers, shrewd cost analysts, savvy lobbyists, and highly paid attorneys. These people sign thousands of defense contracts, hire millions of employees, and gobble up roughly one-seventh of the federal budget each year. It is an industry too vast and important to be shrouded in mystery.

This book is about the arms business, *not* about the relative morality of war or about combat strategies, geopolitical alignments, or nuclear disarmament. It doesn't concentrate on the technology of weapons, though technology cannot be ignored in any examination of the defense industry.

My focus is the *business* of selling arms to the U.S. government. My goal: to present an insider's close-up of the people who sell weapons and the people who buy them, a candid look at the process through which the country arms itself.

I have tried to show how the defense industry operates by describing the methods and motives of the men who have shaped the General Dynamics Corporation, a defense contractor with 99,000 employees that embodies the essence of the industry—a giant among giants. With prime contracts totaling nearly $6 billion, GD was the Defense Department's third largest contractor in fiscal year 1984, the last year for which final figures are currently available.

More important, GD has maneuvered itself into the extraordinary position of supplying all three U.S. military services with major weapons systems. Defense contractors traditionally establish close ties with one branch of the military. The Grumman Corporation, for example, has long been linked to the Navy, the FMC Corporation has sold armored vehicles to the Army for decades, and Boeing has been an important supplier to the Air Force. Occasionally a defense contractor develops links to two services. McDonnell Douglas, for instance, currently sells F/A-18 Hornet fighter-attack aircraft and AV-8B Harrier vertical takeoff and landing aircraft to the Navy as well as F-15 Eagle fighters to the Air Force. But GD is the only contractor that currently sells major ground, sea, and air weapons systems to all three services.

GD sells the Army its principal weapon, the M-1 Abrams battle tank; the Navy its Trident missile-firing submarine as well as attack submarines and sea-launched cruise missiles; and the Air Force its leading lightweight fighter, the F-16 Fighting Falcon, plus ground- and air-launched cruise missiles.

To an unprecedented degree, General Dynamics has become America's most indispensable weapons manufacturer. In recent months it has also become the nation's most controversial defense contractor. Its activities have been criticized by the Pentagon, reviled on Capitol Hill, and investigated by the Department of Justice, the Internal Revenue Service, the Securities and Exchange Commission, and several congressional committees. In many ways, GD's story is the story of the entire defense industry.

# Brotherhood
# of Arms

# Chapter One

# General Dynamics and the Defense Industry

## (1)

David Sloan Lewis, Jr., the seasoned chairman of the General Dynamics Corporation, wrestled with an enormous decision in early 1978: Should Electric Boat, his company's shipbuilding division, openly confront its only customer, the U.S. Navy, by threatening to halt construction on sixteen new attack submarines? Had GD's long-running contract dispute with the Navy finally reached the breaking point?

The two had been fighting for years about who was responsible for the long delays and enormous cost overruns that plagued Electric Boat's shipbuilding program. Each side blamed the other. Electric Boat accused the Navy of supplying faulty submarine designs months behind schedule and then making more than 35,000 costly and time-consuming design changes. The Navy accused Electric Boat of poorly training its workers, grossly underestimating its construction costs, and mismanaging its shipyard in Groton, Connecticut. Admiral Hyman Rickover, who involved himself in almost every aspect of nuclear submarine design and construction, was merciless in his criticism of Electric Boat.

The disagreement had grown more heated in late 1976, when General Dynamics formally submitted a claim to the Navy for more than half a *billion* dollars to cover its unexpected costs. Outraged by GD's demand, the Navy had dragged its feet. Fifteen months later the company's claim was still unresolved.

In the meantime, Electric Boat had suffered losses of more than $370 million and was losing another $15 million each month the dispute dragged on. "We were just running out of money," Lewis recalled. "We all felt the Navy was blackmailing us by forcing our hand to settle."

Lewis was torn. General Dynamics had hired him in 1970 to recapture the prestige and prosperity it had once known. In the eight years Lewis had been chairman he had largely succeeded. When he had taken over, members of GD's board of directors were at war with one another. The company was still suffering from financial setbacks on several weapons programs and a series of bungled commercial ventures.

Lewis had cut unprofitable operations and centralized the management of GD's far-flung industrial empire, and the company had begun to win major weapons contracts again. By fiscal year 1977 GD had ranked eighth in sales among the Pentagon's largest defense contractors. A year later the firm ranked first. That year GD received $4.2 billion in prime contracts from the Defense Department, *more than any other company in the United States.*

Lewis had turned the company around, but he was now worried about the huge ongoing losses at his submarine yard. He knew that any move he made against the Navy might jeopardize GD's coveted position as the nation's leading defense contractor. He had to act, but he didn't know what to do. He had to defend GD's financial interests, but he couldn't bring himself to threaten the Navy publicly. "It was culturally difficult even to contemplate that kind of thing," he recalled later. During thirty-five years in the defense business he had developed a loyalty to his military customers that he couldn't easily disregard.

Only two private shipyards were capable of building nuclear-powered submarines for the Navy: the Newport News Shipbuilding and Dry Dock Company and Electric Boat. Both yards were critical to the nation's defense posture. How in good conscience could Lewis order one of those yards to stop building attack subs?

## (2)

The prominent company Lewis now ran had come a long way since its origin at the turn of the century. GD essentially started as a little firm called the Electric Boat Company, which in 1900 sold the U.S. Navy its first workable submarine, an ungainly fifty-three-foot vessel designed by an Irishman, John Holland.

Holland was a stubborn schoolteacher and tinkerer who had emigrated to New Jersey and spent decades developing and promoting his underwater warship. Initially his ideas met stiff resistance; the senior admirals who commanded America's surface fleet had wanted no part of the comically awkward vessels. "The Navy doesn't like submarines because there's no deck to strut on," Holland once said with a sneer.

The Navy was reluctant, but the public was thrilled by the exotic underwater warships. When President Theodore Roosevelt slipped away from his home at Sagamore Hill in 1905 to spend three hours aboard one of Electric Boat's earliest subs, the newspapers gave the President's daring underwater adventure front-page treatment.

Electric Boat was to become one division of General Dynamics. The Consolidated Aircraft Corporation, a pioneering aircraft company that began in 1923 under the aggressive leadership of Major Reuben Fleet, evolved into another. Through a complex series of mergers, reorganizations, and acquisitions, Consolidated was joined over the years by several other early aircraft manufacturers and their predecessor firms. This cluster of pioneering aircraft companies metamorphosed during World War II into the Consolidated Vultee Aircraft Corporation, or Convair, as it was known, which merged with General Dynamics in 1954.

In many ways the development of U.S. military aircraft and naval submarines followed similar patterns. "The genius of American inventors launched both the submarine and the airplane, yet because of official and public indifference headstarts in both were quickly lost to Europe," observed *Dynamic America,* a corporate history of General Dynamics and its predecessor companies published in 1960. "Submarines and aircraft met with continuing opposition from powerful groups within the armed forces of our country, but also had their fanatical and dedicated supporters in uniform and out of it."

The Army bought its first plane in 1909, but Congress and the War Department took little interest in the military potential of aircraft. The public's resistance to the hazardous new world of flight didn't relax until the introduction of cross-country airmail service and Charles Lindbergh's spectacular transatlantic flight in 1927.

One of the people responsible for getting the aircraft industry off the ground was Major Fleet, an aviation pioneer who, in 1918, organized the nation's first ragtag airmail service. After leaving the Army, Fleet founded Consolidated Aircraft (later Consolidated Vultee), which initially built trainers and seaplanes (then called flying boats) for the military as well as commercial passenger and cargo planes.

During World War II, as the Air Force emphasized long-range bombing, rather than close-in support for U.S. ground troops, the need for suitable long-range aircraft increased dramatically. Consolidated helped meet the need, building more B-24 Liberator bombers and PBY Catalina patrol bombers during the war than any other manufacturer in the United States.

The United States' hasty demobilization after World War II sent Electric Boat and Consolidated Vultee into a business slump, but their forced transition to civilian production was cut short. Soviet actions in Eastern Europe, the disclosure in 1949 that the USSR had also developed an atomic bomb, and the Communist triumph in China the same year alarmed the U.S. defense establishment. When North Korea attacked South Korea in 1950, the U.S. defense industry found itself back in business.

The end of the Korean War brought profound changes to the U.S. economy. For the first time America did not dismantle its war-making machinery after its armed forces had stopped fighting. Instead, the government encouraged the development of a permanent defense industry, comprised of companies dedicated almost exclusively to the design and production of high-technology weapons.

Among the first industrialists to recognize this fundamental shift in America's national security posture was John J. Hopkins, the imaginative lawyer and financier who had taken the helm of Electric Boat in 1947. Hopkins envisioned Electric Boat as a broadly diversified company that could capture as many slices of the nation's emerging defense business as possible. Though his grand vision differed from the more conservative plans of his board of directors, Hopkins usually managed to get his way. "Grow or die" was his business credo and his legacy.

In 1947, shortly after Hopkins had become its president, Electric Boat acquired Canadair, Limited, of Montreal, the largest aircraft manufacturer in Canada. No longer exclusively a submarine builder, Electric Boat changed its name to the General Dynamics Corporation in 1952, retaining the name Electric Boat for its submarine division. Hopkins explained that "General Dynamics" better described his company's role in the development and application of several new forms of energy. Some observers thought Hopkins saw General Dynamics as a new General Motors. Others suggested that he simply wanted General Dynamics to appear ahead of General Electric in the telephone book.

Despite the objections of his board of directors, Hopkins negotiated General Dynamics's merger with Convair in 1954, at a time when the future of military aircraft didn't look particularly bright. "Jonah has swallowed his *second* whale," said one commentator.

"General Dynamics and Convair will represent one of the strongest arms of the free world's defense effort," Hopkins confidently predicted. "We are moving swiftly in the fields of hydrodynamics, aerodynamics and nucleodynamics."

Indeed, General Dynamics had become deeply involved in nucleodynamics. In 1950 Electric Boat was asked by Hyman Rickover, then a Navy captain, to build the world's first nuclear-powered submarine, the *Nautilus*. Although his company had neither the trained personnel nor adequate facilities to do the job, Hopkins jumped at the invitation. Electric Boat desperately needed work during the postwar depression in shipbuilding, and Hopkins was fascinated by the burgeoning field of atomic energy.

On a cold and windy morning in 1955 Electric Boat's *Nautilus* cast off its lines, eased into the Thames River in Connecticut, and radioed back a brief but stirring message: UNDERWAY ON NUCLEAR POWER. It was a triumphant moment for Rickover and Electric Boat. "*Nautilus* did not mark the end of a technological road," Rickover declared. "It marked the beginning. It should be compared with the first airplane that flew at Kitty Hawk."

In the 1950's GD began to thrive. Hopkins created the General Atomic Division in 1955 to undertake applied research in nuclear and thermonuclear energy. He acquired the Stromberg-Carlson Corporation, a major telephone equipment manufacturer that specialized in advanced electronics, to enhance GD's work on aircraft, missiles, submarines, and atomic energy (Stromberg-Carlson was sold in 1982). GD's Convair facilities in California produced aircraft and Atlas intercontinental ballistic missiles for the Defense Department as well as Atlas booster rockets for the nation's fledgling space program. Its Fort Worth plant built B-58 Hustler bombers for the Strategic Air Command. Electric Boat's shipyard designed virtually every new class of nuclear-powered submarine and built more of them than any other public or private shipyard.

By the time Hopkins died of cancer in 1957 he had pieced together one of the most powerful corporations in the defense industry. Before long, however, General Dynamics ran into trouble.

Control of GD passed from Hopkins to Frank Pace, Jr., an Arkansas lawyer who had served as director of the federal budget and secretary of the army. During the next five years Pace guided GD through a bungled attempt to penetrate the commercial jetliner market.

He was succeeded in 1962 by a former Pan American World Airways vice-president named Roger Lewis (no relation to David Lewis). By most accounts, Roger Lewis was an uninspired businessman who had toiled for years in the shadow of Pan Am's charismatic founder, Juan Trippe.

A huge controversy soon erupted when Defense Secretary Robert McNamara selected General Dynamics to build the new TFX fighter-bomber, later designated the F-111. McNamara had overturned the nearly unanimous recommendation of the Air Force brass that he award the TFX contract to Boeing rather than to General Dynamics. The controversy that grew out of

McNamara's decision reflected primarily a Pentagon power struggle between the strong-willed defense secretary and senior military officers, but a later Senate investigation into possible conflicts of interest or illegal influence peddling haunted GD for years. The huge cost overruns and embarrassing technical failures that plagued the F-111's development program only made matters worse for GD.

Roger Lewis insisted on acquiring a commercial shipyard at Quincy, Massachusetts, near Boston, which began to lose a great deal of money. Lewis's decision touched off a small war in GD's Manhattan boardroom, a struggle that pitted Roger Lewis against Henry Crown, one of the wealthiest men in America and the largest individual holder of GD stock. Crown, a self-made multimillionaire who once owned the Empire State Building, lost confidence in Lewis and wanted him out. Lewis, in turn, hoped to force Crown off GD's board. In 1966, under pressure from his fellow directors, Crown reluctantly agreed to sell out his GD preferred shares and relinquish his seat on the company's board. Four years later the canny Chicago financier stunned Wall Street by quietly accumulating great amounts of GD stock and again seizing control of General Dynamics. Crown's return to GD's board of directors in 1970 at the age of seventy-three set the stage for the departure of one Lewis and the arrival of another.

David Lewis was the widely respected president of the McDonnell Douglas Corporation, a St. Louis-based aircraft and missile manufacturing firm that was dominated by its iron-willed founder and chairman, James McDonnell, Jr. Sharp-eyed industry analysts recognized that Lewis deserved much of the credit for the huge success of McDonnell's F-4 Phantom II fighter program in the 1960's and the financial comeback of the California-based Douglas Aircraft Company soon after its 1967 merger with McDonnell Aircraft. But to the public at large, McDonnell, the overbearing chairman—known by friend and foe alike as Mr. Mac—*was* the company.

Lewis, a soft-spoken South Carolinian who had been named president of the corporation at the age of forty-five, prospered under Mr. Mac's regime, but by 1970 he was growing impatient. When Henry Crown offered Lewis the chairmanship of General Dynamics, he was immediately interested. He agreed to leave McDonnell Douglas if GD would relocate its corporate headquarters from Rockefeller Center in Manhattan to St. Louis, where he'd lived since 1946. GD obliged.

Lewis has climbed to the pinnacle of the American defense industry through hard work, tough bargaining with his subcontractors and military customers, and rigorous attention to detail. He isn't a flashy marketing or financial wizard and has little interest in advertising or public relations. Like most top executives in the defense industry, Lewis is and will remain essentially a no-nonsense engineer, fascinated by technology and constantly looking for ways to incorporate that technology into marketable, profitable military hardware. Lewis's relaxed manner can be misleading. He has a sharp mind and a thorough knowledge of every facet of his company's business. Regular visitors to the chairman's twenty-third-floor office soon learn to do their homework and come prepared for an intense grilling.

Under Lewis, General Dynamics has made a remarkable recovery, chalking up one success after another. Its sales have increased steadily for the past twelve years. By 1983 General Dynamics single-handedly accounted for more than 5 percent of all Pentagon prime contracts. The Fort Worth division (which had been split off from Convair) beat out Northrop in January 1975 for a lucrative contract to build the Air Force's F-16 lightweight fighter. A few months later, in what was hailed as the Deal of the Century, a consortium of four NATO allies—Belgium, the Netherlands, Norway, and Denmark—decided to equip their fighter squadrons with F-16's from General Dynamics rather than with Mirage aircraft from France.

The success of the F-16 program was underscored in 1982, when the Air Force awarded its first multiyear contract for a major weapons system to General Dynamics for the production of 480 Fighting Falcons over four years for about $3 billion.

In addition to the F-16, GD has enjoyed considerable success with its newly acquired M-1 tank division, its work on cruise and tactical missiles, its electronic test equipment, and a wide variety of commercial enterprises.

Altogether, GD's future seems bright. It has a backlog of funded weapons orders totaling more than $15 billion. Its profits have almost doubled since 1980, and its return on equity in 1984—a whopping 37 percent—ranked it thirteenth among 1,200 companies surveyed. If the recent defense buildup is sustained in the years ahead, General Dynamics, more than any other contractor, is ideally positioned to benefit.

Although GD's financial prospects may look bright on Wall Street, its reputation has hit rock bottom with the American public. During the past year the company has been bombarded by allegations of fraudulent, deceptive, or improper practices that have supposedly enabled it to bilk the U.S. government of millions—or billions—of dollars.

Most of these charges stem from revelations made by Panagiotis Takis Veliotis, a former general manager of the Electric Boat shipyard who resigned from GD in 1982; was indicted on kickback, fraud, perjury, conspiracy, and racketeering charges a year later; and now lives as a fugitive from justice in

Athens, Greece. Veliotis has provided investigators and journalists with a slew of documents and tapes of secretly recorded telephone conversations he had with other top GD executives during the past decade.

Veliotis's evidence spurred the Justice Department to reopen an investigation of EB's submarine contracts it had closed in 1981, inspired several congressional committees to probe a variety of related allegations, and riveted the media's attention on GD.

The list of GD's alleged crimes and infractions (none of them conclusively proved yet) includes:

• "Buying in" with overoptimistic bids to the Navy in the early 1970's to build eighteen attack submarines
• Submitting a fraudulent half-billion-dollar claim to the Navy in 1976 to recoup its cost overruns on that trouble-ridden submarine program
• Cooperating with a Carter administration plan to exaggerate its financial woes in order to justify to Congress an overly generous settlement of that claim two years later
• Obstructing the Justice Department's four-year investigation of those bids and claims by withholding information from a grand jury in Hartford, Connecticut
• Submitting dubious "insurance claims" to the Navy in 1981 to recover excessive shipbuilding costs that resulted from its own employees' negligence and faulty workmanship
• Withdrawing those controversial claims only after Navy officials promised a higher than usual profit margin on a new contract for another attack submarine
• Discussing a possible GD job with Assistant Secretary of the Navy George A. Sawyer, the official who had helped negotiate the 1981 contract, months before Sawyer left his Navy post
• Giving a pair of diamond earrings and a jade pendant worth $1,125 to Admiral Rickover for his wife in 1977, as well as other gratuities totaling more than $67,000 over the years, and then disguising some of these gifts by falsifying its expense records
• Withholding pessimistic information about higher costs and delayed delivery dates it expected for its Trident submarines in an effort to bolster the price of its stock, in violation of Securities and Exchange Commission (SEC) financial disclosure requirements
• Placing among its overhead charges to the Pentagon such questionable expenses as $4,000 for an executive's twelve-day trip to the 1984 Democratic National Convention, $352 a night for a room at the Waldorf-Astoria Hotel

for Lewis and his wife, and numerous flights Lewis took to his family's farm in Albany, Georgia, aboard a GD corporate jet

• Appointing to its board of directors Lester Crown, a major GD shareholder, without disclosing to stockholders or the SEC that he had been implicated in 1974 in a scheme to bribe Illinois state legislators

• Seeking a top secret security clearance for Crown without informing the Department of Defense of his earlier involvement in the Illinois bribery scandal

• Earning billions of dollars in profit but paying federal income taxes in only one year since 1972

• Failing to support with names and proper details millions of dollars in "undocumented" expense vouchers submitted to the government for reimbursement

• Breaching Navy security regulations by allowing top secret photographs of the interior of its Trident submarine to be seen by unauthorized company personnel

GD officials have categorically denied that the company or its officers acted illegally or fraudulently in any of these instances. "I am not here to say that our company is perfect," Lewis told a subcommittee of the House Energy and Commerce Committee at a highly publicized "showdown" hearing in February 1985. "We do many things well and we make our share of mistakes. But those are human errors. I refuse to accept any portrayal of our company or its people as being dishonest or lacking integrity in our dealings with the United States Government or our many other valued customers."

GD supplied the subcommittee with a detailed forty-six-page explanation of its actions, which generally portrays the company as adhering to the letter, if not always the spirit, of the Defense Department's procurement regulations. Lewis acknowledged that the company occasionally submitted improper overhead charges and sometimes entertained military officers when it shouldn't have, but he insisted that it never intentionally misrepresented its requests for government reimbursement.

The list of accusations grew rapidly in early 1985. It seemed that each morning's newspaper and each evening's newscast focused on yet another example of GD's apparent misbehavior. Lewis objected to the coverage. "Without exception, the hallmark of the adverse material that has been released to the news media about our company has been misrepresentation and exaggeration," he told the House subcommittee.

For a while General Dynamics became the principal focus of virtually every critical story about the weapons business, as if the company had monopolized the field of abusive industry practices. It seemed that every journalist, politician, and military reformer who wanted to take on the defense industry targeted GD. For example, although many major defense contractors (including Boeing, Northrop, Grumman, and Lockheed) take advantage of IRS provisions that essentially allow them to defer their income taxes until their long-term weapons contracts are completed, GD was singled out for special criticism. Although most weapons contractors engage in a running battle with government auditors about the validity of their overhead charges, GD was cited as if its contested charges for hotel rooms, entertainment, and corporate travel were particularly offensive. Although many contractors experience occasional lapses in their security precautions, GD was damned as if its behavior in the Trident photograph incident were without precedent.

GD proclaimed its innocence, but as the political momentum grew in Washington, short shrift was given to GD's convoluted, self-serving, and long-winded explanations. A handful of congressmen enjoyed a field day, accusing the firm of a multitude of sins while aiming their well-rehearsed one-liners at the TV cameras. Even Defense Secretary Caspar Weinberger, who had rarely displayed a hard-line attitude toward the defense industry, took action.

The Pentagon recouped $244 million in disputed overhead charges by withholding progress payments from GD for many of its defense contracts. And in May 1985, Navy Secretary John Lehman, Jr., fined GD $676,283 (ten times the amount of its alleged gifts to Admiral Rickover) and suspended two divisions of the company from obtaining new Navy contracts until GD mended its ways.

Before long GD emerged in the public eye as the nation's most venal and corrupt defense contractor. One pollster discovered in March 1985 that of the 60 percent of Americans who had heard about the allegations confronting GD, four out of five had come to believe that the company "had ripped off the taxpayers and should be made to pay for it."

The company's precipitous fall from grace was captured tellingly in two illustrated covers of *Business Week* magazine. The first, in May 1982, featured a calm and confident David Lewis, sitting with toy models of his profitable tank, submarine, cruise missile, and fighter aircraft, with the upbeat headline STRIKING IT RICH ON DEFENSE. Less than three years later Lewis was back on *Business Week*'s cover, but this time his face had become part of a besieged battle-gray fortress the heavy guns of which were being shelled from all sides. The accompanying headline: GENERAL DYNAMICS UNDER FIRE.

In May 1985, the embattled Lewis announced his plan to retire from GD by the end of the year.

The allegations currently pending against GD are present-day threats to the company. But most of the accusations stem from events that took place years ago.

This book explores the most significant of those allegations, in context, as they unfolded during the course of GD's stormy history. Rather than focus on GD's final guilt or innocence, this book portrays the environment in which the defense industry and the Pentagon operate. Due process will eventually determine whether GD—or any of its employees—has broken the law. The question raised here is whether the institutional demands of the weapons business make such behavior almost inevitable.

## (3)

A handful of civilian officials in the Office of the Secretary of Defense (OSD) and a group of military officers gather regularly in conference room 1E-801 No. 7 in the bowels of the Pentagon to decide the fate of a major new weapons system. This exclusive fraternity of government officials, mostly assistant secretaries of defense clad in conservative business suits, determines which weapons the U.S. government will buy. The group is known formally as the Defense Systems Acquisition Review Council, but in the abbreviation-happy weapons community it is called simply the DSARC (pronounced "dee-sark").

DSARC members sit in armchairs surrounding a horseshoe-shaped imitation wood table the ends of which point toward a slightly raised stage at one end of the room. Military officers can address the council either from that stage or from a podium just below it. The American flag in one corner, the fading green carpet, and the elevated multipurpose projection booth behind a glass window in the rear wall are the type you find in community meeting rooms in any mid-size suburban bank. Only the six overhead microphones, drooping ominously from flexible wires on the two side walls, hint at the importance of the subjects under discussion.

A strictly limited number of officers and military aides are permitted to fill the chairs around the perimeter of the room. DSARC meetings traditionally attract more weapons program officials than conference room 7 can accommodate. Sometimes a low-ranking officer will volunteer to run a Vu-Graph or overhead projector simply to gain admittance to the room.

Military officers, sporting the crisp blue uniforms of the Air Force and Navy or the green attire of the Army, usually appear before the DSARC as advocates and special pleaders. Their mission: to convince the council—and the secretary and deputy secretary of defense to whom it officially reports—that the weapon they are developing has achieved satisfactory technical progress thus far and that further accomplishments lay just ahead. The DSARC's job is to hear the officers' presentations, challenge their performance claims and cost projections, and decide whether the particular weapon warrants the continued support of the Department of Defense (DOD).

This adversarial relationship between the OSD and the military services stems from the structure of the U.S. defense establishment. The National Military Establishment was created in 1947 (and renamed the Department of Defense in 1949) to ride herd on the three existing military departments: the Army, the Navy (which includes the Marine Corps), and the Air Force. Today the military departments act as resource managers for the defense establishment, recruiting and training personnel as well as developing and buying weapons.

The military departments do not serve as combat organizations. In time of war the formal chain of command runs from the President to the secretary of defense through the Joint Chiefs of Staff to the commanders of the nation's combat organizations known as the unified and specified commands. Currently there are six unified commands (European, Pacific, Atlantic, Southern, Readiness, and Central). They are organized geographically and draw troops from two or more services. The three specified commands—Strategic Air, Military Airlift, and Aerospace Defense—are organized functionally and normally draw personnel from only one service, the Air Force.

The Army, Navy, and Air Force procure weapons and oversee the work of defense contractors. The OSD sets defense policy, allocates the budget, and tries to ensure that the services carry out their responsibilities. This institutional arrangement virtually guarantees criticism from both sides. The military services often argue that the OSD doesn't understand weapons technology and shouldn't "micromanage" their acquisition programs. OSD officials accuse the services of seeking too many weapons indiscriminately, often underestimating costs, and insufficiently controlling their contractors. Both sides have a point.

On an organization chart of the Pentagon's weapons bureaucracy, the DSARC sits atop a network of review committees and technical evaluators that regularly monitor the progress of individual weapons programs. It evaluates the status of an individual program only at crucial moments in a weapon's life-span, known in Pentagonese as DSARC Milestones. Long before the council gathers, dozens of review committees and OSD staff members have studied and settled most problems by circulating and "signing off" on position papers formulated to resolve controversial issues. Persistent disagreements that can't be settled on paper are thrashed out by aides to the DSARC members in a series of preliminary meetings known as prebriefings. The DSARC is asked to resolve only the most important or most intractable issues.

Insiders stress that it is the entire DSARC *process*—involving hundreds of Defense Department bureaucrats—not simply the council itself, that shapes most procurement decisions made at the OSD level. The distinction is important. The more people involved in a billion-dollar weapons decision, the more difficult it is for any outsider—be he defense contractor, congressman, or White House official—to influence that decision.

The development of a new weapon, like the maturation of a human being, passes through several well-defined stages of growth. First, you recognize the military need. Next, you select a technical approach for a new weapon and develop a prototype. Then you demonstrate the prototype's capabilities and prepare for its production. Finally, you manufacture the weapon in large quantities.

The sponsoring military service, not the OSD, chooses the defense contractors that will perform most of this work, through a separate, highly stylized process known as source selection. The OSD simply judges the arguments for and against the existence of a particular weapons program and decides if enough technical progress has been made at any given stage to justify further development.

The DSARC serves as the OSD's gatekeeper to determine if—and when—a weapon is ready to move ahead. Conflict is inevitable in view of this division of authority between the services and the OSD. The military service buying a weapon and the defense contractor building it are usually anxious for it to move from one milestone to the next as rapidly as possible. As a result, pressures often build to push a weapon through its development stages before it is ready technically. To counter such institutional pressures, President Richard Nixon's first deputy secretary of defense, David Packard, established the DSARC system in 1969 to apply bureaucratic brakes whenever technical snags emerge, costs escalate, or the Defense Department's weapons priorities change.

Almost everyone in the procurement process feels pressure to hasten the development and production of new weapons. Most participants believe that delays increase costs and that the weapons under development are sorely needed. They also know that rushing a weapon's development can be risky. As a result of these competing pressures, the military services generally act as salesmen for their weapons programs while the OSD serves as the wary consumer.

Most weapons programs formally begin when the Army, Navy, or Air Force recognizes a military requirement for which it has no suitable weapon. The requirement usually stems from several factors, including advances in Soviet weaponry, deterioration and obsolescence of American equipment, or a recent technological breakthrough that seems ripe for exploitation. Soviet tank improvements, for example, might present the U.S. Army with a "requirement" for a more effective antitank shell that can penetrate tougher Russian armor. The Air Force might decide it "requires" a new manned bomber when it realizes how outdated its B-52 bomber fleet is. A dramatic breakthrough in Soviet antisubmarine warfare technology might convince the U.S. Navy that it "requires" a quieter submarine.

In its embryonic stage, a "requirement" will usually kick around a service's development laboratories, long-range planning offices, and the research and development (R&D) departments of competing defense contractors for years before it gathers enough support to inspire a full-blown weapons program. During this time "mission analyses" and concept papers are written, technical ideas are passed back and forth between government and industry specialists, symposia are held, and private contractors sniff out business opportunities. The origins of ideas often blur as one proposal feeds upon another. But gradually there emerges a consensus about what is needed to meet the "threat."

A requirement for a new fighter aircraft to replace the General Dynamics F-16, for example, might evolve from the work of several U.S. Air Force organizations. The Foreign Technology Division of the Air Force Systems Command—along with other elements of the U.S. intelligence community—might report advances in Soviet fighters that warrant an American response. The "user community"—in this case the Tactical Air Command (TAC), which flies the F-16—might support a new aircraft to fill out and modernize its fighter squadrons. Development planners in the Aeronautical Systems Division might contribute ideas on the new fighter's design and capabilities.

These three organizations might recommend that a separate line item in the Air Force budget be set aside for a new fighter aircraft program. "It becomes sort of a ground swell," said one development planner in the Aeronautical Systems Division. "You can do all the studies and everything else, but until you get that funding line established, you're almost blowing smoke."

Aircraft manufacturers play an active role at this stage of a weapon's gestation by promoting their latest technical ideas. "Contractors will always stand taller than us when it comes to wrapping technology around something that's going to fly because that's their game," the Air Force planner acknowledged. "They go into excruciating detail because they have to in order to build it." Even so, defense contractors don't dream up new weapons and foist them on the military services, as many people believe.

Ultimately the service—not the contractors—must decide when a particular "requirement" is important enough to justify the time and money needed to meet it. That decision isn't taken lightly. The service's political appointees and senior officers have to make tough choices from a long laundry list of weapons vying for scarce budget dollars. Despite talk of dramatically increased defense budgets, service officials are always presented with more demands than they can possibly satisfy. If they endorse a new military requirement, they know their future budgets will be stretched even tighter. In the tug-of-war for budget dollars, service officials often opt for weapons already being produced rather than for those that couldn't be deployed for five or ten years. "On any new system they can always say, 'A one-year delay won't hurt you,' " explained another Air Force planner.

However the military service arrives at the conclusion that it requires a new weapon—and this is the subject of much debate—the requirement eventually is reduced to a few sheets of paper and blessed by the service's civilian secretary and senior officers. The service then pitches its new weapons idea to the OSD. The title of the document describing this new military requirement is couched in bureaucratese as a "Justification for Major System New Starts." If the DSARC buys the service's argument, a new weapons program is officially established. The program, having just completed its *requirement validation* phase, passes Milestone Zero—the first in a long series of hurdles.

After Milestone Zero the military officer placed in charge of the new effort, known as the program manager, begins the search for a technical solution. Several options may present themselves. Suppose, for example, that improvements in Soviet air defenses convinced the Air Force it needed a new weapon that could slip past Soviet radar and elude surface-to-air missiles. Among other possibilities, the United States might develop a new manned penetrating bomber that could fly fast enough and high enough to evade enemy detection, or electronic countermeasure equipment that would enable existing bombers to baffle Soviet radar, or small, unmanned cruise missiles that could travel close enough to the ground to sneak under enemy sensors.

During this phase, known as *concept validation,* the sponsoring service might award relatively small study contracts to think tanks or defense contractors to dream up innovative ways to fulfill its new requirement. At this stage, mountains of paper work extolling one technical approach or another are generated by various contractors and "beltway bandits" (nickname for the consulting firms and think tanks located along Interstate 495, which rings Washington, D.C.).

One concept might be eliminated because it is technologically too risky; another, because it indirectly threatens one of the service's beloved military missions. Yet another concept, one that is technically feasible and militarily palatable to the sponsoring service, might win broad support. Contractors work actively at this stage to influence the technical direction a weapons program will take.

"They give presentations on what they see as future fighters or other weapons systems all the way up the line," said an official in the Aeronautical Systems Division. "They not only come here, but go to the air staff [at Air Force headquarters in the Pentagon], they go to TAC, and they go to DOD to try to generate momentum." If their past contracts and current research have emphasized electronic countermeasures, for example, they will do all they can to convince the Air Force to adopt an electronic countermeasures approach to defeating Soviet air defenses.

Company reps will meet regularly with Air Force employees, will provide technical information that supports their case, and might even offer to help a government bureaucrat analyze reams of data or write an official evaluation report related to the program. In short, they'll do whatever they can at this stage to "support" the program on the principle that the more input they offer, the more likely it is the resulting weapons concept will play to their technical strengths.

A weapons program passes Milestone One when its technical concept has been chosen by the service and approved by the OSD at what is called a DSARC I meeting. At this point, often several years after the military requirement has been established, the program moves from its concept validation phase into *advanced development*. The idea has been selected; it's now time to make it work.

By this stage program managers presumably know what kind of weapon they want to develop and how they plan to do it. Their budgets grow. They usually have on hand a pile of plans and theoretical studies and a group of contractors eager to transform the approved concept into a working prototype. Typically the service will now award advanced development contracts to two or three competing companies. For the next several years, during this phase, designers and engineers working for these contractors try to build a prototype weapon that can fulfill the promises made in those early paper studies. They try to transform the ambitious concept approved at Milestone One into reality.

This is rarely easy. By definition, the new concept often draws upon innovations at the frontiers of technology. Contractors attempt to produce weapons that can do things that have never been done before: missiles that can strike distant targets with exceptional accuracy; armor that can withstand the most potent antitank shells; aircraft engines with reduced weight and increased thrust; precision guided munitions that can detect and attack enemy installations. The weapon might require new composite materials, or new integrated circuitry, or new sensors, or new high-energy fuels, or new guidance systems. Designing a new weapon is not like designing a better toaster.

Inevitably different companies experience different degrees of success at the advanced development stage. Generally the prototypes are tested by both the contractors and the service. Additional paper studies document the results of those tests. This work may or may not produce a weapon with genuine promise. Tests often reveal flaws in the original concept. Design changes are made. Ultimately a workable prototype of the new weapon emerges. When the service is satisfied with its contractors' advanced development work, it recommends that the DSARC allow the program to pass Milestone Two and move ahead to the next phase—*full-scale engineering development.*

During this phase the service will probably award full-scale engineering development contracts to one, two, or three of the competing companies, those that designed the most promising prototypes. These companies will train their personnel and prepare their factories and assembly lines to produce the weapon in large quantities. Instead of fashioning a few prototypes by carefully hand-tooling individual parts, the companies build the dies and patterns that they'll need to produce the weapon in large numbers. Where only a few highly skilled machinists and craftsmen might have been required to construct the advanced development prototypes, hundreds or thousands of workers will be employed during full-scale engineering development in preparation for a decision to begin production.

The service tries to determine during this phase which contractors are capable of building large quantities of reliable production line weapons. Quality control on the assembly line, rather than innovative engineering, becomes the critical factor. The weapons are subjected to two types of test during this phase. The first, called development testing, is performed under ideal laboratory conditions, using skilled contractor personnel and highly trained military specialists. A prototype missile, for example, will be meticulously maintained by company engineers and launched by experienced military officers. The second type of test, known as operational testing, is carried out under simulated battlefield conditions, relying exclusively on the type of military servicemen who would actually maintain and use the weapon during combat. Technical problems that might not hamper development tests frequently show up during the more rigorous operational tests.

Competition among the remaining defense contractors often becomes intense during the full-scale engineering phase. Millions or billions of dollars ride on the service's ultimate choice of contractors. News of technical difficulties that plague one contractor's weapon might be leaked to the press or Congress by a competing contractor. Critics of a particular weapon—or of defense spending generally—will often seize upon a technical shortcoming during this phase as sufficient cause to cancel the entire program. Congressional representatives weigh in with impassioned appeals on behalf of contractors in their districts.

The performance, the cost, the continuing military requirement, the enemy's progress in competing technologies, and the weapon's impact on the U.S. defense industrial base all are considered as the program approaches the DSARC's final decision: Should the United States begin full-scale production of this new weapon? Once the service is satisfied that its contractors can build a weapon that fulfills its requirement at a reasonable price on an acceptable timetable, the program will be approved for *full-scale production.* The decision is sometimes made by the DSARC and sometimes by the sponsoring service, depending on the problems it has encountered along the way, but in either case, when the program passes Milestone Three—its final hurdle—production begins.

## *(4)*

It was 1978, and David Lewis still had to decide if Electric Boat should stop building the Navy's attack submarines. In private negotiations with Navy officials he had already threatened to halt construction unless the company's formal claim for $544 million was settled fairly.

"I went to the Navy," Lewis recalled later. "They said, 'If you think this threat is going to make us do anything differently, you're dead wrong. If you think this threat is not going to affect all the rest of your business, you're dead wrong.' "

Both sides dug in their heels, and negotiations ground to a halt. Lewis sensed that GD was sliding toward financial disaster. He had spent the past eight years building GD's financial position, and he wasn't going to allow the Navy to destroy his company now. He had to act.

"The Navy threatened us with everything in the world," Lewis explained. "I just said, 'That's life. You do what you have to do.' " On March 13, 1978, Lewis notified the Navy that Electric Boat would stop building attack submarines in thirty days, at 11:59 P.M. on April 12. He had just declared war.

# Chapter Two

## The Saltwater Enterprise

### (1)

The history of General Dynamics didn't begin in a submarine yard in Connecticut, an aircraft factory in California, or a tank plant in Michigan. It began along the rugged Atlantic coastline of Ireland. There, in 1841, in the village of Liscannor, John Philip Holland, Jr., was born into a Roman Catholic family of modest means.

Holland's lifelong struggle to perfect a workable submarine and peddle it to the U.S. Navy illustrates the technical, political, and financial hurdles that an inventive and stubborn weapons manufacturer had to confront at the close of the nineteenth century. The mighty General Dynamics of today developed from the tiny shipbuilding company Holland founded in 1893. His story is a tale of innovation, secrecy, frustration, triumph, and, finally, betrayal.

As children Holland and his two brothers constantly scrambled up the lush green hillsides of County Clare in southwestern Ireland. Never far from the sea, they sat for hours, gazing across Liscannor Bay or out across the broad Atlantic Ocean.

Life was difficult in Ireland in the decade following Holland's birth. A blight on the potato in the 1840's devastated the country's main crop, causing widespread death. As a direct result of the potato famine, roughly 1.6 million men and women emigrated from the "Emerald Isle" to the United States, where food and jobs were thought to be more plentiful.

Holland's family was insulated from the worst ravages of the famine. His father worked for the British Coast Guard, patrolling the headlands along the Irish coast for smugglers and foreign expeditionary forces. The job offered two advantages. First, part of the compensation included the right to live in a coast guard cottage, so the Holland family never suffered the threat of eviction that many of their impoverished neighbors faced. Secondly, the job required the family to move periodically from town to town, so the children never felt bound to the unyielding soil and were free to study and find work in Ireland's urban centers.

Though young Holland escaped the worst effects of the famine, he couldn't ignore the misery around him. By the time he was ten years old he had seen one brother and two uncles succumb to cholera, his youngest brother suffer from smallpox, and countless hundreds struggle against starvation. His early exposure to death, disease, and hunger no doubt heightened the resentment Holland, like so many other Irish Catholics, felt toward England, which had politically dominated Ireland for centuries.

"Holland's early life had been passed amid the miseries of the devastating famine that caused the great migration of those days from Ireland to the United States, for which British rule rather than nature was held responsible," wrote Frank Cable, a submarine pioneer. "He had imbibed a deep hostility to England; it was a determining factor in turning his thoughts to submarines."

John Holland attended an elementary school near Liscannor run by the Christian Brothers, a conservative Catholic order that never tolerated open calls for rebellion against England among its students or faculty. In any case, Holland's interests were focused not on an incipient Irish uprising but on mathematics, the physical sciences, and the sea. Trips with his father along the coastal headlands and the sight of fishermen readying their gear on Liscannor's lower quay drew his attention constantly back to the sea. He passed a navigation examination at thirteen, and had it not been for his terrible eyesight, he might have become a seaman or ship's mechanic.

At seventeen, when it was clear he would never go to sea, the diminutive Holland joined the Christian Brothers. He spent the next eighteen years teaching. His father's accidental death, by some accounts from a "home remedy" that contained too much potash, reinforced Holland's need to earn money as a teacher.

Poor health required him to be transferred several times before he took up a teaching post in Cork. There he became fascinated by newspaper accounts of the Civil War battles being fought in the United States. In 1862 he pored over a description in the *Cork Examiner* of an electrifying naval battle that had taken place a few weeks earlier between the Union's *Monitor* and the

Confederacy's *Merrimack*. This historic battle was the first showdown between two steam-powered warships protected with iron armor.

The *Merrimack* was a hulking old wooden ship that the Confederacy reinforced by covering its exposed surfaces with iron plates. The vessel was sent out into waters off Hampton Roads, Virginia, to break a harbor blockade that had been established by a Union fleet of wooden ships. Invulnerable to the attacks of its wooden adversaries, the *Merrimack* convincingly defeated two of them and returned to the same waters the following day, confidently expecting similar victories.

This time, however, the Union sent its own "ironclad" into the fray. The *Monitor,* which has been described variously as a tin can on a shingle or a cheesebox on a raft, was designed to ride so low in the water that only its revolving gun turret was exposed to enemy shells. The *Monitor* and the *Merrimack* bombarded each other for more than three hours. Shells and cannonballs bounced off their protective armor, and the combatants eventually withdrew from battle, with neither side claiming a victory.

The *Merrimack*'s decisive victory over the Union's two wooden ships and the following day's stand-off between the two ironclads prompted navies around the world to rethink their strategies. Wrote British Admiral Sir John Hay: "Henceforth the man who goes into action in a wooden ship is a fool, and the man who sends him there is a scoundrel."

Mulling over the pages of the newspaper, Holland wondered how long it would take the British Admiralty to absorb the notion that the clash between the *Monitor* and the *Merrimack* had sounded the death knell for wooden naval ships. Perhaps with innovations like ironclad ships, Irish rebels could threaten the Royal Navy.

When he was twenty-eight, Holland was transferred to the Irish town of Dundalk, where he became a music teacher and introduced the new "do-re-mi" system of musical notation into the country's school system. At Dundalk, Holland spent a lot of time tinkering during his idle hours. He erected a sundial. He introduced his students to the telescope. He studied the aerodynamics of flight. And he wrestled with the same technical problems that had vexed people trying to design a workable submarine for more than 100 years.

Holland constructed a working model of a submarine powered by a small clockwork mechanism and tested it in a large wooden tub. Gradually he became preoccupied with a host of technical questions: How does one calculate the required strength of the submarine's outer shell? How can ballast tanks be used to adjust the submarine's buoyancy? How can diving planes be used to make the craft dive or ascend? What propulsion system is safe, reliable, and effective?

Earlier attempts to develop naval submarines produced some intriguing ideas and a handful of daring prototypes but few genuine success stories. A Dutch inventor, Cornelis Jacobszoon Drebbel, had experimented with a navigable submarine as far back as 1620. English and Spanish inventors tried to perfect various diving bells during the seventeenth century, but most proved dangerous or impractical. It remained for an American to design the first vessel that could propel itself efficiently underwater. In 1775 Dr. David Bushnell, a Connecticut Yankee and Yale graduate, developed the *Turtle,* a hand-propelled submarine shaped like an egg which was used in an unsuccessful attempt to blow up a British ship in New York Harbor during the American Revolution. The plan called for an explosive charge to be attached to the bottom of HMS *Eagle,* but copper sheathing on the *Eagle*'s hull foiled the attack.

Two decades later the American inventor Robert Fulton tried to sell versions of his submarine and torpedo to France, Britain, and the United States. Initially the opportunistic Fulton tried to interest Napoleon Bonaparte in his submarine as a devilish means of destroying the British fleet. Napoleon helped finance the construction of Fulton's sub, which was dubbed the *Nautilus,* but never showed much interest in buying it. The *Nautilus* boasted many of the ingredients of a modern submarine: a ballast system that enabled it to dive, ascend, or stabilize itself while submerged; horizontal and vertical fins that allowed it to steer; a wind sail to propel it on the surface; and a hand-cranked propeller to push it while underwater.

Eventually Fulton soured on the "tyrannic principles of Bonaparte, a man who has set himself above the law." In a shift in allegiance that would make even the most mercenary arms peddler blush, Fulton suggested in 1804 that Britain buy his submarine to attack France. Two years later the British attacked French ships in the French harbor of Boulogne, using Fulton's torpedoes and mines, but not the *Nautilus.* The attack failed.

Rejected by France and Britain, Fulton returned to America in the autumn of 1806. Within a month he had proposed to demonstrate his underwater torpedoes—not his submarine—to the U.S. government. At first his proposal was met with an official yawn, but four years later the persistent Fulton persuaded President James Madison and Congress to appropriate $5,000 to test his torpedoes. The trials held later that year proved inconclusive, and Fulton turned back to commercial steamboats, with which he had been notably more successful.

During the U.S. Civil War the Confederates sent a rudimentary hand-propelled submarine called the *Hunley* on an attack mission against a Union battleship, the *Housatonic,* in Baltimore Harbor. The *Hunley*'s credentials were questionable at best. During sea trials it had sunk several times, drowning thirty-two crewmen. Twice it was found with its bow stuck in the mud. Nevertheless, the *Hunley* was dragged from the bottom, reconditioned, and pressed back into service. In its final nighttime assault on the *Housatonic* it went down one last time, taking the Union frigate and its crew with it.

Apparently this limited success by a Confederate submarine was enough to capture the interest of naval officers in the North. The U.S. government began funding efforts by Oliver S. Halstead to develop a small, hand-cranked submarine named the *Intelligent Whale,* which encountered one mishap after another. "Thirty-nine men were drowned (three whole crews) before the craft was abandoned, brought to shore and set up on the lawn of the Brooklyn Navy Yard—whether as an ornament or a warning was not stipulated," noted submarine historian Edwin P. Hoyt.

Still a teacher in Ireland, Holland eagerly read newspaper accounts of Halstead's experiments in New York Harbor and continued to sketch submarine designs of his own. Though untrained as an engineer, Holland had enough technical knowledge to determine the proper thickness and weight of his submarine's hull. He understood the problems of submergence and buoyancy. His designs reflected a concern with most of the problems associated with operating a submarine underwater (propelling the sub at an even depth, steering it in any required direction, and maintaining an ample supply of compressed air on board for breathing). Holland's sketches were ahead of their time, but he was unable to find anyone willing to finance the construction of a full-scale prototype. "He was regarded as a second Jules Verne; in a word, a dreamer," wrote one of Holland's contemporaries. Discouraged, he stored his designs in a trunk.

### (2)

By the early 1870's the rebellion in Ireland against British rule was gaining momentum, and inevitably Holland was caught up in the fervor. Uprisings took place in Limerick, where his mother lived. His older brother, Alfred, was said to be editing a "semirevolutionary" weekly newspaper in Dublin. His younger brother, Michael, an avowed Irish rebel, had already emigrated to the United States, where Irishmen and their sympathizers were busy rallying support for an armed struggle against the British government.

Concerned for his family's welfare, weakened from a loss of weight and generally poor health, and depressed by the lackluster response to his sub-

marine concepts, Holland decided to emigrate to the United States. Having left
the order of Christian Brothers, he sailed steerage class to Boston in 1873.
Among the few belongings he carried to America was a small battered valise,
inside which he carefully packed the original sketches of what became the
world's first successful submarine.

Shortly after he had arrived in the United States, Holland slipped on a patch
of ice in Boston, broke his leg, and suffered a slight concussion. Laid up for
several weeks, he took the opportunity to rethink his design of the submarine
without reviewing the sketches packed in his valise. To his surprise and delight,
the second set of calculations and sketches matched the originals. Holland was
now certain of their accuracy.

Unfortunately his submarine designs were not putting bread on his table, so
in 1874 he accepted an offer to work again for the Christian Brothers, this time
as a lay teacher at St. John's Parochial School. Reluctantly he put aside his
submarine drawings and settled in Paterson, New Jersey.

While teaching school, Holland made his first contact with the U.S. Navy.
The father of one of his pupils happened to see Holland's submarine designs
and suggested Holland send them to his friend George M. Robeson, the
secretary of the navy. Holland mailed detailed plans for his submarine to
Robeson in February 1875. It was the beginning of a relationship with the
Navy that was to run hot and cold for more than thirty years.

Robeson's reaction was what one might expect of a busy navy secretary. He
referred Holland's designs to an experienced subordinate, Captain Edward
Simpson at the Naval Torpedo Station at Newport, Rhode Island. Captain
Simpson reviewed Holland's design for a 15½-foot one-man submarine that
relied, in part, on air reservoirs fashioned from oiled silk bags. Simpson's terse
response, declaring Holland's design impractical, was enough to dampen the
enthusiasm of a lesser man. The submarine's operator would be unable to see
underwater, Simpson asserted. He would be as blind as a sea captain piloting
a ship in a fog.

Miffed at Simpson's brusque and ill-informed critique, Holland dashed off
a letter to him, bluntly pointing out that the captain obviously had not considered using an underwater compass. Simpson responded a second time, suggest-
ing that the schoolteacher drop the whole submarine idea. No one would ever
go down in such a craft, he declared, and besides, "to put anything through
in Washington was uphill work." Simpson apparently agreed with most naval
officers of his day that submarines were "death traps when they were not toys."

The U.S. Navy had developed a naval strategy in its first 100 years based
primarily on surface warships. Wedded to the idea of surface warfare, its most
senior admirals were usually unwilling even to entertain the notion of under-

water combat. They were not about to accept a submarine that challenged the viability of surface ships or diminished their own status.

There was some logic to the resistance. Traditionally the U.S. Navy had organized itself as a defensive force, capable of protecting America's coastline from enemy attack. Gunboats and light torpedo boats, which operated on the surface, had always been considered adequate vessels for this defensive role. Not until the Navy began to see itself as an *offensive,* as well as a defensive, force would the military potential of submarines be seriously considered.

Despite the icy reception to his designs, the stubborn Holland stuck with his efforts, scribbling new calculations and designs on his school blackboard and meticulously transferring them to paper. One way or another, he intended to transform these designs into a working submarine.

In the same period the Irish revolutionary movement on both sides of the Atlantic was gaining momentum. The Irish Revolutionary Brotherhood was established in Ireland on St. Patrick's Day, 1858, followed a few years later by its American counterpart, the Fenian Brotherhood. The Fenians were unable to agree on a common course of action. Some Irish-American activists advocated open rebellion against Britain, and others supported a more moderate approach. Several splinter groups developed, diluting the strength of the brotherhood.

Meanwhile, in Ireland several Irish leaders arrested by British authorities for allegedly treasonable acts and writings were languishing in British-run prisons. One of the most charismatic of these revolutionaries was Jeremiah O'Donovan Rossa, whom some considered the prototypical Irish rebel. Normally a mild-mannered fellow, Rossa valiantly resisted British prison rules and any attempts to humiliate him. "His most spectacular fight," recalled Irish journalist Desmond Ryan, "was conducted in Chatham Prison, where finally, when Rossa had defied the silence rule by singing all the Irish songs he knew at all hours of the day and night, and hurled his gruel in his jailers' faces and smashed the window in his cell door, he was handcuffed with his hands behind his back for thirty-five days and compelled to lap up his gruel."

Needless to say, acts of defiance like these endeared Rossa and his fellow Fenian inmates to the Irish-Americans who avidly read the newspaper accounts of their resistance and imprisonment. When British Prime Minister William E. Gladstone commuted the sentences of Rossa and thirteen other Irish revolutionaries and "exiled" them from the United Kingdom, they were welcomed in New York City as heroes. Arriving in Manhattan in 1871, the "exiles" were met by effusive Tammany Hall political leaders at the quarantine checkpoint and received by President Ulysses S. Grant on the White House steps.

John Holland never became a "card-carrying" member of the Fenian Brotherhood, but as an Irish-American he couldn't help being moved by the Irish patriotism spreading across the United States. In 1876 Holland was introduced into New York City's circle of militant Irishmen by his younger brother, Michael, who had preceded him to America. Michael was familiar with his brother's efforts to develop a workable submarine and thought the Fenian Brotherhood might be interested in a weapon that could attack British warships and generate enthusiasm for the Irish rebellion.

Holland met the legendary O'Donovan Rossa, who was immediately impressed with the schoolteacher's concept of a submarine and introduced him to newspaperman Jerome Collins, the founder of the Clan-na-Gael, an umbrella group that tried to unite the various Fenian factions. Holland's meeting with Collins had great significance for the future of the submarine, the Electric Boat Company, and ultimately General Dynamics. It marked the first time Holland had come into direct contact with influential people whose interests could be served by his submarine designs and who possessed the money to back him financially. The frustrated inventor described his submarine plans to Rossa, Collins, and other Fenians, one of whom later wrote of Holland: "He was cool, good-tempered, and talked to us as a schoolmaster would to his children."

The Fenians saw Holland's submarine as the ideal weapon with which to terrorize the Royal Navy. It was small enough to be transported clandestinely inside a railroad car and then carried on a ship's deck into British waters. A submarine was the daring sort of project Rossa had in mind when he convinced the Fenian Brotherhood to establish a Skirmishing Fund to collect pennies, nickels, and dimes from Irish-American contributors. "The cost to the Brotherhood would be small compared to the cost to the British should such a vessel be successful," wrote Holland's biographer, Richard K. Morris. "The place to strike John Bull was at sea, not on land."

The Fenians decided to sponsor Holland's submarine project but insisted that their sponsorship be secret. They realized that construction of such an unusual vessel would be difficult to conceal, but they didn't want the public to know who was behind this audacious anti-British endeavor.

With money from the Skirmishing Fund, Holland constructed a thirty-inch model of his proposed submarine, an improved version of the model he had developed years earlier in Dundalk. The new model was still built around a clockwork mechanism, but it featured externally mounted diving planes and rudder. A water ballast system that allowed water partially to fill internal

watertight tanks made it possible to adjust for buoyancy. Holland had worked
out the basic principles of a submarine's operation.

The Fenians gathered one day at Coney Island to watch Holland demonstrate his model. When the miniature submarine performed successfully, they
agreed to fund construction of the full-size submarine. Holland envisioned a
small vessel: 14½ feet long, 2½ feet high, with a 3-foot beam and a weight
of 4,500 pounds submerged. (The Trident nuclear-powered submarine of today
is about 38 times longer and 8,300 times heavier.) Holland hired an ironworks
on Albany Street in Manhattan to build his submarine. His dream was becoming a reality.

The Fenians were now even more insistent than at first that the project's
sponsors be kept secret. Questioned by newspaper reporters who had become
curious about the strange craft taking shape on Albany Street, Holland identified his financial backer only as a "Mr. Jacobs, Sr.," of the fictitious firm
"Jacobs and Company." In keeping with this cover story, John Breslin, the
Fenian assigned to oversee Holland's project, became known as Mr. Jacobs,
Jr., whenever he turned up at the ironworks. In letters among Fenians, the
mysterious project was dubbed the saltwater enterprise.

Construction continued. A new petroleum engine was installed to replace
the foot pedals that had hampered earlier subs. In the spring of 1878 the
cigar-shaped submarine, known simply as *Holland No. 1,* was moved from the
ironworks in New York to a machine shop in Paterson, New Jersey, closer to
Holland's home. Finally, in May, it was ready for the water.

Holland decided to test the unusual vessel on the Passaic River, in the center
of Paterson. Curious mill hands and factory workers heading home from the
clattering silk mills and locomotive works gathered on the bridges and river
banks to watch "Professor Holland" launch the strange contraption. Holland
was assisted by an engineer named William Dunkerly.

Eight pairs of stallions hauled a large wagon carrying the submarine to the
river's edge. As the onlookers grew silent, the rushing sounds from a nearby
waterfall blended with the snorting of the horses and Dunkerly's shouted
commands. While Holland paced nervously up and back on the riverbank, his
first full-size submarine was eased off the wagon and into the river. It floated.
The workers murmured their approval. Then the onlookers gasped as Holland's little vessel slowly sank.

Dunkerly and an assistant pulled strenuously on the disappearing submarine's two towlines, but to no avail. The tiny craft settled ignominiously to
the bottom of the Passaic River. Eventually, after much sweating and straining, the two men managed to drag *Holland No. 1* back onto the riverbank, but
it was hardly an auspicious debut for Holland's saltwater enterprise.

Predictably the newspapers scoffed at Holland's ambitious experiment. DOWN AMONG THE FISHES, said one disparaging headline. Holland wondered what had gone wrong. Had he left a hatch unsecured? Had he miscalculated the buoyancy of the water? Had he misjudged the requirement for compressed air? "Was this to be the alpha and omega of his efforts?" asked biographer Morris. "Would Breslin report the failure; would O'Donovan Rossa call the Trustees of the Skirmishing Fund together; would they vote to shut off the flow of money before he had a chance to learn anything from the little boat?"

As it turned out, two small screw plugs had been missing from the bottom of the sub's hull. Repairs were made quickly, and *Holland No. 1* was readied for a second try a week later. This time, as an added precaution, the submarine was supported on ropes slung between rowboats positioned on either side of it. The odd-looking three-boat flotilla was pulled upstream by Dunkerly's steam-powered launch, out of view of the skeptical onlookers perched on the bridge and along the riverbanks.

Again there were difficulties. Despite assurances from the petroleum engine's inventor, the new engine failed to perform. The sub had no power. Quick to improvise, the ingenious Professor Holland rigged up a hose that connected the boiler in Dunkerly's steam-powered launch to the disappointing engine inside his submarine. Though inhibited by this awkward umbilical cord, the submarine finally managed to get under way with its diminutive inventor cramped inside. Holland tested his vessel's ability to dive underwater and return to the surface. He declared himself satisfied.

By June Holland was ready to demonstrate his submarine for O'Donovan Rossa and several Fenians from Paterson. The professor squeezed himself into *Holland No. 1*'s small turret (which only a slight man could manage) and flooded the two forward ballast tanks with water. Dunkerly's launch again supplied steam power to the submarine.

"The bow went down first, and before we realized the fact the boat was under twelve feet of water," Dunkerly later recalled. "The ropes were a safeguard in case the compressed air should not prove sufficient to expel the water from the ballast tanks. Holland was also given a hammer with which to rap upon the shell of the boat should he find himself in difficulties. After being submerged one hour, Holland brought the boat to the surface, to the great relief of all who were witnessing the test. As soon as the boat came up, the turret opened and Holland bobbed up smiling." Beaming with pride, he grandly offered to let any of the sponsors take a similar test dive. As might be expected, there were no volunteers.

Holland was anxious to safeguard his design, so he decided to scuttle *Holland No. 1* in the Passaic River. He removed the engine and other machinery and sank the historic submarine in fourteen feet of water.

Holland was satisfied with what he had learned. He now had a better understanding of the principles of buoyancy required to maintain stability underwater. He had begun to perfect the principle by which a submarine descends and surfaces diagonally, like a porpoise, rather than straight up and down, like an elevator. Though disappointed with his new engine, Holland was convinced that a perfected petroleum engine would eventually replace foot pedals as the accepted method for propelling submarines.

## *(3)*

Impressed with Professor Holland's first demonstration, the Fenians agreed to sponsor a second, larger boat which they hoped would be able to break a British naval blockade. That second submarine, dubbed the *Fenian Ram* by a reporter for the *New York Sun,* was built at Delamater's Iron Works in Manhattan for about twelve times as much as *Holland No. 1.* Designed to carry a captain, an engineer, and a gunner, it boasted "ramming power" of nearly fifty tons, theoretically enough to destroy an enemy ship's bottom, in the days before double hulls had become commonplace on naval vessels.

Completed in 1881, the *Fenian Ram* was towed across the Hudson River to the little-used Morris Canal Basin in Jersey City, where it was to be submerged for the first time. Holland, who insisted on personally testing his submarines, was at the controls for the first dive in June.

He and his engineer entered the cramped vessel and closed the hatch. Without ventilation, they depended on the submarine's compressed air reserve for their breathing. Satisfied with the oxygen supply, Holland drew back the levers mounted at either side of his head, which were connected to valves on the submarine's bottom. Water rushed into the ballast tanks, and the *Fenian Ram* began to settle. Holland peered through the glass ports in the turret and watched the bow disappear beneath the surface of the water. A few seconds later the inside of the submarine went dark, to be illuminated only by a dim green blur at the ports. Then the sub struck bottom with a slight jar.

In the faint green glow his engineer found everything watertight. Holland was satisfied. He opened the valves on the ballast tanks and heard the whoosh of compressed air forcing water out of the tanks. The green blur at the conning tower grew brighter and brighter as the *Fenian Ram* approached the surface. Suddenly sunlight burst through the tiny glass port, nearly blinding the bespectacled inventor. He threw open the hatch and thrust his head from the tower. The throng of spectators let out a mighty cheer. As Holland recounted later, "We had now demonstrated that our boat was tight, that our air was sufficient for breathing, and that our ballasting system was perfect."

While the popular press speculated on the nefarious purpose of this strange new warship, Holland continued to revise his designs. To incorporate some of these improvements into an actual submarine, he began constructing a third sub in Jersey City—a sixteen-foot, one-ton replica of his *Fenian Ram*.

Meanwhile, bickering and strife within the Fenian movement began to plague Holland's backers. One faction accused another of pilfering money from Rossa's Skirmishing Fund. Arguments broke out over the price Holland had paid for the petroleum engine. Tensions mounted. Concerned that a rival faction might "kidnap" Holland's two submarines from their pier in Jersey City and hold them as payment for the disputed financial claims, John Breslin took preemptive action.

One evening in November 1883 Breslin and a few of his Fenian cohorts forged Holland's signature on phony dockyard passes and gained admittance to the pier in Jersey City. As the unsuspecting watchman stood idly by, a tugboat pulled up to the pier and attached a towline to the floating *Fenian Ram*. Then Breslin and his companions slid the sixteen-foot replica off its support blocks and into the water, where they tied it behind the *Fenian Ram*.

Beneath the darkened sky this bizarre convoy chugged out into New York Harbor. Before they had traveled very far, however, the replica took too much water through its improperly secured turret and sank in 110 feet of water. Undeterred, the "kidnappers" continued towing the *Fenian Ram* up Long Island Sound to New Haven, Connecticut, where it was hidden in another Fenian's riverside foundry.

When Holland learned of the seizure of his two submarines the next day, he was furious, but there was little he could do. After all, the boats had been "stolen" by their financial sponsors. The Fenians tried to operate the sub a few times in New Haven Harbor, but the harbor master considered the odd vessel such a menace to sailboats and small ships that he banned its further use. Impatient with the factional struggles and technical ineptitude of the Irish militants, Holland simply turned his back on his *Fenian Ram:* "I'll let her rot on their hands."

He was so disgusted with the "kidnapping" that he severed his ties to the Fenian Brotherhood. "I received no notice of the contemplated move then, nor was I notified after," he wrote later. "I have no intention of advancing any excuses for the incident, as no official explanation was ever made to me concerning it. As a result, I never bothered again with my backers nor they with me."

Holland recognized that a phase of his life had ended with the theft of the *Fenian Ram*. He had stopped teaching several years earlier to pursue his submarine project full time. Now he wondered if he should return to the classroom. At forty-two, his hairline was receding, and the eyes behind his thick rimless glasses were losing some of their Irish twinkle. He was still convinced that submarines would one day play a major role in naval warfare. But where could he find new backers to finance the conviction?

The answer wasn't long in coming. One of Holland's earliest supporters in the U.S. Navy was Lieutenant Commander William W. Kimball, an enthusiastic advocate of the submarine and an aide to Admiral George Dewey (who became a national hero during the Spanish-American War). Kimball had followed Holland's activities since his initial submission of submarine plans to the Navy eight years earlier. After meeting Holland and discussing his ideas, the lieutenant commander became even more convinced: "Holland was far and away the best submarine man in the United States, if not in the world."

Kimball introduced Holland to Lieutenant Edmund Zalinski, an Army officer with considerable experience in naval gunnery, who saw the submarine as an ideal platform from which to test-fire his own experimental weapons. "The boat may be considered as a floating gun carriage," Zalinski wrote in the *Forum,* an influential journal of opinion. (The founder and president of the *Forum* was Professor Isaac Rice, an entrepreneur who one day controlled John Holland's patents and dominated the submarine business.)

In 1883 Holland teamed with Lieutenant Zalinski and raised enough money to build his fourth submarine, known as the *Zalinski Boat.* This venture proved to be a fiasco. The sub was constructed on the parade grounds at Fort Lafayette on an island off the Brooklyn shore. On the day in 1885 the *Zalinski Boat* was launched, the ramps that were supposed to guide the boat into the water collapsed. The vessel gained too much speed and smashed into some pilings, punching a hole in its bottom. As a result of this calamity, Holland ended his association with Zalinski, just at a time when submarines were slowly beginning to gain acceptance.

Submarines were still being scoffed at by leaders of the world's great navies, but some of the younger, more progressive officers had begun to recognize the potential of underwater warfare. One reason for this change in attitude was the introduction of safe and efficient accumulators (the term then used for electric storage batteries) to provide the power for submarines instead of the dirty and dangerous petroleum engines of the past. The French Navy, in particular, which led the world in the use of accumulators, was actively developing naval submarines.

By 1887 the U.S. Navy's attitude toward submarines had also begun to change. Perhaps in response to developments in France, the chief of the Navy's ordnance bureau began to push for an open competition to find the best design for an experimental submarine, and he urged William C. Whitney, President Grover Cleveland's secretary of the navy, to authorize one. Money hadn't been appropriated for the *construction* of such a sub, but a design competition would constitute an important first step. Holland was informed of the Navy's plans by his friend Kimball, but he held out little hope. Frustrated by his own efforts to catch the Navy's eye, Holland discounted this recent interest in French submarines as unlikely to lead to any substantive U.S. action. He was wrong.

In 1888—thirteen years after Holland had sent his original drawings to Washington—the Navy announced an open competition for the design of a steel submarine torpedo boat. Entrants were asked to design a sub that could travel at fifteen knots on the surface and eight knots underwater (a knot equals one *nautical* mile per hour, which is slightly faster than one standard mile per hour); remain submerged for two hours; maneuver in a circle no more than four times its own length; withstand water pressure to depths of 150 feet; and fire torpedoes armed with 100-pound explosive charges.

In its recitation of the new sub's performance requirements, the 1888 announcement differed markedly from the type of Request for Proposals (RFPs) the Navy might issue today.* In the 1880's the Navy was content to dictate only a proposed ship's performance characteristics.

Holland confidently submitted designs for a submarine that met the required performance specifications. Weeks passed without word from Washington. Then the Navy announced its decision: Holland's design had been chosen for its first submarine.

Unfortunately Holland's celebration was short-lived. The private shipyard that had agreed to build his proposed submarine and guarantee its performance suddenly got cold feet. It wouldn't stand behind the sub's performance. The Navy, in turn, decided to reopen its design competition. Holland was disappointed but not surprised. He had come to expect erratic behavior from the Navy.

A second design competition was held the following year, calling for precisely the same performance characteristics. Holland's sub design was again chosen, but another problem arose. President Cleveland's first term in office expired before Holland could be awarded his design contract. The administra-

---

*The Navy now dictates not only how a ship should perform but also what its physical dimensions, components, and materials should be and how it should be constructed. Like the other military services, today's Navy requires its contractors to build ships and weapons systems that conform to standardized military specifications, known as MIL-SPECs. This rigid procurement practice, designed to maintain uniformly high standards, has frequently been accused of stifling innovation among contractors and boosting the cost of weapons.

tion of newly elected President Benjamin Harrison had different views on how the Navy's money should be spent. Funds that had been earmarked for submarine construction were used to build several surface ships.

Once again the Navy's institutional conservatism had prevailed. Admirals steeped in the strategy of surface warfare weren't willing to yield their slice of the budget pie. "The U.S. Navy has never been accused of excessive doctrinal flexibility," the quarterly journal *Public Policy* observed nearly ninety years later. "It is among the most cretaceous of organizations."*

In 1890 the persistent Holland submitted another unsolicited proposal for a "submergible torpedo boat" to the Navy. His proposal was greeted with silence. An associate of Holland's discussed the Navy's frustrating delay with a young lawyer, Elihu B. Frost, who took a keen interest in the submarine inventor's work and had a profound effect on the rest of Holland's career. A well-connected, ambitious attorney with a keen interest in finance and the law, Frost offered to ask his father, a respected Washington attorney, to find out from Navy Secretary Benjamin F. Tracy why Holland hadn't received a response to his latest proposal.

In 1892 the American electorate decided it preferred former President Cleveland to the current chief executive, Benjamin Harrison. Cleveland's return to the White House, for the only interrupted second term in American history, brought another shift in Washington's attitude toward the submarine. Congress appropriated $200,000 to reopen the submarine design competition in March 1893. On April Fool's Day the Navy announced performance requirements for the proposed sub unchanged from those specified five years earlier.

Holland wanted to enter this third design competition, but he needed financial support. He explained his situation to Frost one afternoon over lunch in a New York restaurant.

"I know I can win the competition and build the boat for the government," Holland predicted. "But I need to raise some money to pay for fees and other expenses in preparing the drawings."

The young lawyer asked how much money Holland thought he required.

"I need exactly $347.19," declared the inventor.

Frost's eyebrows shot up in amazement.

---

*Franklin Delano Roosevelt, who served a stint as President Woodrow Wilson's assistant secretary of the navy before he occupied the White House, arrived at a similar conclusion. "To change anything in the Navy is like punching a feather bed," FDR once complained. "You punch it with your right and you punch it with your left until you are finally exhausted, and then you find the damn bed just as it was before you started punching."

"What do you need the nineteen cents for?" he asked.

"To buy a certain kind of ruler I need for drawing my plans," explained Holland.

"If you have figured it out as closely as all that," said Frost, "I'll take a chance and lend you the money."

Holland pored over his previous drawings for the "kidnapped" *Fenian Ram,* the ill-fated *Zalinski Boat,* the steam-driven submarine that had won the two previous Navy competitions, and the design he had submitted for a "submergible torpedo boat." He reshaped his previous ideas into a new design. On June 4, 1893, Holland signed this latest design and submitted it to the Navy.

## *(4)*

A few weeks before, Holland had incorporated his submarine-building venture in New York State. He named his enterprise the John P. Holland Torpedo Boat Company. General Dynamics is the direct descendant of that fledgling company. Holland became the manager of the company at a salary of $50 per month. E. B. Frost became the secretary-treasurer and was soon the driving political and financial force behind the young corporation. Frost raised the $7,500 deposit required by the Navy to accompany each design submission and obtained the sureties required for a $90,000 bond to guarantee satisfactory performance by the winning designer.

Several weeks later Holland traveled from New Jersey to Washington, D.C., to witness the official opening of the submarine designs. He was asked to sit in a waiting room adjacent to the navy secretary's office, along with several other distinguished-looking gentlemen. Only two other men in the room had submitted designs: Simon Lake, a round-faced young submarine designer from Baltimore who had never before tried to win a Navy contract, and George Baker, a politically well-connected inventor from Chicago.

Simon Lake eventually became one of Holland's major rivals in the submarine business. Unlike Holland, Lake had been experimenting with submarines that employed the even-keel principle—submerging and ascending like an elevator. Some of his early subs, which were intended for commercial salvage work, had wheels that enabled the vessels to roll along the sea bottom. However, Holland's diagonally diving system, when it was finally perfected, was the one most of the world's navies ultimately adopted.

Lake was sitting nervously in the navy secretary's waiting room when Baker's son struck up a conversation.

"Well, I suppose you are here on the same errand as the rest of us," said young Baker, leaning toward Lake. "I see you have some plans, and I suppose you have designs of a submarine boat which you are going to submit."

1. John P. Holland, the Irish-born schoolteacher and tinkerer often
considered the father of the modern submarine, emerges from the conning
tower of the USS *Holland,* the Navy's first workable submarine. His John P.
Holland Torpedo Boat Company was incorporated in 1893 and absorbed six
years later by the newly formed Electric Boat Company, which eventually
became the submarine-building division of General Dynamics. *U.S. Naval
Institute Photo Collection*

"Yes," said Lake, surveying Holland and the others in the room, "and I guess there are going to be a good many plans submitted, judging by the number of people who are here."

Baker shook his head.

"No," he corrected. "I only know of two others who are going to submit plans: there is Mr. J. P. Holland, the gentleman standing over there, and my father, Mr. George F. Baker, of Chicago."

"Well, then, who are all the other gentlemen present?" asked Lake incredulously.

The answer could not have pleased the Baltimore submarine designer, who was inexperienced in the ways of Washington. Baker's son quickly rattled off the names of the senators, congressmen, and influential lawyers in the room, all of whom were present to indicate their support for his father's proposal.

The young designer shrugged his shoulders and thought: "Well, Lakey, it looks as though you were not going to have much of a show here." Sobered by the experience, Lake beat a hasty retreat to Baltimore.

Perhaps less intimidated by Baker's impressive group of boosters, Holland returned to New Jersey, fully expecting to win this third open competition. A month passed with no word from Washington. Then came an unusual request for additional information to document Holland's designs. It appeared the Navy was stalling.

Holland and Frost figured that Baker couldn't possibly win the design competition, but he might be able to exercise enough political clout to delay the decision. After all, it was primarily Baker's lobbying that had persuaded Congress to appropriate $200,000 to finance the submarine competition in the first place. By the end of the summer in 1893 they sensed that Holland's design had withstood Baker's competition when *The New York Times* reported that a Navy selection board had chosen Holland's design for the third time. Frost dashed off a letter to Hilary A. Herbert, the new secretary of the navy, impatiently urging an end to the Navy's foot dragging. "I think I should be pardoned in respectfully asking that the company which I represent be awarded the contract as soon as it may suit your convenience, in order that the building of the boat may be commenced at the earliest moment possible," wrote Frost.

His confidence proved unfounded. Herbert wasn't ready to announce a winner. Perhaps as a result of Baker's influence, the navy secretary decided to spend the submarine money on other construction projects.

Frost and Holland were crushed. Fearing they might never beat Baker's political clout in Washington, they decided to join him. They offered Baker $200,000 worth of stock in the John P. Holland Torpedo Boat Company if he would relinquish his patents and join forces with them. Hoping to smooth the way for this audacious deal, Frost offered stock to Baker's Washington lawyer as a further inducement. But that ploy backfired. The insulted lawyer scorned the transparent bribe attempt, and Frost hastily withdrew the offer.

As autumn turned to winter and Holland's patience wore thin, the navy secretary found other imaginative ways to postpone the announcement of a winning submarine design. Concerned with the disastrous effect a nearby torpedo explosion might have on the occupants of a submarine, the Navy staged a bizarre experiment in late 1893 at the Naval Torpedo Station at Newport, Rhode Island. A watertight diving tank, with a motley crew of a cat, a rabbit, a rooster, and a dove inside, was lowered underwater. A series of guncotton charges were detonated at decreasing distances, the closest exploding within 100 feet of the submerged tank. "Then the craft was brought ashore and found to be undamaged," wrote Frank Cable. "The rabbit and the dove were dead, but the cat and the rooster appeared none the worse for their confinement. The cat fled, highly incensed, with distended tail; the rooster flew out and crowed."

The navy secretary apparently was satisfied that a sub crew could survive a nearby explosion, but he still wasn't ready to buck the admirals who vehemently opposed the underwater vessels. By the end of the year Holland and Frost were no closer to a design contract than they had been five years earlier.

To placate their stockholders, who were growing restless with the firm's lack of success, Frost began a campaign to promote the submarine and obtain patents for Holland's designs in several foreign countries. This highly visible sales and patent effort was also intended to whet the U.S. Navy's appetite. Company representatives were sent to South America, Europe, and Japan. At each stop the reps told their foreign hosts that the Holland company could deliver excellent submarines, but not until one year after it had completed its proposed contract with the U.S. Navy.

The sales mission* Frost organized may have spurred the U.S. government into action. In March 1895, after much foot dragging, the U.S. Navy awarded a $200,000 contract to the Holland Torpedo Boat Company for the construction of a submarine. It had been nearly seven years since the first design competition was announced. A jubilant Frost signed the contract and returned it to the Navy the day he received it.

---

*The international sales trip Frost initiated was different from a sales campaign a defense contractor might mount today. Then private companies could peddle warships and weapons to foreign countries with considerable flexibility. Today such transactions are closely regulated by the U.S. government. American contractors are not permitted to discuss their weapons in detail or provide foreign governments with descriptive literature without the consent of the departments of State and Defense.

The first submarine intended for the Navy, called the *Plunger,* was to be built at the Columbian Iron Works Dry Dock Company in Baltimore. Ironically, Holland found himself working alongside his longtime rival Simon Lake, who was there overseeing construction of his *Argonaut I,* the first submarine intended for the salvage of valuable sunken objects. The two inventors saw each other at the ironworks almost daily, but they seldom talked and never became close.

Lake had an ability to whet the public's appetite for news about the exotic underwater craft he and Holland had developed. One day in 1897, for example, Lake demonstrated his new submarine on the Patapsco River, in Maryland, by taking reporters from twenty-two different newspapers on dives ranging from ninety minutes to four hours.

Within months the strong-willed Holland felt exasperated by the Navy's rigid shipbuilding procedures. He bristled every time officials required a design change that he considered unnecessary. They changed the arrangement of his propellers; they made his boiler so large that the submarine crew would be unable to tolerate the heat. The changes were endless. Pacing back and forth in a smock and a soft felt hat, Holland fumed at orders from officials who knew almost nothing about submarines, experiencing a frustration common among shipbuilders and designers trying to cope with the Navy's cumbersome procurement bureaucracy.

As work progressed on the *Plunger,* Holland became more and more displeased. The submarine was huge—85 feet long and 11½ feet in diameter—and it displaced 168 tons when submerged. The Navy's specifications required four steam engines for running on the surface and two additional electric motors for traveling underwater. This unwieldy configuration of engines, plus a huge mechanism that was supposed to withdraw the smokestack and air tube into the *Plunger*'s superstructure, made the sub unusually heavy and awkward.

Worried that the *Plunger* might never be accepted by the Navy, Holland sought to convince his company's backers to bankroll construction of a new, smaller submarine, his sixth. He figured that a privately financed submarine, free from the Navy's infuriating red tape, could incorporate all his best design ideas. His company would then be able to sell the Navy a superior, privately financed sub in place of the unsatisfactory *Plunger.*

Holland couldn't control the actions of the company that bore his name. As was the case with many inventors before him, his strength was his mechanical aptitude, not his business acumen. He had turned over much of the management of the company to Frost and assigned to it the legal rights to all his submarine patents. In return, Holland had received a large share of stock, but not a controlling interest, in the company. As the prospect of lucrative Navy submarine contracts brightened, and Holland's importance as a submarine designer diminished, his future with the company grew increasingly tenuous.

Even so, company officials decided to follow Holland's latest recommendation. They agreed to finance a new sub, to be known as the *Holland VI,* that might be more attractive to the Navy than the disappointing and ungainly *Plunger.*

With renewed confidence, Holland began building the new sub at a shipyard in Elizabethport, New Jersey. It was designed to be simple but effective, with one torpedo tube, one dynamite gun, and room for only five cramped crewmen. At the stern there would be an ordinary three-bladed propeller, an ordinary rudder, and two horizontal diving rudders, which a journalist from *McClure's Magazine* described as looking "like the feet of a duck spread out behind as it swims along the water." The *Holland VI* represented the distillation of a lifetime's experience with submarines. "I don't think I can improve on the arrangement or general features of the design . . ." wrote Holland of his sixth submarine; "it represents a powerful and effective boat."

Shortly after the *Holland VI* had been lowered into the water for the first time, there occurred an accident that would alter the future of the Holland Torpedo Boat Company. One evening in October 1897, a worker at the New Jersey shipyard inadvertently left open a watertight valve on the floating submarine when he headed home. Water seeped into the hull, and by the time workmen arrived the next morning the *Holland VI* had sunk to the bottom of its slip.

Holland was understandably demoralized. He knew that the salt water could ruin his sub's delicate machinery and electrical system. The sunken submarine was hoisted out of the water within eighteen hours, but the waterlogged electrical system resisted repair. Oil stoves and heaters were used to dry out the electric dynamo, but nothing seemed to work. As a last resort, company officials got in touch with the Electro-Dynamic Company of Philadelphia, the firm that had manufactured the dynamo, and requested the help of its best electrician. An ingenious young man named Frank T. Cable came to assess the trouble. By reversing the electric current running through the dynamo's armatures, Cable cleverly generated an internal heat that dried out the mechanism in less than a week. The *Holland VI* was back in action.

The Holland Torpedo Boat Company thus discovered Frank Cable, who later joined the young submarine firm and eventually replaced John Holland as the principal operator of the company's submarines. More important, this incident alerted Isaac Rice, president of the Electro-Dynamic Company, to the existence of Holland's submarine. Rice's subsequent interest in submarines forever reshaped the U.S. shipbuilding business.

The rehabilitated *Holland VI* took its first successful dive on a sunny St. Patrick's Day in 1898. A Navy inspector reported that in sea trials a few days later the submarine "fully proved her ability to propel herself, to dive, to come up, admit water to her ballast tanks, and to eject it again without difficulty." Company officials settled back and waited for word from the Navy.

Rumors that the latest Holland submarine was part of some foreign intrigue had already spread. The increasing tension between the United States and Spain, inflamed by sensationalist American newspapers, made the rumors even juicier. Each paper had its own theory: Cuban refugees would use the *Holland VI* to escape from their Spanish dominators; Spain would employ the sub to crush the Cuban insurrection; France would acquire the *Holland VI* to further its own sub experiments. Indeed, as the submarine was put through its paces in New York Harbor, foreign governments seemed to show a greater interest in it than the U.S. Navy.

To Holland's regret, the rumors circulating about military plans for his submarine were baseless. The fifty-six-year-old inventor was eager to demonstrate to doubters and skeptics the value of underwater naval warfare but as yet had had no opportunity. The *Holland VI* was simply being built on speculation.

Animosity between the United States and Spain mounted sharply after February 15, the day the American battleship *Maine* was sunk and 260 American lives were lost in the harbor of Havana, Cuba. Though it was never proved conclusively, Spain was widely believed to have been responsible for the attack. President William McKinley was intent on avoiding open conflict but eventually yielded to voices inside and outside his administration clamoring for war. Reluctantly he sent a war message to Congress on April 11.

The day before, Theodore Roosevelt, then assistant secretary of the navy, had recommended that the Navy purchase the *Holland VI*. "Evidently she has great possibilities in her for harbor defense," Roosevelt declared in a personal letter to his boss, Navy Secretary John D. Long. "Sometimes she doesn't work perfectly, but often she does, and I don't think in the present emergency we can afford to let her slip." The Navy postponed deciding whether to purchase Holland's submarine and established a board to evaluate its performance during trials in New York Harbor.

With the Spanish-American War under way, Holland longed for a chance to demonstrate his submarine in battle. But Washington did not encourage him. Desperate to be heard, Holland convinced his firm to stage a remarkable press conference in its New York City office. The little professor, known for his thick glasses, mustache, and derby, announced a bold proposal: "If the government will transport the boat from the Erie Basin [in Brooklyn], where it now is, to some point near the entrance to the [Cuban] harbor of Santiago, and a crew can be secured to man the boat, Mr. Holland will undertake the job of sinking the Spanish fleet, if it be still in Santiago Harbor, commanding the boat in person. If his offer be accepted, and he is successful in his undertaking, he will expect the government to buy his boat."

Washington ignored Holland's outlandish offer, but the newspapers loved it as both fearless and foolhardy. Several papers carried elaborate illustrations showing possible attack routes the courageous Holland might use. The offer also inspired a famous cartoon of an inventor sporting a derby emerging from a submarine's conning tower, asking rhetorically, "What? Me worry?," a model, it would seem, for *Mad* magazine's nincompoop mascot, Alfred E. Neuman.

Denied a role in the Spanish-American War, the *Holland VI* was eventually transferred to a yacht basin in Brooklyn, where a procession of dignitaries came to look at the controversial vessel. As it turned out, none was more important than Isaac Rice, who visited the submarine on July 4, 1898, and took his first trip underwater two months later. Rice emerged from that first dive an enthusiastic supporter of submarines. He was particularly taken with the notion of powering submarines with electrical storage batteries, a commodity for which he virtually monopolized the market.

Later that year, when Holland and his associates decided they would have to alter the design of their sub's propeller, Rice quickly agreed to provide the money for the reconstruction work. Thus, with a relatively minor investment, he entered the submarine business. In 1899 Rice incorporated his own Electric Boat Company, which promptly acquired the assets of the Holland Torpedo Boat Company and some of Rice's other enterprises and soon emerged as the dominant force in American submarine building.

Isaac Leopold Rice was an exceptionally talented lawyer, professor, and financier who, with equal ease, could write a brilliant legal brief in a complex railroad antitrust case, expound on the philosophy of music, devastate a chess opponent with his notorious Rice gambit, or monopolize the storage battery industry. He shifted effortlessly from field to field, impressing onlookers with his agile mind, shrewd business instincts, and stern demeanor.

His strong face was accentuated by penetrating eyes that lurked behind small, oval-shaped spectacles. His full beard, mustache, and thick, unruly hair, which had begun to turn white by the time he met Holland, often needed trimming. A serious, hardworking entrepreneur, Rice seemed obsessed at times by new ideas, new inventions, and new enterprises.

He was born in Bavaria, Germany, in 1850 and emigrated to the United States with his parents when he was six. Having been reared and educated in Philadelphia, he moved to New York City as a young man and was graduated from Columbia University Law School. He became a lecturer in law and political science at Columbia and a noted figure in Manhattan's academic circles.

At twenty-five, he wrote a thoughtful book entitled *What Is Music?*, a treatise on music's cosmic significance that moved one reviewer to describe him as a subtle thinker. "Mr. Rice's speculations are not unfrequently rather fanciful," the reviewer observed, "but they always have the sober cast of true philosophical inquiry and the tone of pure aesthetic feeling."

Rice had been developing that aesthetic sense for many years. As a sixteen-year-old he had spent time studying music in Paris. While there, he developed another youthful passion, chess. For hours on end the intense teenager would hunch over a chessboard at the Café de la Régence, challenging some of France's finest players.

He was never considered a true chess master, but Rice conceived and helped popularize one famous opening, the Rice gambit, in which a player intentionally sacrifices one of his knights at a critical moment in the game. Rice encouraged chess masters of the day to analyze his gambit and helped establish the Rice Gambit Association for that purpose. Another founder of the association told a story that illustrates both Rice's chess-playing style and his competitive personality:

It was in 1882. Mr. Rice was then a member of the faculty of the School of Political Science of Columbia University, New York. Nothing was farther removed from his mind than thoughts of business. Science was his purpose and passion. One day, at Fleischmann's, while contemplatively drinking his cup of tea, he was approached by a stranger, who introduced himself as Mr. L——, and explained that he came on the request of a neighbor of Mr. Rice's, a Mr. R——, to ask Mr. Rice to be counsel for Mr. R—— in a suit. Mr. Rice refused, of course, to consider the proposal, because he was in the academic career, not the active one, of law. After a few weeks Mr. L—— returned, begging Mr. Rice to make an exception in Mr. R——'s behalf, but Mr. Rice declined more strongly. After a few more weeks Mr. L—— again approached Mr. Rice, saying that Mr. R—— would not take "no" for an answer. "Why does Mr. R —— insist on requesting me, a young man without any experience and who does not want any experience, to take up an affair which many able lawyers in this city would be only too glad to take up for him?" asked Mr. Rice, whose curiosity had been aroused. "I will tell you," replied Mr. L——, "it is because Mr. R—— played a game of chess with you in 1869, and from the manner in which you handled the pieces he thinks that you are the only man who can handle this case."

Mr. R—— had found Mr. Rice's weak point. Mr. Rice did actually take his case and completely vindicated that gentleman's opinion.

And so, Mr. Rice became a man of business.

His business interests were wide-ranging and successful. In 1886 he resigned from the Columbia faculty to devote himself exclusively to the burgeoning field of railroad law. America's railroad industry was rife with legal disputes, enabling Rice to distinguish himself with a series of negotiations, reorganizations, and litigations. Each case seemed to enhance his reputation and fatten his wallet.

Before long he turned his attention to the commercial application of electricity. The United States was rushing headlong into the industrial era, virtually bursting with creative energy. Waterwheels had given way to steam boilers, canalboats had yielded to railroads, and sailing vessels had deferred to steamships. The industrialists, financiers, and inventors of America had sniffed the intoxicating aroma of progress. "Nothing could stop their natural exuberance, their confident outlook. Neither the Civil War, nor sporadic strikes, nor agrarian discontent nor spreading slums could shake their belief that progress was not an accident but a necessity. From this time forward, science, invention and industry would shape the course of the nation," wrote the editors of *Dynamic America*.

By the 1880's the era of electricity had begun. In January 1880 Thomas A. Edison was granted a patent for his incandescent lamp. A few months later, William Woodnut Griscom, a businessman and prolific inventor, won a patent for a small electric motor and established the Electro-Dynamic Company of Philadelphia to manufacture them. Griscom's infant company was one day to be swallowed by Isaac Rice.

Rice founded the Electric Storage Battery Company of Philadelphia to sell batteries for use in city streetcar lines, automobiles, taxicabs, and motor launches. He built his company around one essential patent for an efficient and economical battery known as a chloride accumulator. But he sought control of every other patent in the storage battery field as well. "The Electrical Storage Battery [Company] proceeded to fortify its position by absorbing almost every possible competitor and acquiring control of almost every inven-

2. Isaac L. Rice, a brilliant Columbia University professor, railroad lawyer, and industrial entrepreneur, who amassed a fortune in the storage battery business, then founded the Electric Boat Company, which became America's premier submarine builder. *Submarine Force Library and Museum*

tion of merit comprised within the scope of its operations," noted a periodical in 1895.

Eventually Rice controlled every relevant patent except one, which was held by Griscom's Electro-Dynamic Company. Rice offered Griscom $1 million in cash for his patent, but before a deal could be negotiated, Griscom died in a freak hunting accident. Electro-Dynamic floundered and soon came onto the market. Rice purchased it, acquired its key patent, and gained control of the storage battery industry.

Rice had had his initial exposure to submarines after Frank Cable, one of Electro-Dynamic's best electricians, was summoned to repair the dynamo in the *Holland VI*. He immediately saw the submarine's potential and created the Electric Boat Company to capitalize on yet another ripe market.

Holland's inventive genius and E. B. Frost's political maneuvering had not persuaded the Navy to buy the *Holland VI*. A tough, well-connected business-man, Rice took a more direct approach. If the Navy wouldn't come to the *Holland VI*, the submarine would go to the Navy.

Rice organized a thirty-nine-day odyssey from the sub's base in New York, down the East Coast via the Inland Waterway to the Navy's front door in Washington, D.C. He lashed the submarine on pontoons and floated it past admiring crowds all along the route.

This promotional stunt worked beautifully. In March 1900 the *Holland VI* was put through official trials and unofficial exhibitions on the Potomac River. The company distributed programs that hailed its vessel as "The Monster War Fish," "Uncle Sam's Devil of the Deep," and "The Naval 'Hell Diver.' " The next month the Navy purchased the *Holland VI* for $150,000. Within a few weeks it canceled the contract for the cumbersome *Plunger,* and the Holland Torpedo Boat Company returned to the U.S. Treasury the $93,000 it had received for that unsuccessful vessel.

The future finally looked bright for naval submarines. That summer the Navy ordered six similar subs to be delivered during the next three years. It was the beginning of the twentieth century, and the U.S. Navy could boast a submarine fleet of one small boat.

# Chapter Three

## Airborne—the Genesis of Convair

### (1)

Two cavernous industrial buildings with distinctive saber-toothed roof lines sit quietly today on the edge of San Diego's Lindbergh Field. Nothing much seems to be happening. Inside the behemoth structures GD's Convair division manufactures aircraft components, which are later incorporated into complete airplanes by other companies at other locations, and space boosters for NASA. The work that takes place in those buildings has become rather prosaic in recent years, hardly the stuff from which legends are born.

But the activity at Lindbergh Field has not always been so humdrum. In 1944, at the height of World War II, sweaty aircraft workers in the same two buildings churned out more warplanes than any other aircraft factory in the world: B-24 Liberators that carpet-bombed the invasion beaches at Normandy the morning of D-day and PBY Catalina patrol bombers that tracked and helped sink the dreaded German battleship *Bismarck* in the North Atlantic.

These famous U.S. warplanes were built in San Diego by the Consolidated Aircraft Corporation, which had been founded only two decades earlier by Reuben H. Fleet, a former major in the Army Air Corps. Fleet's firm had come a long way. Begun in Rhode Island in 1923 as a tiny company, with total capital of $60,000, Consolidated operated more than a dozen separate manufacturing and modification divisions across the United States by the peak of

48

World War II, employing about 105,000 workers, nearly 40 percent of whom were women. Between the bombing of Pearl Harbor in 1941 and America's declaration of victory in 1945, Consolidated built about 33,000 planes—nearly 13 percent of all aircraft produced in the country.

When the war ended, Consolidated was a giant in the U.S. aviation industry and a household word across America. It was subsequently swallowed by a holding company, merged with another aircraft manufacturer, and renamed Consolidated Vultee Aircraft—Convair for short. When John J. Hopkins orchestrated the merger of Consolidated Vultee and General Dynamics in 1954, Convair's aircraft and missile operation became a division of GD.

The story of Major Reuben Hollis Fleet, the fiercely independent entrepreneur who built Consolidated Aircraft, is more than the tale of a hard-driving industrialist who made good. It is also the story of the pioneering days of military aviation, the methods by which the Army Air Corps purchased its warplanes, and the rapidly evolving role of the U.S. defense industry.

Fleet was an imposing man with a nonstop mouth. Nearly everyone who knew him recalled his fondness for talking. At the drop of an aircraft rivet he would tell the story of his rise in the aviation business, extol the virtues of Consolidated's latest aircraft, or curse the damnable behavior of the Internal Revenue Service. On one occasion Harry S Truman, then a senator from Missouri and chairman of a Senate committee investigating the nation's defense program, turned up in San Diego to look over Fleet's aircraft plant. Weary of his host's interminable blather, Truman cut him off curtly. "God damn!" Truman interrupted. "I want to see your books, Fleet. I'm not interested in your rise from rags to riches!"

To some people, Major Fleet was an insufferable businessman who never dropped an idea once it had lodged in his restless brain. To others, he was an intense individual with limitless energy and an insatiable appetite for getting things done. He stood six feet tall, but his erect military posture made him appear even taller. With sparkling blue eyes and a presence some found charming, he invariably dominated any room he entered. Self-confident, impatient, stubborn, and *boring*—these were the adjectives most often applied to Reuben Fleet.

He was born in 1887 in the tree-covered northwestern corner of the continental United States, in what was then the territory of Washington (it became the forty-second state two years later). His family swung from prosperity during his early years to hardship following a financial panic in 1893, when the value of his father's considerable landholdings plummeted. "From six until I was thirteen I didn't have a decent pair of shoes," Fleet recalled.

Following his graduation from a military academy in Indiana, Fleet returned to Washington, set up a real estate business, joined a local National Guard unit, and soon became the unit's captain.

At the age of twenty-seven, he was elected to the Washington legislature, where he became an outspoken champion of military aviation. When Fleet was a youngster, his interest in aviation had consisted of little more than flying kites and leaping from the second stories of barns, aided only by "wings" fashioned from bed sheets. It was three years after Orville and Wilbur Wright's first flights near Kitty Hawk in 1903 before young Fleet even heard about these historic achievements. In fact, Fleet didn't take his first airplane ride until the year he entered the legislature. He became an instant enthusiast, hitching rides whenever he could with the few pilots operating in the state of Washington. Another young man, who had earlier been a lumberman near Fleet's hometown, shared his newfound love of flying. The man was William Boeing, a name that would link Washington State and aircraft production for decades to come.

When he entered the state legislature, Fleet was named chairman of the lower chamber's Military Affairs Committee in part because he had risen to the rank of captain in the state's National Guard. He used his chairmanship as a platform to promote the use of military airplanes by the nation's armed forces, an idea scorned by most war strategists at the time, who considered the airplane completely impractical for use in combat. Like John Holland, Fleet had to battle the conservative element of the U.S. military for years.

He wasn't deterred. In a dramatic gesture to draw attention, he convinced a local pilot to fly his seaplane to Olympia and circle the State Capitol for thirty-five minutes. Legislators, reporters, and the citizens of Olympia gawked at the aerial spectacle, and Fleet savored the resulting publicity.

The young legislator promptly introduced a bill that would require the state to appropriate $250,000 for the Washington National Guard to purchase planes and initiate aviation activities. It was an audacious request—$250,000 was more money than the federal government had appropriated that year for aviation activities throughout the entire United States. Nevertheless, with Fleet's energetic backing, the bill was approved by the legislature's lower chamber.

Word of Olympia's startling action reached the officials in Washington, D.C., responsible for the U.S. military aviation program. Still in its embryonic stage, that group had been organized only seven months earlier and humbly named the Aviation Section of the Signal Corps of the U.S. Army. After Fleet's $250,000 appropriation bill had whizzed through the legislature's lower chamber, Lieutenant Colonel Samuel Reber, head of the Aviation Section, traveled across the continent to learn what was happening in Olympia. Colonel Reber told a joint session of the legislature that it was folly for a single state to be spending more than the entire federal government on military aviation.

As head of the Military Affairs Committee Fleet began the interrogation of their visitor from the East.

"Colonel, are you really the head of the Aviation Section of the Army Signal Corps?" Fleet remembered asking.

"I am," Colonel Reber answered.

"Are you, yourself, a flier?"

"No, I am not."

"Have you ever been up in the air?"

"Yes, twice."

"Couldn't you see, when you were up in the air, where the 'enemy' was; how wonderful aviation is as a new source of information which is helpful to those below who are supposed to engage the enemy?"

"No, I couldn't see a thing."

"Why couldn't you see anything?"

"Because my eyes were closed."

"Why were they closed?"

"Because of the wind. I was terrified."

"What were you doing?"

"I was holding on to two braces and praying to God to get me down."

"Did you ever make any other flights?"

"Yes, I made one other flight."

"What did you do then?"

"I did the same thing. My eyes were closed and I didn't see anything. I just wanted to get down alive. If the Lord had intended mankind to fly, he would have given him wings. There isn't one man in a million who could ever learn to fly."

Fleet saw a different future. He told Colonel Reber that the U.S. Army had failed to comprehend aviation's possibilities. He urged the federal government to keep pace with the Europeans, who were then the innovators in the aviation field.

Perhaps Fleet's pep talk emboldened Colonel Reber when he returned to Washington. The following year Congress appropriated more than $13 million for Army aviation activities, a huge jump from the paltry sum of $225,000 earmarked the year before. Included in that $13 million budget were funds to train one national guardsman from each state to fly. Fleet was selected as one of the first eleven guardsmen in the country for that pilot training.

In the spring of 1917, at the age of thirty, he closed his prosperous real estate business and headed for San Diego, where the Army had established a pilot training school on North Island, a flat, sandy island in San Diego Bay.

The First World War was already raging in Europe, and the United States was soon to be drawn into the conflict. When Fleet reported for pilot training, the Army's Aviation Section wasn't much to brag about. It possessed only seventy-three planes, thirty of which were assigned to the flight school. Fleet took his maiden flight as a student pilot on April 5, 1917. The next day the United States declared war on Germany.

He was immediately transferred from the National Guard to the Regular Army. Student pilots were being taught to fly Curtiss JN-4D Jenny and Martin TT trainers. The declaration of war had heightened the sense of urgency at North Island. Fleet was awarded the country's seventy-fourth pair of pilot's wings and was promoted from captain to major, a rank that stuck with him informally long after he stepped out of uniform.

At the beginning of 1918 Fleet was assigned to the headquarters of the Army's Aviation Section in Washington, D.C., where he spent the next four years managing the production and procurement of Army aircraft. Flying was still a young and dangerous field. Airplanes crashed with alarming frequency. Of the seventy-three pilots who had earned their wings before Fleet, about two-thirds had already died while flying. Planes were structurally weak, engines frequently failed, and aircraft control systems were notoriously unreliable. In fact, before Fleet's pilot training had begun, flying was deemed so risky that only bachelors under thirty were considered eligible.

The United States produced relatively few military aircraft before World War I because Congress hadn't appropriated much money. The dramatic hike in the Army's aviation budget from $225,000 to $13 million didn't receive congressional approval until August 1916. As a result, U.S. aircraft production during the war itself was confined primarily to the Curtiss Jenny and the De Havilland DH-4, a British-designed observation and reconnaissance aircraft built in the United States by the Dayton-Wright Company. Most of the pursuit planes and bombers used in World War I by American fliers were built in France or Great Britain.

## (2)

The U.S. war effort gained momentum in the spring of 1918. The Aviation Section, which had been upgraded and renamed the Army Air Service, was busy with aircraft production, pilot training, and combat operations in Europe. Consequently, it came as a great shock to the service when Secretary of War Newton Baker publicly announced on May 3, 1918, that in a mere twelve days the U.S. Army would initiate the world's first regular airmail service from Washington to Philadelphia to New York City.

The Air Service was caught completely by surprise. It had fewer than two weeks to assemble its pilots, purchase and modify its aircraft, select landing sites in the three cities, coordinate logistics, and organize an impressive inaugural ceremony scheduled for May 15. The notion of establishing an airmail service had been kicking around the Cabinet for several months as a means of fostering the development of commercial aviation in the United States. President Woodrow Wilson wanted it. Thus, A. S. Burleson, the postmaster general, wanted it. Thus, Otto Praeger, the second assistant postmaster general in charge of mail transportation, wanted it.

Some people thought that using Army Air Service fliers to initiate such a postal service would offer the young pilots invaluable flying experience. In fact, the government had nowhere else to turn. The U.S. Post Office had solicited bids from private aviation companies capable of running an intercity airmail operation, but no bidder had stepped forward. As a result, the Post Office and the War Department agreed to assign the task to the Army Air Service. Congress appropriated $100,000 to begin the service. Everything was unfolding according to plan, except for one hitch: No one had bothered to inform the Air Service.

On the recommendation of Colonel Henry "Hap" Arnold, an aeronautics officer who later became a five-star general and the father of the U.S. Air Force, Major Fleet was placed in charge of the new airmail program. He had a lot to do and little time in which to do it.

The air distance from New York to Philadelphia to Washington, D.C., was 218 miles. Unfortunately the Air Service didn't own any planes that could fly either leg of that journey without stopping for fuel. Furthermore, gaining access to suitable airfields would be difficult. Bustleton Field, near Philadelphia, was available. But in New York the Army didn't want its pilot training at Hazelhurst Field, near Mineola, Long Island, interrupted by a new airmail service. And in Washington, D.C., there simply was no suitable landing strip.

On May 6, Major Fleet was summoned by Secretary of War Baker to discuss the new airmail service. Fleet bluntly suggested postponing the service's inauguration to allow the Army enough time to obtain modified Curtiss JN-6H aircraft with enlarged fuel tanks. Baker summoned Postmaster General Burleson.

"Burleson went into a rage over the suggestion for deferment, stating he had already announced to the press that an Army Aerial Mail Service would get started on 15 May," Fleet wrote years later. "It had to start then, even if war work suffered."

Left with no alternative, the major picked up a phone in Baker's office and instructed one of his subordinates in the Air Service immediately to order six JN-6H's from the Curtiss Aeroplane and Motor Company on Long Island.

Under normal circumstances the Jenny would be equipped with a nineteen-gallon fuel tank that would enable it to fly approximately ninety miles, at about sixty-five miles per hour. For this unique mission, however, Curtiss was asked to remove the seat and controls from the front cockpit and use the extra space to store fuel, oil, and a special mail hopper. The six planes had to be delivered to the Army airfield in Mineola within eight days. Curtiss accepted the order by phone on the condition that the "rush" project could take precedence over its other war production work.

The absence of suitable landing strips in New York and Washington required novel solutions. First, Fleet phoned an old friend, August Belmont, a banker and transportation tycoon who owned the Belmont Park racetrack on Long Island. Belmont granted Fleet permission to use his park as a New York landing strip. Then Fleet set his sights on the polo field in the District of Columbia's Potomac Park. The grassy playing area was surrounded by a racetrack and offered an ideal landing strip were it not for a single tree standing hazardously in the middle of the field. With only four days left before mail service was set to begin, Fleet contacted the local parks commission to request permission to remove the offending tree.

"By when will you need it removed?" asked a commission official.

"Three days," said Fleet.

"But it will take three months for the Commission to act," said the official.

Not one for bureaucratic niceties, Fleet hung up the phone, went immediately to the polo field, and personally ordered a workman to cut down the tree.

Five pilots were needed to launch the airmail service. Fleet chose three of them from the Army Air Service. The Post Office, which had its own political interests to look out for, recommended the other two pilots, Lieutenant James Edgerton and Lieutenant George Boyle, both from the Air Service.

Lieutenant Edgerton, a recent flying school graduate, happened to be the son of the Post Office's purchasing agent. He was assigned to fly the first airmail *into* Washington on May 15. Lieutenant Boyle was engaged to Margaret McChord, daughter of Charles McChord, the interstate commerce commissioner who had just sided with the Post Office in its ongoing battle with private parcel post companies. Boyle was slated to fly the first mail *out* of Washington.

By May 14 Curtiss had delivered only two planes to the Army Air Service on Long Island. Anxious to witness the inaugural ceremony in Washington at 11:00 A.M. the next morning, Fleet flew out of New York, where he had been supervising last-minute details. He headed for Bustleton Field in Philadelphia, flying an ordinary Jenny trainer, equipped with a standard-size fuel tank. Another Air Service pilot flew alongside in a modified Jenny.

"The weather was so frightful; it was so foggy we pilots could not see each other after take-off; the masts of boats in New York Harbor were in fog," wrote Fleet in a detailed reminiscence. "I climbed through the fog and came out at 11,000 feet, almost the ceiling of the airplane. I flew by magnetic compass and the sun until I ran out of gasoline and the propeller stopped."

Fleet glided his crippled Jenny toward Philadelphia, dropped out of the clouds at 3,000 feet, and was forced to land in a farmer's field. After pouring a few gallons of the farmer's fuel into his tank, the irrepressible Fleet took off again. "I inquired where Bustleton was, took off, flew toward it, ran out of gasoline again, and landed in a meadow two miles from Bustleton Field. As no telephone was available, I commandeered a farmer to drive me to Bustleton Field. . . ." He ordered the accompanying Air Service pilot to fetch his plane.

The next morning Fleet again set off for Washington. He arrived at the polo field at 10:35 A.M., just twenty-five minutes before Lieutenant Boyle was scheduled to take off. A crowd of about 2,000 people had gathered in Potomac Park for the inaugural ceremony. President Wilson, Postmaster General Burleson, and second Assistant Postmaster General Praeger all were there. So was Margaret McChord, with an armful of red roses.

The dignitaries were assembled and eagerly awaiting the historic moment. But there was one minor oversight: Nobody had thought to bring aviation fuel for Lieutenant Boyle's plane. Frantically Fleet and his subordinates drained fuel from three planes standing nearby. As 11:00 A.M. drew near, workmen were still pouring gasoline into Boyle's aircraft. Fleet strapped a map to the young pilot's leg and corrected his compass course for Philadelphia. Margaret McChord admired the helmet, goggles, and leather jacket of her handsome pilot, then moistened his cheek with a farewell kiss.

With Major Fleet at his side, President Wilson smiled as the modified Jenny taxied down the polo field and took off precisely on schedule. Twelve maddeningly hectic days had culminated in a bone-wearying triumph for Fleet. As the JN-6H lifted off the grassy runway, President Wilson turned to Fleet and said nonchalantly, "Tomorrow I want to extend the service to Boston."

To the assembled crowd the first day of airmail service seemed an unblemished success. Lieutenant Edgerton landed at the polo field on schedule that afternoon, carrying mail from New York and Philadelphia. The letters were distributed throughout the District by local Boy Scouts in a mere thirty-three minutes. Newspapers carried laudatory accounts. Everyone was satisfied. Everyone, that is, except young Lieutenant Boyle and his irate boss, Reuben Fleet.

Unbeknownst to the general public, Boyle's historic flight from Potomac Park turned out to be an abysmal failure. Twenty-five miles north of Washing-

3. Major Reuben H. Fleet of the Army Air Service organized the nation's first official airmail service in May 1918, with flights in both directions between Washington, D.C., and New York, via Philadelphia. After leaving the Army, he founded the Consolidated Aircraft Corporation, which built more than 33,000 planes during World War II and eventually became the Convair division of General Dynamics. *Reuben H. Fleet Collection—San Diego Aerospace Museum*

ton, Boyle had lost his way, landed in a plowed field in Waldorf, Maryland, flipped the plane on its back, and snapped its propeller. The young pilot had no choice but to telephone Fleet, who ordered him to bring the mail quietly back to Washington for delivery the following day.

The Post Office asked that Lieutenant Boyle be given a second chance to redeem himself as a pilot.

"On this trip," recalled Fleet, "I accompanied him in another airplane 40 miles on the correct compass course, cut my throttle, asked him if he was okay and could carry on. He yelled back, 'I'm okay.' " Boyle's luck was no better the second time around. "He landed, lost and out of gas, near the mouth of the Chesapeake Bay, retanked with gasoline and took off for Bustleton Field. He crashed near [the] Philadelphia Country Club without hurting himself, breaking a wing of his plane." Lieutenant Boyle eventually delivered the mail to Philadelphia . . . by truck. Despite the Post Office's fervent pleas, that flight marked the end of Boyle's career as an airmail pilot.

Immediately following the inauguration ceremony Major Fleet had strongly recommended against extending airmail service to Boston the following day. He and Secretary of War Baker met with President Wilson in the White House that afternoon, with Baker backing Fleet's recommendation. Airmail service to Boston began instead three weeks later. As planned, Major Fleet completed his airmail duties a few weeks after that. For its part, the Army Air Service delivered airmail successfully until the middle of August 1918, when it turned its responsibilities over to the Post Office.

With the conclusion of World War I most U.S. servicemen shed their military uniforms and returned to civilian jobs. Major Fleet chose to remain in the Army and became a contracting officer who negotiated with private aircraft companies on the Air Service's behalf. He quit in 1922 to accept a job as general manager of the Gallaudet Aircraft Corporation, a company that was rich in history but poor at the bank.

He helped Gallaudet terminate several of its money-losing aircraft contracts, but Fleet had grander plans. After securing the rights to a trainer aircraft from the Dayton-Wright Airplane Company and luring away one of Dayton-Wright's best aircraft designers, Fleet set off on his own.

## (3)

Fleet established the Consolidated Aircraft Corporation in 1923 with about $15,000 of his own money and $10,000 from his sister and brother-in-law. Before long Consolidated won the Army trainer contract Fleet had expected, a $200,000 award for twenty TW-3 trainer aircraft and the equivalent of three additional planes in spare parts. Consolidated was off and running.

At the same time the company entered an Army competition for a new primary trainer that was expected to replace the wartime Jennies. The winning plane would probably become the Army's principal trainer for years to come. Fleet wanted the contract badly.

A competitive fly-off was staged at the Air Service's primary training school in San Antonio, Texas, during the summer of 1924. Consolidated entered a newly designed trainer it called the Camel. After the scores had been tabulated, Consolidated walked away with its second Army contract: an initial order for 50 Camel trainers, which the Army named Trusty and designated PT-1 (for first primary trainer). The Trusty was ugly, but it was so rugged and easy to operate that even the clumsiest student pilot could learn to fly it safely.

Fleet was pleased with the Army's first order of 50 trainers, but he hoped for more. He made an enticing offer to the chief of the Air Service's supply section: If the Army doubled its order, Fleet would relocate Consolidated

Aircraft to San Antonio, where it could respond more promptly to the Army's aircraft requirements. Also, Consolidated would deliver all 100 trainers during the next two years, in batches of 10. If the Army noticed any technical problems in the aircraft that required design changes, Consolidated would incorporate those changes in the undelivered airplanes at no additional cost. It would initially charge $11,000 for each trainer. When the Army was satisfied and froze the design, the company would cut its price by $2,500 and receive $625 per plane as a bonus.

Fleet knew he could buy component parts and materials for 100 planes at lower unit costs than for 50. He also knew that a 100-plane order probably meant that more planes would be left to build after the design had been frozen. His offer to absorb the cost of all design changes was a big gamble. The thorny question of continual design changes—and who should pay for them—was already troubling aircraft manufacturers by the 1920's. (The same issue brought the Navy and its private shipbuilders into bitter conflict during the 1970's.)

The Army rejected Fleet's proposal, so he signed the original contract for 50 trainers and abandoned the idea of relocating to San Antonio. (It was seventeen years before Consolidated made it to Texas, as operator of a new B-24 bomber plant the government built in Fort Worth.)

Fleet knew he needed larger quarters for his expanding company. His Rhode Island factory already had to recruit aircraft workers in New Haven, Boston, and New York City, sometimes at higher salaries than he paid his local employees. He decided to relocate to Buffalo—midway between the skilled craftsmen of Rhode Island and the manufacturing center of Detroit. He leased space in a sprawling one-story government-built factory that the Curtiss Aeroplane and Motor Company had used during World War I. Major Fleet arrived in Buffalo in 1924 in a Model T Ford, followed by three railroad boxcars filled with Consolidated Aircraft's physical assets.

Consolidated was building the 50 PT-1 trainers in Buffalo when the Army instructed the company to provide its designs to rival aircraft manufacturers that might want to bid against Consolidated for future orders. The Army had received appropriations from Congress for 100 additional trainers and planned to seek competitive price quotations.

Fleet was outraged. "We cannot but regard such an arrangement as disadvantageous, if not disastrous, to both the Government and ourselves, and unnecessary in peace time," he complained to the Army. He was even more vituperative when he discussed the subject in *The New York Times* eight years later.

"Every company employing a staff of designers and engineers knows that under the present system any worthy model it has created may be torn from its creator and turned over to an underselling, pirating competitor to manufacture . . ." Fleet argued. "And when its product is taken away by the very government it has tried so hard to serve, and turned over to another to make it, it is spirit-killing, discouraging beyond words, unethical and unfair."

Throughout 1925 Fleet peppered the Army with reasons why Consolidated should be awarded the next 100 PT-1's. His company had designed the plane, it could build them more cheaply, and he was figuring a modest profit of only 15 percent. He argued that while fighter planes might need to be upgraded continually, trainers were a different breed. "Constant improvement in performance is not necessary; birds learn to fly the same way they always did," he wrote.

His arguments did not convince Major General Mason Patrick, chief of the Air Service. Patrick insisted on seeking bids from rival companies, thereby forgoing whatever savings Consolidated might achieve by purchasing its materials in large quantities.

Fleet was not ready to give up. He was convinced he could build his trainer for less than any competitive company, so he ordered enough material to build 150 trainers. It was a big gamble. Consolidated would find itself with an awful lot of unneeded material if one of its competitors won the second or third trainer contracts. This time Fleet's gamble paid off. Two months after the Army had placed its initial order for 50 trainers, it handed Consolidated a second order for 50 more, and a third order for the remaining 50 planes followed two months later.

Before long the Navy began buying Consolidated's trainers, and the company was doing a brisk business. Its order book showed sales of approximately $211,000 in 1924, its first full year in business. That figure nearly tripled the following year and topped $1 million in both 1926 and 1927. During those four years the company earned about $800,000 in profits.

The company's early success backfired in 1927. General Patrick of the Army Air Corps (its name had been changed again) wasn't pleased that Consolidated had earned so much money. He maintained that $300,000 of the company's $800,000 in earnings represented "excess profits" that ought to be returned to the Army and Navy. Fleet vehemently disagreed. "It was nobody's business what we made since our bid was the lowest and since we had the best plane," he told an Associated Press reporter years later. He considered $800,000 the proper reward for Consolidated's shrewd purchase of aircraft materials in larger than normal quantities and its cost-cutting production methods.

In contract disputes such as these, however, the government often prevails. Consolidated's board of directors reluctantly agreed to return $300,000 to the government. But General Patrick didn't want the repayment in cash. He suspected that a cash reimbursement from Consolidated would be grabbed by the Treasury Department and would never show up in the Air Corps's budget. Instead, Patrick insisted that Consolidated supply the Army and Navy *free of charge* fifty trainers worth about $6,000 apiece.

Major Fleet was livid. He went to Washington to tell General Patrick face-to-face that he refused to supply the planes free of charge. A heated argument erupted. Fleet claimed that profits in the aircraft industry were wildly unpredictable, and that Consolidated's earnings history was not much different from that of other aircraft companies. He emphasized that his firm had taken business risks and maintained that its earnings weren't excess profits.

Indeed, between 1926 and 1934, profits in the aircraft industry rose and fell erratically. A War Department official told a House Military Affairs Committee in 1934 that published accounts of "fabulous profits" in the aircraft business were unjust and misleading. The average profit of companies selling to the Air Corps between 1926 and 1934 had been 19.8 percent, but during the last three and a half years of that period the profit rate had slipped to less than 9 percent, the official explained.

Given the vagaries of his industry, Fleet was adamant. He and General Patrick negotiated stubbornly behind closed doors, and it appeared that the two strong-willed men might never reach an accord. Then the door to the general's office swung open, and a smiling Major Fleet strolled out. He had agreed to *sell*—not *give*—the fifty planes to the services for $1 each!

Though it had purchased trainers from Consolidated and would have been entitled to thirteen of the $1 aircraft, the Navy declined to accept any form of payment from Fleet, suggesting instead that Consolidated was entitled to whatever profits it had earned. "It is the opinion of this office that, having procured aircraft from the Consolidated Aircraft Corporation after due competition, the Navy Department is not in a position to question the profits that the company may have made," Rear Admiral W. A. Moffett explained in a letter to General Patrick.

General Patrick thought otherwise. He demanded the Army's thirty-seven $1 planes and the Navy's thirteen as well. Fleet was bitter. Partly as a result of the fifty $1 planes, Consolidated didn't pay dividends to its stockholders for more than nine years. To taunt General Patrick, Fleet intended to send fifty separate $1 invoices to the Army and mount the fifty checks he received on his office wall. But the Army would have none of Fleet's little plan. It paid for Consolidated's fifty planes with a single $50 check.

The year 1927 was important for Consolidated for reasons other than the $1-plane fiasco. The designer of Consolidated's original Trusty trainer left the company that year. Fleet hired Isaac "Mac" Laddon, the Army's principal designer of large aircraft. And Consolidated decided to enter the heavy-aircraft market.

It was also the year of Charles Lindbergh. On May 20 and 21, 1927, the photogenic airmail pilot flew his single-engine *Spirit of St. Louis* from New York to Paris and into the hearts of adoring admirers around the world. "This boy is not our usual type of hero," humorist Will Rogers declared a few days later. "He is all the others rolled into one and multiplied by ten. . . ." The world had a new hero, and the aircraft industry had a celebrity. Aircraft sales shot upward as the public's fascination with flying spread rapidly. Good times seemed assured. Then, without warning, the stock market crash of 1929 and the subsequent depression threw the aircraft industry, and the entire U.S. economy, into a disastrous tailspin.

The military aircraft business was still young and unpredictable. Interest in a particular type of aircraft often rose and fell in unexplained ways. Consolidated had tried to crack the night bomber market but lost out to a field of competitors. Now it was looking for another, "hotter" type of military aircraft to build. It found it in the Navy's long-range patrol bombers. In order to expand its reconnaissance patrols up and down the Atlantic coast and across the Pacific Ocean to Hawaii, the Navy required a durable seaplane, sometimes called a flying boat, with a range of about 2,000 miles.

The Navy chose the winning design for this aircraft in a unique way. For the first time the Navy's Bureau of Aeronautics didn't provide the aircraft industry with a finished design of the plane it wanted built. Instead, it designed only the hull and left the rest of the plane for the competing companies to design. The Navy's aircraft factory in Philadelphia designed and built its own version of the plane for comparison with the industry's submissions.

Consolidated had a leg up on its competition. Coincidentally Laddon's bosses had given him permission to design a flying boat for Boeing while he was working for the Army. Consolidated's revisions of Laddon's earlier designs won the Navy competition for the new long-range patrol plane. The company was awarded a $150,000 contract in February 1928 to build a prototype patrol plane, designated the XPY-1. It was a major victory for Consolidated, which went on to become the largest and most respected builder of flying boats in the world.

Fleet named the XPY-1 the Admiral after Admiral Moffett, the Navy officer who had declined to accept any $1 planes from Consolidated. The plane was developed just as U.S. commercial airlines were beginning to carry passengers overseas, and so Consolidated designed the Admiral to serve either military or commercial markets. As a military patrol bomber the enormous plane with 100-foot wings and watertight pontoons could carry a pilot, copilot, navigator-bomber, radio operator, and mechanic-gunner. As a commercial aircraft it could accommodate thirty-two passengers.

## (4)

Construction of the first Admiral prototype began in March 1928. By December it was ready for delivery to the Navy. The plane may have been ready, but the weather in Buffalo wasn't. Blocks of ice choked Lake Erie and the Niagara River, preventing the seaplane from taking off. Fleet ordered his workers to disassemble the flying boat into three large sections, which were loaded on railroad flatcars and transported to Washington overland.

After numerous design changes had been made, and several defects corrected, the Navy decided to order nine more flying boats. It could have awarded a production contract to Consolidated, which had designed the XPY-1 and built the first prototype, but instead, it solicited bids from any qualified aircraft manufacturer. Just as Fleet had fumed when the Army had decided to "compete" the award for fifty PT-1 trainers which his company had designed, so he now railed at the Navy's plan to "compete" the flying boat contract. In this case, however, the consequences of losing were far greater.

Consolidated had already invested about $500,000 of its own money in the Admiral's development, on top of the $150,000 it had received under the Navy's prototype contract. In addition, Fleet had already ordered enough material to build the initial production run. Now he was worried. Consolidated had to recoup those material costs, or it would suffer financially for years. But a competing aircraft manufacturer, which hadn't spent $500,000 to develop the flying boat, might be able to underbid Consolidated for the production contract.

One of them did. The Glenn L. Martin Company won the Navy's contract for the first nine flying boats with a bid about half a million dollars lower than Consolidated's. It was small consolation to Fleet that Martin damaged its reputation in the industry by taking far longer than it had promised to build those aircraft.

In the meantime, Consolidated's designers modified their XPY-1 design. After losing the initial production contract to Martin, Consolidated leaped back into the flying boat business two years later, when it won a second Navy contract to develop an advanced model of its Admiral. The new aircraft was given the designation XP2Y-1. As Fleet put it, that XP2Y-1 contract marked the last time Consolidated found itself "sucking hind teat" in the flying boat business.

Although Consolidated won the XP2Y-1 prototype contract, Fleet wanted to recover the huge investment in engineering and materials it had made for the Admiral. Because the plane had been designed for commercial as well as military use, Fleet began searching for a commercial customer for his long-range plane.

He found it in the New York, Rio & Buenos Aires Line, a newly established airline that carried mail and passengers between New York and many of the burgeoning cities along South America's east coast. Fleet recognized the possibility of selling flying boats to the new airline and agreed to provide some of its start-up capital. NYRBA, as it was known, once boasted the longest airline routes in the world, but it eventually succumbed to Pan American World Airways, the commercial juggernaut fashioned by airline mogul Juan Terry Trippe. By the time the airline was bought out by Pan Am, Consolidated had sold it fourteen flying boats, named Commodores, and twenty smaller aircraft. Fleet was satisfied. Those transactions had earned Consolidated $208,000 in profits and absorbed its original development costs and unused materials from the Navy's Admiral project.

## (5)

Like many businessmen "married" to their companies, Fleet seemed to spend more time with his secretary than with his family. His first marriage, to his hometown sweetheart, Elizabeth Girton, had ended in divorce. Now he fancied his secretary, Lauretta Golem, who was married to a machine shop foreman employed at Consolidated Aircraft. That didn't seem to deter Major Fleet.

"I think there was some general understanding among Reuben Fleet's associates that he expected to marry Lauretta—that the relationship was a personal one as well as a business one," wrote Lauretta Golem's niece, Dorothy Mitchell. Ironically Mitchell herself later became Fleet's secretary and, eventually, his second wife.

Before that twist of fate could occur, Fleet and his secretary set off on a monthlong cross-country sales tour in the summer of 1929 in the Fleet, a commercial two-seat trainer they were anxious to promote. The trip went beautifully. The Fleet was greeted enthusiastically by aircraft dealers and flying schools, while Fleet and Golem enjoyed each other's airborne companionship.

One leg of their journey took them to San Diego, where Fleet had learned to fly twelve years earlier. The city had become an aviation center since that time and had constructed a new municipal airport, called Lindbergh Field, on tidelands near the center of town. The local Chamber of Commerce knew that Fleet wanted to relocate Consolidated Aircraft someday to a city with sunnier weather than Buffalo's. Even so, he surprised a Chamber of Commerce audience with a bold offer: "If the municipality will sell Lindbergh Field, I'll purchase it at any time for $1,000,000 cash." San Diego officials turned down his offer, and another five years passed before Fleet began seriously negotiating for a West Coast home for Consolidated.

The final leg of the sales trip, from Detroit to Buffalo, was made in September 1929—on Friday the thirteenth. Fleet sat in the front cockpit, as usual, while Golem piloted the plane from the rear cockpit. To avoid the longer route south of Lake Erie or the riskier route across the water, she steered the Fleet north of the lake, over Ontario, Canada.

After they'd flown eighty miles, the plane's engine suddenly sputtered. A valve on one cylinder had failed. Fleet grabbed the controls with the plane at 750 feet. He searched frantically for a suitable place to land. The plane lost altitude. At 475 feet Fleet knew he'd have to land either by flying with the wind or by reversing direction and flying into the wind. The engine was choking. Fleet chose to bank the plane into a 180-degree turn. Two menacing trees loomed in his path. He gunned the engine, hoping to skip over the tops of the trees. But the plane gasped, lost speed, veered sharply to the left, and plummeted toward the ground. A Canadian farmer watched as the stricken plane crashed into his field. "The plane struck some obstruction in the field and overturned, pinning its occupants beneath it," *The New York Times* reported. An ambulance rushed Lauretta Golem to a nearby hospital, where the thirty-one-year-old secretary died the following day of a broken neck and spinal cord injuries. Fleet spent the next seven weeks in the hospital recuperating from his injuries.

Fleet's hospitalization interrupted negotiations that Consolidated had begun to purchase the Thomas-Morse Aircraft Corporation of Ithaca, New York. One of the pioneering aviation companies in the United States, Thomas-Morse had become financially troubled.

To the confusion of many, the three principals of the original Thomas Brothers Aeroplane Company all had been born in England and were all surnamed Thomas, but only two of them, William and Oliver, were brothers. The unrelated member of the triumvirate was named B. Douglas Thomas. William Thomas had come to the United States from London in 1909 to work for Glenn Curtiss. Three years later he left Curtiss to organize his own company in the city of Bath in upstate New York. His brother Oliver soon arrived from England to join the new enterprise. William Thomas was a jack-of-all-trades who designed, built, and flew the company's first plane. The firm met success quickly with a three-passenger plane known as the TA, which became popular among aerial acrobats of the barnstorming era.

B. Douglas Thomas had a background similar to that of the Thomas brothers. He, too, came from England. He, too, began working in the United States with Glenn Curtiss. He, too, was an aircraft designer, having worked with such firms as Vickers and Sopwith Aviation before leaving Britain. The colorful Jenny trainers of World War I fame represented the marriage of the Model J. which B. Douglas Thomas had helped design, and the Model N, which Curtiss had created.

In 1914 Thomas Brothers moved its headquarters to Ithaca, New York, and B. Douglas Thomas joined the company as chief engineer. The firm met little success. It designed innovative aircraft, but few of these won production contracts from the military services. By 1916 Thomas Brothers needed outside capital to remain in business. Frank Morse, its neighbor in Ithaca, who owned the Morse Chain Company, and Herman Westinghouse, who manufactured air brakes, came to their rescue. The injection of cash enabled Thomas Brothers to reorganize in 1917 as the Thomas-Morse Aircraft Corporation, with Morse in control.

The new financing allowed the company to survive until World War I, when aircraft orders began to flow more rapidly. The company designed the S-4 Tommy Scout, an advanced trainer, and built more than 600 of them during the war. Thomas-Morse became the nation's fourth-largest aircraft producer during World War I, with a payroll peaking at 1,300 workers. Then, when the armistice was declared, the bottom dropped out. Government orders for 533 Tommy Scouts were abruptly canceled, and the company had to lay off workers.

In 1919 the company built a pursuit plane, the MB-3 Hawk, that could reach the sizzling speed of 177 miles per hour. When General William "Billy" Mitchell chose a Hawk as his private plane, its stature was instantly enhanced. When the Army ordered 50 Hawks, Thomas-Morse boldly invested in manufacturing jigs, dies, and tooling in the hope of winning a second contract for 200 more planes. The investment was a big mistake, similar to the error Fleet made years later when he overconfidently counted on the Navy's order for Admiral flying boats and purchased materials to build them. In this case there was a double irony: The contracting officer who awarded the Hawk production contract to the low bidder, Boeing, was none other than Army Major Reuben Fleet.

The MB-3 award to Boeing was a setback from which Thomas-Morse never fully recovered. It continued to design experimental planes but never landed another production contract. When Thomas-Morse unveiled its O-2 observation biplane in 1929, the Army liked the aircraft but wasn't convinced that the company had the financial resources to produce it. Instead, the Army encouraged Consolidated Aircraft to consider buying out Thomas-Morse.

Consolidated was interested in Thomas-Morse's design for the O-2 plane but not in its manufacturing facility. Consolidated gave 6,000 of its shares to Thomas-Morse for its designs, plus another 4,000 shares to B. Douglas Thomas for his services. The tall, wiry B. Douglas Thomas was named president of Consolidated's newest subsidiary, the aircraft production of which was merged with Consolidated's operation in Buffalo.

Despite its loss to Martin on the Navy's Admiral contract, Consolidated was fully committed to flying boats. Fleet believed that he had redeemed himself nicely with his sale of fourteen commercial flying boats to NYRBA and that Consolidated could win a significant piece of the military's flying boat business. The company had modified its original XPY-1 design several times, catering to the Navy's expressed interest in seaplanes with longer ranges.

These flying boat projects were often hampered by Buffalo's long winters, ice-choked Lake Erie and Niagara River, and truncated flying seasons. In 1931, for example, the company built an experimental patrol bomber version of its Admiral flying boat that the Navy designated the XP2Y-1. This three-engine prototype was assembled outdoors in March on a concrete apron at Buffalo Marine Airport, next to the launching ramp into the Niagara River. Its maiden flight had to be cut short when dangerous chunks of ice floated toward the takeoff area.

Buffalo's weather was becoming intolerable to Fleet. Not only were takeoffs and landings delayed, but hordes of company pilots waiting to ferry Consolidated planes to Texas or Florida were racking up enormous bills while biding their time at the Buffalo Athletic Club.

Fleet realized he had three alternatives: stop building flying boats, make them smaller and more easily transportable, or relocate his factory to warmer climes. He spent years scouring the East and West coasts for a suitable location. He investigated the Florida coast from Jacksonville to Miami. He surveyed the Seattle area, in his native Washington, which was already home to William Boeing's aircraft company. But his choices eventually narrowed to Los Angeles and San Diego.

San Diego had become a city of aviation firsts: Glenn Curtiss had demonstrated the first practical seaplane in the city in 1911 and had established a flying school on North Island. The first aerial photograph was taken the same year, when a pilot held a camera over the side of an aircraft soaring high above

San Diego. In 1913 Lincoln Beachey, a famous aerial stunt man, performed the first loop-the-loop above the city.

In 1923 the first transcontinental, nonstop flight ended at San Diego's Rockwell Field. The first round-the-world flight began and ended in San Diego, and in 1927 "Lucky Lindy" began his historic journey to Paris there. The next year the first aerial appendectomy was performed by a doctor and nurse on a female patient in a Ford Trimotor while flying above the city, after which the patient recovered satisfactorily. Finally, in San Diego a first-class glider pilot's license was granted for the first time in 1930 to a woman: Anne Morrow Lindbergh.

Even before Consolidated's board of directors chose a new location, Major Fleet heard that Franklin Roosevelt, then the governor of New York, was objecting to the company's leaving the Empire State. Fleet immediately flew to Albany to meet with FDR. He told the governor about Buffalo's intolerable climate and his desire to relocate Consolidated south of the Mason-Dixon Line, for the good of the country in case of war and for the benefit of his stockholders. FDR didn't object.

Like most businesses in the United States, Consolidated suffered economically during the early 1930's. During its first five and a half years (1923 through 1928) it had earned about $2.1 million. Those profits almost disappeared during the four subsequent years, when the company just managed to break even.

In 1932, the year FDR was first elected President, Consolidated sold only 100 planes for a disappointing $1.3 million. The company laid off hundreds of employees, including Fleet's son David, then a pilot and service manager. Employees lucky enough to retain their jobs endured 20 percent pay cuts.

Despite the drop in sales, Consolidated's design work continued. Its commercial flying boat was redesigned for Navy use. The improved model, dubbed the Ranger, was first delivered to the Navy in 1933. Consolidated built itself largely upon the success of this plane.

Groups of Rangers made headlines when they set off on long-distance formation flights to demonstrate the ability of the U.S. armed forces to leapfrog around the globe. On their first formation flight a group of Rangers flew nonstop from Norfolk, Virginia, to the Panama Canal Zone—more than 2,000 miles. Five Navy patrol planes then flew north in formation, stopping at Acapulco, San Diego (for three months), and San Francisco. Finally, the Navy patrol squadron set off from San Francisco for its longest flight yet: 2,408 miles nonstop across the Pacific Ocean to Pearl Harbor. It flew some twenty-five hours through a thick, overcast sky in January 1934. When the six Ranger flying boats appeared in the sky above Pearl Harbor, a jubilant crowd awaiting their arrival broke through the restraining barricades at the airfield to congratulate them. FDR sent his congratulations for a "magnificent accomplishment," and in Tokyo a spokesman for the Imperial Japanese Navy noted the beneficial effects such an achievement would have for humankind.

Japan had more than a casual interest in the Ranger's long-range patrol capability. Its navy purchased one Ranger, the rudder pedals of which had to be extended to accommodate short-legged Japanese pilots, to test alongside its own flying boat designs. Consolidated sold Rangers to the U.S. Navy, Argentina, and Colombia and went on to design the most successful flying boat of all time, the famed Catalina.

By the spring of 1933 businessmen in Long Beach and San Diego, California, were actively trying to lure Consolidated to their cities. Long Beach offered twenty-two and a half acres free of charge at the city's municipal airport, but Consolidated would have to haul its seaplanes overland for several miles to reach the nearest water. San Diego offered land adjacent to Lindbergh Field, with access to the city's municipal seaplane ramp. It also promised better highways, capital improvements at the airfield and harbor, and more housing for Consolidated's workers, Fleet's son David recalled. In addition, San Diego promised to charge less for electricity than Long Beach.

Before he reached a final decision, Fleet visited both cities with his second wife, Dorothy. "Long Beach was in the throes of an oil boom," she later wrote, "and the stench of the wells was nauseating." Later that day her reaction to San Diego was much more favorable. "The majestic sweep of the Coastline, the acres of orange groves, the palm trees, the gardens, flamboyant with bougainvillaea and oleander and hibiscus, combined to create a world far removed from Buffalo, New York," she wrote, in an understatement.

Fleet had already made up his mind on less aesthetic grounds.

"Long Beach or San Diego? Where do you want to live, dear?" he asked while the couple was still in San Diego.

"I prefer to live here," she announced without hesitation.

"So be it," said Fleet.

In May 1933, ten years after Consolidated had been organized in East Greenwich, Rhode Island, its board of directors decided to relocate to San Diego. The United States was mired in the Depression, but Fleet remained optimistic about the future of the aircraft business. The company sent a $1,000 check as a binder on a fifty-year lease for thirty acres of property at Lindbergh Field. The businesslike sales campaign of San Diego's Chamber of Commerce, Fleet's fond memories of his early days at the Army's pilot school on North

Island, and the sweet smell of hibiscus and bougainvillaea had carried the day for San Diego.

## (6)

The Navy wanted a new flying boat with a range of 3,000 miles to replace the Ranger. The longer range and increased bomb-carrying capacity of the new plane would allow the service to develop more ambitious plans for its patrol bomber fleet. In addition to patrolling the oceans for enemy warships, these planes could coordinate their operations with carrier-based aircraft to form a potent striking force against enemy ships and bases.

Rear Admiral Ernest King, head of the Navy's Bureau of Aeronautics, described the role he envisioned for Navy patrol bombers in a classified memorandum to the chairman of the Federal Aviation Commission in December 1934. Patrol bombers, operating alongside U.S. warships overseas or from strategically located bases such as San Diego, San Francisco, Seattle, Alaska, Narragansett Bay, Norfolk, the West Indies, the Canal Zone, Manila, and Pearl Harbor, could search for enemy ships or attack enemy bases, airdromes, or supply depots, King explained.

"An important feature of the patrol-bombers' usefulness lies in the fact that these planes require no prepared operating field other than sheltered water and tenders," he continued. If the U.S. fleet could establish a base anywhere within 1,000 miles of the enemy's home territory, the patrol bomber force could be used to raid that territory, Admiral King wrote. The planes could also monitor approaches to the United States for signs of hostile forces.

King's memo outlined a Navy plan to operate 300 patrol bombers in peacetime and about 1,000 by the end of the first year of a war. Consolidated wanted a large chunk of that business. In October 1933 the company won one of two development contracts to design an experimental aircraft that could meet the Navy's patrol bomber requirements. The second contract was awarded to the Douglas Aircraft Company.

The competition allowed Consolidated to distill all its knowledge of building such flying boats as the Admiral, Commodore, and Ranger. Laddon was pleased with the result. "I'd taken advantage of all the mistakes I'd made on the previous ones," he said later. It worried Fleet and Laddon that Douglas's entry made it off the drawing board and into the air six weeks before Consolidated's XP3Y-1 prototype. But Consolidated had designed the sleekest seaplane ever built.

Its engines were mounted on the leading edge of the wing—rather than above or below the wing—to reduce drag. Its flotation pontoons, which were mounted beneath the tips of the wings, could be folded up after takeoff to become an extension of the wing surface. In this way they would enhance the plane's lift rather than add to its drag. Finally, Laddon designed integral fuel tanks that allowed the use of sealed portions of the wing structures for the storage of gasoline instead of separate, heavier fuel tanks.

Both planes met the Navy's performance specifications during flight tests. In fact, they performed so well the Navy changed the plane's designation from P (for patrol plane) to PB (for patrol bomber). The choice between Consolidated and Douglas ultimately came down to price, and on that criterion Consolidated won. In June 1935 it received the largest military production contract the U.S. government had awarded since World War I: $6 million for sixty seaplanes, known as PBY-1 Catalinas.

Consolidated had also landed an Army contract for fifty pursuit planes six months earlier. The lean years of 1931 and 1932 gave way to years of rapid growth. By 1935 the company had a huge backlog of military orders. Both aircraft were to be built in its new facility at Lindbergh Field in San Diego.

First, the company had to transport its manufacturing equipment, material, and personnel across the United States—perhaps the biggest corporate move up to that time. Consolidated had moved its belongings from Rhode Island to Buffalo in 3 railroad boxcars in 1924; it required 157 freight cars to haul its possessions across the country eleven years later.

At the Buffalo plant Consolidated's employees kept working until the middle of August 1935, so production would be interrupted for as short a time as possible. The company paid moving expenses for 311 of its best employees and offered jobs to another 100 workers if they relocated to California at their own expense.

Meanwhile, the specter of lost jobs and an empty aircraft factory haunted the city fathers of Buffalo. A group of local businessmen approached Lawrence D. Bell, the executive who had served as general manager at Consolidated since Fleet's plane crash. They asked if he'd be willing to remain in Buffalo and organize his own aircraft company from the remnants of Consolidated. Bell seized the opportunity and founded the Bell Aircraft Corporation, which was helped at the outset when Fleet steered a few million dollars' worth of subcontracting work its way.

In October 1935 Fleet addressed a huge crowd in San Diego that had gathered for the dedication of Consolidated's new headquarters. He said his long search for a city with fine weather, an adequate labor supply, and a publicly owned waterfront had culminated in "a factory of our own in a city of our choice.

"No holding company owns or controls us," he continued, in words that were to sound ironic only a few years later. Consolidated had $9 million in unfulfilled orders and 874 employees when its new factory was dedicated. Fleet expected that payroll to swell to 3,000 workers within twelve months. Much of that growth was the result of Consolidated's world-famous PBY series of flying boats.

The Navy had awarded Consolidated its first Catalina contract three months before the company moved west. Before long the Navy handed the firm a second contract, this time for fifty improved PBY-2 models for $4.9 million. Before Consolidated could catch its breath, it received a third contract in July 1936, to develop a prototype for an even larger patrol plane with a longer range. That prototype led to an order for sixty-six more flying boats.

The firm was quickly emerging as a major American manufacturer. Its airplane orders and its need for additional factory space continued to grow. Its stock on the New York Curb Exchange, which had sunk to $6 in 1933, rebounded to $33.50 by March 1937. Later that year shares were traded on the New York Stock Exchange for the first time. By the end of 1937, after nine years of public trading, Consolidated announced its first dividend: fifty cents per share. Consolidated was on a roll.

The PBY patrol bomber answered the Navy's need for a long-range aircraft that could project U.S. air power throughout the Pacific Ocean, stretching from Alaska to Hawaii to the Canal Zone. The Catalina became a household word, hailed for its military and civilian achievements. In a highly publicized expedition noted naturalist and explorer Dr. Richard Archbold flew a stripped-down Catalina to far-off New Guinea. "We made 168 flights in and around New Guinea from June 15, 1938 to May 10, 1939, carrying 568,000 pounds of food and equipment over jungle impassable on foot," he later wrote. The connection between the Catalina and Archbold's exotic adventure left an indelible impression on the public's mind.

The plane was also used in a daring attempt to rescue a group of Russian pilots who had been lost somewhere in Canada's vast polar region after failing to complete a 4,000-mile flight from the Soviet Union to Fairbanks, Alaska. The Catalina raced back and forth across the rough, uncharted terrain, logging more than 19,000 frozen miles in just over a month. The Russian fliers were never found, and the mission failed, but the PBY Catalina polished its reputation as a hearty American workhorse of the air.

The praise accorded the PBY during Archbold's expedition to New Guinea and the polar rescue attempt was minor compared with the accolades Consolidated received when a squadron of Catalinas helped sink the 35,000-ton German battleship the *Bismarck* in the North Atlantic in May 1941.

Seven months later, when the United States declared war on Japan and Germany, the Consolidated Aircraft Corporation played a key role in the nation's mobilization efforts. Fleet was eased out of the company by officials in Washington who found his one-man style of management unsuited to the tremendous wartime demands that would be placed on Consolidated. They pressured him to sell out his interest in the company he had built. Consolidated was merged with Vultee Aircraft, another California airplane builder, and renamed Consolidated Vultee, or Convair. In 1944, the peak year of production, Convair outproduced every other aircraft manufacturer in the world. Altogether, between Pearl Harbor and V-E day, Convair churned out an astonishing 33,000 planes. By the time it merged with General Dynamics it had captured a unique place in the hearts of most Americans who had lived through World War II.

# Chapter Four

## The Dynamic Duo

### (1)

In late summer 1952 a team of *Business Week* reporters fanned out across the United States to speak with corporate executives building armaments for the Korean War. When the magazine's editors on West Forty-second Street in Manhattan reviewed their reporters' notes, they reached an eye-opening conclusion: "For the first time in its history, the U.S. is getting a full-time, national-scale arms industry—an industry that's about as individual and experienced as automobile manufacturing or food processing."

Companies that had previously shifted in and out of weapons production with the rise and fall of international military tensions perceived for the first time an ongoing demand for their armaments and munitions. Like their counterparts in Europe—longtime arms manufacturers like Krupp, Bofors, and Skoda—American firms had come to regard war production as a normal state of affairs and had taken steps to capture a piece of this new market. "Many of them created separate divisions, headed by key executives, to work exclusively on government contracts," *Business Week* reported. "Some of them have even built separate munitions plants."

A fundamental shift in the U.S. economy was under way. "What it all adds up to is that the U.S. now has a functioning, experienced arms industry—not merely a group of commercial plants that, with much sweating and straining, can be twisted into military production in case of war."

At 445 Park Avenue fresh signs were being painted and crisp letterheads were being printed to identify the Manhattan headquarters of a weapons manufacturer that had just changed its name. At the insistence of its indefatigable fifty-eight-year-old chairman and president, John Jay Hopkins, the venerable Electric Boat Company had recently become the General Dynamics Corporation. The new name, Hopkins declared, would be more appropriate for a company with wide-ranging activities in shipbuilding, aircraft production, electrical equipment manufacturing, and nuclear power. The company no longer confined its business to submarines or electricity; it would prosper among a new fraternity of American arms makers by excelling in many different fields. Indeed, the little-noticed birth of General Dynamics in April 1952 both reflected and fostered the growth of a permanent arms industry in the United States.

Hopkins, a husky, square-faced executive with slicked-back hair, recognized that the U.S. armed forces required huge stockpiles of sophisticated weapons that could be supplied only by a permanent defense industry. After World War II he expanded Electric Boat's line of products to garner a larger slice of this expanding defense market. "Instead of switching from guns to gadgets, he decided to stick to guns—but to make as many varieties as possible," *Newsweek* noted.

Hopkins's background wasn't typical of those in the munitions industry. He had no engineering training, and his military experience consisted of little more than a brief stint as an ensign during World War I. That Navy tour of duty had interrupted studies at Harvard Law School, which he promptly completed after the war. As a young attorney Hopkins left his native California for the stodgy New York law firm of Cravath, Henderson, Leffingwell & de Gersdorff (which eventually became Cravath, Swaine & Moore, the epitome of a corporate law firm). After four years at Cravath, and another eight years practicing law on his own in New York and Los Angeles, Hopkins followed his longtime Republican sympathies into the Hoover administration. During the final year of Herbert Hoover's presidency he served as a special assistant to Treasury Secretary Ogden L. Mills. By the time Franklin Roosevelt moved into the White House in 1933 and swept Washington clean of Republicans, Hopkins had become a wealthy lawyer with considerable legal, financial, and political skills.

Handsome and debonair, Hopkins led a comfortable life. An avid golfer, he would frequently shoot in the low seventies at the Burning Tree Club outside Washington, D.C., or the hallowed Royal and Ancient Golf Club of St. Andrews in Scotland. (He later founded the International Golf Association to foster goodwill around the world through golf.) When in Manhattan, Hopkins would stop by the Fifth Avenue Presbyterian Church occasionally to listen to the organist rehearse. His first encounter with Electric Boat occurred in that church when he met a fellow congregant who was an EB vice-president and director. Through that acquaintance Hopkins was invited to join EB's board of directors in 1937.

At the time Electric Boat was limping through a lean period. For thirteen grim years, between 1918 and 1931, it hadn't received a single submarine contract. Instead, the company tried to keep busy building commercial ferries and tugboats, repairing ships, and performing assorted foundry work and odd jobs. At one stage Electric Boat built the bridges for Connecticut's Merritt Parkway. "Indeed, the company that had helped 'to make the world safe for democracy' was happy to repair hair curlers for a beauty parlor," observed *Dynamic America.*

Hopkins played a minor role for five years, serving only as a member of Electric Boat's board of directors. Then, in 1942, when a flood of World War II submarine contracts suddenly poured in to the shipyard, he was asked to take charge of the company's financial and contractual matters and become a full-time vice-president and the head of EB's Washington office. For the next fifteen years, as vice-president and president of Electric Boat and founding chairman of General Dynamics, Hopkins sought to broaden the scope of the company's activities. GD's current preeminence in so many facets of the defense industry is a testament to his vision.

Since Hopkins's death in 1957, two men have had the most impact on General Dynamics. Henry Crown, as noted, has dominated GD's board of directors for nearly a quarter century. David Lewis, his handpicked chairman, has led GD through a minefield of problems to its present position at the top of the defense industry.

## (2)

Five men and four women pulled on their jogging suits and headed for the 200 block of Hamilton Street in Evanston, Illinois, an affluent suburb along Lake Michigan immediately north of Chicago. At first glance the nine runners attracted little attention from residents in the quiet neighborhood because joggers were a familiar sight along the parks and beaches on the lakefront. But these were no ordinary joggers. The five men and four women were members of a Puerto Rican terrorist group, the FALN. And this day, April 4, 1980, the terrorists had set in motion a bold plot.

In a few minutes the group planned to rendezvous on Hamilton Street with two other FALN members, who had just held up a nearby Budget Rent-a-Car office and escaped with a fourteen-foot rental truck. In the name of Puerto Rican independence, the eleven members of the Fuerzas Armadas de Liberación Nacional were about to kidnap and hold for ransom a living symbol of American capitalism.

Their target lived a few blocks away, at 900 Edgemere Court, in a seventeen-room mansion. He was an eighty-four-year-old multimillionaire who had once owned the Empire State Building outright. He controlled the Chicago, Rock Island & Pacific Railroad. He owned more stock in the Hilton Hotels Corporation than anyone but the Hilton family. He had investments in hundreds of companies, including banks, coal mines, shipyards, sugar plantations, and real estate. He and his friends and family owned some $400 million worth of stock in General Dynamics, thereby dominating one of the nation's mightiest defense contractors. He was one of the richest men in America. His name was Henry Crown.

The FALN terrorists had carefully planned to abduct Crown as he took his daily stroll along the beachfront. They equipped themselves with a dozen handguns, a rifle, a shotgun, two-way radios, binoculars, and ski masks. Some of the men disguised their faces with false mustaches. They had at their disposal three vans and other vehicles, at least one of which could serve as a crash car to block a street and thwart any attempt to break up the kidnapping.

But their plan went awry. A woman in the neighborhood became suspicious of the nine "joggers" as they moved furtively between two parked cars and a van and called the police. Within minutes the nine Puerto Rican terrorists had been arrested, and the audacious kidnapping of Henry Crown had been aborted. A few hours earlier police had arrested two other FALN members toting weapons between the stolen truck and two vehicles that had pulled up alongside.

The terrorists had planned to hold Crown hostage in a nearby "safe house" and demand a multimillion-dollar ransom that would help finance their terrorist activities. Perhaps even more important, the FALN members were counting on Crown's abduction to generate a barrage of media attention for their political cause. "If they had kidnapped him," observed Charles Neubauer, a Chicago newspaper reporter, "it would have made a hell of a splash." But the terrorists bungled the operation, and their scheme was derailed. Eleven FALN members were tried, convicted, and jailed.

Crown wasn't told about the kidnapping plot for several months. "I'm satisfied that my security people knew about it," he said later. "They thought it better that I didn't know." Worth more than half a billion dollars, Henry Crown doesn't take his personal security lightly. His home burglary alarm system is wired directly into the Evanston police station. "We have every base covered and have had for years," he maintained. But if the FALN terrorists had somehow managed to kidnap him, he claimed he would have urged his family *not* to meet their ransom demands. Henry Crown had worked hard for more than seventy years to amass his private fortune. He wasn't about to part with it easily.

At eighty-nine, Crown still dominates General Dynamics. Along with his son Lester and a handful of business cronies, he controls more than 23 percent of the 50 million outstanding shares of GD, a large enough block for Crown to wield enormous clout at the company's monthly board of directors' meetings in St. Louis. He also serves as chairman of GD's Executive Committee, a seven-man subgroup of the board that sets the company's basic policies.

Far from an absentee landlord in Chicago, Crown is on the phone with David Lewis almost daily. While Lewis is clearly in charge of the company's day-to-day operation and deserves most of the credit for fashioning GD into the nation's premier defense contractor, no one doubts that the ultimate authority at GD is still Henry Crown. His influence among his fellow board members is enormous, not only because of his huge financial holding but also because of his exceptional business savvy. "When the colonel says something, we listen," reported Nathan Cummings, the former chairman of the Consolidated Foods Corporation who had been a longtime Crown ally on GD's board before he died in February 1985. "He's keen as can be. If he made a recommendation, we'd pretty damn near say, 'Yes, we'll do it.' "

Crown doesn't act impulsively. He believes quick deals are for suckers. Instead, he likes to study a business transaction, roll it around in his mind, and find answers to all his questions. "When the colonel gets into a deal, he knows the size of your underwear," said one admiring real estate operator. At GD board meetings, if doubts exist or issues remain cloudy, Crown is not afraid to suggest further thinking. "He doesn't feel compelled to jump into a decision, just for the sake of making an 'executive' decision," said Wallace Persons, who served with Crown on GD's board in the early 1970's. "Henry is a real wizard at quietly unfolding facts. He participates as a very acute listener. When all the facts are out, Henry will often come up with the answer."

Loyal to friends and longtime employees and unusually generous to those who stick by him, Crown can be unforgiving to business rivals who cross him. For decades he reportedly held a grudge against A. N. Pritzker, patriarch of the fabulously wealthy Chicago family that has controlled the Hyatt Hotel chain, Braniff Airlines, and real estate, for a deal Pritzker allegedly stole from under his nose.

Crown's life reads like a classic rags-to-riches novel. He was born in Chicago

4. Henry Crown, a Chicago-based industrialist and financier who earned
millions in the construction materials business in the 1950's and once owned
the Empire State Building, quietly dominates GD's board of directors. After
recapturing financial control of GD in 1970, he ousted board chairman
Roger Lewis and replaced him with David S. Lewis. *The New York Times*

in 1896, one of seven children of impoverished Latvian immigrants, Arie and
Ida Crown. His father made men's suspenders for years and then eked out a
living as a kitchen match salesman. The family lived above the Ashland
Avenue warehouse where his father's matches were stored until a nearby
department store fire spread to the warehouse, ignited the match inventory,
and destroyed their home.

As a kid on Chicago's tough Near North Side Crown also sold matches door
to door and earned fifty cents a day delivering neckties for a local factory. He
quit grammar school to earn $4 a week as a shipping clerk for the Chicago Fire
Brick Company, a building supplies firm. He was hired by his older brother,
Sol, the company's sales manager, but fired the following year when he bungled
a customer's order. By inadvertently dispatching two loads of sand to a construction site when the contractor had ordered one load of sand and one load
of gravel, he forced the contractor to shut down for the day. The mistake cost
Crown his job, but it taught him a valuable lesson: Give your customer exactly
what he wants precisely when he wants it.

There was never enough money in the Crown family in those early days. Crown regularly had his teeth fixed by students at a local dental college because his family couldn't afford a licensed dentist. As a result, his teeth still trouble him more than half a century later.

He never finished high school. At sixteen he worked for the Union Drop Forge Company during the day and studied bookkeeping and other commercial subjects at night. His bookkeeping instructor asked each pupil to create a hypothetical company and maintain its fictitious accounting books for one year. "Most of the class modestly established their businesses with a capital of a few thousand dollars and a profit to match," Crown recalled years later. "I started my mythical company with a million dollars and netted $200,000 the first year." Crown always thought big, and he was unafraid to borrow large sums of capital, provided he had figured out a way to pay it back.

In 1919 Henry and Sol Crown pulled together $10,000 and incorporated the building supplies company that would generate Henry Crown's first fortune. They gave their company a prosaic name: Material Service Corporation. Before long Sol Crown died of tuberculosis, leaving the fledgling sand, cement, and gravel business in the hands of his twenty-five-year-old brother. Henry Crown began searching for Material Service's first large account, knowing full well that in the building supplies business, *service* was everything. Because the building products had to comply with standardized specifications, service was what distinguished one material supplier from its competitor.

Young Crown thrust his business card into the hand of a potential customer and promised him vastly improved service.

"Why do you think you can do better?" asked the skeptical contractor, who had never heard of the Material Service Corporation.

"The fact that I will personally follow it and the fact that our yard is closer to you than anyone else," Crown answered. In those days building supplies were hauled by horse and wagon, so delivery distances were crucial. The contractor turned to Crown with a half smile.

"You know, kid, you've got all the answers. Someone must have thrown these questions at you before, so you've memorized them." Material Service landed the order. Other orders followed, and the company began to prosper. But in the years following World War I it was usually in need of cash.

In 1922 Crown had his first run-in with the Internal Revenue Service, which challenged his valuation of the Material Service Corporation and demanded additional taxes. Crown battled the IRS for months before reaching a financial settlement. During the process he learned an important lesson. "I eventually managed to come up with the back taxes," he said later. "But at least I could use the money during the months we negotiated." The importance of sound tax planning became clear. "What good is it to make money so it's taxed away?" he asked rhetorically. Ever since, Crown has been a bulldog on taxes. At GD he studies the tax angles of any proposed transaction with religious fervor.

He often turns to another longtime crony, Milton Falkoff, sixty-nine, for tax advice. A former official with the IRS, Falkoff is a shrewd tax specialist whose persnickety obsession with details occasionally irritates his colleagues on GD's board. Crown lured Falkoff away from the IRS years ago with a blunt offer: "A year from now you're either going to be worth twice as much as I'll pay you now, or you won't be with me." Falkoff is still with him. He has become a wealthy man and one of Crown's right-hand operatives. Along with Gorden MacDonald, the company's executive vice-president, the Crown-Falkoff combination provides GD with some of the keenest tax avoidance advice in the defense industry. (Despite its millions in profits, GD has paid *no* federal income taxes since 1972, a fact that outraged several congressmen when it became widely known earlier this year.)

In the 1920's Crown also recognized the value of borrowed money. At one stage he borrowed $200,000 *with no collateral* to build in suburban Chicago a one-mile feeder rail line that would connect his inland sand and gravel pits to waterborne barges. With the barges he could transport his building materials more cheaply than could the competing railroads.

Crown began his close association with the huge First National Bank of Chicago in 1931, when the bank swallowed a smaller financial institution that had lent Material Service about $1 million, without collateral, before it went bankrupt. To demonstrate his good faith to First Chicago, which could easily have demanded that Material Service put up commercial assets as collateral, Crown pledged his company's receivables, his life insurance, and his house to secure his loans. First Chicago's chief lending officer was impressed with Crown's guts. The bank and the expanding Crown empire have been business allies ever since.

The Material Service Corporation prospered during the late 1930's, when war erupted in Europe and America's participation looked inevitable. By 1940 the company was worth about $4 million and free from debt for the first time. Crown toyed with the idea of selling out and retiring comfortably, but World War II intervened.

He was commissioned a lieutenant colonel in the Army Corps of Engineers in the Chicago area and placed in charge of procuring about $1 billion worth of supplies and equipment each year. His wartime service left him two souvenirs: the title Colonel, which has stuck with him ever since, and widespread contacts among Chicago builders, suppliers, and contractors.

In the postwar years Crown's contacts helped Material Service ride the construction boom in the Midwest that was rapidly transforming Illinois farmlands into mile after sprawling mile of Chicago suburbs. The company's familiar red and yellow tugboats could be seen shoving barges laden with sand and gravel up and down the branches of the Chicago River, while its red and white mixing trucks were busy delivering what Colonel Crown liked to call "s'ment" to dozens of dusty construction sites.

Inevitably Colonel Crown's success in business has led a variety of journalists and "crime watchers" to accuse him of bribery, influence peddling, and all manner of collusion with Chicago's Democratic machine. In a city infamous for the mutual backscratching of its business, political, and criminal elite, the Material Service Corporation, which garnered much of its revenue from city construction contracts, was bound to become the target of widespread suspicions. The fact that Henry Crown has never been convicted of a crime only reinforces the suspicions of those who believe he has insulated himself with loyal friends in high places.

Crown denounces as indecent and untrue the rumors and accusations that have been hurled his way. He acknowledges that he is a Chicago Democrat —like most businessmen in that overwhelmingly Democratic city—but considers himself a Republican in national politics. He denies he has enriched himself in criminal or corrupt ways. "Mr. Crown's reputation is more important to him than any possession," declared a flattering *New York Times* profile some years ago. "His handshake is as good as a signed contract. He prides himself on never lying, and he thinks that children shouldn't be told about Santa Claus because that, in a way, is a lie."

Nathan Cummings dismissed the notion that his friend Crown might be dishonest or condone fraudulent activities by GD's executives. "We know we're clean," he said. "We wouldn't do anything that isn't dignified or honest. Henry Crown and Nate Cummings don't need anything done that's dishonest to make a buck. We're way above and beyond that, and we wouldn't even think of it."

The net worth of Material Service was mushrooming. Before long Crown's enterprise had become the largest distributor of cement and building supplies in the Chicago area. In 1951 he parlayed other people's money into a spectacular acquisition. He bought a controlling 25 percent interest in the Empire State Building with $10 million borrowed from the First National Bank of Chicago, which had originally discouraged the purchase. The building was making money not from its office rentals but from the visitors to its observation deck and from fees from the television tower atop its 102d floor. Three years later Crown acquired full ownership, still without investing a penny of his own money. The total cost: about $33 million.

The building provided Crown with a lofty, high visibility plaything that enabled him to entertain Queen Elizabeth II, Nikita Khrushchev, Fidel Castro, and other VIPs when they visited the world's most famous skyscraper. Crown claimed he felt no special pride of ownership in the Empire State Building—"not that I *mind* owning it, of course." He said that he planned to pass the building on to his grandchildren, but in 1961 he sold it for $64 million.

While the Empire State Building was making Crown's reputation, Material Service was making his fortune. Throughout the 1950's profits continued to swell. From its first year in business, when it earned about $3,000 profit on sales of $200,000, the Material Service Corporation had grown to the point that it earned $7.9 million in 1957 on sales of $103 million. The company's audit report for 1957 was so healthy it seemed to beg for some bold initiative.

Crown casually sought the advice of a friend, the vice-president of a large insurance company. "Just out of curiosity, to see what he would say about it, I threw the audit over to him and asked him to read it, but particularly the last page," which traced the company's financial history. "He blinked when he looked at that last sheet and asked me what was our objective. I said I didn't have any except to continue building the company up. He then asked me whether I didn't feel the situation would be improved if our stock were listed. That's how we threw in with General Dynamics."

With cash flooding into the Material Service Corporation in the late 1950's Colonel Crown realized he had to act. "We either had to swallow or be swallowed," he recalled later. "We started looking more like a bank than a building materials company." As he scanned the horizon for a likely merger candidate, General Dynamics came into view.

In 1959 GD was being run by Frank Pace, an Arkansas lawyer and former secretary of the army. From the outside it looked like a well-managed firm with limitless prospects in defense and energy-related markets. Crown considered GD the most progressive corporation in the country, an ideal company to buy Material Service and manage its continuing operations. Besides, Crown would still run Material Service as a GD subsidiary.

## (3)

The deal offered advantages to both sides. GD was able to add Material Service's reliable earnings to its books. Crown, in turn, gained tenuous control of GD. The transaction was structured with several intriguing aspects. In exchange for his and his family's stock in Material Service, Colonel Crown was given about $125 million worth of convertible preferred shares in the General Dynamics Corporation. The shares eventually could be converted to roughly 16 percent of GD's outstanding common stock.

Unlike preferred shares issued by many other companies, Crown's shares enjoyed equal voting privileges with GD common stock and entitled him to three seats on the thirteen-member board of directors, enough for him to exert a strong, if not controlling, voice in GD's affairs. Unlike GD's common shares, each of Crown's preferred shares was to earn a fixed annual dividend of $2.90. That meant GD was obliged to pay Crown about $1.8 million annually in dividends on his initial holdings.

There was another interesting aspect of the transaction: GD's management retained the right to require Colonel Crown to convert his preferred shares into GD common stock or cash at some time in the future. Crown could opt for either the cash (in which case he'd be liable for considerable capital gains taxes) or the common stock.

When he first moved onto GD's board of directors, Crown disavowed any interest in personally running the company. He was under family pressure to ease back on his business activities or retire altogether. "With General Dynamics I hope to become interested in their situation purely as a director, not as an officer," he declared. "I'll continue to operate Material Service."

However, it wasn't long before Crown found himself the dominant force in GD's affairs. As chairman of the Executive Committee he began commuting frequently between Chicago and GD headquarters in New York. He pushed the board to shut down several money-losing operations and oversaw a major management shakeup.

Pace had been eased out as chairman as a result of the financial beating GD took when it tried to enter the commercial airliner market. Its loss of more than $400 million was the worst debacle any U.S. company had suffered up to that time.

Crown's handpicked replacement for Pace, the former Pan American World Airways executive named Roger Lewis, fared little better. Within a few years of Lewis's arrival his relationship with Crown had deteriorated. Lewis felt Crown cramped his style as GD's chairman by taking too active a role in the company's day-to-day business. Crown, for his part, had become convinced that Lewis simply wasn't shrewd enough to lead a huge defense, shipbuilding, and aerospace conglomerate.

Nathan Cummings took an even less charitable view of GD's chairman. "Roger Lewis was fit to be an office boy," he remembered. "I didn't have any use for Roger, and the colonel didn't have any use for him either because he just wasn't smart. He was a dumbbell."

Tensions mounted when Lewis insisted on buying the Fore River shipyard in Quincy, Massachusetts, from the Bethlehem Steel Company despite Colonel Crown's reservations. As Crown feared, the shipyard lost money.

By the spring of 1965 it became obvious that Crown and Lewis were heading for a confrontation. Crown could probably have mustered enough support on GD's board to oust Lewis. But Lewis wasn't sitting idle, waiting for his pink slip. He was gathering support for a bold plan of his own.

At the time Crown and his allies controlled virtually all of GD's 1.6 million preferred shares. These shares entitled Crown's forces to annual dividends of more than $5 million, an ongoing financial burden that Lewis would have liked to eliminate.

GD still retained the right, from its 1960 merger agreement with Material Service, to insist that Crown convert his preferred shares into GD common stock or cash. If Lewis could persuade the board of directors to exercise its contractual right, Crown would face a difficult choice: He could convert his shares to common stock, thereby forgoing annual dividends of more than $5 million, or he could accept more than $100 million cash for his preferred shares, thereby losing control of his Material Service Corporation and facing capital gains taxes of about $32 million.

Lewis figured that if pushed, Crown would convert his preferred shares to common stock rather than pay the IRS $32 million in capital gains taxes. In 1966 the GD board went along with Lewis's strategy by insisting that Crown either convert his preferred shares to common stock or sell out for cash. It was a bold gamble. And GD lost.

Crown chose to sell out. "I warned Roger [Lewis] we'd take cash," he later explained. "And I said I thought it was foolish for them to think of exchanging equity for interest-bearing debt. They had the damn fool idea they could borrow $100 million to buy us out. As it turned out, they were lucky to borrow $40 million. They took the rest from working capital, which hurt their ratios terribly."

In one sense Lewis had dearly lost because GD was suddenly strapped with a large unexpected debt on which it had to pay interest. In another, more personal sense Lewis won. He had rallied the board of directors to his strategy and dramatically forced Colonel Crown off GD's board.

But Henry Crown didn't give up easily. By selling their preferred GD shares, he and his allies collected a total of $132 million, from which they paid the IRS capital gains taxes of approximately $32 million. The remaining $100 million were used to retire a few debts and invest in various companies and railroads. Crown also began buying GD common stock on the open market, at cheaper prices than his own conversion rate. He amassed about 8 percent of GD's outstanding shares before he stopped buying.

To outsiders it appeared as though Colonel Crown weren't interested in regaining control of General Dynamics. Perhaps not. But something happened three years later, in 1969, that seemed to galvanize him into action. It might have been vindictiveness, a quality not alien to Crown, or it might have been pride. Perhaps it was a careful analysis of GD's business outlook or the sudden death of his son Robert. Whatever it was, Crown couldn't stop thinking about General Dynamics.

One Friday afternoon in Paris he decided to take action. He was sitting in the Hôtel Athénée, an elegant hostelry along the Rue Montaigne, sharing drinks with his old pal Nathan Cummings. Their friendship spanned more than thirty years, back to the first deal they had struck together while vacationing in Honolulu. Crown's Material Service Corporation had been growing rapidly, and Cummings had been enjoying similar success with Consolidated Foods. The two businessmen had bought a chain of movie theaters, held the chain a few years, then sold it back to its original owners for a handsome profit.

They once went to Israel and paid a visit to Golda Meir. "I gave a half a million dollars to Israel and the Colonel gave a million," Cummings recalled later, "because he was a much richer man than I am."

That afternoon in the Hôtel Athénée Colonel Crown had something on his mind. He leaned across the table and made Cummings a simple proposition: "If you want to come in with me as a partner, I'd like to go back into General Dynamics."

Cummings put down his drink. "Let me think about it," he said. "That's a pretty big bite, and I'm not as rich as you are."

Cummings promised to sleep on the idea. The two men hadn't talked dollars and cents. They hadn't even doodled numbers on a cocktail napkin. They didn't have to. Cummings probably had figured out 100 deals in his life and acted on half of them. He made his business decisions intuitively. "You do them instinctively," he explained. "You *feel* whether the circumstances are right. You feel whether the guy is right. It's a combination of stuff up here," he added, tapping his temple. "Who the hell knows?"

The next day the two men met again in the hotel. Cummings spoke first. "I can invest up to $12 million," he said. "That's my limit."

"All right, let's go in as partners," said the colonel, who placed no ceiling on the amount of money he was prepared to invest.

With that the two men quietly decided to take control of General Dynamics.

Back in New York, they met with André Meyer, the brilliant financier who was a senior partner in the investment banking firm of Lazard Frères & Company. They authorized Meyer to accumulate as much GD common stock as possible for them without arousing any suspicions on the New York Stock Exchange. In December 1969 GD shares were trading at about $25, and they didn't want the price to be artificially inflated. Meyer would arrange for the purchase of, say, 1,000 shares and have 500 delivered to Crown and 500 to Cummings. Only four people knew of this confidential buying spree: Meyer, his assistant who handled the buying and distributing, Crown, and Cummings.

On January 2, 1970, the Crown-Cummings group filed a report with the Securities and Exchange Commission, revealing it had acquired 1,113,477 shares of General Dynamics. Within three weeks the group had purchased another 236,000 shares, pushing its total ownership to 13 percent of GD's outstanding stock. By the end of February the Crown-Cummings forces had amassed more than 1.8 million GD shares—18 percent of the outstanding stock.

At this point Meyer negotiated on behalf of Crown and Cummings. Roswell Gilpatric, the former deputy secretary of defense from the Kennedy administration, represented Roger Lewis and the rest of GD's board. "Mr. Meyer used to go into a rage with me," Gilpatric recalled, "blaming not me but my principals at General Dynamics. I had some stormy sessions with him. He'd lash out with all sorts of expletives about [Roger] Lewis and his people." Eventually Crown and Cummings won six seats on an expanded fourteen-man board of directors.

Crown's successful tactics were hailed as a "personal triumph" by *The New York Times.* Having been squeezed out of GD in 1966 and having been paid over $100 million for his preferred shares, Crown had just recaptured control of the corporation for well under $50 million. Crown and Cummings seized control of the company at GD's annual stockholders meeting in Fort Worth in April 1970. One of Crown's first moves after reasserting his dominance at General Dynamics was to contact David Lewis, the president of McDonnell Douglas.

## *(4)*

David Lewis understands the psychological power of silence. He intimidates employees and government officials by waiting patiently for *them* to speak. He rarely argues or loses his temper, and he rarely has to. Ever since he was a child, Lewis has understood that people often respect him more for what he *doesn't* say than for what he does say. In his presence, people sense they're dealing with someone who knows his business. They can't bluff him or outwit him. If they try, he'll look at them gently and steadily, with tired eyes partially obscured by drooping eyelids, and announce with great courtesy, "I don't believe that." He's usually right.

Lewis doesn't tolerate superficial preparation by his subordinates. When he first took over at General Dynamics in 1970, he and Gorden MacDonald, the new chief financial officer he had recruited from Hughes Aircraft, began to grill each of GD's division managers about his specific weapons program. "We'd go around and ask the general manager something," Lewis remembered. "Then we'd start probing into that program, and pretty soon we'd run him out of gas. Then we'd get in somebody else, and we'd run *him* out of gas. Finally, we'd find that the guy who *really* knew what the hell was going on in some of these divisions would be at about the fourth level. Generally he was somebody with insufficient experience to make decisions."

Lewis does his homework. He often knows more about his managers' programs than they do. In view of his background, his obsession with details and his centralized style of management are not surprising. Lewis matured as an aerospace executive in the tightly disciplined environment created by James S. McDonnell, Jr., founder of the McDonnell Aircraft Corporation and one of the giants of American aviation. "McDonnell got into enormous detail, down to the bottom of the bucket—if you were with him and didn't understand what you were talking about or your knowledge was superficial, you better not be there," Lewis recalled later.

Today Lewis has a well-established reputation as a quiet, demanding boss. When a GD employee is summoned to the chairman's corner office on the twenty-third floor of the modern Pierre Laclede Center, he expects to be questioned closely. If there is bad news, he had better report it. There is a palpable pressure in that office to be candid. By all accounts, Lewis brings out the best in his staff. They admire him. They fear him. And they respect him.

"With definite traces of magnolia and mint julep in his voice, and the charm of Leslie Howard in his carriage, Lewis cloaks his iron hand in a Southerner's velvet glove," wrote one journalist.

Unlikely as it may seem, David S. Lewis, Jr., the chairman of America's leading defense contractor, comes not from one of the academic or industrial regions of the United States known for their technological sophistication but from the tradition-bound South Carolina of magnolias, palmetto trees, and *Tobacco Road.* His career has taken him a long way from the broad and sluggish Savannah River that meanders lazily through the Horse Creek Valley of western South Carolina. It was in that valley, in the modest suburban community of North Augusta—just across the river from Augusta, Georgia —that Lewis was born on July 6, 1917.

His father, known to most people as Dick Lewis, supervised civil construction projects as a young man and then took a job with the powerful Esso oil company in South Carolina. He began working in Esso's asphalt department, based in Charleston, a gracious city where the Lewis family had enjoyed upper-crust status for decades. Their elite stature was, perhaps, best reflected in their long-standing membership in the St. Cecilia Society, the state's most prestigious social organization.

The junior Lewis spent his youth in Charleston and attended the city's schools, where he was known as a soft-spoken, good-looking, ambitious student. He wasn't an outstanding athlete and rarely asserted himself among friends, but his sharp mind and pleasant personality made him welcome in virtually any group. Girls were fond of him because he was well dressed, quiet, and genteel. Boys liked him because he was easygoing and flexible, willing to attend any dance, visit any party, or while away the lazy afternoon and evening hours.

The Great Depression devastated South Carolina's economy but largely spared the Lewis family. As David Lewis was beginning his final year of high school, his father was placed in charge of Esso's retail oil and gasoline sales throughout the state. The promotion required the family to relocate from Charleston to Columbia, the state capital, a move they welcomed. Dick Lewis soon emerged as an influential businessman in a state beset by mounting unemployment and economic hard times. He'd swap jokes and anecdotes with state legislators and local politicians who regularly dropped by for drinks at the hospitality suite Esso maintained in the Jefferson Hotel near the State Capitol.

Despite his increasing clout within South Carolina's business community, Dick Lewis was regarded as a man of integrity and fair play. As head of Esso's statewide sales effort, Dick Lewis regularly rented commercial billboard space throughout South Carolina. One year he decided to carry Esso's advertising message to the thousands of fans who crammed into Columbia's Carolina Stadium, home of the University of South Carolina's football team. The stadium needed a huge new scoreboard with fancy flashing lights, a clock, and plenty of room for Esso advertising.

"I want the best you can build," Dick Lewis told the youthful president of a struggling outdoor advertising firm. "Just give me a price." The president came up with a competitive price and won the contract. Unfortunately the task proved far more complicated than he had expected, and he had to subcontract out a large portion of the work. Eventually the scoreboard was completed and functioned as the billboard president had promised, but his company had taken a financial beating.

"How did you make out on that job?" Dick Lewis later inquired.

"I lost on it," the advertising man admitted sheepishly.

"Well, refigure your cost on it," said Lewis, "and then add in a thousand-dollar profit for yourself."

David Lewis was graduated from high school in Columbia in 1934. He had his eye on the Massachusetts Institute of Technology, where he could pursue his boyhood interests in airplanes and engineering, but MIT's high tuition made that idea prohibitive. Instead, Lewis enrolled at the University of South Carolina in Columbia, a lovely, tree-covered campus not far from his family's home. He earned money to help cover his college expenses by working as a cabin boy on a commercial oil tanker during summer vacations.

His years at USC were a blend of academic course work (mostly sciences, engineering, and mathematics), chatting with friends at a local beer joint, and socializing with his Sigma Alpha Epsilon fraternity brothers. Lewis fitted in comfortably with this group of bright, ambitious, hard-partying, self-confident achievers. But he rarely stood out. More often he shunned the center stage among these friends, deferring to the backslapping raconteurs among the group.

In an uncharacteristic moment, however, Lewis could occasionally grab the spotlight. There was a time he and a group of college friends were sitting in his parents' home, recounting the outrageous exploits of Huey Long, the larger-than-life senator from Louisiana.

"Let's call him," said Lewis impulsively, reaching for the telephone. "Operator, get me Huey Long in Washington," he barked authoritatively. For a few minutes Lewis savored the quiet admiration of his friends. Then the phone rang, and Lewis's self-satisfied grin shriveled as the operator announced, "Sir, Huey Long is on the line."

After three years at USC Lewis transferred to the Georgia Institute of Technology in Atlanta, where his studies focused on engineering. Then, as now, Georgia Tech was considered one of the best engineering schools in the South. In 1939 Lewis was graduated with a Bachelor of Science degree in aeronautical engineering. He immediately accepted an offer to join aviation pioneer Glenn L. Martin's aircraft company in Baltimore.

Martin, nicknamed the Flying Dude because he liked to don his Sunday best whenever he piloted an airplane, was one of America's earliest and most innovative fliers. He made his first flight in 1909, six years after the Wright brothers' historic achievement near Kitty Hawk, in a plane he had fashioned from silk, bamboo, and wire with the help of his mother. (A lifelong bachelor, Martin attributed much of his business success to his mother's unending enthusiasm.) During the early days of aviation he crisscrossed the country, earning a reputation as a racer and a seat-of-the-pants barnstormer. In 1912 he made aviation history by piloting America's first *overwater* flight, from Catalina Island in the Pacific Ocean to Newport Harbor, California, a distance of more than twenty miles.

The year before, Martin had settled into the less adventurous business of manufacturing aircraft. In Santa Ana, California, Cleveland, and then Baltimore, he produced civil aircraft for the embryonic commercial aviation market and warplanes for the U.S. armed forces. Among his many firsts were the first Army bomber, the first Army trainer, the first pursuit plane, and the first twin-engine bomber. In 1921 General Billy Mitchell, the Army's outspoken champion of air power, used seven MB-2 bombers built by Martin to demonstrate that bombs dropped from an airplane could indeed sink a battleship.

By the time David Lewis was hired in 1939 the Glenn L. Martin Company* had begun building powerful clippers, including the famous China Clipper, which carried passengers across the Pacific Ocean. However, when World War II began, the company again turned its attention to military aircraft, churning out hundreds of B-26 Martin Marauder bombers.

David Lewis spent seven years at the Glenn L. Martin Company, rising rapidly from a draftsman to a project aerodynamicist. While there, he met James McDonnell, briefly his co-worker, later his mentor and father figure at the McDonnell Aircraft Corporation, and finally his defense industry competitor. Lewis left Martin in 1946 to join McDonnell Aircraft in St. Louis as chief of aerodynamics. The final notation in Lewis's personnel folder at the Glenn L. Martin Company, now almost forty years old, consists of three words: "Eligible for Rehire."

James McDonnell had worked at Martin for five years, rising to the position of chief engineer, before he left in 1939, shortly after Lewis had arrived. With $165,000 in start-up capital ($10,000 of which came from his college friend Laurance Rockefeller), he rented space in the American Airlines building at the St. Louis airport and established the McDonnell Aircraft Corporation.

---

*In 1961 Martin merged with the American Marietta Company, a cement and chemicals concern, to form the Martin Marietta Corporation, which has its headquarters in Maryland. However, like several other former aircraft producers, Martin Marietta no longer builds complete aircraft. Instead, the company builds targeting and night vision systems for the Army's AH-64 attack helicopter program and is the prime contractor for the controversial Pershing II nuclear-tipped missile deployed in Western Europe —enough defense work to earn it the number twelve spot on the Pentagon's 1983 list of leading prime contractors.

Martin Marietta's image today stems largely from its dramatic and highly publicized takeover battle with the Bendix Corporation in 1982. In that Wall Street showdown Bendix's aggressive young chairman, William Agee (with advice from his wife, Mary Cunningham), attempted to swallow Martin Marietta, only to have the Allied Corporation step in as a "white knight" and seize control of Bendix instead. In the aftermath Agee was squeezed out of Bendix, and Martin Marietta managed to protect its cherished independence.

McDonnell was no newcomer to aviation. He had received his pilot's wings from the Army Air Service in 1924, after earning a bachelor's degree in physics from Princeton and a master's degree in aeronautical engineering from MIT. For fifteen years he had bounced from job to job in the aircraft industry, working as a stress analyst, draftsman, and engineer.

In 1939 his attempt to launch his own company proved successful. The first twelve months of McDonnell Aircraft weren't terribly auspicious (sixteen proposals submitted with dismal results, and a net loss of $3,892), but the company's future looked bright. At first, it won subcontracts from other aircraft producers that were swamped with World War II orders. Eventually it was awarded a major prime contract when other firms were too busy to handle any more orders.

In 1943 McDonnell Aircraft was chosen by the Navy to develop the first jet fighter capable of operating off an aircraft carrier. Three years later, the year Lewis became the company's chief of aerodynamics, it delivered the innovative jet fighter the FH-1 Phantom. Since then McDonnell has earned a worldwide reputation for fighter aircraft and healthy profits from its succession of Phantoms, Banshees, Demons, Voodoos, and Eagles.

Unwilling to limit his growing company to military aircraft, McDonnell moved aggressively into missile research in the 1940's and the space program during the late 1950's. The company began experimenting with missiles on its own in 1943, won a Navy development contract to design a radio-controlled dive bomb the following year, and successfully fired that missile, named the Gargoyle, by the end of 1945. Even before NASA awarded McDonnell a prime contract in 1959 to build the Mercury space capsule, the company had begun designing a manned orbital spacecraft of its own. McDonnell capsules carried Alan Shepard, Jr., into space and John Glenn into orbit around the earth.

James McDonnell was an outspoken foe of totalitarianism who championed America's military strength. As such, he fitted the mold of the postwar American industrialist who helped shape the mindset of the country's permanent defense industry. Virtually everyone who knew James McDonnell, and many who didn't, called him Mr. Mac, as noted earlier. The nickname was a term of affection, respect, and awe. Mr. Mac dominated his company, and his employees, as few American businessmen did. He called all the shots. Once, when the company was planning a small party for a group of employees, the question arose as to how many shots of liquor should be purchased for the festivities. Mr. Mac immediately pulled out his slide rule, figured exactly two and one-quarter drinks per person, and calculated *precisely* how many bottles of liquor should be ordered.

He expected his employees to be available twenty-four hours a day seven days a week. If an idea or a concern struck him, he didn't hesitate to rouse a slumbering employee at 3:00 A.M. The only time McDonnell's immediate staff thought they might enjoy an uninterrupted weekend was if he was away from St. Louis. Even then he could telephone unexpectedly, demanding explanation, justification, or information. Mr. Mac rarely delegated authority. He needed to know every detail. He demanded to read every press release before it was issued and he wanted to sign all of the company's letters.

Four years after joining McDonnell Aircraft, Lewis was offered a job in the company's design engineering department, where paper theories were translated into actual airplanes. It was an exciting new position, though it paid less than he was earning. Lewis was reluctant to accept a pay cut. He asked his uncle Robert Walton for advice. His uncle gently tapped his temple with his middle finger. "Mr. Mac has something in mind for you, David. Take the job."

## (5)

Indeed, it seemed Mr. Mac did have something in mind for Lewis, an up-and-coming protégé he referred to as his baby-faced assassin. Lewis's rise through the company's organizational chart was meteoric. In 1950 he became a design engineer. Two years later he was named chief of preliminary design in the airplane engineering division. In 1955 he was promoted to manager of sales. In each position, he demonstrated two talents essential to success in the aerospace business: an ability to conceive of a new aircraft ahead of the competition and an ability to build that aircraft while holding its manufacturing costs in line.

The following year Lewis was appointed company-wide project manager and placed in charge of McDonnell's F3H Demon fighter program. The defense industry's project manager, like the military's program manager, is responsible for developing and producing the promised weapons system on time and at the agreed price. If the program succeeds, the glory is his. If the program runs behind schedule or over budget, the blame lands at his feet.

In the summer of 1957, having just celebrated his fortieth birthday, Lewis was appointed vice-president of project management for the entire McDonnell Aircraft Corporation. That autumn he was elevated to the company's board of directors.

Perhaps the high point of Lewis's career at McDonnell Aircraft was his role in the development of the Demon's successor, the F-4 Phantom II fighter, one of the mainstays of the U.S. air war over Vietnam. "The most successful military airplane McDonnell ever built and perhaps destined to become the best ever produced by any free world aircraft company is the F4 Phantom,"

5. David Sloan Lewis worked for twenty-four years for James "Mr. Mac" McDonnell, Jr., at McDonnell Aircraft (later known as McDonnell Douglas) as an aerodynamic engineer, project manager, rising executive, and president before accepting the number one job at General Dynamics in 1970. A respected figure in the defense industry who built his reputation on McDonnell's hugely successful F-4 Phantom fighter, Lewis has been tarnished recently by allegations of contract fraud at his Electric Boat division and GD's improper overhead charges. *St. Louis Post-Dispatch*

the hometown *St. Louis Globe-Democrat* reported enthusiastically in 1967, "currently responsible for McDonnell's record employment of over 46,000 persons. . . ." Lewis was widely praised for helping formulate the original concept of the Phantom, peddling it to the U.S. Navy, Marine Corps, and Air Force, and enhancing its technical capabilities so that it eventually brought in hundreds of millions of dollars to McDonnell Aircraft. By the late 1970's the three services and nine other nations had received more than 5,000 of these planes. The success of the Phantom earned McDonnell huge profits and David Lewis an outstanding reputation in the aerospace industry.

Clearly headed for the top, Lewis was chosen as senior vice-president—the company's third-highest job—in 1959. Two years later he was named general manager of McDonnell Aircraft, reporting only to Mr. Mac himself. And finally, in July 1962, sixteen years after he had arrived at McDonnell Aircraft, Lewis was elected president and chief operating officer. All that stood between Lewis and the number one slot was his boss, the sixty-three-year-old McDonnell, who showed precious little interest in retiring.

McDonnell received most of the acclaim for his company's extraordinary growth in the 1960's. "You would read a lot about old Mac," recalled Wallace

Persons, once the chairman of the Emerson Electric Company in St. Louis and a former GD director, "but those of us in this community knew that David [Lewis] was behind a lot of what was happening at McDonnell."

Among the things happening there was Mr. Mac's growing desire to seize control of the Douglas Aircraft Company, the ailing airplane manufacturer in Santa Monica, California. Douglas had fallen on hard times. Production disruptions on its DC-8 and DC-9 jetliners resulting from labor difficulties and parts shortages had cost Douglas $27.5 million in 1966. If Mr. Mac could consolidate the two firms, it would be the biggest aerospace merger in U.S. history, combining Douglas's capabilities in commercial aircraft with McDonnell's strength in military and space work. The resulting company would become the nation's fourth-largest aerospace concern—behind the Boeing Company, North American Aviation, Inc. (later Rockwell International), and the Lockheed Corporation.

Begun in 1920 by Donald W. Douglas, Sr., who designed one of his earliest airplanes in the back room of a barbershop, Douglas Aircraft had prospered during the previous four decades on the basis of its World War II fighter-bombers and transports and its postwar commercial jetliners. By the mid-1960's, however, the company was plagued with financial problems. It had introduced into the airline market so many versions of its DC-8 and DC-9 jetliners ("DC" stood for "Douglas Commercial") that it couldn't produce any of them efficiently. Hunting for a merger candidate, Douglas had considered General Dynamics and North American Aviation before focusing on McDonnell.

"Paradoxically, the news of Douglas searching around for a partner came at a time when the company already had a huge backlog of civil aircraft orders —but the fact was that they had been in financial difficulties since about 1963 and had been unable to make their DC-9 machines pay," noted John Godson, author of *The Rise and Fall of the DC-10.*

Now, as James McDonnell and David Lewis eyed Douglas, the California firm looked like an ideal turnaround opportunity. In 1966 McDonnell decided to pursue Douglas with the understanding that Lewis, his right-hand man, would immediately relocate to California to try to restore Douglas Aircraft to profitability while amalgamating the division into an expanded McDonnell Douglas Corporation. In a sense, the assignment to California may have been Mr. Mac's final test of Lewis's executive talents. Since Lewis had been named McDonnell's president four years earlier, sales and profits had tripled and employment had more than doubled to some 44,000. If he could further prove himself on the West Coast, Lewis would surely succeed Mr. Mac as the corporation's next chairman.

McDonnell already held about 300,000 shares of Douglas—more stock than anybody, including the Douglas family. So the takeover effort proceeded smoothly. The two aerospace firms announced they would merge in January 1967. Actually, it was clear all along that McDonnell had swallowed Douglas and that virtually all decision-making power would be exercised from St. Louis. Initially both companies stressed that Douglas Aircraft and McDonnell Aircraft would continue to function separately, as distinct components of a newly formed McDonnell Douglas Corporation. Donald W. Douglas, Sr., the founder, would be given the title honorary chairman of the new corporation and retained as a consultant. His son, Donald W. Douglas, Jr., would remain president of the Douglas Aircraft division.

However, David Lewis was named board chairman and chief executive officer of Douglas Aircraft, while Mr. Mac retained those titles for the parent corporation, leaving little doubt where the real power would reside. The fact that the elder Douglas's annual pay was cut from $116,700 to $50,000 and that his son's compensation was shaved from $154,200 to $100,000 reinforced this impression.

Lewis moved to California. His new assignment at Douglas was challenging —"the high point in my life"—and liberating. Back in St. Louis, all McDonnell Aircraft executives toiled under the increasingly penny-pinching scrutiny of Mr. Mac. They drove small, economical cars and entertained on frugal expense accounts. "The old man wouldn't stand for anyone living high on the hog," said Ted Schafers, veteran St. Louis newspaperman and a longtime McDonnell watcher. By contrast, Lewis lived royally in California, using a sleek corporate helicopter to hop between his lavishly appointed home and the Douglas aircraft factories.

Within a matter of months Lewis had managed to pull Douglas Aircraft back from the brink of bankruptcy by streamlining its tangled production of DC-8 and DC-9 commercial jets. From January to August 1968, on the DC-9 production line alone, the number of employees working on final assembly was cut from 2,400 to 1,600. Further cuts were made in Douglas's engineering and support staffs. "It was the first time Dave had ever coped with commercial planes," commented one industry friend, "and he rose to the occasion."

Dragged down by losses at Douglas, the new McDonnell Douglas Corporation showed a minuscule net income of $7.5 million in 1967. Twelve months later Lewis had helped boost the corporation's earnings to more than $98 million—a thirteenfold increase. Before long McDonnell Douglas displaced Lockheed as the Defense Department's leading prime contractor.

Lewis returned to St. Louis headquarters in triumph and was named chief operating officer of the parent corporation. But he remained number two behind the indomitable James McDonnell, a status that began to frustrate him. As long as McDonnell remained at the helm, Lewis's new title added little to his actual authority. Other problems began to bother him. He wasn't happy with the costly cutthroat competition that had developed between the three-engine Douglas DC-10, which McDonnell Douglas had begun developing soon after the merger, and Lockheed's rival L-1011 Tristar. In their desperate lunge for sales to major U.S. airlines, McDonnell Douglas and Lockheed had slashed their prices and divided the market to the point where neither company could build planes profitably. "It was a destructive competition, and neither company is likely ever to recover fully from its effects . . ." observed John Newhouse in his book on the commercial aircraft business, *The Sporty Game.*

The counterproductive competition with Lockheed troubled Lewis, but his growing malaise at McDonnell Douglas seemed to come more from within. At first he couldn't put his finger on his gnawing discontent, his uneasiness, his sense that his life was somehow drifting away. "I was about fifty-three, and I had time to make some kind of a mark," he later recalled feeling. For the first time in his twenty-four years at McDonnell he had lost his enthusiasm for working. His relationship with Mr. Mac remained excellent. But since his return from California something intangible had changed. On the West Coast he had run the entire aircraft operation; back in St. Louis he was once again eclipsed by McDonnell's enormous shadow. Eventually his frustration became clear. "At McDonnell I was the number two man. Mr. McDonnell was in charge. I wanted to be the chief executive officer," he later explained; ". . . it's as simple as that."

If he could wait for the top spot at McDonnell Douglas, Lewis would have been satisfied. But there was no guarantee that day would ever arrive. By 1970 there were still no signs that Mr. Mac was ready to step aside. In fact, the company's board of directors had waived its mandatory retirement age so he could continue working beyond his sixty-fifth birthday. At seventy-one, Mr. Mac was still remarkably fit and worked longer hours than almost anyone.

Like other empire builders who had built phenomenally successful businesses from scratch, James McDonnell was reluctant to let go. Lewis understood and empathized with his mentor's worries: "He's just determined that no one is going to ruin the company he worked so hard to build." Was Lewis willing to wait another seven, eight, or nine years?

One day, as he pondered such questions, the phone rang. It was Sidney Salomon, Jr., a friend and local businessman who was chairman of the St. Louis Blues, a professional hockey team. Salomon suggested the two men get together. Lewis didn't know that Salomon was also a friend of Henry Crown's and that this phone call was the first step in some carefully orchestrated corporate diplomacy.

Crown had recently moved back onto GD's board of directors and was actively looking for some high-powered executive talent. He invited Lewis to meet with him in Chicago on the Sunday of Labor Day weekend. At first Crown offered Lewis the presidency of GD, but Lewis said he wasn't interested in leaving McDonnell Douglas to take the number two post at an inferior company. A few weeks later the two men agreed that David Lewis would join GD as chairman, supplanting Roger Lewis, who would stay on as president. The "Dynamic Duo" of Crown and Lewis had taken the reins.

Lewis made the right move. James McDonnell remained chairman at McDonnell Douglas until he died at the age of eighty-one, in 1980—ten years after Lewis had resigned to take the helm at General Dynamics.

# Chapter Five

## Tug-of-War—Electric Boat
## Versus the Navy

### (1)

David Lewis's dramatic announcement on March 13, 1978, that Electric Boat would stop building attack submarines in thirty days climaxed a bitter struggle with the Navy that had been developing for years. EB and the Navy had been quarreling over who would pay for the shipyard's unexpectedly high costs of completing eighteen new fast attack submarines it had contracted to build. Each side blamed the other for the construction delays and price increases. In December 1976 Electric Boat had tried to recoup its mounting financial losses by submitting a formal claim to the Navy for more than half a *billion* dollars. But for fifteen months the Navy had been unwilling, or unable, to settle the claim. Lewis had now run out of patience. Either the Navy would resolve EB's outstanding claim or the shipyard would stop working.

Electric Boat wasn't alone in its confrontation with the Navy. In recent years several major shipyards had taken similar actions as their relations with the Navy deteriorated. During the Nixon and Ford administrations, the price tag on ships had escalated at frightening rates. Ship construction timetables had slipped badly. Worker productivity at the private shipyards had fallen off sharply. Bitterness and acrimony had replaced trust and cooperation as the hallmarks of the naval shipbuilding business. Even the Shipbuilders Council of America, the trade association of private shipyards, acknowledged that its members and the Navy had developed "an adversary attitude" during the preceding decade.

The Navy's most troublesome problem was the mountain of contract claims it confronted from its three largest shipbuilders: Electric Boat, Newport News, and Ingalls. The three yards argued that the unusually high costs they incurred in the construction of submarines, destroyers, and assault ships were caused largely by the Navy's actions and inactions, not by the shipyards' own mistakes or mismanagement. Accordingly the three yards were demanding that the Navy cover their unanticipated costs to the tune of $2.3 billion.

Those three claims—$544 million from the Electric Boat division of General Dynamics; $742 million from the Newport News Shipbuilding and Dry Dock Company, a subsidiary of Tenneco; and just over $1 billion from the Ingalls Shipbuilding division of Litton Industries—plus other claims from smaller yards that pushed the total to $2.7 billion, threatened to sink the Navy's entire shipbuilding program. If the shipyards weren't paid a substantial portion of their out-of-pocket costs, they might stop building the Navy's ships.

Contract claims from shipbuilders had grown at an alarming rate in recent years. Before 1968 shipbuilders had submitted only a handful of small claims. During the next decade claims totaling nearly $1.5 billion had been settled with relative ease. But by the time the Carter administration took over in 1977 unresolved claims totaled $2.7 billion, more than half the Navy's annual shipbuilding budget. The sharp rise in such claims prompted one Navy official to declare that shipbuilders' claims had become "the most dysfunctional element in the business of Navy ship acquisition." He was putting it mildly.

Ship claims had begun to poison the entire shipbuilding process. As the claims controversy reached a climax in 1978, more than money was at stake. "The problem is not just one of evaluating the legal validity of shipbuilding claims," warned Charles Duncan, Carter's deputy secretary of defense. "It really concerns the whole future relationship of the Navy and the private shipbuilding industry."

To many observers, the dispute went deeper than a disagreement over outstanding claims. The claims were merely symptoms of a profound revolt by the powerful conglomerates that owned the shipyards and refused to have their day-to-day management decisions dictated by the Navy. "The current shipyard owners have financial strength, managerial depth, political clout, and tenacity," wrote one Navy captain who studied the situation. "They are strong enough to survive without future business from the U.S. Navy; therefore, they have set out to make the shipyards into the profitable 'cash flow machines' which were envisioned when they were acquired."

What caused the naval shipbuilding industry to run aground in the mid-

1970's? Who was to blame? How did the shipbuilders' claims spotlight deeper problems in the Navy's procurement system? And how was the animosity finally resolved? Describing the origin of these multibillion-dollar disputes, particularly the $544 million claim submitted by Electric Boat, helps answer these interwoven questions. By retracing the conception, design, and construction of the Navy's SSN-688-class of high-speed attack submarines (also known as the Los Angeles class after the first ship of that type), one can witness how EB's half-billion-dollar claim grew out of an unfortunate confluence of events. Changes in the Navy's procurement process, a deepening mistrust of defense contractors, the fear of an expanding Soviet Navy, a tightening U.S. defense budget, and an overburdened and mismanaged Electric Boat shipyard—all contributed to a tense showdown between General Dynamics and the Navy.

The Navy's approach to shipbuilding has changed dramatically since World War II. During the war and into the 1950's the Navy relied on both government-owned shipbuilding facilities, such as the naval shipyards in Brooklyn, Boston, Portsmouth, New Hampshire, and Mare Island, California, and privately owned shipyards, such as Electric Boat, Bath Iron Works, and Todd, to construct its new naval ships. Contracts generally were distributed among these public and private yards on the basis of their available shipbuilding capacity, not formal bids or competitive prices. The Navy was more concerned with keeping the country's largest shipyards busy and with maintaining a healthy "mobilization base" that could be tapped in case of war than in finding the lowest shipbuilding prices.

By the 1960's a shift in procurement practice began. New ships and the weapons systems designed for them were becoming technologically more sophisticated. As this advanced technology outstripped the Navy's internal design capability, the Navy began to scale back the activity at its own shipyards and to depend more heavily on private yards to design and construct new vessels. At the beginning of the decade the role of Navy-owned yards was limited to building only nuclear-powered submarines, auxiliary ships, and landing craft. This role was to shrink still further as the private shipbuilding industry competed vigorously for Navy business.

A few years later the Shipbuilders Council of America hired the accounting firm of Ernst & Ernst to compare shipbuilding costs at public and private yards. Not surprisingly the completed study determined it would be cheaper for the Navy to have its ships built in private shipyards because of their lower labor and material costs and their higher worker productivity. This conclusion by the shipbuilders' association was later corroborated by a separate Navy-sponsored study. Armed with this comparative report, the private shipbuilding industry effectively lobbied Congress and the executive branch for a larger slice of the naval shipbuilding pie. In 1967 the Navy's yards were cut out of the shipbuilding business altogether when President Johnson decided that all future naval ships would be built in private shipyards. No major ship construction contract has been awarded to a Navy shipyard since 1967. Instead, the publicly owned yards have confined themselves to repair and overhaul work.

As the Navy's shipbuilding business was shifted from public to private yards, it was gobbled up by a handful of major firms. By the time the claims controversy erupted in the mid-1970's there were twenty-seven private shipyards in the United States capable of building oceangoing merchant or naval vessels, but only nine were actually engaged in Navy shipbuilding. Of those, three shipyards—Electric Boat, Newport News, and Ingalls—clearly dominated the field.

Since 1960 sales to any one of the three yards topped the *combined* sales to the rest of the naval shipbuilding industry, including such familiar firms as National Steel & Shipbuilding Company, Todd Shipyards, Bath Iron Works, Lockheed Shipbuilding and Construction Company, and Avondale Shipyards. Over the last two decades the Big Three has built more than 40 percent of the Navy's 401 new ships.

Electric Boat was the leader. Since 1960 the General Dynamics division had logged Navy orders of $7 billion for submarines, including Polaris, Poseidon, and Trident ballistic missile submarines and several classes of diesel- and nuclear-powered attack submarines designed to hunt down and destroy enemy subs and surface ships. EB launched the world's first nuclear-powered submarine in January 1954, moments after First Lady Mamie Eisenhower smashed a bottle of champagne on the vessel and declared, "I christen thee *Nautilus.*"

EB was not only the busiest submarine builder but also the Navy's leading sub designer. Since the *Nautilus,* EB was the only private shipyard to serve as design agent for a nuclear-powered sub. Measured in terms of its backlog of submarine orders, its historical tradition, and its design talent, it was the nation's premier shipyard.

Newport News, the country's only private shipyard capable of building nuclear-powered surface ships or aircraft carriers, was the Navy's second-busiest contractor, boasting sales of $6.6 billion since 1960. Unlike Electric Boat, which constructed submarines exclusively, Newport News was a diversified yard that had built aircraft carriers and submarines as well as guided missile cruisers, amphibious cargo and command ships, and submarine tenders.

Ingalls ran third, having landed $5 billion in Navy orders for fifty-four destroyers, attack submarines, assault ships, sub tenders, and assorted smaller vessels. In 1961 the shipyard was acquired by Litton Industries, one of the most aggressive conglomerates of the decade.

As it redirected its shipbuilding dollars from public to private yards, the Navy took a lot more interest in the price it was paying for each new vessel, and it changed its ship procurement strategy to reflect this concern. It began awarding firm fixed-price contracts to the shipyard that had submitted the lowest bid for a particular ship design or construction project. Under fixed-price contracts, the winning shipyard promised to design or build a new ship by a specified date for an agreed-upon price. If the yard spent less than the fixed price to complete the contract, it earned a profit. If it spent more, it swallowed the loss. Thus, the shipyard, not the Navy, took the financial risk.

It didn't always work out that way, however. A shipyard would frequently attempt to buy into a shipbuilding contract by submitting an unrealistically low bid for the initial design work on a new class of ship with the expectation that the yard would also win the subsequent contract to build the ship. The yard might lose money on its early design and development work, but it expected to recoup those losses by charging the Navy an exorbitantly high price under its follow-on contracts to construct the new ships. This abusive practice of buying in was well known in shipbuilding circles—indeed, similar ploys have been used throughout the defense industry—but Pentagon officials had a hard time finding a way to stop it.

In 1969 the Navy tried to prevent shipbuilder buy-ins by adopting a weapons procurement procedure developed earlier by former Defense Secretary Robert McNamara known as Total Package Procurement. Under this concept, contractors were to be asked to bid one overall price for the total package—the design, development, production, and logistical support of a complete new weapons system—rather than to submit separate bids for each successive phase of the program. By forcing companies to compete, McNamara hoped to extract the lowest possible price from the contractors for the complete weapons project and to thwart buy-ins.

The idea performed better on paper than in the defense marketplace. Contractors submitted bids for the weapons package from start to finish but often discovered they couldn't complete their contractual obligations at the price they had quoted.

The Ingalls shipyard at Pascagoula, Mississippi, for example, won two Total Package Procurements from the Navy: one in 1969 for nine amphibious assault ships (later reduced to five), the other in 1970 for thirty Spruance-class destroyers, named after the World War II admiral Raymond Spruance. The shipyard signed a contract to design, build, and support these ships for a total of $2.5 billion. Before long, however, the Navy and the shipyard discovered they had underestimated the total costs of designing, building, supporting, and outfitting the warships over dozens of years. Cost overruns emerged. Critics accused Ingalls of bidding too low in the first place. The shipyard maintained that it was impossible to forecast accurately its costs so far into the future. In the end, the Total Package Procurement concept was blamed for many of Ingalls's cost problems.

Total Package Procurements required competing contractors to submit fixed-price bids for an enormous quantity of technically sophisticated work, stretching over many years. The cost of that work was difficult to predict. It's not surprising that in a competitive environment many companies bid too optimistically and then suffered cost overruns. Total Package Procurement seemed to invite such optimism.

Burned by its experience at the Ingalls shipyard, the Navy retreated to its traditional practice of awarding separate contracts for the design and construction of its new ships.

## (2)

The trust and businesslike ethics that had characterized the relationship between the Navy and its private shipbuilders in the 1950's and 1960's were being replaced by suspicion and rancor. "In the old days Navy personnel and shipyard executives would traditionally sign their contracts and then walk down to the end of the pier and drop them in the water," said one industry veteran, recalling the days when a handshake was valued more highly than a written contract. Those days were long gone.

One man, Admiral Hyman G. Rickover, was widely viewed as the cause of much of the bitterness that permeated the naval shipbuilding business in the 1970's. A brilliant, stubborn, demanding, fiercely honest naval officer, Rickover had earned a niche in the nation's history by fathering the nuclear-powered submarine *Nautilus*. He is widely credited with almost single-handedly persuading the Navy and the Atomic Energy Commission (AEC) to support the development of nuclear-powered submarines.

In the decades that followed, he succeeded in countless ways in imposing his deep-seated mistrust of defense contractors—particularly shipbuilders—on the rest of the Navy. He was in a unique position to do so.

Since the early days of the Navy's nuclear propulsion program Rickover had simultaneously held positions in two separate agencies of the U.S. government. In the Navy itself he held a fourth-echelon position as deputy commander for nuclear propulsion, within what became the Naval Sea Systems

6. Vice Admiral Hyman G. Rickover, often called the father of the nuclear Navy, visits the USS *Nautilus,* the world's first nuclear-powered submarine, the development of which he spearheaded. Before he was forced into retirement in 1982, the irascible admiral battled publicly for decades with Electric Boat and other Navy shipbuilders that he considered greedy and incompetent. *U.S. Navy*

Command (NAVSEA). In that post he was responsible for the design, production, and maintenance of the propulsion systems installed on all nuclear-powered Navy ships. Theoretically he reported to the commander of NAVSEA, who reported to the chief of naval material, who reported to the chief of naval operations. (The chief of naval operations—called the CNO—is both the Navy's senior officer and its representative on the Joint Chiefs of Staff.) In reality Rickover often communicated his strongly held views to whomever he wished.

Rickover also held a fourth-echelon position within the AEC and later within the Department of Energy. In those capacities he was responsible for the research, development, manufacture, and safety of any nuclear reactor intended for a Navy ship. Deftly switching roles to fit the occasion, Rickover often was able to get his way by playing one of his agencies off another. "He was a master at blurring the line, pretty fuzzy to begin with, between the two jobs," explained former CNO Elmo Zumwalt, Jr., who had to contend with Rickover's inordinate power. If Rickover was angered by a proposed Navy action, for example, he might correspond with his many allies in Congress using an AEC letterhead, rather than Navy stationery, thereby bypassing the naval chain of command. "In short, Rick doffed his admiral's suit whenever he found himself in conflict with Navy policy, and sniped at the Navy in civvies," Admiral Zumwalt remembered.

To an extraordinary degree, Rickover's intense personal involvement in virtually every facet of the nuclear submarine program—and much of the surface shipbuilding program as well—altered the manner in which the shipyards carried on their business with the service. Some admirers considered Rickover a tireless public servant who strove heroically to prevent the private shipyards from gouging the Navy. Other observers thought he was an obsessive, ego-driven autocrat whose suspicion of defense contractors had at some stage passed the point of rationality. Many officers and civilians who worked closely with Rickover praise and cuss the "Old Man" in the same breath. "As long as he stayed on the operational side, the design side, and the side of building nuclear submarines, I don't think he had an equal in the world," said William P. Clements, a former deputy secretary of defense. "But when he goes astray and wanders into fields where he lacks that expertise, like contract law, Rickover can cause some problems."

Rickover disputes the notion that he was once a supremely effective officer but somehow "lost it" in his later years. "I've always been crotchety," the eighty-three-year-old admiral insisted in 1983, the year after President Reagan had pushed him into retirement. It's the shipbuilders who have changed, he said. Executives at Electric Boat, Newport News, and the other major shipyards once cared deeply about the quality of their vessels, the admiral continued, but the shipbuilding industry has changed dramatically since the 1950's, with multibillion-dollar conglomerates having swallowed the major yards. (Indeed, between 1959 and 1968 six major independent shipyards, including Avondale, Ingalls, National Steel & Shipbuilding, and Newport News, were acquired by conglomerates.) Now, according to Rickover, the Navy is forced to deal with corporate financial experts more concerned with bottom-line profits than with building first-class ships. He once declared bitterly that the shipyards would sell the Navy a cow turd as soon as they would sell it a ship, so long as they made their profit.

Among the revelations that surfaced when Takis Veliotis turned on his former employer was word that GD had given gifts and gratuities to Rickover in 1977. The gifts included jewelry for his wife worth $1,125, which GD allegedly attempted to conceal by falsifying its expense records. The gratuities consisted primarily of food and other provisions, which came to be known as the "Rig for Rickover List," which the admiral insisted be available whenever he rode a new submarine during sea trials.

A Navy Gratuities Board established by Navy Secretary Lehman concluded that GD had given Rickover at least $67,283 worth of jewelry, trinkets, and mementos between 1961 and 1977. In response, Lehman announced in May 1985 that he was fining GD $676,283, canceling two GD contracts worth about $22.5 million, temporarily suspending future contracts at two GD divisions, and placing a punitive letter of censure in retired Admiral Rickover's personnel file.

GD had admitted giving Rickover the gifts but insisted company officials had never intended to win any favors from the cantankerous admiral. "The admiral was a unique person in his commanding position in the Navy's nuclear propulsion program," Lewis explained. "He was difficult. He was feared but respected. He was impossible to get along with, but he already was legendary in the years while he was still in active service. . . . In the desire to get along with him, it was easier to comply with his petty or idiosyncratic requests and to get on with the building of submarines," Lewis continued, "than to waste time resisting those requests."

Unfortunately, while relations between the private shipyards and the U.S. Navy were deteriorating, the Soviet Navy was growing more ominous. This was particularly true of the Soviet Union's rapidly expanding fleet of attack submarines, which by 1968 was more than twice the size of the U.S. fleet. The rapid improvement in Soviet attack subs caught some U.S. planners off guard. "Having scored a first a number of years ago in the practical application of nuclear energy for submarine propulsion, the United States considered itself so technologically advanced, and, therefore, qualitatively superior, that any serious challenge to that supremacy could not possibly occur for years to come," a Senate Armed Services subcommittee observed in 1968. "Unfortunately, that meaningful and serious challenge has taken place." The newest Soviet attack submarines were running faster, prowling more quietly, tracking enemy subs with better sonar equipment, and diving deeper than their predecessors. Planners in the U.S. Navy were understandably worried.

The primary purpose of a U.S. attack submarine is to track down and destroy an enemy attack submarine that might threaten the U.S. fleet or disrupt U.S. sea-lanes. In such one-on-one underwater duels, superior technical capabilities can provide the margin of victory. The three most important capabilities are speed, quiet operation, and depth. The submarine with greater speed can pursue a fleeing enemy, can fire its torpedoes and dash off, or can outmaneuver its opponent at close range. The sub that makes less noise can approach an enemy submarine more closely without being detected and can "listen" for the enemy with its own sonar system more effectively. The sub that is structurally stronger can operate at greater depths in the ocean and confound its enemy by "hiding" in different thermal layers of water that exhibit different sound-conducting properties. Designing a new submarine with optimal capabilities requires a careful trade-off among these factors. As one increases the power of the propulsion system, for example, the sub becomes noisier; as one increases the strength of the hull to withstand the pressure at greater depths, the sub becomes heavier and thus slower.

Confronted by vastly improved Soviet attack subs, U.S. Navy submarine admirals, led by Rickover, began pushing in the mid-1960's for a faster attack sub to replace the latest SSN-637 Sturgeon-class subs, which had not yet entered service. The proposed new high-speed attack submarine, later designated the SSN-688 class, would boast a more powerful nuclear propulsion system and improved weaponry. As originally envisioned, it would travel underwater at about forty knots, compared with the SSN-637-class sub's top speed of approximately thirty knots.

Rickover and his allies had to fight for the high-speed sub within the Navy, the OSD, and Congress. "It was very hard to sell," recalled retired Vice Admiral Joe Williams, Jr., who helped spearhead the campaign. In the Navy the SSN-688 class was opposed by many surface admirals who preferred to spend Navy money on surface ships.

In the OSD John Foster, Jr., the influential director of defense research and engineering, was convinced that the proposed high-speed sub would be noisier than the Sturgeon class. "He was dead set against the speed," Admiral Williams recalled later on. A classic confrontation developed between cost-conscious civilian analysts in the Navy and the OSD, who questioned the value of a few extra knots of speed, and the Navy commanders, who had to depend on their submarine's capabilities. "*You* go to sea for a few years, *you* go nose to nose with the Soviets, and you'll find out what a ship's weapons systems can do," Admiral Williams would say to himself as he debated the issue with young civilian analysts. "Until you've done this, don't be so brash as to assume that the military man that's talking to you from across the table is just pushing a cause for the hell of pushing it."

Rickover appeared on Capitol Hill repeatedly to warn Congress of the Soviet Navy's habit of churning out one menacing new class of attack sub after another. "Six years ago, when I began to push for the U.S. to build submarines with higher speeds, the Soviets began to design several high speed classes," he once reminded a House subcommittee. "Today, when we still do not have firm approval to proceed [with the SSN-688 class], the Russians have many high speed units operating and under construction."

Eventually Rickover's personal influence and dogged persistence were enough to carry the day. Secretary of Defense Clark Clifford, who had succeeded Robert McNamara four months earlier, approved the development of a high-speed sub in July 1968. Congressional funding of the new SSN-688-class program followed a few years later.

The Navy's desire for new high-speed attack submarines—as well as other warships—coincided with a period of tightened U.S. defense budgets. Contract awards to private shipyards plummeted from $1.4 billion in 1967 to $456 million the following year and $313 million in 1969. As a result, the Navy felt compelled to squeeze its private shipbuilders, demanding more work in a shorter period of time at a lower price. These demands inevitably strained the shipyards and further soured their attitudes toward the Navy.

The tightened Navy budget affected shipbuilding in other ways as well. Since the 1960's the Navy had performed less and less design work in-house, relying instead on the work of commercial naval architecture firms. NAVSEA, the organization primarily responsible for acquiring ships, chose not to replace its older, experienced ship designers as they retired. Gradually the Navy lost its ability to design new ships.

Some NAVSEA personnel who had formerly designed new ships were assigned to review the plans drawn by private architectural firms. Others were assigned to approve or disapprove the thousands of proposed design changes that constitute a large part of the ship construction process. Before long the shrinking group of former ship designers had more review work than they could handle. The Navy grew more dependent on outside design firms and took longer to approve and implement proposed design changes.

Rickover had sold the Navy, the Defense Department, and Congress on his SSN-688-class submarine. Now it was time to get it designed and built. The admiral bemoaned the fact that the Navy had allowed its traditional in-house ship design capability to atrophy. He was particularly unhappy that only one private shipyard, Electric Boat, had ever designed a nuclear-powered submarine. Rickover didn't doubt EB's technical capabilities. That competence had been demonstrated repeatedly for more than sixty years, most recently on the widely praised Sturgeon class. Rather, Rickover bristled at the notion that EB, or any shipyard for that matter, might take advantage of its monopoly as the nation's only submarine designer. He worried that EB felt few competitive pressures to hold down its design costs.

Eager to topple EB's monopoly, Rickover looked to the Newport News Shipbuilding and Dry Dock Company as a possible competitor. The sprawling Virginia shipyard had constructed more than a dozen nuclear-powered submarines from plans drawn up by Electric Boat or the Navy but had never designed a nuclear submarine on its own. If Rickover could induce Newport News to challenge EB for the upcoming design contract, he could introduce a new competitiveness into the SSN-688-class sub program.

The SSN-688-class submarine, like other ships before and after it, was designed in a traditional process that flows step by step from an idea to a concept to rough plans to detailed drawings to the completed vessel. Designing a ship is different from designing another major weapons system because ships themselves are different. "Ships are *constructed* as opposed to being produced or assembled," Navy Captain Brady Cole has written. "They include complex weapons systems such as missiles, combat information sensors, and guns. In reality, constructing a Navy ship is not unlike building a self-sustaining, self-regenerating city with its maze of facilities, all integrated by streets and miles of wires and piping passing overhead and underground."

Long-range planners toiling anonymously in the Navy bureaucracy are continually thinking about new ships. Even before senior admirals focus on a specific type of ship they might want to acquire, mid-level planners have been brainstorming in general about possible ships and emerging weapons technologies. These planners constantly gather information that can help answer an endless parade of questions: Can new advances in sonar technology improve U.S. submarines? Can better hull designs lead to lighter and stronger surface ships? How should the changing composition of the Soviet Navy alter the U.S. Navy's military mission? Will improvements in enemy antiship missiles require new defensive systems aboard U.S. vessels? The conceptual analyses undertaken to answer these questions lay the groundwork for the development of a specific new ship.

First, the Office of the Chief of Naval Operations, known as OPNAV, spells out the formal requirement for a new ship that says, in essence, "Given the enemy threat and the available technologies and funds, the Navy should design and build this vessel."

Secondly, feasibility studies are performed to establish the gross physical dimensions, performance characteristics, and costs of the proposed new ship. For example, the new ship, a destroyer, might be required to travel at thirty-five knots yet weigh less than 3,000 tons. To meet these demanding performance goals, experts must first answer a series of fundamental design questions: Should the ship be powered by gas turbine, steam turbine, or diesel engines? Should it use a monohull, catamaran hull, or an air-cushion design? Should it be armed with Tomahawk, Harpoon, or Standard missiles? Typically, the dozens of feasibility studies generated at this stage by the Navy designers, private think tanks, and naval architecture firms offer recommendations on these basic design issues.

Thirdly, NAVSEA spends about a year developing a preliminary design that defines which weapons will be used, the arrangement of the major pieces of equipment to be installed onboard, and the rough layout and approximate weight of various sections of the new ship. "It is this stage of design where the major characteristics and the 'personality' of the ship are fixed," one ship design expert has written. Because the technology of modern weapons moves much faster than the technology of ship construction, fundamental decisions about the structure of a new vessel are generally dictated by the choice of combat systems it will carry. This preliminary design work for major combatant ships is often done in-house by Navy personnel.

Fourthly, the Navy—usually with the assistance of outside naval architecture firms—prepares a contract design which describes in great detail the dimensions of the interior spaces of the ship and the placement of equipment and subsystems. It also spells out the performance standards required of such major components as the engines, pumps, and generators. When these designs are given to the competing shipyards hoping to build the new ships, they serve as the basis of the shipyards' initial cost estimates.

For this reason, the contract design represents a crucial stage for potential subcontractors trying to sell their components or heavy equipment for use on the ship. Each company wants the contract design to specify its product by name. If, for example, the contract design specifies "General Electric LM-2500 gas turbine engine, *or better,*" GE will have the upper hand when the Navy chooses its engines. A rival manufacturer somehow will have to demonstrate that its engine is better than the LM-2500, while GE doesn't have to prove anything.

If, on the other hand, no product is specifically identified, prospective suppliers hope the dimensions and performance criteria spelled out in the contract design will at least allow their equipment to compete against other contenders. In the worst case, a contract design will specify some performance, weight, or size requirement that eliminates a disappointed manufacturer altogether. The last thing an engine manufacturer wants to see is a contract design calling for a ten-foot-square engine room when the smallest engine it produces is eleven feet long.

During the final stage of the process, called the detailed design, working drawings, the set of plans from which the shipyard will construct the ship, are prepared. Generally, this work is performed by a private naval architecture firm, as either a contractor to the Navy or a subcontractor to a shipyard.

Since every shipyard uses different manufacturing equipment and different production methods, it's important that the designers take into account the capabilities of the shipyard that will actually build the ship. For instance, one shipyard may have equipment capable of bending heavy metal plates into all sorts of odd shapes. A detailed design that calls for frequent bending of metal plates could be accommodated at that shipyard, but not at a yard that didn't own that piece of equipment.

Similarly, a detailed design that calls for a lot of intricate welds could be built at a shipyard that still does most of its welding by hand, but not at one that uses automated welding equipment. When a "follow" shipyard is awarded a contract to build a ship from designs drawn up originally for a different shipbuilder, it frequently is necessary to modify the working drawings to accommodate such idiosyncrasies. The choice of a design agent is crucial to the success of any shipbuilding effort, particularly a program in which submarines will be constructed by more than one shipyard.

*(3)*

Admiral Rickover saw an opportunity to pressure Newport News on the SSN-688 design issue one day in 1967. He was aboard the *Ray,* the newest SSN-637-class submarine built by Newport News, for the first day of sea trials. (Rickover insisted on witnessing some portion of the sea trials for each nuclear submarine—usually the first two days, when the nuclear propulsion systems were tested.) Also aboard that day were executives from the Newport News shipyard. Albert Kelln, then the commanding officer of the *Ray* and now a retired rear admiral, has recalled the conversation that took place in the wardroom of his new submarine.

Rickover asked the shipyard executives if they planned to bid on the upcoming SSN-688-class submarine design contract. He was obviously looking for an affirmative answer from the hesitant shipbuilders. Newport News would have to take a risk to seek the design contract. The yard would have to acquire new equipment and employ a highly specialized team of submarine designers. The cost would be high and the gamble large because even if Newport News decided to bid, there was no certainty that it would win the contract.

The admiral couldn't simply hand the design contract for the new high-speed attack submarine to Newport News, but when it came to nuclear subs, he had a habit of getting what he wanted. Besides, he could minimize the Virginia shipyard's financial risk. If Newport News didn't win the SSN-688-class design contract, Rickover could probably steer enough other design work its way to keep its new design team busy.

Unwilling to disappoint their most important customer, the shipbuilders said yes, indeed, they intended to assemble a team and bid on the design contract. And who, the admiral asked, was going to head that team? Rickover wanted an indication that Newport News would be deeply committed to the project. He knew it was one thing to go through the motions of preparing a bid and quite another to put one's best people on the project and work tirelessly to win the contract.

The executives named a few of their most talented designers as possible candidates to head the project. Rickover mulled over the names, obviously satisfied with the caliber of potential project leaders. No commitments had been made, but messages had been communicated: Rickover was ready to end Electric Boat's monopoly on the design of nuclear submarines, and Newport News was willing to respond to the admiral's invitation.

When the Navy announced that its newest high-speed attack submarine would be designed by the Newport News shipyard, not Electric Boat, Rickover had chalked up another victory.

The shipyard that lands the design contract for a new class of ship traditionally wins the subsequent contract to build the first ship in that class, commonly called the lead ship. To no one's surprise, Newport News was awarded a contract to build the lead ship in the SSN-688 class in February 1970. What was surprising was that rather than require Newport News to sign a cost-plus contract, in which the Navy reimburses the shipyard for all its allowable expenses, the Navy required the shipyard to sign a fixed-price contract. It did so largely at Rickover's urging. A brief foray into the arcane world of government contracting will help explain the significance of this crucial decision.

Essentially the Army, Navy, or Air Force signs one of two types of contracts with a private company: a fixed-price contract or a cost-plus contract. A fixed-price contract, as has been pointed out, obligates the company to perform a specified amount of work for a fixed price. For example, a tank manufacturer might sign a fixed-price contract to supply the Army with 250 tanks in one year for $500 million. Regardless of the company's actual cost of building and delivering those 250 tanks, the Army will pay only $500 million. (Under certain circumstances the price of a fixed-price contract can be altered; more on that later.) If the company builds the 250 tanks for $450 million, it keeps the $50 million difference as its profit. If it spends $600 million because it was delayed by a labor union strike or can't obtain the components it needs from its own subcontractors, or if its original cost estimate proves to be overoptimistic, it must absorb the $100 million loss.

Under a cost-plus contract, the military agrees to reimburse the company for all the allowable expenses the company incurs in the process of performing the required work. In addition, the government pays the company a fee—its profit—on top of its reimbursed expenses. For example, an aerospace manufacturer might sign a cost-plus contract with the Air Force to develop a new heat-seeking missile intended to be launched from a fighter aircraft. In three years the company might spend $300 million in allowable costs. Under a cost-plus contract, the Air Force is required to pay the company $300 million to cover those costs, plus a fixed or sliding fee of perhaps another $20 million. The method of calculating the fee would have been negotiated when the original contract was signed. In this case, the Air Force, not the missile manufacturer, has assumed the financial risk involved in development. If costs escalate beyond everyone's expectations, the Air Force picks up the tab, and the contractor has nothing to lose.

The key ingredient in a cost-plus contract is the definition of allowable costs. Naturally contractors want as many of their expenses as possible to be deemed allowable. The Defense Department attempts to limit the allowable costs by requiring contractors to adhere to a voluminous set of rules called the Federal Acquisition Regulations. For example, the money a missile manufacturer might spend for steel, engines, or gyroscopes is allowable. The salaries of employees who work directly on the missile program—such as managers, assembly-line workers, and quality-assurance experts—are allowable. The chief engineer's travel expenses to and from Washington, D.C., to consult with Air Force officials on the status of the program are allowable. Those direct costs all are attributable to the particular missile program.

There is also a category of indirect costs—known as overhead—that are not tied to any specific program but are part of the company's ongoing costs of doing business. Typically, overhead costs include rent, utilities, taxes, general and administrative expenses, and the salaries of employees whose work affects the entire company rather than any specific weapons program. Under a cost-plus contract a company will be reimbursed for all its allowable direct costs plus an appropriate share of its total overhead expenses.

Costs that are not allowable include money a contractor spends to run a four-color advertisement in *Time* magazine extolling the virtues of its newest missile, money a company spends to defend one of its executives in court against a government indictment for contract fraud, and money a firm spends on a Washington representative whose sole responsibility is to lobby Congress on behalf of its weapons programs. In short, money spent to perform work required by an ongoing contract is allowable, and money spent to win new business or defend employees in court is not.

How does a military service decide whether it should award fixed-price or cost-plus contracts to the companies that design and build its weapons? There are no firm guidelines. In general, a military program manager tries to sign a fixed-price contract with a company when both sides have a clear idea how much the required work is going to cost. If a tank manufacturer has been building the same tank for ten years and is reasonably sure it can produce 250 more tanks in the coming year for less than $2 million apiece, the company might be willing to sign a fixed-price contract for $500 million because it doesn't think it is taking an undue risk. In that instance a fixed-price contract makes sense.

   The situation is completely different with a missile manufacturer that agrees to design and develop a completely new heat-seeking missile. Neither the manufacturer nor the Air Force can estimate accurately how much it will cost to develop the missile. The company is trying to develop a new weapon, with advanced capabilities, that can perform certain air-to-air tasks that have never been performed before. On the basis of its past development work, the contractor might be able to come up with a ball park estimate of how many man-hours of designing, engineering, wind tunnel, redesigning, and testing time the project will require, but the estimate is only an educated guess.

   A company hoping to win a research and development contract tries to predict costs, but most executives acknowledge privately that they really don't know what it will cost to perform an open-ended R&D project. How could they? They don't know how long it will take for their engineers to hit upon a promising technical approach, they don't know how long it will take to translate a technical concept into working prototypes, and they don't know what problems they will encounter along the way. They just don't know.

   Most companies won't accept the financial risk associated with a fixed-price contract; they don't want to tie themselves to a fixed amount of money for an unpredictable amount of work. Presumably the Air Force program manager would also recognize that the amount of work involved in developing a new heat-seeking missile was difficult to forecast. He wouldn't try to force a company to sign a fixed-price contract because an overoptimistic prediction could place one of his major contractors in financial jeopardy. He would probably conclude that a cost-plus contract was fairer to the missile manufacturer during a period when the company's costs were largely unpredictable. However, once the missile has been developed and the company has begun producing them at a stable price, the Air Force program manager might try to sign a fixed-price contract for future purchases.

   In short, fixed-price contracts are generally considered appropriate when costs are predictable and the financial risks to both government and contractor are minimal. Cost-plus contracts are better suited to development programs or initial production contracts when the costs of performing the required work cannot be accurately estimated.

   Actually fixed-price and cost-plus contracts are not the only types used by the military services. They represent the extreme ends of a spectrum, with several hybrid versions in between. As one moves along this contracting continuum, essentially one question is being asked: Who bears the greater financial risk on this contract, the company (at the fixed-price end) or the government (at the cost-plus end)?

   The feature that most distinguishes one hybrid contract from another is how the contract calculates the company's potential profit. If a fixed fee is written into the contract, the company's profit won't be affected by changes in the overall cost to complete the contract. The company knows up front what its profit will be. For instance, the missile manufacturer might sign a cost-plus fixed-fee contract under which all its allowable costs would be reimbursed and it would earn a fixed fee of perhaps $10 million.

In other cases, the contract contains an incentive fee, which varies in size depending on the total cost to complete the work. The incentive fee increases if the company completes its contract for less than a specified amount, called the target price, and decreases if the company's costs exceed it. Incentive fees are designed to encourage contractors to hold down costs. Because incentive fees entail greater financial risks, they can sometimes grow larger than fixed fees.

Incentive-fee contracts have one other element: a ceiling price. The ceiling price, which is always higher than the target price, is the point beyond which the military service refuses to spend any more money. For example, a shipyard might sign a fixed-price incentive-fee contract with the Navy to build one aircraft carrier at a target price of $2 billion, a figure that both agree is reasonable. The ceiling price might range anywhere from 10 to 50 percent above that target price. Let's say that at 10 percent the ceiling price is $2.2 billion. Suppose the contract is structured so that the shipyard earns a fee of 15 percent of its costs if it delivers the completed carrier at the target price. Under that contract the shipyard could earn a profit of 15 percent of $2 billion —or $300 million. If the shipyard spends less than $2 billion to complete the carrier, its fee will be even higher because it will be allowed to share with the Navy some of the money it saved.

On the other hand, if the final cost of the carrier exceeds $2 billion, the shipyard's fee will gradually be reduced from $300 million. The yard will be forced to share with the Navy the extra costs it incurred above the $2 billion target price. If this sharing were pegged at sixty-forty, for example, the Navy would keep sixty cents out of every dollar saved below the target price or would pay sixty cents out of every dollar spent beyond the target price. The shipyard would pick up 40 percent of the savings or pay 40 percent of the additional costs. The split between the Navy and the shipyard, known as the share line because it is commonly represented as a sloping line on a graph, varies from contract to contract.

When costs run over the target price, this sharing continues up to the point at which the shipyard's total costs exceed the ceiling price—in this example, when they top $2.2 billion. At that point the Navy stops paying. Every dollar the shipyard spends beyond the ceiling price to complete its contract comes out of its own pocket. Needless to say, defense contractors dread this predicament.

## (4)

After awarding the lead submarine in the SSN-688 class to Newport News, but before detailed designs had even been completed, the Navy solicited bids from U.S. shipyards to build the intial batch of eleven subs, known as the first flight. Electric Boat and Newport News submitted bids. In January 1971 the Navy decided to award seven of these subs to Electric Boat and four to Newport News. Again, at Rickover's insistence, the Navy required both shipbuilders to sign fixed-price, rather than cost-plus, contracts. Electric Boat agreed to construct seven subs at a ceiling price of $428.1 million, or about $61 million each. Newport News signed a similar fixed-price contract for $249.5 million, or about $62 million apiece.

The Navy's decision to require fixed-price contracts marked a dramatic departure from its past procurement practice. Normally, on a new class of ship the Navy would offer cost-plus contracts to its shipyards until both sides had a clear idea of the costs involved. With the SSN-688's, however, Rickover pushed vigorously for fixed-price agreements. He was convinced that the nation's shipyards could not be trusted to build naval vessels under cost-plus contracts.

Although the detailed designs for the new SSN-688 class had not been completed by Newport News, Rickover considered the new sub essentially an advanced version of the SSN-637 class, not a completely new design. Therefore, he reasoned, Electric Boat and Newport News should be able to come up with accurate estimates for building the new subs, on the basis of their costs for building earlier SSN-637-class subs. If they could accurately predict their costs, the shipyards should be required to sign fixed-price contracts, the admiral concluded. Many Navy procurement officials disagreed, sensing a disaster in the making, but Rickover again prevailed.

Why, you might ask, were Electric Boat and Newport News willing to commit themselves to such risky fixed-price contracts? Several explanations present themselves. First, like Rickover, both shipyards initially viewed the Los Angeles class as a stage in the evolution of the Sturgeon-class design, not as a significantly new submarine. If they were right, it shouldn't be too difficult to calculate the cost of building the new subs.

Electric Boat used the traditional method of estimating costs for an undesigned new class of ship. It applied historic ratios of man-hours of labor per linear foot of cable or pound of construction in various portions of the proposed sub. Previous experience may have indicated, for example, that each foot of cable in the power and lighting system of a submarine requires 4 man-hours of labor, while each foot of cable in the more complex weapons control sections of the ship requires 8 man-hours of work. Because the configuration and weight of each section of the new Los Angeles-class sub had not yet been defined, Electric Boat based its cost estimates on its earlier experience building Sturgeon-class subs. Those estimates proved woefully optimistic. EB originally figured it would take 3.8 million man-hours to build its first SSN-688-class sub, but it wound up taking 7.1 million man-hours, or almost twice as much effort.

Secondly, both shipyards were hungry for work. Opportunities to build commercial vessels for the U.S. or international merchant fleets were few and far between. The U.S. shipbuilding industry, with its high labor costs and meager government subsidies, was a weak competitor in the world market. American yards had constructed less than 2.3 percent of the world's gross tonnage during the decade ending in 1977. With naval ship orders also scarce in the post-Vietnam era, Electric Boat and Newport News recognized that the high-speed submarine program might be their best hope for work during the next ten to fifteen years.

Finally, the shipyards may have figured that the Navy would bail them out financially if their costs exceeded the ceiling prices on their fixed-price contracts. Or they may simply have resigned themselves to losing money on the construction of the lead ship and first eleven subs in the expectation they could recoup their losses on subsequent contracts.

Rickover didn't care whether the shipyards accepted the fixed-price contracts out of excessive cost optimism, economic necessity, or a conscious buy-in attempt. "It was the propensity of Admiral Rickover to squeeze the shipyards out of every penny he could," Admiral Williams recalled. "He didn't believe in those people making very much profit." As far as Rickover was concerned, Electric Boat and Newport News were run by shrewd businessmen who knew what they were doing. No one forced the shipyards to bid on the SSN-688's, he later argued. "They took the contracts, didn't they?"

## (5)

Both shipyards began building their submarines in earnest in the early 1970's, even as Newport News continued to work on the detailed designs. If, during those early years, there were schedule delays or unusual cost increases caused by inflation, neither the shipyards nor the Navy expressed much alarm. The SSN-688 program was finally under way, and no one was complaining.

By 1973, however, clouds began to gather. After dire warnings from Rickover and much behind-the-scenes wrangling, Congress appropriated additional funds, and the Navy invited Electric Boat and Newport News to bid on a second flight of eleven more SSN-688-class subs. As with the first flight, the Navy planned to divide the subs between Electric Boat and Newport News to foster competition and hold the price down.

But Newport News's relations with the mercurial Rickover had soured dramatically during the two years since the first flight awards. Nelson Freeman, chairman of the board of Tenneco, which owned Newport News, was fed up. He loathed the onerous inspection system and intrusive management approach the admiral had instituted. Eventually he ordered his executives to throw Rickover out of the shipyard if the admiral showed up again.

Needless to say, this kind of acrimony didn't help Newport News in its bid on the second flight contract. The yard that Rickover had wooed into the submarine design business a few years earlier had fallen from grace. The Navy ruled that the Virginia shipbuilder's bid on the second flight was noncompetitive.

Electric Boat had received only a small portion of the completed drawings from Newport News when it came time to submit its bid for the second flight contract. The cost estimates it prepared, based on those partial drawings, did not anticipate that Newport News's final design would be far more complex than earlier subs EB had designed. The shipyard submitted a bid, which in retrospect was overly optimistic. But because Electric Boat had expended only 11 percent of the man-hours it had forecast on the first flight, the Navy had little evidence with which to refute the shipyard's second flight bid.

The Navy eventually awarded fixed-price contracts for all eleven submarines to Electric Boat. (Rickover later accused EB of trying to defraud the Navy by *intentionally* underestimating its projected costs when it submitted that second flight bid. From his self-imposed exile in Greece Veliotis has also accused GD of buying in to that second flight contract. Veliotis has claimed that Lewis made the decision to submit a fraudulent bid in meetings at GD corporate headquarters. GD, in turn, points out that Veliotis wasn't even working at EB at the time that second flight bid was prepared.)

EB's order book was filling up rapidly. In fewer than three years the shipyard had signed fixed-price contracts worth more than $1.2 billion to construct eighteen SSN-688 attack subs over the coming decade. That huge backlog of contracts raised eyebrows at the Groton shipyard and at General Dynamics headquarters in St. Louis. A few Navy officers warned against awarding the entire second flight to Electric Boat for fear the shipyard would be swamped with work. The contract was signed anyway, on a wave of optimism.

It wasn't long before that optimism wore off at Electric Boat. The shipyard began to fall behind schedule, and its costs began to soar. As Gorden Mac-Donald, the general manager, put it, "Thousands of engineering changes and design modifications, delays, and inflation have caused monumental difficulties for the company." The combination of these problems threatened to bury Electric Boat.

One of the first problems to surface in the SSN-688 program was the difficulty with the sub's designs. Newport News, as design agent, had never drawn up plans for a nuclear submarine. It was frequently six to nine months late delivering finished drawings to Electric Boat. This tardiness was compounded by similar delays by the Navy, which was also late delivering construction specifications and data known as Government Furnished Information (GFI) to Electric Boat. (General Dynamics later argued that the Navy's delay in delivering GFI to Electric Boat disrupted the shipyard's construction schedule and added millions of dollars to its costs.)

Communications between Newport News and Electric Boat degenerated quickly. Neither company seemed interested in helping the other succeed in the attack sub program. EB officials resented the loss of their monopoly on the design of nuclear submarines; and Newport News wasn't anxious to be blamed for whatever design problems cropped up.

In a traditional shipbuilding program the design agent that draws up the plans and the shipyard that builds the vessel have to cooperate closely, as interdependent participants in a very intricate process. Construction of a nuclear submarine takes approximately five years. The process can be divided into three basic phases: hull fabrication and erection, installation and outfitting, and final outfitting and testing. During the first phase, which consumes the first few years, skilled steel tradesmen construct the frames, cylinders, major tanks, and structural assemblies. During the second phase, which takes place in the second, third, and fourth years, shipfitters, pipe fitters, and electricians install the major equipment and machinery, piping, and electronics gear. Then, during final outfitting in the fifth year, painters, carpenters, and sheet metal workers install the interior fixtures while test technicians rigorously check all systems and components.

Construction normally begins months or years before the detailed designs and working drawings have been completed. As the drawings are finished, they are sent to the shipyard's engineering department so that the necessary materials and parts can be ordered well in advance and future work can be scheduled.

When shipyard workers spot the errors that inevitably appear in any new set of plans, they're expected to send recommendations for changes back to the design agent. Unless the design agent and shipyard are communicating amicably, the entire project can bog down at this point in acrimonious finger pointing. Such was the case between Newport News and Electric Boat.

To top it off, Electric Boat had to contend with a staggering number of design changes. It is common for thousands of design changes to add millions of dollars to the cost of most new ships. But the changes that plagued the SSN-688 program caused enormously long delays and added tremendously to the subs' costs.

Design changes are made for all sorts of reasons: to eliminate recently discovered safety hazards, to introduce technological improvements, to strengthen a part or component that failed during testing, to switch vendors, to satisfy a demanding Navy contracting officer, or, in years past, to placate Admiral Rickover. Every time a design is changed, one or more working drawings have to be revised to incorporate the change.

Newport News eventually delivered 5,368 detailed drawings to Electric Boat for the first flight of the SSN-688 subs. The General Accounting Office (GAO) counted some 35,000 revisions made to these drawings. Some were major changes that required substantial engineering and, perhaps, ripping out previous work. Others were minor clerical changes or simply the renumbering of blueprint pages. "Maybe there were only five thousand changes that really ripped something out and replaced it with something else," conceded David Lewis. "But the cumulative effect of all that in purchasing, procurement, manufacturing, planning, and so on was enormous." Worse yet, according to GD's chairman, is the confusion created in the shipyard by introducing design changes at the wrong time. "If you put in a change in a chaotic situation, it will cost you far more than if you put it in during smooth, tranquil production," he added.

Whenever a design change is proposed, several questions arise: Is the change necessary? If it's necessary, should completed work on earlier ships be ripped out to incorporate it? Should the Navy, the design agent, or the shipyard pay for this extra work? Does the Navy approve too many design changes? There aren't any easy answers to these questions.

Submarine technology advances at a bewildering pace. Improvements in materials, electronics, onboard weapons systems, optics, guidance and control systems, and "human engineering," to name but a few areas, emanate from government research facilities, the design agent's engineering department, and, most frequently, the companies that supply parts and subcomponents to the shipyard.

What happens when there is a technological improvement? Let's say, for example, that a manufacturer of metal piping used to carry high-temperature liquids perfects a process that increases the life-span of its piping, thereby enhancing the safety of the submarine. In passing the performance data along to the ship's design agent, the supplier will probably recommend that the new piping be substituted for the original piping. After evaluating the piping's probable costs and benefits, the design agent may recommend the piping for Navy review. After carrying out its own cost-benefit analysis, the Navy will decide if the proposal is worth the extra money and whether it should be installed only in future submarines or retrofitted in submarines for which piping had already been installed.

Institutional pressures to approve recommended design changes are ever-present in the U.S. Navy, in part because of the steady improvements being made in the Soviet Navy. Pentagon planners understandably want each new U.S. submarine to be as technically advanced as possible when it enters the fleet because it may be ten or fifteen years before the Navy has a chance to develop its next class of submarine.

A second school of thought says the Navy would be better off making fewer design changes on its submarines in order to build them faster and less expensively. "One of the things we have to do is be far tougher on the change orders and just go with the original design," testified Rhode Island Senator John Chafee, who wrestled with the dilemma of design changes as President Nixon's first secretary of the navy. "It is nearly irresistible, and yet it is the change orders that kill you. I think that for better or worse, when we go with a design, we might as well go with it and stick with it."

Chafee's advice has not been taken. In the current environment the design for a modern submarine is no longer seen as a static set of blueprints from which ten or twenty identical submarines can be built, like cookies stamped from a cookie cutter. Instead, they are viewed as an evolving set of blueprints, continually revised to incorporate technical improvements or eliminate flaws. The changes inevitably add to the cost and postpone the delivery of new submarines, making it even more important that each completed vessel be as capable as possible. The circular nature of this policy obviously tends to perpetuate itself.

Design changes fall into two broad categories, directed and constructive changes. Directed changes are those that the Navy orders the shipyard to make to correct a deficiency, meet some new requirement, enhance the ship's safety, or cut costs. The service expects to pay extra money if a directed change adds to the shipbuilder's costs. The Navy and the shipyard try to negotiate a fair price to cover those extra costs. If agreement is reached, the Navy raises the target and ceiling prices in its contract with the shipyard by that amount. Thus, the price of the ship increases, but the Navy agrees to pay the extra sum. Sometimes, when the shipyard can't quickly arrive at a cost estimate for the extra work or the two sides can't agree on a fair price, the Navy will order the design change to be made anyway. Both sides operate with the understanding that a price adjustment will be negotiated later.

For example, if Navy officials decided in the midst of a vessel's construction that a change in its hydraulic system was required, their decision would constitute a directed change. Similarly, if the Navy determined that an electric generator had to be covered by a protective shield to improve its safety, the modification would be another directed change. In each instance the Navy would instruct the shipyard to draw up what's known as an engineering change proposal, which spells out the work to be done and the costs involved. The Navy's acceptance of the shipyard's engineering change proposal constitutes its agreement to cover those added costs. Some outside observers might call the resulting price increase a cost overrun. Navy officials wouldn't. They would explain that the extra money was paying for a more capable ship and that the cost had risen at the express direction of the service.

Constructive changes, on the other hand, are changes caused *unintentionally* by some Navy action or inaction that affects the shipbuilder's costs. Because they are not explicitly ordered by the Navy, constructive changes are much more difficult to document and thus are much more controversial than directed changes.

Suppose, for example, the Navy supplies a shipyard with a contract design for a new ship that calls for three boilers of a specified size to be installed in a boiler room of certain dimensions. The shipyard prepares its cost estimate on the basis of this design. If the three boilers turn out too large to fit inside the boiler room, substantial design changes will be required. They'll cost extra money. Worse yet, if the walls of the boiler room have already been constructed, they might have to be ripped out and rebuilt. That will cost even more money. The shipyard would justifiably consider this design error by the Navy a constructive change and would seek additional funds to pay for the extra work.

Or suppose a Navy inspector on duty at a shipyard arbitrarily requires a shipbuilder to replace one clearly specified grade of piping with a higher grade. The shipyard would probably be entitled to additional payments for installing the more expensive piping.

Finally, suppose a shipyard is forced to suspend work while it awaits long-overdue approval from the understaffed Navy of some pending change proposal. The extra payroll costs, as workers sit idle, might also be reimbursed by the Navy as a constructive change.

Constructive change orders can be abused by both sides. The Navy sometimes denies that its actions or inactions have added to its shipyard's costs when in fact they have. The Navy might acknowledge that it delivered some Government Furnished Information behind schedule, for example, but might challenge the shipyard's contention that the delay represents a constructive change that cost it extra money. On the other hand, shipyards have been known to submit spurious requests for reimbursements for extra costs that they brought upon themselves.

A shipyard formally requests the Navy to pay for direct or constructive changes by submitting a contract claim. During the 1970's such claims had become a familiar part of the naval shipbuilding process. Even so, many officers in the Navy's ship procurement community, including Admiral Rickover, bitterly resented them. "Some shipbuilders are trying to turn their [fixed-price] contracts into cost plus transactions simply by claiming that all their costs must have resulted from Government actions," Rickover told a congressional committee in 1977.

Indeed, shipbuilders and the lawyers that represent them in the drawing up of contracts with the government can dream up imaginative cross-impact claims that describe how a Navy action or inaction on one program has affected adjacent shipbuilding programs in the same shipyard. A disruption on one ship in the yard might prevent a team of workers from moving to another ship on schedule; a suspension of work might cause a "loss of learning" among new employees that hurts their future productivity; a lengthy delay might necessitate overtime work or allow inflation to increase the cost of performing certain work.

One critic accuses a handful of Washington, D.C., law firms of indirectly costing U.S. taxpayers millions of dollars. "The firms create claims that can't be settled quickly, developing endless points of contention, obscuring the merits of the case," journalist James Cramer has argued. "The settlement that comes out of such a process is more of a horse trade than an intelligent estimate of the project's actual cost."

Of course, the Pentagon is hardly a defenseless midget in the weapons marketplace. It controls the purse strings. The notion that weapons manufacturers sometimes have to fight the government for their legitimate contractual rights may seem farfetched, but it is true. The military services take advantage of their contractors as often as contractors take advantage of the services.

In one sense, contract claims can be seen to benefit the government. If contractors had no way to recoup the unexpected costs they might incur as a result of government actions, they inevitably would protect themselves by increasing their cost estimates on all new weapons. The government avoids such price hikes by including standard clauses in its contracts that allow a company to recover legitimate, unanticipated cost increases only when they occur. "Thus, despite the 'bad press' it sometimes receives, 'claim' is not a four letter word," according to Robert Martin and Fred Geldon, two Washington lawyers. "Rather it is an essential part of the government contract structure."

## *(6)*

Electric Boat's headaches were made even worse by the shortage of skilled workers. The shipyard was straining to keep up with its work on eighteen attack submarines when, in July 1974, the Navy awarded it an additional contract to build the nation's first Trident missile-firing submarine, the *Ohio*. These Trident subs were designed by Electric Boat to replace the Navy's Polaris and Poseidon ballistic missile subs, which had been in service since the 1960's. Under normal circumstances the initiation of a second major submarine program at Electric Boat would have been cause for celebration, but in this case the Trident work threatened to overload the yard.

The shipyard's labor force grew from 12,000 workers in January 1971 (when the first flight contract for the attack subs was awarded) to 18,800 workers by January 1975 to almost 30,000 by mid-1977, a population explosion that created chaos. "The Defense Department, the Navy and congressional investigators are in rare agreement about what went wrong at the Groton shipyard," *Fortune* magazine later reported. "As the work force was doubled to a peak of 30,000 in mid-1977, the yard suffered the corporate equivalent of a nervous breakdown."

The work force was not only expanding but undergoing a traumatic change in its composition. The shipyard had entered the 1970's with an experienced labor force of pipe fitters, electricians, carpenters, shipfitters, welders, painters, and scrapers. "It was basically an all-male work force of Italian and Puerto Rican background, tough, hard-drinking, clannish men who enjoyed the challenge and excelled at a rough and dirty job," reported Long Island's *Newsday*.

But the boom in submarine orders at EB in the early 1970's changed that. The shipyard had a difficult time recruiting enough skilled workers largely because U.S. shipyards have traditionally paid their production workers less than other comparable industries pay. (The average weekly paycheck for a shipyard production worker in 1976 was about $247; the same worker could have earned 15 percent more, or about $285 per week, from a building construction company.) At one stage Electric Boat chartered as many as fifty buses a day to transport workers to its Connecticut shipyard from as far away as Boston and New York. But EB still fell short of its recruiting goals as pressure mounted from the Navy to keep on schedule. Inevitably the shipyard lowered its skill standards.

7. The first Trident nuclear-powered ballistic missile submarine, *Ohio,* sits in a dry dock at the naval submarine base in Bangor, Washington, in 1983, undergoing preparations for its first patrol. The Electric Boat shipyard was plagued by cost overruns and schedule delays during the 1970's under the strain of simultaneously building Trident missile-firing submarines and Los Angeles-class attack subs. *U.S. Navy*

Electric Boat turned to CETA, WIN, and various antipoverty programs to find unskilled workers. It hired thousands of the untrained women, blacks, and other minority applicants who turned up at its employment office through these training and affirmative action programs. The percentage of skilled workers at the shipyard plummeted from 80 percent in 1972 to 35 percent four years later. These green workers, young men and women supervised by the old-timers, soon overwhelmed their mentors. Normally three learners watched one skilled employee. As the work force swelled, however, as many as twelve new workers were being trained by one experienced employee. "What happened was we lost a good welder and got a bad supervisor," recalled one Electric Boat manager.

EB also had to contend with the high turnover rate that traditionally afflicts the shipbuilding industry. Most private shipyards maintain a small, steady cadre of highly skilled senior craftsmen but must cope with the fact that 13 percent of their employees, on the average, either start or stop working in any given month. By contrast, the turnover in the fabricated metals industry is 8 percent, in the primary metals industry 6 percent, and in the aircraft industry 3 percent.

"Marijuana and pills were introduced by younger workers who care little about Rickover's screaming and Navy deadlines," *Newsday* reported. According to *The Wall Street Journal*, "They would work only three or four days a week, ignoring overtime and requests for top priority projects." A shipyard manager asked one production worker why he showed up only three days a week. "Because I can't get by on two," answered the impertinent employee.

Stanley Eno, Jr., a former supervisor of labor relations at Electric Boat, told a congressional committee about the labor problems the shipyard had experienced. In its eagerness to find new workers it had hired indiscriminately and failed to train its new employees adequately. The introduction of women into the predominantly all-male environment, Eno noted, had inevitable consequences. "When women walked by bra-less with their T-shirts bouncing—and I'm not trying to be funny—production slowed down because everybody stopped what they were doing to take a look." Alcoholism, shipyard brawls, sex, and racial incidents cut further into the productivity. "We had every problem of a major city right within our shipyard," Eno recalled.

In sum, many factors—unrealistic cost estimates, slow delivery of plans from Newport News and Government Furnished Information from the Navy, continual design changes, the deleterious effects of inflation, and the explosive growth of Electric Boat's unskilled work force—contributed to skyrocketing costs and schedule delays for the *fixed-price* SSN-688-class submarine program. The question was: Who was going to pay?

8. Thousands of Electric Boat workers and guests applaud the launching of the attack submarine *Hyman G. Rickover* at GD's Groton, Connecticut, shipyard, while the Trident submarine *Alabama* sits on an assembly platform behind them. *General Dynamics*

In February 1975 General Dynamics went on the offensive against the Navy. Electric Boat's costs to build the first seven attack subs had risen sharply. GD submitted a contract claim for $220 million, arguing that the Navy's tardiness in supplying detailed drawings and Government Furnished Information had caused unavoidable delays in the SSN-688 construction program for which EB was not financially responsible. In essence, the shipyard was saying, "Despite the fixed-price contract we signed, these construction delays are not *our* fault, but the Navy's. For that reason, it should cover the extra costs we have incurred."

A Navy panel of technical experts conducted a legal and financial review of EB's claim, called an entitlement analysis, to determine how much, if any, was justified. Fourteen months later, in April 1976, EB and the Navy agreed to settle the $220 million claim for $97 million—roughly 44 cents on the dollar, a figure that came as little surprise. At the same time the Navy agreed to extend by one year the scheduled delivery dates for each of EB's uncompleted SSN-688-class submarines in recognition of the delays the government had caused. Also, the shipyard agreed to submit by December 1, 1976, any further claims it planned to file against the Navy for work it had already performed on its attack submarine contracts.

The $97 million settlement was reached without great fanfare. The shipyard was disappointed at the size of the settlement but pleased that the Navy had acknowledged its role in the delays. The service was more concerned with future claims in the SSN-688 program than with the size of the $97 million settlement it had just reached with Electric Boat. Its concern was well founded. On December 1, 1976, one month after Jimmy Carter had defeated Gerald Ford for the presidency, General Dynamics submitted a second claim against the Navy. This time it was for more than half a *billion* dollars.

The shipyard had two complaints: First, the Navy's incessant design changes were costing EB millions of dollars. Secondly, the Navy took unreasonable risks by not scheduling the usual two years between the design and construction of the lead submarine by Newport News and the construction of the first follow submarine by Electric Boat. "Those risks have in fact materialized," EB later argued, "resulting in mammoth delays to the entire program and huge increases in projected costs."

The yard justified its claim with stacks of documents. The bottom line: Electric Boat claimed $544 million—$121 million from the Navy on its first flight of seven submarines and another $423 million on its second flight of eleven submarines.

The Navy was shaken. Electric Boat wasn't alone in its discontent. Newport News and Ingalls had submitted similar contract claims. All three shipyards had fallen behind their construction schedules, spent more than they had expected, suffered negative cash flows, and turned to their corporate parents for help. The number of claims, nonexistent a decade earlier, now threatened to sink the Navy.

Procurement officials were particularly upset because the mounting claims focused attention on a fact they would have preferred to ignore: It was the Navy that had pressured the nation's shipyards to build too many ships in too short a time for too little money with too little Navy management expertise.

In October 1977, to cope with the chaos that was overwhelming his shipyard, David Lewis appointed P. Takis "Taki" Veliotis, one of his toughest executives, general manager of Electric Boat. In that capacity Veliotis would oversee operations at both the Groton, Connecticut, and Quonset Point, Rhode Island, submarine facilities. A Greek-born shipbuilder, fifty-one-year-old Veliotis had resuscitated GD's sagging commercial shipyard at Quincy, Massachusetts. There he completed the first tankers in the United States designed to haul liquefied natural gas and managed to steer the shipyard back onto a profitable course.

Veliotis was a large, colorful, hard-nosed manager, with a thick face and a pencil-thin mustache, who tolerated no interference in his shipbuilding operation. Some people said he was a shrewd supershipbuilder. "He was a good organizer, he was an impressive leader, he was a good engineer, and he was a good shipbuilder," said Admiral Williams, who worked briefly under Veliotis at Electric Boat after retiring from the Navy.

On his first day as general manager at Electric Boat, Veliotis fired 3,410 employees. "I could have let employees go piecemeal, but that is the Chinese torture way," he explained. "I chose to cut clean." All hiring was stopped immediately; newly employed workers who arrived for their first day on the job were sent home. As one admirer described Veliotis, "a Prince Charming he isn't."

Within a few days Veliotis had struck again. He demoted twenty-three top managers; dismissed Harold Foley, the yard's director of operations who was once thought to be heir apparent at Electric Boat; and placed eight trusted executives from the commercial shipyard (the Quincy Eight) in senior positions. Veliotis defended his controversial firings by insisting that the dismissed employees were white-collar or managerial personnel, not production workers. "I am going to maintain my delivery schedules," he insisted. Senior management at Electric Boat was shaken by all the sudden changes. "People are making their own organizational charts on the back of envelopes," observed one engineer.

In November 1977, a month after Veliotis had taken over at the Electric Boat shipyard, troubles with the Trident program set off alarm bells in Groton, Connecticut, and St. Louis. The Navy held a press conference on November 29 to disclose that it expected a cost overrun of $400 million on the Trident program, primarily caused by problems at Electric Boat.

GD officials were horrified. They had been telling stockholders for years that the Trident program was profitable. This Navy announcement was certain to have a devastating effect on the price of the company's stock. Furthermore, the Navy's presentation of information had left the erroneous impression that the entire $400 million loss was attributable to EB when the Navy and GD knew that only $114 million of the loss should have been allocated to GD.

Electric Boat officials hastily conferred by telephone with Gorden Mac-Donald in St. Louis. They agreed to issue the following day a press release aimed at correcting the misimpression caused by the Navy's press conference and halting the skid in GD's stock price. GD's draft press release focused on the cost of the Trident program and mentioned the anticipated delivery dates only as a secondary issue. The release said GD expected the delivery of the first Trident, *Ohio,* in October 1979, while acknowledging that the Navy had predicted delivery wouldn't take place until April 1980, about six months later.

In fact, most GD executives believed that the Trident wouldn't be delivered by October 1979, as the release predicted. But there was no agreement on a more realistic date. Veliotis had initiated a major review of the Trident program's construction schedule shortly after arriving at EB, but the review wouldn't be completed for several months.

Veliotis told MacDonald that he wasn't comfortable announcing the excessively optimistic delivery date of October 1979. In a telephone conversation he secretly taped and later made public, Veliotis said that the October 1979 date was "not real" and that the actual delivery probably would occur more than a year later. Then, in a remark that has come to haunt him, MacDonald told Veliotis that Lewis "understands that. But he wanted to go ahead anyway only to stop our stock from sliding."

(Since fleeing from the United States to his native Greece, Veliotis has accused MacDonald and Lewis of intentionally trying to manipulate the stock market when they issued that press release. GD has defended itself by claiming that there was no consensus at the time among GD executives about a more realistic delivery date for the *Ohio* and that the crux of their press release dealt with the overall cost of the Trident program, not with its delivery schedule. They have tried to discredit the notion that they engaged in stock manipulation by noting that when the Navy announced an additional seven-month delay in the Trident program in March 1978, GD's stock price remained essentially unaffected. The overall *cost* of the Trident program was significant to the investment community, Lewis has argued, but the *delivery date* of the *Ohio* was not.)

Veliotis was born and educated in Greece and claims to have served as an officer in the Royal Hellenic Navy during World War II while still in his teens. After the war he spent five years as an engineer in his father's shipping business, E. G. Veliotis Shipowners, before emigrating in 1953 to Canada. There he worked his way up from draftsman to general manager and president of Davie Shipbuilding Ltd., of Quebec, a firm that constructs large oceangoing vessels.

In the early 1970's GD's Quincy shipyard was under contract to build ten liquefied natural gas tankers designed to haul gas from Indonesia to Japan. GD's chairman, David Lewis, wanted to install a new management team that could shape up the antiquated yard and introduce modern shipbuilding methods. At the suggestion of a former chief of naval operations Lewis turned to Veliotis. Impressed with Veliotis's credentials, he offered him the general manager's post at Quincy in 1973.

By 1977 Veliotis had distinguished himself as one of GD's most effective executives and a possible candidate to succeed Lewis when the fifty-nine-year-old chairman decided to step down in a few years. Veliotis has since claimed that Lewis promised him the company's number one job by 1982 in a frank face-to-face conversation the two men had in May 1977, a few months before Veliotis took over at Electric Boat. "I was the fella who was going to take over Lewis's job," Veliotis said. Lewis remembers things differently. "We never discussed the matter," said Lewis of Veliotis's chances for the CEO position. "I felt he was ambitious and would go on up in the company, but I did not see Taki as a CEO for GD."

As Veliotis moved up the ladder in the shipbuilding world, his domineering personality became his most recognizable trademark. "I believe in controls," he declared shortly after taking the reins at Electric Boat. "At the beginning I would like to control practically everything."

He began by grabbing control of his work force. In the past EB workers had moved about the yard as they pleased, often without the knowledge or permission of their overburdened supervisors. Veliotis quickly changed that. He issued new time cards that workers were required to carry at all times. Foremen were ordered to describe each of their workers' primary and backup job assignments on the backs of their time cards. "Anytime I'd see a worker walking around, I'd say, 'Where are you supposed to be?' recalled one EB manager. "He'd tell me, and I'd say, 'Let's see your time card.' " In a matter of days Veliotis had a firm grip on his workers.

Another area in desperate need of control was the parts inventory. Millions of spare parts were scattered in warehouses throughout Connecticut and Rhode Island. No one really knew which parts were where. When design changes altered the specifications for particular parts, they should have been purged from the inventory but usually weren't. Thus, millions of obsolete parts occupied valuable storage space, confusing everybody.

When Veliotis assumed command, he brought production at the yard to a screeching halt. He mounted an around-the-clock inventory that lasted seven days and identified every part located on every ship and in every warehouse. After another three or four weeks the information had been fed into the shipyard's computer. For the first time in years managers knew which parts were required and which parts were actually on hand. Obsolete parts were thrown out. New parts were ordered or built. The inventory was soon up-to-date.

Veliotis was the classic turnaround executive, who could walk into an abysmal business situation and quickly straighten things out. He exuded confidence. He could throw his arms around a mind-boggling inventory problem and wrestle it to the ground. He could intimidate a work force. And he could command the attention of corporate executives back in St. Louis when it came time to finance expensive capital improvements at Electric Boat. The big question was whether he could make these changes fast enough to save the yard from financial ruin.

Once Electric Boat had submitted its $544 million contract claim, the atmosphere at the shipyard changed dramatically. EB officials and Navy officers became even more distrustful of each other, as both groups feverishly gathered data to support their side in the claims dispute. "During that period EB management was totally absorbed with the claims issue," Admiral Williams remembered. "Nobody had time to worry about what was going on in the engineering part of the plant or on the waterfront. All management talent was tied up arm wrestling with the government: justifying this, reading that, drafting papers to answer this, gathering statistics to prove that—everything but building ships."

An attempt was made during the Ford presidency to resolve the claims issue, but little came of it. Ford's deputy secretary of defense, William Clements, Jr., informed Congress in April 1976 that he intended to settle some $1.8 billion in claims from four shipyards at an additional cost of $500 million to $700 million. But Newport News and Litton balked at the proposed settlement figure. Displaying what Clements considered "an adamant, set-in-concrete attitude," the Navy refused to make a more generous offer. Both sides dug in their heels, and the claims problem grew worse.

Clements's continuing negotiations with the shipyards were publicly criticized by Senator William Proxmire as likely to lead to a corporate handout. Ultimately Clements abandoned the idea of a single, sweeping settlement package. Instead, he set up a Navy Claims Settlement Board, headed by Rear Admiral Francis "Frank" Manganaro, to handle shipbuilders' claims individually. As the Ford presidency drew to a close, the new Carter administration stood to inherit one of the thorniest problems that had ever confronted the U.S. shipbuilding industry.

# Chapter Six

## Tough Bargaining

### (1)

Shortly after Jimmy Carter's election as the nation's thirty-ninth President, the telephone rang in Edward Hidalgo's Washington, D.C., law office. Hidalgo's caller was his longtime friend and the former chairman of Southern Railways W. Graham Claytor, Jr., whom Carter had just asked to become the next secretary of the navy. Hidalgo and Claytor, both sixty-four, had known each other since 1936, when they served as law clerks at the U.S. Circuit Court of Appeals in New York City. Claytor, a recent graduate of Harvard Law School, had clerked for the esteemed Judge Learned Hand. Hidalgo, fresh out of Columbia Law School, had clerked for another Columbia alumnus, Martin Manton, the senior judge in the second circuit.

Fortunately the legal troubles of Judge Manton, who became one of the only sitting federal judges to be convicted of accepting bribes, didn't tarnish the career of young Hidalgo. Born in Mexico City, Hidalgo matured into a dignified, silver-haired attorney whose courtly manner fitted his role as the scion of one of Mexico's wealthiest families.

His career had taken him in and out of government. He was an aide and confidant to Navy Secretary James Forrestal, who became the country's first secretary of defense in 1947 and committed suicide in a fit of depression two years later. As a private attorney Hidalgo had represented U.S. corporations involved in a variety of joint ventures with Latin American and European companies. More recently he had served as general counsel and congressional liaison for the U.S. Information Agency.

Over the years Hidalgo had developed a reputation as a silky, smooth negotiator. Familiar with the levers of power in the country's national security apparatus and sensitive to the concerns of the Fortune 500, he was at home in that rarefied territory where the interests of government and big business overlap.

Claytor met with Hidalgo to discuss the issues he would face as the new secretary of the navy. "One of the dreariest problems in the Navy today are those shipbuilding claims," Claytor lamented. He realized that an equitable solution to the stalemate, one that would be generous enough to keep the shipyards solvent yet stingy enough to avoid a congressional outcry of "corporate bailout," had to be found.

"Ed, you're a damn good negotiator," said Claytor. "I'll take the secretary's job if you'll come with me."

Hidalgo found Claytor's challenge irresistible. He accepted and soon became the assistant secretary of the navy for manpower, reserve affairs, installations, and logistics. His primary task was to be the settlement of those enormous ship claims.

In his new role Hidalgo met with the new secretary of defense, Harold Brown, a savvy bureaucrat who had gained his weapons procurement expertise as director of defense research and engineering under Kennedy and as secretary of the air force under Johnson. But Brown had little direct experience with Navy shipbuilding and no specific recommendations for Hidalgo on settling the intractable ship claims dispute. Hidalgo was essentially left on his own. He was to report his progress, if any, to Navy Secretary Claytor and to Brown's deputy, Charles Duncan, a former president of the Coca-Cola Company.

Thus, with only the vaguest of guidelines Hidalgo began groping his way through the bureaucracy for what he calls the "pockets of power, difficulty, and prejudice" that were inflaming the multibillion-dollar claims controversy. "There seemed to me to be an unbridgeable chasm between the two sides— an inability to discuss, to communicate, to do anything except pile up resentments," he later recalled.

By the time Hidalgo became involved the dispute had become three-sided. On one side were the shipyards (principally Electric Boat, Newport News, and Ingalls), their government-contracts lawyers in Washington, and their political allies in Congress and their home states. On another side was the Navy, beset with its internal disagreements. And on the third side were the congressional opponents of any settlement package that looked like a corporate bailout, notably Democratic Senator Proxmire, who had adopted the Rickover approach to the claims issue.

The Navy's internal difficulties presented a separate problem. At the Navy's highest levels, political appointees like Claytor and Hidalgo felt an obligation to settle the dispute, on the best possible terms, so the service could push ahead with its faltering shipbuilding program. These people felt that the monetary cost of a settlement and the integrity of the Navy's claims procedure were of less importance, perhaps, than putting the whole irritating issue behind them.

At lower levels in the bureaucracy, in what is sometimes called the permanent Navy, the struggle with the three shipyards was seen as part of an ongoing procurement battle rather than as a political embarrassment to be dealt with expediently. Officers in the Naval Sea Systems Command were prepared to analyze the claims Electric Boat had submitted but were unwilling to reimburse the shipyard for all its supposed costs. To many of these officers, the claims were totally unjustified. They bitterly resented their political superiors' going over their heads to reach an agreement with the shipyard's executives. "This was a highly charged environment," recalled one management consultant who became involved in the claims issue. "A lot of Navy people had their noses out of joint."

Admiral Rickover took a hard line. Rather than seek any accommodation or compromise with the three shipyards, the abrasive Rickover insisted repeatedly that the Navy enforce its fixed-price shipbuilding contracts to the letter. However, by 1977 Rickover's influence, if not his energy, had begun to wane. He sent dozens of memorandums warning that a harmful precedent would be set if the shipyards' claims were settled too generously, but few of them were officially answered, and it became clear that Rickover was more of a spoiler than a constructive voice.

David Lewis reviewed Electric Boat's troubling situation in his office in St. Louis. The design contract for the SSN-688's had been yanked from his shipyard for the first time—largely at the instigation of Old Man Rickover—and handed to the rival Newport News yard. Even so, with the help of some very optimistic bids on the first and second flights, Electric Boat had garnered the lion's share of the Navy's attack submarine business.

However, the shipyard was running into all sorts of problems with endless design changes, its inadequate labor supply, its disorganized inventory control system, and the Navy's shipyard inspectors. Running a private shipyard was enormously complicated. Managers had to distribute a broad range of technical assignments among thousands of workers. Hundreds of separate tasks had to be perfectly synchronized. In addition, the shipyard had to cope with a raft of new laws and regulations relating to the nation's social goals, including the Occupational Safety and Health Act, equal employment opportunity, and the Longshoremen's and Harbor Workers Act. On top of that were never-ending demands for information from the Navy and other government agencies. At a time when the Navy believed the decline in worker productivity to be the fault of shipyard management, Lewis was convinced that the Navy was intruding too far on his own prerogatives.

The Electric Boat executives who had considered the original SSN-688 bids overoptimistic were now being vindicated as costs escalated. Relations with the Navy, particularly with Rickover's nuclear propulsion staff, were deteriorating. Journalists were throwing a harsh spotlight on the chaos, delays, and cost overruns at Electric Boat.

Worst of all, from Lewis's vantage point, the cash flow at the shipyard had flipped from positive to negative. And there was no relief in sight. Labor and material costs were running far higher than expected. The operation at EB had already lost more than $300 million and was losing $15 million more each month. All of GD's repeated requests for some provisional payment from the Navy, pending the resolution of its $544 million claim, had been denied.

It was obvious the eighteen attack submarines would cost at least half a billion dollars more to complete than EB had originally estimated. The Navy would have to raise the overall ceiling price for the eighteen submarines, or the shipyard couldn't afford to complete its work. Lewis expected the ceiling price to be raised but didn't know if it would be high enough to cover the huge cost increases that confronted his shipyard. He knew Electric Boat would probably have to swallow part of the costs.

This troubled him. If the shipyard accepted a fixed loss on the SSN-688-class subs, he would have to report that bad news to GD's stockholders. GD hadn't paid a cash dividend to its shareholders since 1970, and a huge loss on the attack sub program would only make matters worse. Acknowledging the inevitability of such a loss was a task Lewis would rather avoid.

There were other problems. The manner in which General Dynamics had been describing its claims in reports to its shareholders could have attracted the attention of Securities and Exchange Commission (SEC) investigators. By forecasting revenues of $98 million in 1976 and $135 million in 1977 from its unresolved claim, GD could have been accused of painting a rosier financial picture than was justified. Such optimism could push GD's stock prices to artificially high levels.

Rickover objected whenever defense contractors predicted unusually generous claims settlements. "The amount of income a company books against an outstanding claim is a judgment which even certified public accountants cannot evaluate effectively," the admiral argued. "Thus, through large claims the company can effectively control the amount of profits or losses it reports publicly and the timing of their disclosure." Having the SEC breathing down his neck would only add to the urgency of Lewis's current situation. (In fact, the SEC initiated just such an investigation in 1978 but closed its file without recommending any enforcement action four years later.)

Lewis had left the presidency of McDonnell Douglas seven years earlier to try to turn the ailing General Dynamics around, and he now faced losses that would cast a shadow across GD's annual reports for years to come. That possibility was disturbing, but Lewis was more concerned with the daily cash drain at the shipyard. He had to bring money into the company quickly.

While Lewis was pondering GD's financial dilemma, Herbert Fenster was mulling over the same situation at his law office in Washington, D.C. Fenster, forty-two, was a partner in Sellers, Conner & Cuneo, one of the leading Washington law firms that specialized in representing defense contractors in their claims against the government. Fenster led the team of lawyers working on Electric Boat's claim. He also represented Ingalls—and informally advised Newport News—in their similar claims against the Navy, so he was a key behind-the-scenes player throughout the claims controversy.

From the beginning Fenster recommended a more aggressive strategy than the shipyards had adopted. A tough negotiator, experienced in legal battles, Fenster framed the claims issue in its narrowest contractual terms. He considered the Navy's refusal to reimburse his clients for their shipbuilding costs a clear-cut breach of contract. On this ground, he urged the shipyards to stop building its ships.

If the shipyards took his advice and threatened to stop work, Fenster was convinced the Navy would immediately turn to the courts and seek an injunction compelling the shipyards to continue working. That would be fine. Fenster thought that a federal court, when presented with legal arguments on both sides, would probably order the shipyard to continue working "in the interest of national defense." But he also predicted that a judge would order the Navy to pay the shipyard for all or most of the construction costs it had incurred while the larger claims question was being resolved. In other words, he was confident that a federal court would insist that the Navy, rather than the shipyard, carry the financial burden while the disputed claims were being negotiated. If he were right, the shipyards would instantly increase their bargaining power because the Navy would have to pick up the financial tab for as long as the claims negotiations dragged on.

At first GD was unwilling to go along with this aggressive legal strategy. "Defense contractors are remarkably patriotic," Fenster told me. "There is something that even transcends patriotism. They have a loyalty to their customers that is extraordinary. My perspective, as a claims lawyer, is to provide them their best legal protection. No one has asked *me* to be patriotic. I *am* patriotic, but that's not the role I've been asked to play."

Shipbuilders are far more comfortable accommodating themselves to their customers' wishes than confronting them with unwelcome claims. Even the most diversified defense contractor has only four possible customers: the Army, Navy, Air Force, and Marine Corps. A shipbuilder has only one: the Navy. Few defense contractors can antagonize their customers and prosper. The nature of their business inevitably breeds coziness, flexibility, and cooperation with the Pentagon, rather than open conflict.

Accustomed to an adversarial posture, Fenster pressed a similar strategy on Ingalls's corporate parent, Litton Industries. In June 1976 Litton heeded his advice and threatened to stop work at its Pascagoula shipyard on five amphibious assault ships. Just as Fenster had expected, the Navy sought a temporary restraining order from a federal district court in Mississippi.

The court in Mississippi responded by issuing a temporary restraining order that required Ingalls to keep working, as Fenster had anticipated. It ordered the Navy to make to Litton progress payments that would cover 91 percent of the shipyard's costs for work it had already performed and for work it would perform while its claim was being negotiated. Progress payments are regular payments a military service makes to its contractors to reimburse them for their allowable costs. As one might expect, contractors habitually plead for higher progress payments, say, 95 percent or 98 percent, so that they can minimize their own financing costs. The military traditionally prefers to withhold part of a contractor's progress payments so it retains some financial leverage over the company until it has completed its work satisfactorily.

Litton viewed the federal court ruling in Mississippi as a major victory. The order that the Navy make 91 percent progress payments meant an immediate injection of cash into the shipyard for its past expenditures and shifted the ongoing financial burden to the Navy. Unhappy with the ruling, the Justice Department appealed the Mississippi judge's decision.

Fenster was delighted with the success of his legal tactic. He advised General Dynamics to issue a similar threat to stop building the Navy's SSN-688 attack submarines. He predicted that a federal court in Connecticut would probably prohibit Electric Boat from shutting down and require the Navy to make progress payments to the shipyard of approximately 91 percent. Such a court order would represent a victory for General Dynamics. Again, David Lewis demurred. GD executives still hoped they could negotiate a settlement of their claims against the Navy without resorting to the courts.

The claims submitted by GD and Newport News had been referred to the Navy Claims Settlement Board, headed by Admiral Frank Manganaro, for their formal entitlement analysis. Litton's claim had been referred to a separate team of NAVSEA analysts.

Hidalgo was ready to begin one-on-one negotiations with each of the three shipyards, but before he could open such talks, Litton's legal troubles in Mississippi had to be cleared up. The Navy couldn't negotiate Litton's $1 billion ship claim as long as another government agency, the Justice Department, was pursuing an appeal against the private company in a federal court in Mississippi. Hidalgo met with Jimmy Carter's attorney general, Griffin Bell, to try to work out a delicate intragovernment compromise. Sympathetic to the Navy's effort to solve its ship claims problem, Bell agreed to set aside Justice's pending litigation against Litton.

In return for the opening of negotiations on its $1 billion claim, Litton agreed to accept progress payments of 75 percent instead of the 91 percent the court had ordered. Litton's willingness to accept reduced progress payments represented a victory for Hidalgo, for it cleared the way for negotiations with each of the shipyards. Hidalgo had also won a side bet with Graham Claytor, who had wagered a dollar that his assistant secretary could never convince Litton to accept progress payments of less than 80 percent.

Closed-door talks began. GD was represented occasionally by David Lewis but more regularly by Max Golden, a former general counsel of the Air Force who had become GD's corporate vice-president for contracts. Representing the Ingalls shipyard was Frederick O'Green, president of Litton. Negotiating on behalf of the Newport News yard was John "Jack" Diesel, president of the shipyard, but yet not an officer of the parent Tenneco corporation.

Hidalgo met individually with these men at least once a week.

The assistant secretary sought similar solutions to the GD and Litton claims because both shipyards faced huge losses and similar circumstances. He decided to handle the Newport News negotiation separately partly because the shipyard wasn't confronting huge losses but also because of the personalities involved. Hidalgo was able to deal amicably with Golden of GD and O'Green of Litton, but not with the abrasive Diesel of Newport News.

Newport News and its corporate parent, Tenneco, were playing hardball. Tenneco had acquired the shipyard in 1968 in part because it anticipated an increased demand for ships to handle its Alaskan North Slope oil and perhaps to transport liquefied natural gas to the Soviet Union. A decade later, with Newport News accounting for only 10 percent of the oil conglomerate's revenues, Tenneco could risk confronting the Pentagon. Diesel openly blasted the Navy. "The Navy's 10-year pattern of coaxing, cajoling, bullying, and arm-twisting shipbuilders and suppliers to take marginal, high-risk and frequently

unprofitable business—all with promises of future rainbows if they acquiesce
and economic disaster if they refuse—is just about over," he had told a House
subcommittee a few years earlier.

Hidalgo, the assistant secretary of the navy, later recalled laying down the
ground rules at his first meeting with each of the shipyard's representatives.
"You're going to undress financially for me," he warned them. "If you have
any resistance to that, let's stop all the meetings. We're going to get into your
whole financial structure, where you are if you take this kind of loss. What is
that going to do to your commitments to your banks? Are you going to get
to the edge of the precipice? I want to know how much of a loss you can take
because I don't want to get blood out of you . . . at least not more than you
can possibly give."

Hidalgo's first significant meeting with David Lewis took place in Deputy
Secretary Duncan's office on October 18, 1977. The two men, one representing
a company with 70,000 employees, annual sales of $2.7 billion, and a shipyard
that had built more nuclear submarines than any yard in the world, the other
representing the U.S. Navy, sat opposite each other. As Hidalgo settled back
in his seat, he reminded himself to remain firm. Nothing would be more
counterproductive than to play the role of a patsy. At the same time he recalled
a Spanish proverb: *Lo cortez no quita lo valiente:* "Courtesy does not negate
valor." Hidalgo spoke softly but unequivocally. The Navy obviously had
tremendous problems dealing with private shipyards, he began. "My first job
is to change things so that this doesn't happen again."

Lewis was despondent. At first he saw Hidalgo as a well-dressed, ebullient
dandy who didn't know anything about shipbuilding. "We'll sit around here
for a year," Lewis said to himself, "while Hidalgo tries to straighten out all
the Navy's regulations so this doesn't happen again, and we'll go belly up in
the process." Lewis was more concerned with GD's immediate troubles.

Hidalgo soon turned to that subject. Again he made his position clear: GD
must accept the notion of a severe fixed loss on its SSN-688 submarine program. No other solution was possible. He mentioned the possibility of an
investigation of General Dynamics by the SEC as yet another reason for the
two sides to reach agreement on the claims.

Hidalgo had familiarized himself with the arguments on both sides. True,
the Navy had insisted upon thousands of changes in the submarine's design
that boosted costs. And double-digit inflation had added hundreds of millions
of dollars to the shipyard's estimated expenses. But it was also true that the
inept management and plummeting productivity at EB could not be tolerated
or excused. This was a mess for which both sides were responsible, Hidalgo
believed. GD would have to acknowledge its share of the blame, or there could
be no settlement.

David Lewis was equally adamant: General Dynamics would *not* consider accepting a fixed loss on the attack subs. The shipyard was in this financial crisis because of the Navy's cumbersome shipbuilding practices. Why should GD have to swallow part of the loss? GD would have no part of it and was prepared to stop building the Navy's attack submarines if its claims weren't resolved quickly.

Lewis took a firm position in his meeting with Hidalgo, but actually he was ambivalent. He didn't want EB to stop building the submarines; he took GD's national defense responsibilities too seriously for that. Besides, he didn't want to jeopardize EB's share of the Navy's five-year shipbuilding plan.

Each year the President submits to Congress a request for the naval ships he wants in the coming fiscal year, plus his *planned* requests for the four following fiscal years. The five-year plan Jimmy Carter had sent to Congress in March 1978 called for seventy ships to be ordered between fiscal years 1979 and 1983. Of those, six were Trident submarines, all of which would go to Electric Boat, and five were SSN-688-class attack submarines, many of which were also likely to go to Electric Boat.

Lewis knew that Carter's most recent five-year shipbuilding program would probably change many times before the arrival of the second, third, fourth, and fifth years of the plan—known as the out years. Traditionally, by the time an out year arrives, the President's budget request for that year has been shaved substantially. Even so, Lewis was tantalized by the prospect of ten or eleven more submarines over the next five years and was reluctant to challenge the Navy openly.

At the same time Hidalgo recognized that GD could easily throw the dispute into a federal court if it threatened to stop working on the attack subs. He had winced at the Mississippi ruling and had no reason to think a federal judge in Connecticut would rule any differently. Hidalgo, an experienced attorney, knew of the maddening delays and astronomical legal costs any prolonged litigation would require. His boss, Navy Secretary Claytor, felt the same way.

"I am an old trial lawyer, and litigation does not frighten me," Claytor once told Congress, "but I know what its disadvantages are, and it sure includes taking the time of the productive people in testimony, in hours and hours and days and days of depositions, in answering extensive and difficult interrogatories, and in doing almost everything except getting on with the job of building ships."

Thus, reluctant to push the ship claims dispute into court but equally reluctant to play the role of a patsy, Hidalgo found himself walking a thin line in the negotiations. He didn't know how far the Navy could push GD or how much of a fixed loss David Lewis could sell to his own board of directors.

Before that meeting broke up, Hidalgo promised that the Navy would accelerate its entitlement analysis of EB's $544 million claim, an analysis that had
already consumed ten months. Hidalgo didn't offer much, but it was enough
to dissuade Lewis from issuing an immediate stop-work order at Electric Boat.

One-on-one meetings took place sporadically in Hidalgo's Pentagon office
during the fall and winter of 1977 and into the spring of 1978. Many of them
ended with Max Golden's threatening to break off the talks. The financial
picture at Electric Boat was deteriorating. Morale at the shipyard was plummeting as groups of fretful workers gathered to discuss the likelihood of
massive layoffs or a total shutdown of EB's Groton and Quonset Point facilities.

Faced with a loss of about $350 million, which was mounting at the rate of
$15 million a month, Lewis decided he had to act. No matter how much loyalty
he felt toward the Navy, he couldn't allow his company to suffer such a
financial strain. On March 13, 1978, General Dynamics announced that it
would stop building its remaining sixteen SSN-688 submarines after 11:59 P.M.
on April 12 and lay off 8,000 workers in Connecticut and Rhode Island. "We
regret most sincerely the necessity for our having to take this distasteful
action," Veliotis explained in a twenty-one-page letter to Vice Admiral C. R.
Bryan, NAVSEA's commander, "especially with respect to our only customer,
but we have no alternative as a prudent, responsible management."

The simmering dispute, which until now had been carried on discreetly in
Hidalgo's office, suddenly boiled over in public. Ella Grasso, Connecticut's
governor, was shocked by the specter of thousands of Electric Boat workers
laid off simultaneously. She placed an urgent telephone call to Connecticut's
senior senator, Abraham Ribicoff, to warn him of the coming economic disaster.

Ribicoff had been aware of the negotiations under way between the Navy
and Electric Boat, but he had demonstrated surprisingly little interest in the
claims dispute. Though shipbuilding wasn't a critical component of the U.S.
economy (as an industry it ranked fortieth in size and contributed only 0.3
percent of the GNP in 1978), it was enormously important in Connecticut.
Now that Electric Boat had threatened to dismiss 8,000 workers, Ribicoff was
spurred into action. He called Navy Secretary Claytor and described the dire
consequences a shutdown at Electric Boat would have on the defense-oriented
Connecticut economy. Claytor assured Ribicoff that "come hell or high water,
the yard was going to stay open." He also offered to accompany Hidalgo to
the senator's office that afternoon to brief the Connecticut and Rhode Island
congressional delegations on the claims issue. Before he hung up, Ribicoff had

one final thought for Claytor on the Navy's search for an equitable settlement; it was part warning and part plea. "In *no* way," said Ribicoff, "could this thing fail."

Ribicoff called David Lewis at GD headquarters in St. Louis and Henry Crown in Florida. Assuming the role of statesman, the senator urged the executives to meet with Claytor in his Pentagon office. The two men from General Dynamics were willing to meet with the secretary, but not in his office. They insisted on meeting unobtrusively, on "neutral ground," away from cameras and publicity.

A meeting was set for March 21 on "neutral ground"—Ribicoff's office. Claytor arrived with Hidalgo and Deputy Secretary Duncan. Lewis arrived with Crown and Golden. The Navy urged GD to postpone its stop-work threat and resume discussions of its half-billion-dollar claim. Claytor urged the company to accept the notion of swallowing a large fixed loss on its SSN-688 contracts. Lewis refused. EB was desperate for cash, but he would not acknowledge the company's role in the shipyard's rapidly escalating costs. EB had never been a big money-maker. It had logged sales of $3.5 billion during the decade ending in 1976 but had earned profits of only $125 million during that time—a modest 3.5 percent.

Even so, Lewis was in no mood to back down. It appeared as if this meeting, too, would end without any progress. Hidalgo was dissatisfied. The three government officials conferred privately and then made two offers to GD.

First, the government would adjust its inflation forecast in GD's favor. The Navy would lower GD's anticipated cost to complete the eighteen attack subs by arbitrarily reducing the inflation rates it had been using to project GD's future costs. (The government forecasts the rate of inflation for future years and uses those rates to calculate the cost growth it expects in its defense contracts. If the government were to reduce its projected inflation rates, the anticipated costs of those contracts would automatically drop.)

Of course, reducing the inflation rates wouldn't affect GD's actual costs, but it would cut the apparent size of GD's *projected* loss from $981 million to $843 million. Lewis presumably would welcome any bookkeeping maneuver that trimmed the size of his potential loss. The Navy also offered to rewrite the escalation clause in the current SSN-688 contracts so that EB's costs would be fully covered in case *future* inflation ran higher than the government's revised projections.

Secondly, and more important, the Navy offered GD a quick infusion of money: progress payments of $12.4 million a month to help cover the shipyard's construction costs during the next two months. This wasn't the Navy's first offer of money on the $544 million claim. Back in September 1977 it had offered the company a "provisional payment" of approximately $12 million on its $544 million claim, but GD had spurned the offer as a "token sum" which only called into question the Navy's true desire to reach a settlement. However, the shipyard's financial problems had worsened since then. Hidalgo and Claytor thought Lewis might be more receptive this time.

In return for its two-part offer, the Navy expected GD to postpone for sixty days its April 12 stop-work order at Groton and Quonset Point. In the meantime, both sides would continue discussing the shipyard's unresolved claim until the new deadline of June 11 arrived.

Lewis was reluctant to accept the Navy's offer of roughly $25 million. He thought it might compromise the company's legal case if the claims dispute ever wound up in federal court. But the shipyard had to stem its hemorrhaging losses somehow. Claytor, Hidalgo, and Duncan pressed for an agreement.

"Come on . . . we've offered you twenty-five million dollars," urged the Pentagon officials. "Take it. . . . It gives you a little infusion . . . a little cash flow right now."

Ribicoff's office fell silent as Lewis, Golden, and Crown considered the Navy's offer.

"All right, I'll take it," said Lewis, and a deal was struck.

Two days later Senator Ribicoff, who had adroitly positioned himself as an honest broker between the Navy and General Dynamics, unveiled the interim agreement. Electric Boat would not shut down on April 12. Shipyard workers in Connecticut and Rhode Island breathed sighs of relief. Their jobs were safe for at least another sixty days.

Hidalgo and Max Golden resumed their talks at the Pentagon. The claims dispute had attracted widespread press attention, and the interim agreement had brought the two sides back to the negotiating table, but little had actually changed. The Navy and GD were as stubborn as ever.

Golden presented one argument after another why the shipyard should not have to bear a fixed loss on its SSN-688 submarines. The problem of inflation was only partially resolved if the government revised its inflation estimates for future years. What about past years? Neither GD nor the Navy had expected runaway inflation when they signed the original SSN-688 contracts in 1971 and 1973. Why not change the escalation clause in those contracts *retroactively* to accommodate the staggering double-digit inflation of 1974 and 1975? Golden argued. U.S. shipyards had paid 83 percent more for their construction materials between 1970 and 1977, compared with a jump in consumer prices of only 56 percent in the same period. If the Navy applied realistic inflation clauses, Golden maintained, the $843 million loss facing Electric Boat could be cut in half. Hidalgo balked.

Well, Golden continued, the Navy should not overlook the recent $150 million capital investment the Electric Boat division had made with its own money, particularly since the equipment and facilities would be used exclusively on Navy shipbuilding programs. These investments included a launcher and a 60,000-square-foot pontoon graving dock, used to take a vessel out of the water, at the Groton shipyard as well as fabrication, steel processing, and storage buildings at its Quonset Point site. Again, Hidalgo balked.

Time and again, Golden marched out of Hidalgo's office, with no date set for a return engagement. But sooner or later the two men would find themselves talking again.

Meanwhile, the Navy Claims Settlement Board's analysis of GD's claim was progressing slowly under the supervision of Rear Admiral Manganaro. In an entitlement analysis, a team of Navy specialists tries to determine who is responsible for the extra costs associated with each aspect of a shipbuilder's claim. The final figure that results from this analysis is known as the entitlement. Naturally the shipyard wants it to be as high as possible.

Rickover managed to place a few of his staff members on Manganaro's entitlement team, but their work was confined largely to the few parts of EB's claim directly related to the submarines' nuclear propulsion systems. So Rickover's influence on the final entitlement figure wasn't very significant.

Hidalgo had been meeting with Manganaro about four times each week but wasn't happy with the admiral's attitude. "I always felt there was a wall there," Hidalgo recalled. Manganaro may have been equally disenchanted with the assistant secretary's search for a "political" solution. Hidalgo was concerned that the board might arrive at an entitlement figure that was too low for David Lewis to accept. He knew that as the entitlement figure grew larger, the size of the remaining loss that GD would have to swallow grew smaller, and a settlement became more likely.

Hidalgo also had to contend with a delicate political dilemma. Any agreement he reached with GD would have to be sold to Congress, where opponents of anything resembling a bailout were lying in wait. To a few representatives, senators, and staffers, the Navy's entitlement figure represented the *maximum* the service should pay the shipyard to settle its claim. Anything above that figure would smack of a sellout to the nation's all-powerful military-industrial complex.

In late 1977, in an effort to ensure that the entitlement figure be as generous as possible, Hidalgo went to his boss, Graham Claytor, with a proposal.

"Look, I'm having the evaluation of the Litton claim done by a real pro who doesn't have a Rickover ax to grind," he said. "I want to bring the Electric Boat entitlement under a similar arrangement, directly under my aegis."

9.  Edward Hidalgo (right), the dapper assistant secretary of the navy and point man in the acrimonious ship claims dispute, chats with Senator John C. Stennis of Mississippi, then the powerful chairman of the Senate Armed Services Committee and the Senate Defense Appropriations Subcommittee. Hidalgo paved the way for the settlement of the Navy's dispute with GD and two other shipbuilders in 1978 by convincing Stennis and other key lawmakers of the need for a financial compromise. *U.S. Navy*

Before long, members of the Manganaro panel learned of Hidalgo's plan to usurp their authority. Word leaked to Senator Proxmire, an ally of Rickover and the "permanent Navy," who quickly accused the Navy's civilian leadership of trying to subjugate its own entitlement panel. Rather than lose any precious goodwill in Congress on that particular battle, Hidalgo promptly backed off and allowed Manganaro to continue operating independently.

In January 1978 the Navy Claims Settlement Board announced its entitlement finding: $125 million. Thus, under its strict interpretation of the contract terms, it determined that the Navy should offer GD $125 million on its $544 million claim—a relatively low 23 cents on the dollar.

The term "entitlement" is a misnomer that leads people to misunderstand the process it describes. Use of the word "entitlement" implies that the dollar figure the Navy analysts arrive at is the maximum amount of money a shipyard is *entitled* to be paid. However, some observers believe the entitlement is actually the Navy's opening offer in a negotiation with a contractor, not the service's final word on the subject. "This is one party's determination of what he would be willing to pay," Secretary Claytor later told a Senate committee. "Usually one does not make a determination of that kind without being pretty sure that you are not going too far."

The final judgment on the value of a contractor's claim against the military is made either within the Defense Department by the Armed Services Board of Contract Appeal or in a civilian court. Most observers recognize it is patently unfair for one party in a contract dispute to determine unilaterally how the dispute ought to be settled.

Proxmire considered the Navy Claims Settlement Board the appropriate panel to evaluate GD's claim. He opposed the administration's attempt to settle the dispute outside the existing procedural channels. Paying a dime more than the entitlement, in Proxmire's view, was tantamount to a corporate handout. He was concerned that the authority of the Navy Claims Settlement Board and the integrity of the permanent Navy would be compromised if GD received more than the entitlement figure.

Rickover couldn't exert much influence over the entitlement analysis, but Hidalgo worried that the "Old Man" might sabotage his negotiations with GD by speaking directly to the former officer on the nuclear submarine *Sea Wolf* who now occupied the White House. "It was always my dread that I'd be going along, doing the best I could, and then be undercut completely by Rickover talking to the President," Hidalgo acknowledged years later.

Jimmy Carter respected, admired, obeyed, and feared Rickover more than any man in his life, with the possible exception of his father, James Earl Carter, Sr. Once, in 1972, while Carter was still a little-known governor, he told a group of Georgia broadcasters how he received phone calls from President Nixon or Vice President Agnew with complete equanimity. "But when the operator says, 'Governor, Admiral Rickover is on the phone,' I break out in a cold sweat, because he still watches very closely what I do and some days he is proud of me and on some days he says he is ashamed."

Hidalgo could envision Rickover condemning his proposed claims settlement package, calling it an outrage, a sellout, a bailout. "We've got contracts with the shipyard," Rickover might say to President Carter. "We must enforce those contracts to the letter." Hidalgo feared just such a conversation taking place in the Oval Office. He could imagine Carter agreeing with the indomitable admiral and torpedoing his negotiations with the shipyards.

Hidalgo need not have worried. Rickover never communicated his private views on the ship claims controversy to Carter. In fact, the President became directly involved in the claims issue on only one occasion, during a meeting in the White House Cabinet Room with Hidalgo, Claytor, Duncan, and Admiral Bryan in February 1978. The President was accompanied by David Aaron, his deputy assistant for national security affairs. Aaron sat silently as Carter, well prepared as usual, peppered his guests from the Pentagon with questions.

The President had no game plan of his own to foist upon the Navy; he wanted to leave it enough maneuvering room to negotiate effectively with the shipyards. Hidalgo considered Carter's position a vote of confidence.

## (2)

The Navy and GD were supposedly negotiating EB's formal claim for $544 million, but by the spring of 1978 the estimated cost overrun had grown to $843 million. Both sides were trying to determine how much of that loss the shipyard was going to absorb. Because the Navy's entitlement figure came in at $125 million, everyone assumed GD would be paid at least that much, leaving $718 million still to be divided. The question was: How much of that $718 million was GD going to pay? For months Lewis had refused to pay *any* of it, arguing that the entire cost overrun was caused by the Navy. He thought the service was trying to take advantage of GD. "They were not negotiating honestly and fairly," he said.

A crucial meeting on Capitol Hill radically altered Lewis's thinking. He and other GD executives were invited to a closed-door meeting with the congressional leadership at which Representative George Mahon, the conservative Texas Democrat who chaired the House Appropriations Committee and its defense subcommittee, acted as spokesman. Mahon courteously informed Lewis and his colleagues there was no way politically for General Dynamics to emerge from this contract dispute without swallowing some financial loss. There was no room for debate. "I urge you, Mr. David Lewis, to find some way because we want to help you," drawled Mahon, who had been in Congress for forty-three years. "We know that some of this inflation is beyond your control and beyond the Navy's control. . . . I urge you to find a solution, but don't look for one that's General Dynamics, a hundred percent, and the government, zero."

Lewis recognized the futility of GD's position. The Navy ultimately would have to look to Congress to appropriate the money to settle all three shipyards' outstanding claims. If the congressional leadership wouldn't even contemplate a settlement that reimbursed Electric Boat for 100 percent of its unexpected costs, it was time for Lewis to change his negotiating stance.

GD finally yielded in May 1978. Max Golden told Hidalgo that the shipyard would accept the principle of absorbing a loss on its SSN-688 contracts. In the same breath, Golden said his company would not go beyond a certain dollar figure, an amount that has not been disclosed. Hidalgo dismissed Golden's figure as absolutely unacceptable; GD would have to swallow a much larger loss. The impasse quickly shifted from the principle of accepting a fixed loss to the question of a dollar amount.

Talks continued on an irregular basis, but there was little cause for optimism as Electric Boat's stop-work deadline of June 11 approached. GD was preoccupied with its negative cash flow, and the Navy insisted that the shipyard accept a larger part of the loss. Hidalgo rarely missed an opportunity to remind Golden that Congress would never approve a claims settlement that didn't stick GD with a substantial loss.

Hidalgo was in a bind. He was confident that Claytor and Duncan would back him if he broke off negotiations, but he wanted desperately to settle the dispute and prevent the Navy's leading submarine builder from shutting down.

One week before the deadline Hidalgo met again with Golden. It was a tense session. Hidalgo made GD a bold, new offer, one he hoped would carry enough intangible "charisma" to clinch an agreement. He offered to split the $718 million loss down the middle: The Navy would pay the shipyard an extra $359 million if GD would swallow the remaining $359 million.

"Absolutely not," responded an incensed Golden. "We won't even think of it." With that, GD's vice-president marched out of Hidalgo's office and broke off the negotiations.

As it happened, Hidalgo was scheduled to address a civilian organization that Monday, June 5, in Chicago—less than 300 miles from GD headquarters in St. Louis. The trip would provide him one last opportunity for a settlement with GD. He called Claytor.

"Graham, I've got a wonderful pretext for setting up a meeting with David Lewis and Max Golden at the Naval Air Station in Glenview, Illinois. Why don't you come along for the ride?"

"The hell with it," said Claytor, who saw little hope for a last-minute agreement. "It's a waste of time."

Hidalgo persisted. He wanted one last chance to reach a compromise.

"All right, I'll do it," said Claytor, yielding to his friend of forty years.

Hidalgo phoned Golden in St. Louis.

"Max, I'm going to be out in Chicago. Why don't we all sit down together? I know we broke off negotiations, but I'm going to take Claytor with me. Why don't you bring Dave? At least we'll have a farewell coffee and we'll call it quits. Let's part like friends who've made a decent, valiant effort to settle this goddamn thing." Golden agreed to a meeting in Glenview, twenty miles north of Chicago.

As their plane headed toward Chicago, Hidalgo and Claytor reviewed their bargaining strategy.

"Graham, what we've got to come up with is some front end money. I'm not going to budge from that three hundred and fifty-nine million, and don't you budge. But on the front end, let's offer them a carrot," Hidalgo recommended.

Claytor nodded.

The four men gathered in the commander's office at the naval air station, where the atmosphere was pregnant with compromise. Supposedly they had come to terminate their unsuccessful negotiations. Instead, Hidalgo made a final two-part offer. First, he repeated the Navy's willingness to split the projected loss on EB's eighteen attack submarines. Secondly, Hidalgo offered to pay GD $300 million *immediately* as the first installment on the Navy's $359 million reimbursement. This was the first time Hidalgo had broached the possibility of paying GD a large chunk of its claim up front, an offer that would save the company sizable interest payments. Whenever Lewis or Golden mentioned the idea in the past, Hidalgo had dismissed it out of hand.

GD was already carrying losses estimated at $370 million. A $300 million payment would go a long way toward sopping up the red ink. Lewis and Golden recognized that the Navy was making a significant concession. A $359 million fixed loss would wipe out all the gross profits Electric Boat had earned since it began building nuclear submarines in the 1950's. That wasn't easy to accept, but Lewis could at least tell his board of directors and his stockholders that the Navy had agreed to split the loss fifty-fifty. A settlement would put this bitter disagreement behind them and allow Electric Boat to mend its tattered relationship with the Navy.

Lewis thought of the advice he had been getting from Washington. GD's claims lawyer, Herbert Fenster, urged the shipyard to carry out its threat, stop building the attack submarines, and force the Navy to take the dispute into federal court. Lewis was reluctant to follow Fenster's advice. He quietly pondered Hidalgo's offer.

"Well," he said after a long silence, "this is something I'll report to my board of directors. We'll be in touch with you."

Hidalgo's offer made sense for the Navy as well as for GD. If the company accepted half of the $718 million anticipated loss, the Navy would have a far easier time selling the settlement package to Congress. The front-end payment of $300 million to the shipyard, which Hidalgo had just offered, would not be a huge additional burden for the Navy. Eventually the service would pay EB the $359 million anyway; paying $300 million of that amount sooner rather than later was not that onerous. And of course, an agreement signed by both sides would avert a shutdown at the shipyard, a restraining order, possible progress payments of 91 percent or more, and years of acrimonious and expensive litigation.

Yes, the deal finally made sense for both sides. Hidalgo conferred with Golden by phone half a dozen times on Tuesday and Wednesday. On Thursday, June 8, GD accepted the Navy's offer.

On Friday, June 9, two days before the stop-work order was to go into effect, Lewis flew to Washington to sign the official memorandum of decision in Claytor's office. Max Golden was there. So was P. Takis Veliotis, EB's general manager who had played only a minor role in the claims negotiations.

GD was satisfied. The Wall Street financial community also seemed pleased, as GD's stock jumped 4⅜ points a few days later to $67.50 per share, its highest price in a decade. "Though its $359 million write-offs on these subs will plunge General Dynamics far into the red this year, Chairman David Lewis describes the future as 'very bright'—and in general that is true," observed *Fortune* magazine.

Claytor was also relieved by the agreement. "I think it's the most important thing from the standpoint of the Navy we've accomplished since we've been in office," he later declared. Hidalgo beamed with pride. He considered the agreement a personal triumph.

Hidalgo's personal triumph was somewhat tarnished years later when reports surfaced that he had accepted at least four consulting assignments from GD after he had returned to private law practice in Washington in 1981. Hidalgo has charged more than $70,000 in consulting fees for helping GD try to sell F-16 fighters and tanks to the Spanish government, without success. But he vehemently denies ever favoring GD during the protracted ship claims negotiations. "I will defend those settlements to my dying day," he said. "I have nothing to conceal or apologize for."

The terms of the 1978 ship claims agreement were simple enough to be spelled out in one and a half typed pages.

• The Navy would pay Electric Boat the full $125 million recommended by its Claims Settlement Board as a result of the entitlement analysis.

• The overall cost of building the eighteen subs was estimated to be $718 million higher than originally agreed to by the Navy. Of that $718 million, 50 percent would be paid by the Navy, raising its total price tag $359 million from $2.309 billion to $2.668 billion. The other half of the $718 million would be covered by Electric Boat, with no reimbursements from the Navy. "That is unrecovered costs, not the amount of claims settlements," Deputy Secretary Duncan assured Congress. "That's *loss.*"

•If costs for the eighteen subs continued to rise above the new estimate of $2.668 billion, the shipyard and the Navy were to share them equally for the next $100 million. Any additional costs would be paid for entirely by GD. The company and the Navy would share any savings on a fifty-fifty basis in the unlikely event that Electric Boat completed the eighteen submarines for less than $2.668 billion. These new pricing arrangements meant two things for Electric Boat: It had a strong incentive to finish the eighteen submarines for less than $2.668 billion and an even stronger *disincentive* not to exceed that figure by more than $100 million.

•The contracts were amended to account more realistically for inflation. The Navy agreed to cover through 1984 any increases in labor costs that topped 7 percent annually or increases in material costs that exceeded 6 percent annually. "If our increase gets worse than that," Claytor said, "we're all going to be in bad shape."

•GD also agreed not to submit any additional claims related to its SSN-688 submarine program for events occurring up through the date of the settlement. And, in a bigger concession, it promised not to submit any claims against the Navy asserting that the delays in the attack submarine program had disrupted work on the Trident subs under construction in the same shipyard. GD's disavowal of such cross-impact claims came as a big relief to several worried Navy procurement officials.

•Finally, the shipyard promised to estimate promptly the extra costs involved in implementing future Navy-imposed design changes. Such promptness might prevent a backlog of unpriced changes that could lead to another round of claims.

Not surprisingly Rickover was dissatisfied with the claims agreement. "I would have liked a deal like that if I were General Dynamics," he observed years later. He thought the Navy should have paid GD no more than the $125 million specified by the entitlement analysis.

All that remained was the tacit approval of Congress. Technically the agreement reached between the Navy and GD required the two SSN-688 submarine contracts to be restructured at higher target and ceiling prices. This restructuring was to be accomplished under terms of a 1958 statute, Public Law 85-804, which allows the Defense Department to take extraordinary contractual actions in cases such as this to "facilitate the national defense." An agreement reached between the DOD and a contractor under provisions of PL 85-804 becomes effective automatically unless one or both chambers of Congress pass a resolution of disapproval within sixty legislative days.

Some critics of PL 85-804 argue that it has frequently been used by the DOD to bail out undeserving companies that have mismanaged their defense contracts. The restructuring of Lockheed's C-5A aircraft contract is often cited as just such a case. Defenders of PL 85-804 argue that it allows the government to make equitable adjustments to defense contracts when no better solution exists. Senator Proxmire opposed the use of PL 85-804 in GD's case, preferring instead that the dispute be elevated to the Armed Services Board of Contract Appeal or the court system if the company wouldn't accept the $125 million entitlement figure.

Hidalgo didn't anticipate any serious problems. He had been in quiet meetings for months, lining up the support of key figures in both chambers. "Hidalgo was personally driving the 85-804 wagon over the Navy's dead body and, particularly, over Rickover's dead body," recalled Lewis. "He looked on this as a solution." Hidalgo was so committed to the PL 85-804 approach that he has since been criticized for trying to ram it down GD's throat. Internal GD memorandums, which have surfaced in Jack Anderson's column, suggest that Lewis was more reluctant to have GD portrayed in dire financial condition than was Hidalgo. Even so, their decision to pursue the PL 85-804 solution seems to reflect the political realities of Washington more than a concerted effort to deceive Congress.

On the House side, Democrat Charles Bennett of Florida, the chairman of the Seapower Subcommittee of the House Armed Services Committee and a longtime friend of the Navy, had indicated his support for the use of PL 85-804 to grant the shipyards "extraordinary contractual relief." On the Senate side, Hidalgo had lined up Democrat John Stennis of Mississippi. Stennis had keen interest in the ship claims issue, particularly the portion of the settlement package that concerned the Ingalls shipyard, Mississippi's largest employer. A strong advocate for the Navy, Stennis felt it was sometimes necessary to go over the heads of the uniformed admirals to reach a political compromise between the service and its major shipbuilders.

"With all deference to the Navy," Stennis drawled in a courteous understatement, "I have found out that they are naturally more interested in getting new ships and more ships than they are in settling old claims." The seventy-seven-year-old senator wielded enormous influence in the defense procurement arena by serving as chairman of both the Senate Armed Services Committee and the Defense Subcommittee of the Senate Appropriations Committee. In this unique situation, Stennis's voice dominated the panels that *authorized* defense expenditures and *appropriated* the money to fund them. (Stennis relinquished both chairs when the Republicans took control of the Senate in January 1981.)

Congressmen and senators from Connecticut and Rhode Island applauded
the compromise with GD that averted a shutdown in Groton and Quonset
Point. Senator Ribicoff spoke of his crucial role in patching together the fragile
negotiations. "There is no way this settlement can be called a bailout for
General Dynamics," he maintained. Senator Barry Goldwater of Arizona
ruminated about the problem of continual design changes' raising the cost of
modern weaponry and then switched the topic—as he often does—to his
favorite subjects, tactical air power and aircraft production. In the aircraft
field, as in shipbuilding, Goldwater warned that excessive design changes by
the Air Force were pushing manufacturing costs through the ceiling.

Senator John Chafee of Rhode Island, who had once occupied Claytor's
desk as secretary of the navy, enthusiastically supported the claims agreement.
Rhode Island's other senator, Claiborne Pell, had an answer for those critics
who said the PL 85-804 restructuring would set a dangerous bailout precedent
that other defense contractors might wish to follow. "No sane contractor
would choose the claim process merely to achieve the kind of relief provided
by this settlement," Pell concluded bluntly.

Proxmire was the Senate's lone critic of the agreement. He called the package "a form of backdoor welfare" that rewarded the shipbuilders for their
waste and mismanagement and would establish a harmful precedent. "The
message the Navy is sending out is this," said Proxmire. "If you are a large
contractor and you dominate an important portion of the defense market, file
an inflated claim and the Navy will pay the true value plus as much as 50%
of the remaining portion."

A publicity-conscious phrasemaker, the Wisconsin senator accused the
Navy of "turning military muscle into fat." By restructuring the SSN-688
contracts under PL 85-804, it would divert budget dollars from buying new
ships to settling illegitimate old claims. Proxmire criticized the Navy for
yielding to the shipyards' stop-work threats and for extracting no assurances
from the shipyards that they wouldn't submit any new claims in the future.
He viewed the settlement as a sellout of the Navy and the taxpayers' interests,
not as a hard-fought agreement between two obstinate organizations, each
with compelling arguments on its side.

Despite Proxmire's vigorous protestations, neither chamber of Congress
mustered strong opposition to the proposed settlement packages. In addition
to the pact with GD, the Navy hammered out similar agreements to settle the
Litton claim for $447 million and the Newport News claim for $165 million.
Thus, the long dispute between the Navy and its three largest shipbuilders
finally seemed to be resolved.

# Chapter Seven

## The Weapon Nobody Wanted

### (1)

*Creating a new weapon without service support and seeing it through to procurement is rather like the proverbial dog who walks on his hind legs; the wonder is not that he does it so poorly, the wonder is that he does it at all.*

—Henry D. Levine, "Some Things
to All Men: The Politics of
Cruise Missile Development"

General Dynamics, like other major defense contractors, succeeds or fails on the basis of its individual weapons programs. We've traced the origins of GD and examined the company's ship claims dispute with the Navy. Now it's time to take a closer look at three of GD's most important products: cruise missiles, fighter aircraft, and tanks. The story behind each weapon illuminates a different aspect of the procurement process.

The Pentagon's approach to the development of cruise missiles during the 1970's illustrates the importance of technical inventiveness and the hindrance of interservice rivalry. The history of the F-16 fighter program demonstrates how the concept of a new weapon can change dramatically over time. And

GD's acquisition of the M-1 tank program from the Chrysler Corporation underscores the clout that the Army and Department of Defense continue to wield over even the mightiest defense contractors.

On the afternoon of January 6, 1977, the Defense Systems Acquisition Review Council (DSARC) gathered in the basement of the Pentagon to decide the fate of the nation's cruise missile program. A multiple showdown was about to take place in conference room 1E-801 No. 7 between the Air Force and the Navy; between both services and the OSD; between the Defense Department and Secretary of State Henry Kissinger; between the arms controllers on Capitol Hill and those who advocated a hard line in the ongoing strategic negotiations with the Kremlin; and between several billion-dollar corporations with huge financial stakes in the outcome of the cruise missile program.

Cruise missiles are unmanned small aircraft that can deliver nuclear or conventional warheads on enemy targets. They are powered by "air-breathing" turbofan jet engines, rather than by ballistic missile rockets, and travel at relatively slow speeds (less than 500 miles per hour) and low altitudes. Terrain contour matching (TERCOM) guidance systems, which compare the topographic features of the land beneath them to a programmed map in their onboard computers, enable ground-hugging cruise missiles to make in-flight corrections, "sneak" under enemy radar, and strike distant targets accurately. The missiles are relatively cheap to build and extremely difficult to defend against. Accordingly they have become an important element in the U.S. nuclear weapons arsenal.

The parallel development of cruise missiles in the United States by the Navy and Air Force represents a classic example of interservice rivalry. At first neither the Navy nor the Air Force showed much enthusiasm for these exotic new weapons. Both saw the cruise missile as a potential threat to their traditional military missions. "The Air Force and the Navy went right up the wall," recalled William P. Clements, Jr., a vigorous advocate of cruise missiles while he was Nixon's deputy secretary of defense. "The Air Force said, 'You're going to kill our B-1,' and the Navy said, 'You're going to kill our aircraft carriers.' " Both services dragged their feet developing the new missiles. Only after the OSD had pressured the Navy to develop a *sea*-launched cruise missile did the Air Force feel compelled to develop its own *air*-launched version. The Air Force wasn't about to cede exclusive responsibility for cruise missiles to a rival service.

The DSARC meeting that January afternoon marked a turning point in the history of the cruise missile program. Each service was well along in developing its own version of the missile. At earlier meetings the DSARC had approved the military requirement for the weapons and the technical approaches that would be pursued—the equivalents of Milestone Zero and Milestone One. (Precise DSARC terminology has a tendency to change from one administration to the next, although the concept of periodic OSD review at critical points in a weapon's life-span remains the same. For the sake of consistency, I am using only one set of DSARC terms, even if the proper terminology may have been different in the period being described.) By 1977 both efforts had "matured" to the point where the DSARC had to determine if the country needed both services working on separate cruise missiles. If not, which program should move forward into full-scale engineering development and which should be canceled?

At the Pentagon these questions were of monumental significance. The rivalry between the Navy and the Air Force over custodianship of the cruise missile program at times seemed more heated than the rivalry between the United States and the Soviet Union. The DSARC's decision would certainly make or break the careers of several Air Force colonels and Navy captains. More important, it might reshape each service's military mission.

Within the defense industry the DSARC's decision would be no less profound. Different companies had aligned themselves into subcontracting teams in support of one service or the other. As the DSARC members began their closed-door meeting, executives with those aerospace firms still vying for a piece of the cruise missile program—General Dynamics, Boeing, McDonnell Douglas, Williams, and others—waited anxiously for news. The council's decision would affect the fate of billions of dollars' worth of defense contracts.

## (2)

To understand the situation that confronted the DSARC that afternoon, it will be useful to review the curious history of the cruise missile program. How could a weapon that had been nearly abandoned by the United States in the 1950's rebound in the 1970's and become such an enticing opportunity for defense contractors? How did a program which began life as a wayward orphan, with neither the Air Force nor the Navy showing much interest, suddenly become the darling of both services? How did General Dynamics, Vought, and Boeing emerge as the leading contenders for lucrative prime contracts? The story of the cruise missile is not only a textbook case of interservice rivalry but also an excellent illustration of the roles that strong personalities, geopolitical strategists, and shrewd legislators can play in the development of a new weapon.

The search for answers begins in the blackened skies over London during World War II. By most accounts, today's cruise missile traces its heritage to

Hitler's dreaded V-1 buzz bombs, launched against Britain and Belgium in 1944. The V-1, an abbreviation for *Vergeltungswaffe Eins* ("Reprisal Weapon One"), could fly approximately 150 miles, at speeds of 400 miles per hour, carrying a one-ton explosive warhead. It was essentially an unmanned, slow-moving, gyro-stabilized aircraft, with a buzzing jet engine, which crashed and exploded indiscriminately as soon as its fuel ran out. Buzz bombs possessed none of the range, accuracy, or explosive power of current cruise missiles, but they were psychologically devastating. More than 10,000 were fired at the United Kingdom, and about one-quarter reached their targets, injuring nearly 15,000 people. To this day the memory of unmanned bombs smashing into London rooftops haunts countless Britons.

The first rudimentary efforts to develop an unmanned flying missile in the United States predated the German V-1, beginning as far back as World War I. During that conflict the Navy awarded the Sperry Gyroscope Company a contract to develop what it called a flying bomb, essentially a primitive cruise missile capable of carrying explosives. At about the same time the Army turned to inventor Charles Kettering, cofounder of the Dayton-Wright Airplane Company, to design a similar flying torpedo, later dubbed the Kettering Bug. Comprised of cardboard-covered wings and a forty-horsepower engine built by Henry Ford, the ingenious Bug was aptly described as half player piano and half cash register. Its first flight, at Dayton's South Field in 1918, was spectacular, if not successful. Instead of flying horizontally, as expected, the aerial torpedo climbed vertically to about 800 feet, flipped over, plummeted toward a group of horrified military guests, and buzzed them several times before crashing ignominiously. The Bug's flying ability was improved, but World War I ended, and the early work on cruise missiles was set aside.

By the mid-1930's the Navy's interest in unmanned aircraft had been renewed. This time it tried to develop training targets for antiaircraft gunners by installing radio controls in pilotless planes, known as drones. The first successful flight of a full-size radio-controlled target drone, an aging Stearman-Hammond JH-1 airplane with no pilot aboard, took place before Christmas of 1937. Once the radio controls had been perfected, Navy officials began designing more sophisticated onboard devices, such as radar, miniature television, and sound-activated and heat-seeking guidance systems, that might allow unmanned drones to serve also as *offensive* weapons. The technical challenge was to develop a cruise missile powered by a small engine that could deliver a heavy payload of explosives over long distances with dependable accuracy.

At the height of World War II, while Germany was launching its buzz bombs, the U.S. Navy established the Gorgon missile program to wed its guidance and propulsion technologies. "The target drone program gave us a radio-controlled aircraft and the assault drone program gave us a guidance system," the Navy's Gorgon program director wrote years later. "Finally, the Gorgon program gave us a guided missile that could be launched from a combat aircraft, ships, or shore, and clearly became the credible ancestor of the cruise missile."

With the end of World War II a new type of offensive weapon, the ballistic missile, began to receive more attention in the United States than the cruise missile. A ballistic missile is essentially a wingless projectile propelled into space by a brief, powerful thrust from a rocket booster. Its flight path—like the trajectory of a tossed stone—follows a parabolic arc determined by its speed and direction at the time its booster rocket quits. Its guidance system is used primarily to steer it onto its trajectory. Once the missile's booster stops, its downward path is determined largely by gravity and aerodynamic drag, not by the minor mid-course adjustments its guidance system can make. By contrast, a cruise missile remains in the earth's atmosphere throughout its flight and employs a jet engine and stubby wings to provide aerodynamic lift, much like a manned aircraft. Its onboard guidance system steers it all the way to the target.

In the 1940's and 1950's ballistic missiles held the promise of traveling farther and faster than cruise missiles, with heavier payloads, greater accuracy, and less vulnerability. Consequently R&D money in the defense budget shifted from cruise to ballistic missiles. When the Soviet Union used a ballistic missile in November 1957 to launch Sputnik, its first earth-orbiting satellite, alarmed Pentagon officials placed even greater emphasis on developing an American intercontinental ballistic missile (ICBM) that could strike the USSR.

Even so, low-key efforts to improve U.S. nuclear and conventional cruise missiles continued. A few of these weapons even made it into active use. One of the most notable was a Navy missile that could be launched from a submarine or surface ship. That weapon, named Regulus I, could carry a nuclear warhead nearly 600 miles. It was fired experimentally more than 1,000 times and eventually entered the Navy's active inventory. A follow-on version, called Regulus II, which could exceed Mach 1, was fired from a submarine successfully in 1958. (Mach 1, the speed of sound, is about 700 miles per hour at sea level.)

The Regulus cruise missiles developed a cadre of loyal Navy supporters, as one might expect. Whenever a weapon is deployed by one of the services, its future within that branch is considerably brightened. Officers who become familiar with the weapon's capabilities in the field tend to favor it when they are promoted to headquarters staff assignments or weapons procurement jobs. However, this support couldn't save the Regulus program when an unexpected event occurred in the skies above the Soviet Union.

On May 1, 1960, a high-flying Lockheed U-2 spy plane flown by CIA pilot

Francis Gary Powers was intercepted by a Soviet surface-to-air missile and crashed near the city of Sverdlovsk. "When my U-2 was shot down," Powers later wrote, "a number of our most cherished illusions went crashing down with it: that the United States was too honorable to use the deplorable enemy tactics of espionage; that we were incapable of acting in our own defense until after being attacked." He failed to mention another U.S. illusion that crashed that day. As the crippled U-2 plane fell more than 68,000 feet, the future of the cruise missile plummeted with it. The technical rationale for cruise missiles —that they could elude Soviet surface-to-air missiles—had been dramatically shattered. If the Soviets could shoot down a swift, high-flying U-2, they could certainly shoot down a slower-moving cruise missile. Shaken by the incident, the U.S. missile development community focused its attention exclusively on long-range ICBMs.

Other ancestors of today's cruise missile included Martin's Matador and Mace ground-launched missiles, designed to be fired from the back of a truck; Northrop's Snark, the first U.S. missile of intercontinental range; North American Aviation's air-launched Hound Dog, which carried a nuclear warhead; and McDonnell Douglas's Quail decoy missile, designed to fly patterns that resembled a B-52 bomber on enemy radar screens. "In general, these and other first generation U.S. cruise missiles shared a number of handicaps," declared the Institute for Foreign Policy Analysis, a Cambridge, Massachusetts, think tank. "All were hindered in their performance by the use of large and heavy warheads, inefficient turbojet engines and heavy power-demanding guidance systems that were, in any case, grossly inaccurate."

A fortuitous marriage of technology and politics resurrected cruise missiles in the United States in the 1970's. Breakthroughs in the development of compact turbojet engines, miniaturized warheads, and microelectronic circuitry had made sleek new cruise missiles with vastly improved guidance systems technologically feasible. But the political catalyst for America's renewed interest in cruise missiles occurred on the other side of the world.

On October 22, 1967, four months after the conclusion of the Arab-Israeli Six-Day War, the Israeli naval destroyer *Elath,* with 202 crewmen aboard, was patrolling near the northern coast of the Sinai Peninsula. A Soviet-built Egyptian patrol boat bobbed quietly in the harbor of Port Said, thirteen and a half miles away, its crewmen scanning radar screens and tracking the position of the unsuspecting *Elath.* While the United States had suspended its efforts to develop cruise missiles in favor of ballistic missiles, the USSR had been busy perfecting a series of air-launched, ground-launched, and sea-launched cruise missiles. Mounted on the deck of the Egyptian patrol boat was the fruit of that effort, a Soviet-built Styx subsonic cruise missile capable of guiding itself to targets more than twenty miles away. It was armed with a 1,000-pound explosive warhead. The crewmen set the Styx missile's autopilot on a deadly course toward the *Elath* and fired it.

The warhead smashed into the *Elath*'s midsection. A few minutes later a second Styx struck the destroyer's engine room, wrecking its engines and boilers. Fires blazed, the ship's control system was crippled, and the electricity was knocked out. An hour and a half later a third missile smashed into the burning Israeli vessel and sank it. A fourth Styx arrived a few minutes later, adding to the casualties when it exploded in the water nearby. Altogether at least seventeen Israelis died in the attack.

While the two countries traded accusations and denials that the *Elath* had violated Egypt's territorial waters, the rest of the world pondered the military significance of these sophisticated new Soviet cruise missiles. A few self-guided antiship cruise missiles had sunk a mighty destroyer from thirteen and a half miles away.

Within the U.S. Navy the sinking was enough of a shock to stimulate new thinking about U.S. naval strategy, which had long held that major surface ships could be adequately protected by carrier-based aircraft. Just as General Billy Mitchell had had to demonstrate to a skeptical Army Air Service in 1921 that a bomber could sink a battleship from the air, it took the disastrous *Elath* incident to convince the U.S. Navy that a cruise missile could sink a major surface ship.

Israelis considered this incident the worst military setback their country had suffered since independence in 1948, and they pledged to correct the dangerous imbalance in weapons technology. The day after the sinking, at a Tel Aviv news conference, Israeli military officials described the attack on the *Elath* and assessed its military significance. "It's a milestone," acknowledged one Israeli officer. "It's the first time they fired sea-to-sea rockets, probably the first time in the world these were used." The officer was asked what lessons Israel had learned from the unexpected attack. His answer probably echoed through the halls of the Pentagon, 6,000 miles away. "What lessons did we learn?" repeated the Israeli officer. "We learned that we need proper tools—and there are proper tools."

## (3)

The sinking of the *Elath* sent a shock wave through the Navy's missile development community. Suddenly pressure to build an American antiship cruise missile began to mount. The attack on the Israeli destroyer helped the

U.S. Navy pry money out of Congress for stepped-up cruise missile research. "That strike was something we could dramatically point to and say, 'See, *this* is what we're talking about,' " one admiral recalled.

However, not everyone in the Navy embraced the idea of developing cruise missiles. The attack on the *Elath* dramatized the destructiveness of antiship cruise missiles, but it also gave the admirals who commanded the surface fleet something to worry about. If cruise missiles could effectively sink a major combatant, wouldn't they spotlight the vulnerability of surface ships?

Similarly cruise missiles won little support among naval aviators. Pilots based on U.S. aircraft carriers traditionally had three missions: defending the U.S. surface ships they accompanied, attacking enemy ships, and striking enemy land targets. If new antiship cruise missiles could attack enemy ships and long-range cruise missiles could strike distant land targets, wouldn't they sharply reduce the role left for Navy fliers?

Only the submariners felt relatively unthreatened by the new weapon. Cruise missiles would enable a U.S. attack sub to operate farther from enemy ships, reducing the likelihood of its being detected, but they wouldn't threaten the sub's primary mission of stalking and destroying other subs.

Different power centers within the Navy began tugging the program in different directions. Various weapons development offices vied with one another for leading roles in the new effort or the adoption of their own technological ideas. The embryonic cruise missile program floundered for years in this bureaucratic tug-of-war until Admiral Zumwalt was named chief of naval operations, in July 1970. He was an outspoken advocate of cruise missiles who considered the Navy's cancellation of the Regulus II in the 1950's the worst weapons decision the service had made during his career. "That decision was based on the theory that our carriers were so effective that we did not need cruise missiles," Zumwalt believed, "though some have suspected that the reluctance of the aviators' union to give up any portion of its jurisdiction played a large part in the decision."

The CNO was convinced the Navy was allocating too large a slice of its R&D and procurement budgets to Admiral Rickover's ultraexpensive nuclear-powered submarines and surface ships and not enough to cheaper ships and missiles that it could afford to buy in larger quantities. In the early 1970's Zumwalt aligned himself with a controversial approach to weapons procurement known as the high-low mix. This concept envisioned the development and procurement of a combination of highly sophisticated, expensive new weapons and an impressive quantity of low-technology weapons. Theoretically the Navy would be able to challenge the Soviet Union's most advanced armaments with high-cost, high-technology weapons while it simultaneously covered vast oceans and engaged in attrition warfare with numerous low-cost ships and weapons.

In Zumwalt's view, the proposed new antiship cruise missile, later dubbed Harpoon, was a low-cost weapon that the Navy urgently needed to counter threats from enemy ships armed with similar missiles. He demonstrated his commitment to such a weapon by appointing Captain Claude Ekas, Jr., one of the procurement community's rising stars, project manager for the fledgling effort.

Captain Ekas had to make some basic choices about Harpoon. Advocates within the Navy and the defense industry had coalesced around three possible technological approaches to the design of the new weapon. Ekas had to choose one.

The first approach was to develop a new antiship cruise missile by modifying the guidance system on the Navy's Standard missile then being built by the Pomona division of General Dynamics. The Naval Ordnance Systems Command, the agency that acquires naval guns and other surface weapons for the fleet, had developed the Standard missile. Naturally it favored an approach that drew upon its earlier success. Lined up with the Ordnance Systems Command was the Applied Physics Laboratory of Johns Hopkins University, a nonprofit research and development organization that traditionally assists the "surface" admirals.

A second approach was to modify new Condor air-to-surface missiles being built by North American Rockwell so they could be fired from ships as well as from airplanes. An early backer of this approach was the Naval Air Systems Command (NAVAIR), which develops the service's aircraft and airborne weapons, including the Condor. Supporting NAVAIR was the Naval Weapons Center at China Lake, California, an R&D lab that had earned an outstanding reputation on the success of its Sidewinder, an air-to-air missile intended for short-range aerial dogfights.

A third option was the clean-slate approach—a fresh start on cruise missiles that would leave all technical options wide open. Advocates of this approach were somewhat harder to identify, but they included the Navy's technologists, those designers, engineers, and planners who usually favored the most advanced, innovative (and generally costly) solution to any technical challenge. NAVAIR was a hotbed of Navy technologists, but they could also be found throughout the service.

Technologists argued that by starting with a clean slate, the officials responsible for the cruise missile program could design a weapon precisely tailored to their requirements. They would not have the problem of adapting an air-launched missile for use on a ship or of replacing the guidance system on an existing missile intended for a different purpose. The clean-slate approach offered freedom in overcoming any technical obstacle. It also placed technical considerations above costs. This approach naturally attracted the support of those contractors that were "out in the cold," with no current missile work, and were looking for new contracts.

Each of the contractors interested in the Navy's Harpoon program was promoting its favorite approach with government officials at all levels. General Dynamics was building a case for a modified version of its Standard missile. North American Rockwell was arguing in favor of an adaptation of its Condor missile. McDonnell Douglas and other companies without any current missile contracts were extolling the virtues of approaching the Harpoon program with a clean slate.

Navy bureaucrats began to line up behind one technical approach or another, but they rarely identified the defense contractors connected with each approach. Though officials generally know which company stands to gain from each suggested approach, there is an unwritten rule among Pentagon bureaucrats *not* to discuss specific contractors by name. To do so might convey the impression that a bureaucrat has abandoned his objectivity or been co-opted by one of the competing companies.

Government officials are reluctant to acknowledge it, but informal alliances between bureaucrats and defense contractors inevitably develop over time. It's not surprising. Bureaucrats behave like people who follow a professional sports team, learn about the individual players, identify with the club's victories, and eventually become fans. In much the same way Pentagon employees come to identify with defense contractors they've worked with closely over the years.

While Captain Ekas and his program officials pondered which technical approach to follow, competing contractors worked feverishly to argue their cases. Selling a weapons system is a process of winning allies by encouraging individual bureaucrats to adopt one's solution to the military problem. "After a while they feel it's *their* solution," explained one insider. To accomplish this, defense contractors will talk to anyone remotely connected with "their" program, often working from vertical organization charts that identify every government decision maker involved in a particular weapons program, from the secretary of defense down to the lowliest engineer or long-range planner. Company reps gather "market intelligence" from engineers in the weapons laboratories, political appointees running the Defense Department and the services, National Security Council (NSC) staffers, State Department officials, and staff members of the key congressional committees.

"Their pitch typically will be a technical pitch," said one congressional staffer, describing the standard approach a lobbyist might use to plug one of his company's missiles. "They come in and say, 'Here is our vehicle. Here is its range. Here is the payload. Here's how it is carried. Here's how the Strategic Air Command maintenance people will repair the system.' The last chart of the briefing will be the cost—how much it's going to cost."

Meetings with committee staffers tend to be technical. They aren't clandestine sessions in which contractor reps pry into staff members' briefcases or twist their arms. Contractors gain information that enables them to focus their R&D work and marketing efforts in areas that interest the Pentagon. Committee staffers receive the technical data, cost estimates, and promotional material they need to evaluate weapons programs competing for scarce budget dollars.

Before the Navy program office could choose among the three competing technical approaches, yet another policy question arose: Should the United States buy an existing foreign missile from one of its allies rather than develop a cruise missile of its own? Cooperation among NATO allies was being promoted on both sides of the Atlantic, so this possibility was being discussed more and more in Washington. On the whole, U.S. officials paid only lip service to the notion of working with their Western European allies in the production of common weapons. They rarely bought weapons abroad, for several reasons.

First, the U.S. military exhibited a deep prejudice, sometimes called the not-invented-here syndrome, that foreign-built weapons could not perform as well as their American-built counterparts. Secondly, foreign-made weapons don't normally conform to the military specifications (MILSPECs) that outline requirements such as weight, size, power, and mandatory subsystems. Buying a foreign weapon could necessitate redrafting and recertifying hundreds of these MILSPECs, a bureaucratic task of nightmarish proportions. And buying weapons abroad is more complicated and time-consuming for the U.S. bureaucrats who must complete the necessary paper work. The language barriers, long distances, logistical uncertainties, and international red tape are more cumbersome than most officials care to tolerate. Thirdly, the creation of more jobs for foreign defense manufacturers and fewer jobs in the United States is an inevitable by-product of overseas weapons purchases that wins few friends in Congress.

At least two foreign candidates were offered to the U.S. Navy: a German-French air-launched missile called the Kormoran and the French Exocet missile, which grabbed worldwide headlines a decade later when Argentina used one to sink the British destroyer HMS *Sheffield* during the war for the Falkland Islands. Executives of the giant French firm Aérospatiale, which built the Exocet, tried to persuade the Navy that it could save time and money by procuring their missile "off the shelf."

Ultimately the Navy decided it would neither purchase a foreign weapon nor develop its cruise missile on the basis of an existing American weapon. Instead, it would start its Harpoon program with a clean slate, ready to explore any avenue that seemed promising. The decision was a clear-cut victory for McDonnell Douglas, which now stood a good chance to win the development contract. General Dynamics had backed a losing technical alternative, but it decided nonetheless to compete with McDonnell Douglas for the contract.

GD's effort was handicapped by disagreements among its own personnel about which technical approach the company ought to push. Some employees wanted to promote a semiballistic missile like the Standard, which could be fired from a ship and would follow a low arc en route to the enemy target. The trouble with this concept was that the missile's guidance system would have difficulty identifying enemy ships against a background of water. The Navy was partial to the sea-skimming approach used by the Exocet, in which the missile flies low over the water and picks out its target against a background of sky. While some GD employees were pushing the Standard missile approach, others tried to fashion a proposal more in tune with the Navy's preferences. The internal dispute at GD was apparent to Navy officials during technical negotiations, and the Navy didn't like it.

General Dynamics's dilemma was not uncommon in the defense industry. Employees often become so wedded to an idea they have been developing for years that they can't bear to drop it, even after the idea has lost favor in the government. A company with shrewd management will "shoot the dissidents" or quickly reassign them, so that frustrated employees don't muddy communications between the company and its military customer. In this case, General Dynamics didn't shoot its dissidents. Diehard proponents of the Standard missile approach were kept on GD's cruise missile team.

*(4)*

The process by which companies are awarded development or production contracts varies from program to program but follows a general pattern. After a military requirement has been formally acknowledged, companies are invited to submit their ideas for fulfilling it, along with a description of the management team they plan to assemble and the costs they expect to incur. The government's formal invitation is known as a Request for Proposals (RFP). Most defense contractors become familiar with the details of an upcoming RFP well before it is announced in the federal government's official bulletin of business opportunities, *Commerce Business Daily*. In some instances the government circulates draft RFPs to enable companies to comment before final versions are issued.

If a contractor's intelligence network has been working, the firm may have been able to influence the definition of the military requirement. Also, if its representatives have been talking to the right people in the program office, it may have been able to shape the language of the formal RFP to favor its proposal. And if the company's reps have been unusually persuasive, they may have helped draft an RFP that virtually "wires the contract" by specifying a technical solution that only one company—*their* company—has the expertise to deliver.

After competing companies have submitted their proposals, separate panels of government specialists are established to evaluate the voluminous documents. A group of engineers and technicians will review the companies' technical ideas, auditors and financial experts will evaluate the cost estimates, and a third panel of program officials will study the contractors' management proposals to assess how committed the companies are to this particular weapons project. Have they suggested innovative technical solutions? Will they assign their best employees to this program? Have they devoted adequate production facilities and manufacturing equipment to this task?

If the government is selecting a company for an advanced development contract and if no prototype of the proposed weapon is available yet for evaluation, procurement officials may have to choose the winning contractor on the basis of proposals alone. More commonly, program officials first invite executives from the competing companies to separate technical negotiation sessions. There company representatives can defend their proposal, answer the program manager's questions, and listen to the government's concerns.

After the program office has reviewed submissions and grilled competing companies, a separate source selection evaluation board gathers additional information and prepares evaluation reports that award points for each aspect of the proposal. These evaluation summaries are forwarded to another panel of senior officials, the source selection advisory council, that consolidates the information, compares the proposals, and recommends a winner. The final decision is made by one top official, known as the source selection authority, who has not been a member of either panel. When a major weapons contract is being awarded, the civilian secretary or the head of the service's procurement organization usually serves as the final source selection authority.

Contrary to popular belief, the selection process is generally objective and fair. Because the members of both panels and the source selection authority usually have not communicated with the competing contractors, they are able to reach independent judgments, unaffected by the natural pressures that arise in personal relationships. The selection process is further insulated by the fact that dozens—or hundreds—of Pentagon officials are involved in every major decision. Congressmen, contractors, and interested public officials occasionally try to influence the outcome of a source selection, but these efforts are most often futile. "What quite a few people don't realize, and wouldn't believe if I told them," said William Perry, the undersecretary of defense for research and engineering during the Carter administration, "is that the integrity of the source selection process is really maintained very well in the Pentagon." Legislators, lobbyists, and public officeholders have a better chance of affecting the size of an existing weapon's annual budget or of blocking an attempt by the Pentagon to cancel an ongoing program than they do of influencing the selection of a contractor for a new weapons system.

The government tries to choose the contractor with the best overall proposal. However, a particular aspect of the proposed new weapon sometimes takes on more significance during the selection process than it deserves. In a tank program, for example, the ability of the tank's gun to lock onto a distant target while the vehicle speeds along bumpy terrain might become the chief focus of the selection process. In a cargo aircraft program the plane's ability to use rugged, "austere" runways might be credited with greater military significance than it deserves. In effect, the tail wags the dog. In much the same way, the guidance system for the Navy's Harpoon was treated as the most significant component during the source selection process. Any contractor that could sell the Navy on its guidance system could probably sell its whole cruise missile. General Dynamics recognized the opportunity and tried to capitalize on it.

It selected as subcontractor for its guidance system Bendix, a firm that had also been chosen to develop a sophisticated new guidance system for an unrelated program. GD probably believed that naming Bendix as a subcontractor would enhance its proposal in the eyes of the source selection advisory council. The reverse was true. Guidance specialists on the council reacted negatively to GD's obvious ploy. McDonnell Douglas was declared the winner and awarded a contract to develop the Navy's new Harpoon antiship cruise missile.

While the Navy was initiating its Harpoon program in response to technical breakthroughs and the sinking of the *Elath,* the Air Force was beginning a cruise missile effort for different reasons. The Air Force had been relying on its Boeing B-52 Stratofortress bombers as the air-breathing leg of the country's strategic triad since 1955.* U.S. nuclear strategy has long depended upon three distinct weapons systems (triad) that can deliver nuclear warheads on the

---

*The term "air-breathing" refers to either manned aircraft or cruise missiles that are powered by air-breathing jet engines, as opposed to land-based or submarine-launched intercontinental ballistic missiles that are powered by rocket engines.

Soviet Union: manned penetrating bombers, land-based intercontinental ballistic missiles (ICBMs), and submarine-launched ballistic missiles (SLBMs). There is no magic reason, of course, why the United States needs three different delivery systems, but it has become an article of faith among strategic planners that three complementary systems will deter a Soviet nuclear attack whereas one or two "legs" might not.

As the B-52's aged during the 1950's and 1960's and the Soviet Union improved its air defenses, the Air Force leadership believed it had to take steps to ensure the viability of its manned bombers. To that end, it began deploying on its bombers missiles containing electronic decoys that would confuse Russian defense officials by showing up on Soviet radar screens as B-52's. In 1967 SAC, which operates the nation's strategic bombers, concluded that even its most advanced decoy, the Quail, had grown obsolete and a better decoy was needed. This set the stage for a new Air Force decoy program, one that would incorporate the latest advances in microprocessors and small jet engines.

While these new decoys were confusing Soviet radar, B-52 bombers would be able to launch nuclear-tipped air-to-surface missiles such as the GAM-77 Hound Dog or the newer short-range attack missile against targets in the USSR. The bombers would also be able to penetrate Soviet airspace and deliver conventional bombs on enemy targets. The decoy program was formally titled the Subsonic Armed Cruise Decoy and more commonly known as SCAD.

The birth of SCAD illustrates two unwritten rules of the weapons business. First, the development of a new technology frequently leads to the creation of a new weapon that can exploit that technology. Secondly, a weapon is more likely to win the support of a military service if it doesn't directly threaten that service's primary military mission.

The development of SCAD began with technological breakthroughs made by the Williams Research Corporation, a small engine manufacturer based in Walled Lake, Michigan. Williams had developed an air-breathing turbofan engine that was far smaller and more powerful than any predecessor. It had begun working on its engine in the mid-1960's, under a contract with the Defense Advanced Research Projects Agency (DARPA), a corporate R&D lab for the Defense Department. Williams was trying to design an engine small enough to strap around a man's waist, à la Buck Rogers. The jet flying belt project never came to fruition, but Williams's efforts pushed compact engine technology to a new plateau. The Defense Department had an impressive engine on its hands, but no weapon to wrap around it. Like the proverbial vacuum waiting to be filled, the engine sat begging to be used. It soon dawned on the Air Force that it could install a Williams engine in a cruise missile decoy.

The original concept behind the Air Force's cruise missile decoy—to make a B-52 bomber less vulnerable to Soviet air defenses—posed no particular threat to the *raison d'être* of the Strategic Air Command. At first the new decoys seemed to enhance the value of manned bombers. It was only when the cruise missile came to be seen as a possible substitute for the manned bomber that the Air Force became alarmed. "The Air Force would always describe the cruise missile as 'a useful adjunct to the manned bomber,' " recalled a retired Air Force colonel and former cruise missile program manager. "It was never viewed in the Air Force as a replacement to the manned bomber."

Ever since World War II the ability to fly strategic bombers into Soviet airspace and deliver nuclear attacks on the USSR has been the hallowed mission of the U.S. Air Force. Generations of American pilots have spent their careers in SAC paying homage to the mystique of the manned bomber.

It is no exaggeration to say that a threat to the special role of the manned bomber is viewed by many Air Force officers as a direct attack on the soul of their organization. "We all felt—we all *knew*—that the Strategic Air Command had a manned bomber, and by God, they were going to have a manned bomber for years to come," said one retired officer. It was this kind of stiff institutional resistance that the SCAD cruise missile had to buck in 1972.

The Boeing Company of Seattle, Washington, which had built the B-52 bombers and the short-range attack missiles they carried, was awarded the Air Force contract to develop SCAD. Williams was brought on as a subcontractor to supply its impressive new engine.

Thus, by the early 1970's the Navy and Air Force had initiated parallel efforts to design cruise missiles, each with a different military mission and neither particularly welcomed by the service that was building it.

The SCAD program limped along in its early years with small budgets and little support in Congress. The Air Force tolerated its fledgling SCAD program but resisted all recommendations to improve the decoy's accuracy. If its accuracy were improved, SCAD might be useful as an *attack* missile as well as a decoy, and that possibility was too much for the Air Force to accept. Above all else, the service wanted to ensure the future of its new strategic bomber, the B-1, which was still in development, and bitterly opposed anything that jeopardized the B-1's chances of succeeding the B-52. Thus, when SCAD program officials recommended fitting their new decoys with nuclear warheads, the Air Force reluctantly agreed to arm only enough to force the Soviet Union to take the incoming decoys seriously.

Meanwhile, the submarine branch of the Navy was getting itchy for a specially designed cruise missile of its own. If the surface admirals could have an antiship cruise missile, why not the submariners? Vice Admiral Rickover had his own motives for promoting the development of a large tactical cruise missile that could be launched from a submarine. He envisioned a cruise missile larger than a Harpoon, some thirty inches in diameter, called an advanced cruise missile. It would be too fat to fit inside the torpedo tubes of the Navy's latest SSN-688-class attack subs. Instead, a behemoth new submarine, powered by a huge 60,000-horsepower nuclear reactor, would be required to carry them.

Appearing before the Defense Subcommittee of the House Appropriations Committee in 1971, Rickover called his proposed cruise missile-carrying submarine the "single most important tactical development effort the Navy must undertake." Some of Rickover's critics at the time accused him of being more interested in promoting the huge new attack submarine than the new cruise missiles it would carry.

One of his allies was Joe Williams, Jr., now a retired vice admiral. Like Rickover, Williams had no real incentive to develop a new cruise missile that could fit, with its wings folded, inside the twenty-one-inch torpedo tube. "I was a little bit biased in that because I really didn't want to get it down to twenty-one inches," Williams acknowledged years later. "If I got it down to twenty-one inches, I knew I'd have to live with the ship I had, the torpedo tubes I had, and the environment in which we were working."

Despite Rickover's support, or perhaps because of it, the proposal for a new submarine was dropped a year later. Admiral Zumwalt, the CNO, had opposed Rickover's recommendation. "Zumwalt didn't want Rickover's big missile because he didn't want Rickover's big submarine," explained a retired Navy officer. Once the idea of a 60,000-horsepower submarine had been dropped, little more was heard from Rickover on behalf of the advanced cruise missile.

Weapons programs do not develop in isolation. To flourish, they usually need active boosters within their own military service, within the OSD, and within Congress. On rare occasions, however, events that unfold outside the procurement community can play an important role in a new weapon's popularity. Such was the case when Harpoon and SCAD, two equally obscure and unsupported programs, got swept up in the politics of the Strategic Arms Limitation Talks (SALT).

On May 26, 1972, at a summit meeting in Moscow, President Richard Nixon and Soviet leader Leonid Brezhnev signed two documents known collectively as SALT I: a treaty limiting the antiballistic missile (ABM) systems each country could operate and an interim agreement setting a cap on their offensive strategic weapons. The treaty had to be ratified by the U.S. Senate. Henry Kissinger, then Nixon's national security adviser who had helped hammer out SALT I with the stubborn, hard-nosed Russians, still had to persuade two equally obstinate power centers: the Pentagon and the Senate.

To accomplish that, Secretary of Defense Melvin Laird had to placate the Joint Chiefs of Staff (JCS) with concrete proof that the United States wasn't about to disarm unilaterally. Public endorsement of SALT I by the JCS was crucial if the agreement was to have any chance of Senate approval.

Like the Joint Chiefs, Laird had a long history of mistrusting the Soviet Union. He got his start in politics in 1946, successfully campaigning *in his Navy uniform* for a seat in the Wisconsin State Senate. During eight terms in Congress, including long service on the defense appropriations subcommittee that he eventually chaired, Laird polished his image as a hard-line defense expert.

Now, as Nixon's first secretary of defense, Laird wanted to send a stern warning to Moscow. He asked his weapons analysts to identify some strategic weapons programs already in development that could be accelerated in a highly visible way. Two candidates were immediately obvious: the B-1 bomber, being developed by Rockwell, and the new Trident nuclear-powered ballistic missile submarine, taking shape at GD's Electric Boat shipyard. Laird submitted to Congress in June 1972 a supplemental budget request for $1.2 billion to speed up the two weapons. "Laird's position is that the Trident submarine and the B-1 bomber projects, in particular—which have a collective long-term price tag of at least $25 billion—were under way before the [SALT I] accords were signed and that they are necessary to eventually replace current Polaris-type submarines and B-52 bombers to preserve the U.S. deterrent," *The Washington Post* reported.

A third candidate for "acceleration" was less obvious: something Laird's weapons specialists were calling a strategic cruise missile—a cruise missile with a range long enough to deliver a nuclear warhead on targets in the Soviet Union. This would be different from the Navy's Harpoon, which was intended to attack enemy ships, with a maximum range of about seventy miles. It would also be different from the Air Force's SCAD, which was still viewed as an electronic decoy to help protect a penetrating B-52 bomber. Actually Laird's strategic cruise missile didn't exist, but the concept seemed to offer something for everybody.

Kissinger favored a strategic cruise missile because it would provide him with a valuable chip he could trade for some Soviet concession during the upcoming SALT II negotiations. He would later kick himself for supporting the new weapon when Defense Department officials became committed to strategic cruise missiles and stubbornly refused to surrender them. "Those geniuses," Kissinger once said, gesturing across the Potomac River toward the Pentagon, "think the goddamn thing is a cure for cancer and the common cold."

Two different staffs within the OSD supported the strategic cruise missile for different reasons. The Office of the Director of Defense Research and Engineering (DDR&E), the unit that oversaw the services' weapons programs, had long been a home for high-tech solutions to military requirements. The strategic cruise missile appealed to its officials because it allowed the United States to challenge Soviet weaponry in terms of quality rather than quantity.

Another unit within the OSD, the Office of Program Analysis and Evaluation (PA&E), also favored the strategic cruise missile. PA&E was the lineal descendant of the Office of Systems Analysis established by John Kennedy's defense secretary, Robert McNamara. The "whiz kids" who had arrived with McNamara brought a new religion to Pentagon decision making, the gospel of systems analysis. "Scientists and economists invented new techniques of systems analysis, linear and dynamic programming and game theory," wrote Arthur M. Schlesinger, Jr., "devising ingenious tools by which to formulate problems, break them down, distinguish alternatives, establish their quantitative equivalents, compare the effects of different decisions and seek the most favorable results in situations characterized by a great mass of variables."

In determining if a particular weapon should be developed, for example, OSD decision makers identified, for the following year and for the life-span of the program, all projected costs for the weapon itself as well as for its spare parts, maintenance, and logistical support. Then they tried to quantify the benefits that would be realized from that weapon, in terms of such factors as firepower, durability, and ease of handling. By comparing the cost-to-benefit ratio calculated for that weapon with cost-to-benefit ratios for other options, McNamara's analysts arrived (in theory, anyway) at the most "rational" weapons choices. In essence, comparison shopping had replaced gut instincts.

The fact that some benefits defied quantification rarely deterred the systems analysts. For many years the "whiz kids," such as Charles Hitch, Harold Brown, and Alain Enthoven, bamboozled the older generals and admirals with their bewildering analyses and statistical sophistry. By the early 1970's, however, systems analysis had lost much of its mystique. One of the few remaining strongholds of such cost-benefit studies was the downgraded and renamed PA&E.

Today PA&E serves as a home for maverick thinkers and independent weapons analysts who act as thorns in the sides of the military, poking holes in proposals sent to the OSD by the services and defense contractors. As one reporter put it, PA&E "is supposed to act as the manure separator for the defense secretary and his top civilian deputies."

When asked by Laird to suggest weapons to include in his saber-rattling supplemental budget request, PA&E also recommended the strategic cruise missile. It saw the long-range cruise missile as a relatively inexpensive weapon that could be carried by stand-off aircraft and still penetrate Soviet air defenses —a cost-effective alternative to the Air Force's expensive B-1 bomber. To PA&E, the strategic cruise missile would be a bargain-basement weapon that could bolster the arguments against a new bomber.

The Navy had an indirect interest in the strategic cruise missile. It had begun work on the Harpoon, but that tactical antiship missile program was not being generously funded by Congress. Some admirals figured their tactical cruise missile could benefit from many of the same subsystems developed for the strategic missile, in effect, hitching a ride with the better-funded strategic program.

There was another reason why the Navy supported the strategic cruise missile. Under SALT I the United States agreed to a ceiling on the number of SLBMs it could carry aboard its submarines. Each time the Navy sent new Trident SLBMs to sea aboard a new Trident submarine, it was required to retire some of the older SLBMs carried by its aging Polaris subs. Ultimately its ten oldest Polaris subs would be stripped of their SLBMs and rendered obsolete. Cruise missiles, however, weren't covered under this SALT I ceiling. The Navy could replace old SLBMs with new strategic cruise missiles without violating the agreement. In effect, the strategic cruise missile program might help save the Navy's Polaris fleet.

The Air Force wasn't alarmed by Laird's original plan because the strategic cruise missile would be launched only from Navy ships. At first the new missile appeared to pose no threat to the Air Force's cherished B-1.

Thus, the notion of a strategic cruise missile (SCM) won support in a surprising number of Washington power centers. Laird asked Congress for $20 million to initiate an SCM program in addition to the $1.2 billion requested for the B-1 bomber and Trident submarine.

"Congress was not sympathetic to the request for funds to begin SCM development—only $6 million of the $20 million request was appropriated— but Laird had his new program, Kissinger his bargaining chip, DDR&E a new toy, PA&E an entering wedge for a standoff bomber and initial work on a cost-effective weapon, the Navy a *Polaris*-saver and peg on which to hang its sought-after tactical cruise missile, and the Air Force its freedom to ignore the whole thing," wrote Henry D. Levine in *Public Policy*.

*(5)*

Laird and his staff hadn't gotten all they wanted on Capitol Hill, but the ball was rolling. Admiral Williams remembered how word reached the Navy. "When Laird got back down from there, they called the Navy and said, 'Start that cruise missile program,' and that was the birth of Tomahawk." The year was 1972. Navy Captain Walter Locke, the deputy program manager for the Harpoon missile, was chosen to head the new strategic program, which was later named the Tomahawk sea-launched cruise missile (SLCM, pronounced "slick-em").

In the decade that followed, Locke established himself as the most knowledgeable and widely respected cruise missile expert in the government. Trained as an engineer at the Naval Academy, he had worked aboard a destroyer, with a carrier-based fighter squadron, and with an aircraft flight testing group prior to joining the Harpoon program. He was a savvy technologist, whose disjointed thinking and rambling conversations often camouflaged his sharp intelligence. Some detractors have criticized Locke for trying to run the complex Tomahawk program as a one-man operation, but everyone agrees he was deeply committed to cruise missiles and extraordinarily successful in inspiring others to share his dream.

Defense contractors are traditionally cautious about competing for new weapons contracts. Their marketing representatives, engineers, designers, and financial analysts can spend millions of dollars to prepare an elaborate bid and proposal (B&P)—much of it at the company's expense—with no guarantee of winning anything. Worse yet, after all that company effort, the program itself might fizzle out or be canceled. Contractors are hesitant to get involved with a new weapons program if they doubt it has enough support within its own service, in the OSD, or in Congress to thrive.

Sometimes defense contractors don't have to risk their own money on early research and development work on a new weapons program. They can spend money allocated to it by the Defense Department under a controversial program called Independent Research and Development (IR&D). Under this program, the Defense Department tries to inspire innovation and competition by allowing its major defense contractors to perform research work in areas of their choosing. The companies' expenses are considered reimbursable overhead costs. That means the Pentagon pays the contractor for its IR&D work, just as it pays for other legitimate overhead expenses, such as telephones, maintenance, and utilities.

The suggested research must have some potential military relevance to qualify for reimbursement, a somewhat loose standard that most proposed

IR&D work seems to meet. "More than 90 percent of the IR&D projects undertaken annually are directly relevant to DOD interests," Richard DeLauer, President Reagan's first undersecretary of defense for research and engineering, told Congress in 1982.

The amount of IR&D money available to each company is directly related to the size of the production contracts it received during the previous year. Huge companies, working on major production contracts, receive the largest portion. Any company allocated more than $4 million in IR&D funds must reach an advance agreement with the Defense Department that spells out its planned projects for the coming year. These agreements are less formal than a traditional Pentagon development contract, which specifies the tasks a company must carry out. In fiscal year 1983 approximately $1.5 billion was paid to contractors as IR&D reimbursements, compared with direct R&D contracts that totaled $6.3 billion.

The net effect of the IR&D program is to provide a pool of government money that contractors can use for a variety of development efforts, but critics of the program claim the Defense Department and the services are lax in ensuring that IR&D money is spent on relevant military research. "What is to prevent a turbine manufacturer from studying fruit flies since fruit is eaten by the piccolo player of a military band?" asked Admiral Rickover, an ornery opponent of "ill-founded and wasteful" IR&D expenditures. "What if the contractor decides to develop a new blend of coffee—obviously this would have a potential relationship with the eating habits of the military." Rickover and others have accused the Pentagon of neither screening nor supervising IR&D projects carefully enough. The admiral has recommended that the Defense Department finance relevant military research exclusively through direct contracts, not through IR&D reimbursements.

The IR&D program doesn't enable the Pentagon to control the defense industry's R&D agenda as rigidly as it could with direct contracts, but supporters claim IR&D reimbursements offer other advantages. The Pentagon pays approximately one-third of its contractors' total expenditures for independent military *and commercial* research. The remaining two-thirds of those costs come out of the companies' pockets. For its one-third reimbursement, however, the Pentagon gains some influence over—and significant access to—most of the IR&D work its contractors perform.

More than a dozen contractors were interested in Tomahawk. Like its competitors, General Dynamics tried to foresee the future market for cruise missiles. David Lewis saw a mixed picture. On one hand, he sensed that cruise missiles might one day represent more business to GD than the nuclear-powered submarines Electric Boat was building. On the other hand, he was concerned that both the sea-launched and air-launched versions were likely to run into stiff opposition in their respective services. Lewis wasn't certain which version would ultimately emerge with the larger budget.

GD initially focused on winning the Navy's Tomahawk contract, but the possibility of capturing the air-launched version was never far from Lewis's mind. (GD eventually won contracts for sea-launched, air-launched, and ground-launched versions of the cruise missile.)

Boeing had been awarded the Air Force contract to develop the SCAD decoy. It stood a good chance of winning the Tomahawk award as well. McDonnell Douglas, which the Navy had chosen earlier to design its Harpoon antiship missile, would be a third strong contender.

Designing a cruise missile that could be launched from a submarine involved enormous technical obstacles. "It had to fly like an airplane, swim like a fish, and be handled as roughly as a steel bar," explained Captain Locke. Inside the submarine the cruise missile would be handled roughly by crewmen, like an ordinary steel-enclosed torpedo. Once ejected from the torpedo tube, it would be propelled by a booster rocket to the surface of the water, at which time its turbofan engine would take over for the duration of the flight. Thus, one challenge was making the missile strong enough to withstand rough handling and possible enemy depth charge explosions but light enough to fly. No projectile fired from a torpedo tube had ever flown more than 25 miles, yet this cruise missile was expected to fly 1,500 miles.

Locke decided to "pick the brains" of the aerospace business by awarding study contracts of approximately $100,000 each to several companies that hoped to devise a technical solution. Twelve companies expressed an interest in the Navy's RFP. The list read like a Who's Who of the defense industry: Bendix, which had built the Talos ship-launched missile first fired in 1959; Boeing, the diversified civilian and military aircraft manufacturer that had won the Air Force's SCAD development contract; the Goodyear Aerospace Corporation, which had developed the submarine-launched SUBROC missile for use against enemy subs; Grumman, an aircraft builder on Long Island, New York, the fortunes of which had long been tied to the U.S. Navy; the Lockheed Missiles and Space Company, which had built the Navy's Polaris and Poseidon SLBMs and had won a contract to develop a larger, more powerful Trident SLBM; Martin Marietta, the predecessor of which, the Martin Company, had built the Matador "pilotless bomber" in the late 1940's as well as a derivative known as Mace; McDonnell Douglas, which had developed the Quail decoy that SAC deemed obsolete and which was now working on the Navy's Harpoon; North American Rockwell, which had built the strategic

Hound Dog missiles deployed on B-52's since 1961, six years before North American Aviation merged with Rockwell-Standard and a dozen years before the enlarged corporation took on the name Rockwell International; Northrop, the aggressive Los Angeles-based fighter aircraft manufacturer that had developed Snark, the first U.S. missile of intercontinental range; Teledyne Ryan, which built some of the best target drones in the world; and the Vought division of the Texas-based Ling-Temco-Vought (LTV) conglomerate, which had developed the Regulus sea-launched missile.

The twelfth company to express interest was General Dynamics. GD's Pomona division picked up the RFP, but the Convair division in San Diego took over the project in midstream and actually submitted the company's proposal. Perhaps that was because Convair was in greater need of defense work at the time. The San Diego plant was building commercial DC-10 fuselages under a subcontract to McDonnell Douglas as well as Atlas and Centaur space boosters for NASA, but it wasn't nearly as busy as GD's Pomona division. The Pomona facility east of Los Angeles was churning out several variants of its successful Standard surface-to-air tactical missile as well as prototypes for a shoulder-fired antiaircraft missile called Stinger and a new "close-in" shipboard gun system known as Phalanx.

Six of the twelve companies eventually submitted proposals to the Navy. After Locke's program office had eliminated Goodyear because it had virtually no experience designing aircraft, the field was narrowed to five semifinalists, which were awarded three-month study contracts running from December 1972 through February 1973. Boeing, Lockheed, McDonnell Douglas, Vought, and General Dynamics each received nearly $100,000 from the Navy to design a Tomahawk sea-launched cruise missile.

Locke sought innovative technical solutions in a novel way. Rather than invite representatives from the Navy's various weapons laboratories (who would probably suggest ideas that had originated with the competing contractors), he called in the company representatives themselves. Each company was allowed to brief the Tomahawk program office on its proposed approach for one hour and then answer questions for another hour. Locke's method served two purposes: It enabled the Navy to evaluate the rival companies, and it signaled the defense industry that the Navy was, indeed, committed to this new strategic cruise missile program. The approach illustrates a key point: A program office often has to sell its weapon within the government and the defense industry just as vigorously as contractors have to sell their products to the Pentagon.

Each of the semifinalists received about $100,000 from the Navy, but all five spent far more than that—perhaps as much as half a million dollars apiece—

from their pool of IR&D money. They were willing to dip into those funds because they believed they were getting a clear message from the Navy that a full-fledged cruise missile program lay just ahead.

Other observers sensed that the Defense Department had not yet decided what kind of cruise missile it wanted. The situation was certainly confused. The Air Force was developing a decoy but resisting any suggestion to upgrade SCAD into an armed, long-range cruise missile that could attack Soviet targets. The Navy, until recently, had been funding three overlapping efforts: the Harpoon antiship cruise missile, Rickover's short-lived advanced cruise missile, and the strategic cruise missile. Even after the latter two had been consolidated and renamed Tomahawk, the Navy and Air Force seemed headed in divergent directions.

As with every weapons program, rival contractors speculated endlessly about the possible motivations of the OSD and the services. The Boeing Company, for example, thought it saw some logic behind the Defense Department's apparent confusion over cruise missiles. Boeing reasoned that the OSD was interested primarily in obtaining an air-launched rather than sea-launched strategic cruise missile. An air-launched missile could be fired from a stand-off aircraft flying outside Soviet territory. Such a missile would have to penetrate Soviet air defenses to hit key targets in the USSR, but the pilot could remain safely out of range of Russian surface-to-air missiles.

The Air Force's adamant resistance to an air-launched cruise missile made the OSD's task more difficult but not impossible. In Boeing's scenario, the OSD was supporting a sea-launched naval missile as a temporary ploy to pressure the Air Force into the cruise missile field. The OSD knew that interservice rivalry would compel the Air Force to pursue an air-launched cruise missile if only to avoid yielding the field exclusively to the Navy. Eventually the Air Force would bend to the OSD's pressure and initiate a competing strategic cruise missile program.

Once the Air Force had entered the picture, Boeing executives speculated, a series of events would unfold. The Air Force would capture the strategic cruise missile mission from the Navy, and support would dry up for the sea-launched Tomahawk. The Navy would then cancel its Tomahawk, leaving the program's defense contractors out in the cold. In Boeing's view, Captain Locke's Tomahawk program didn't have much of a future.

On the basis of such reasoning, the company decided in the spring of 1973 to drop out of the five-way competition for the Tomahawk development contract and instead concentrate on winning the development award for an air-launched cruise missile *if* the Air Force ever chose to build one.

A confrontation between the OSD and the Air Force grew imminent. During the early 1970's, while the Navy was making technical progress on its Tomahawk, the Air Force was dragging its feet on its decoy program, SCAD. The OSD decided to twist the Air Force's arm. The Defense Systems Acquisition Review Council (DSARC), evaluating the SCAD program in 1973, ordered the Air Force to develop a long-range armed version of SCAD in addition to its decoy version. Those orders were precisely what the Air Force didn't want to hear. The more potent SCAD became, the more it might erode support on Capitol Hill for the B-1 bomber.

The Air Force retaliated with two new studies of its SCAD program. One concluded that the B-1 would be able to foil Soviet air defenses even without SCAD, thus reducing the necessity for the pesky little cruise missile. The other study indicated that the projected overall cost for SCAD had more than doubled between January and July of 1973, from $285 million to $700 million, making it much less attractive. This forecast came as little surprise. The military services can be remarkably candid with pessimistic cost estimates when it serves their purpose.

As expected, Boeing won the Air Force's prime contract to develop SCAD. Williams and Litton were signed as subcontractors to supply the engines and inertial navigation systems respectively. Boeing had played its cards astutely, dropping out of the Tomahawk competition to concentrate its energy on the Air Force's program.

But the Air Force and Congress were growing increasingly disenchanted with SCAD. In the summer of 1973, with the Air Force's quiet acquiescence, Deputy Secretary of Defense Clements, a millionaire oil driller from Texas, yielded to congressional pressure. He cut $50 million from SCAD's $72 million budget request and pushed the program back to an earlier stage of development. A month later the Defense Department moved to kill SCAD altogether. Clements may have looked like an opponent of cruise missiles, but he soon established himself as the Defense Department's strongest supporter of these new, cost-effective weapons. In some circles he was even dubbed the Godfather of Cruise Missiles.

With his blessing, the Navy was handed the lead on all cruise missiles. The mission of its Tomahawk missile was suddenly broadened to include launches not only from submarines but also from airplanes and possibly from surface ships. "Here we are, in the summer of '73," recalled Locke, then head of the tiny Tomahawk program office, "and we're the only game in town." *Aviation Week & Space Technology* magazine noted that the engine, guidance system, and decoy package used in the decimated SCAD program were still compatible and might be used in a redesigned cruise missile. "Chances are, however, they would be used in a Navy-sponsored family of missiles if they are re-constituted," the trade publication predicted.

The Air Force responded to Clements's order by suspending its contractors' work in a clever way. It terminated Boeing's contract to develop the decoy version of SCAD as well as Litton's contract for the navigation system. But it issued only stop-work orders for the two SCAD contracts that might some-day lead to an air-launched cruise missile: Boeing's contract to design the SCAD airframe and Williams's contract to build its engine. Unlike termina-tion notices, stop-work orders were considered temporary. Boeing and Wil-liams could hold together their engineering and design teams in the hope that the stop-work orders might soon be lifted.

If the Air Force were coerced by the OSD to develop a strategic air-launched cruise missile (ALCM, pronounced "al-kum"), it could promptly "turn on" its contracts with Boeing and Williams by lifting the stop-work orders. There would be no need for revised RFPs or the selection of new contractors. The Air Force was trying to have it both ways. It hoped to resist the OSD's pressure to initiate an ALCM. But if it had to yield, it wanted to revive Boeing and Williams quickly to keep ahead of the Navy's Tomahawk program.

Boeing wasted no time building a case for a strategic ALCM with Kis-singer's National Security Council staff. Boeing executives pointed out that an ALCM would be a valuable weapon—and a useful bargaining chip—when the United States entered the next round of SALT negotiations with the Soviets. Cruise missiles had not been prohibited under the SALT I agreement, the company emphasized, and recent technological improvements made their de-velopment scientifically possible and politically desirable.

At least partially as a result of Boeing's energetic marketing, Kissinger encouraged the Air Force to revive its cruise missile program. In July 1973 Kissinger recommended to Clements that the United States proceed with a long-range version of the cruise missile. "I argued to Clements that a long range bomber-launched cruise missile program makes sense strategically and could help our SALT position," Kissinger later wrote. Clements enthusiasti-cally agreed, and in the autumn of 1973 the Air Force finally yielded. It resuscitated its SCAD effort and renamed it the air-launched cruise missile. The Air Force's decision was a triumph for Boeing and a direct challenge to the Navy's Tomahawk. Even the name of the missile represented a victory for Boeing, which had been actively promoting a generic air-launched cruise missile around Washington and had become identified with that phrase.

In one sense, Deputy Secretary Clements had achieved his primary goal: inducing the Air Force to develop an air-launched cruise missile. In another sense, he had created a costly two-headed monster that some critics in Con-gress refused to support. Why should taxpayers sponsor parallel efforts by the Navy and the Air Force to develop similar strategic cruise missiles? To placate these cost-conscious critics, Clements pledged that both cruise missiles would use many of the same components and subsystems to save money.

"We would have *commonality*," Clements later recalled, using a beloved Pentagon buzz word. "The guidance system, the engine, and the fuel cell would be exactly the same in both missiles. That means, from a production standpoint, it's very cost-effective. And you're using existing systems; you're not starting a brand-new ball game."

The ALCM program utilized much of the early design and test work already completed for SCAD. This didn't please the Navy. Both services wanted their programs to complete development and enter production as quickly as possible. The question that haunted Captain Locke was whether the Navy's Tomahawk had been used to manipulate the Air Force into starting its own strategic cruise missile program. If so, what would happen to Tomahawk once the Air Force's ALCM gained momentum? Would the OSD step in and cancel the Navy's program?

By the spring of 1973 Captain Locke had set aside that troubling question in order to concentrate on his Tomahawk semifinalists: Lockheed, McDonnell Douglas, Vought, and General Dynamics. Locke didn't have enough money in his budget for additional tests or development work, but he wanted more data from the four contractors to help him select his two finalists. He invited the companies to use the wind tunnel facility at the Navy Ship Research Development Center in Carderock, Maryland, to test the Tomahawk models they had built at their own expense. "We will pay for the wind tunnel if you bring your models," he told the four contenders. "We'll let you play in our backyard if you bring the toys."

As noted earlier, one of the trickiest design problems of the Tomahawk was making it sturdy enough to withstand rough treatment and enemy depth charge explosions but light enough to fly thousands of miles. Three of the contenders proposed encasing a heavy steel cruise missile inside a protective capsule that would fall away like a banana peel once the missile had been launched. General Dynamics had the clever idea of encasing a much lighter *aluminum* cruise missile inside a rugged stainless steel capsule that could withstand any rough handling by the sub's crewmen. The entire unit would be loaded inside the torpedo tube, but the stainless steel capsule would remain behind when the cruise missile was fired. "This was a joke in the eyes of the Navy at the outset," GD's Lewis remembered. "But we wanted a missile that could fly a long way. We were looking right then at the idea of carrying the things on an airplane."

After evaluating the four companies' proposals, the program office whittled the field to two finalists and awarded GD and Vought development contracts for $1 million each. Intense competition began in January 1974. Each company was asked to build ten prototype missiles that would compete in a carefully supervised fly-off. The prototypes would undergo shock tests that simulated depth charges, wind tunnel tests, electronic tests that measured the radar "cross sections" they emitted, and underwater launches from mock torpedo tubes. This phase of development and testing was to consume more than two years.

The problem created by having separate cruise missile programs under development in the Air Force and Navy was coming to a head. Some OSD officials, having successfully pressured the Air Force into building its own cruise missile, were ready to kill the Navy's Tomahawk just as Locke had feared. Others favored long-range air-launched cruise missiles in both services. Still others called for a *joint* program office that would develop a common missile for both services.

A meeting of the DSARC was scheduled in February 1974 to resolve this question and determine how far each program had progressed. On the basis of the council's recommendations, Deputy Secretary Clements would decide if one service, or both, would continue developing strategic cruise missiles. He would also determine if either program was ready to pass Milestone Two and move from advanced development into full-scale engineering development.

Most DSARC meetings at the time were chaired by the director of defense research and engineering within the OSD, then a former Hughes Aircraft Company executive named Malcolm Currie. The meetings were usually held in conference room 1E-801 No. 7 in the Pentagon's basement. This meeting, however, was chaired by Clements himself. It was held in a private conference room between his and Defense Secretary James Schlesinger's offices on the third floor of the Pentagon's outermost corridor, known as the E ring, over-looking the Tidal Basin and the Washington Monument.

Boeing executives hoped Clements would bar the Navy from working on an air-launched variant, leaving that mission exclusively to the Air Force. It also hoped for Clements's permission to begin full-scale development of its ALCM. GD and Vought, still competing in the Tomahawk fly-off, pegged their hopes on the Navy program.

As usual, the service representatives, Navy Captain Locke and an Air Force colonel, arrived with Vu-Graphs, flip charts, and upbeat, positive attitudes. The OSD officials sitting around the table adopted skeptical, tight-fisted postures. Whenever Locke and his Air Force counterpart highlighted the strengths of their programs, the OSD interrogators focused on areas of doubt or weakness.

Even so, Captain Locke was satisfied with his presentation. He was confident that the Navy had accomplished more in recent months than the Air Force. Locke knew that the fly-off he was staging between his two finalists would please Clements, who strongly favored competition among contractors. The Air Force's decision to award the ALCM prime contract to Boeing without further competition was unlikely to please the deputy secretary.

As the meeting progressed, it became clear that the Air Force didn't have enough data on hand to document its technical progress. Its request to enter full-scale engineering development seemed to be unraveling. An enthusiastic fan of cruise missiles, Clements was bothered by what he sensed was a reluctance by both services to build them. In particular, he didn't trust General David Jones, soon to become the Air Force chief of staff and later the chairman of the JCS, to support the ALCM program. "Davey Jones fought the program every way in the world he knew how to fight," Clements recalled years later.

## (6)

After the DSARC meeting, but before Clements's decision was announced, hundreds of defense industry executives and government officials gathered at a strategic weapons symposium in Monterey, California, sponsored by the American Institute of Aeronautics and Astronautics. At one point during the conference a handful of somber Boeing employees gathered in a corporate hospitality suite to discuss the recent DSARC meeting that would determine the fate of their air-launched cruise missile. One observer likened the Boeing executives to a group of bereaved mourners.

Having plunged optimistically into cruise missiles, Boeing braced for the ramifications of Clements's decision: the cancellation of its program. Even if the ALCM survived, its chances of progressing into full-scale development seemed remote. The situation was grim, but the Boeing executives weren't ready to give up. They enlisted the help of an assistant secretary of defense. He agreed to speak with Clements on Boeing's behalf when the deputy secretary arrived in Monterey to address the symposium.

Clements had seriously considered canceling the Air Force's ALCM program, a move Boeing vehemently opposed. He also had considered amalgamating the Air Force and Navy cruise missile programs under a joint office that would develop a common missile for both services. Since the Navy had already begun working on sea-launched, ground-launched, and air-launched versions of its Tomahawk missile, it would have been the logical service to head such a joint office. Boeing vigorously resisted this idea as well, convinced that its ALCM would suffer if the Air Force's program were subsumed within a Navy-run joint office.

Hoping to head off Clements's decision, Boeing turned to its longtime champion, Senator Henry Jackson, an influential Democrat from the company's home state of Washington. Jackson bypassed Clements and pressed Boeing's case directly with Defense Secretary Schlesinger. Like many defense secretaries before him, Schlesinger listened closely to the "senator from Boeing."

Schlesinger and Clements were strong-willed men, whose policy disagreements occasionally surfaced in public. In this instance, however, Clements yielded to Schlesinger and decided not to cancel Boeing's ALCM program. The company wasn't able to dictate Clements's final decision, but it accomplished the next best thing. It ambushed the most intolerable aspects of the decision and delayed the final announcement for three months. By that time many of the most onerous parts of Clements's ruling had been forgotten within the Pentagon bureaucracy.

When Clements's official directive finally appeared, ALCM had been kept alive, and the Air Force left in charge. Boeing—and the other foes of a joint program office—had triumphed. Clements hadn't approved the Air Force's request to move its ALCM program into full-scale development, but that was only a temporary setback. At a second DSARC meeting in December 1974, the ALCM again was to be considered for full-scale development.

Clements's decision was a mixed blessing for the Air Force. On one hand, it was a victory because the Air Force preferred not to have the Navy dominate cruise missile development. On the other hand, the Air Force wanted to be rid of cruise missiles altogether. But that wouldn't happen, the Air Force realized, until Bill Clements left the Pentagon.

The Air Force's ALCM program was scheduled for review by the DSARC in December 1974 to see if it was ready for full-scale development. The Navy's Tomahawk was slated for an informal program review at the same meeting. As the DSARC session approached, familiar arguments for canceling the ALCM or establishing a joint program office were heard again within the OSD.

Clements didn't attend this DSARC meeting but met privately with the council's chairman, Malcolm Currie, immediately after it had broken up. Within an hour the rumor that Clements had decided to cancel Boeing's cruise missile and to create a Navy-run joint office was circulating among Washington's cruise missile community.

Boeing moved swiftly. The company urged the Washington State congressional delegation to appeal directly to the White House to reverse Clements's decision. Fortunately for Boeing, the DSARC had convened shortly after a summit meeting between Soviet leader Brezhnev and Gerald Ford, who had assumed the presidency in August. That summit had been held outside the

Siberian port city of Vladivostok at the Okeanskaya Sanitorium, a health spa that Ford described later as looking like an abandoned YMCA camp in the Catskills. As he walked the grounds of the sanitorium, Secretary of State Kissinger may not have appreciated the ALCM's technical complexities, but he recognized the weapon's political utility at this delicate moment in U.S.-Soviet diplomacy. He wasn't about to abandon the ALCM unilaterally.

Meanwhile, Boeing was presenting several arguments on behalf of its ALCM: The United States should confront the USSR with more than one cruise missile threat; the sea-launched Tomahawk version wouldn't fit on a B-52 bomber; it was necessary to maintain competition among defense contractors; and a decision to cancel the air-launched version might indicate that the United States lacked the political resolve to match the Soviet Union's steady arms buildup. For Kissinger, the most compelling argument was the Kremlin's obvious nervousness about these new American missiles. Kissinger was never a diehard supporter of U.S. cruise missiles, but if Moscow was so worried about the new weapons, he certainly wasn't going to take them lightly.

It was agreed at Vladivostok that the United States and the Soviet Union should each be allowed to deploy no more than 2,400 "strategic delivery systems," a term that proved difficult to define. The United States said the agreed-upon ceiling covered ICBMs, SLBMs, and strategic bombers, but *not* cruise missiles. The Soviets maintained that cruise missiles were included. As long as the disagreement persisted, Kissinger felt the United States could continue developing its strategic cruise missiles.

The events in Vladivostok plus Boeing's lobbying efforts turned the tide. Clements's decision to cancel the ALCM was overruled by Schlesinger before it was officially announced in January 1975. ALCM had survived another round, but again it wasn't a total success for Boeing. The DSARC decision paper, signed by Malcolm Currie, declared that the missile would not move ahead to full-scale engineering development until it had proved itself technically. Moreover, while the Air Force and Navy programs would continue to function separately, the two services were instructed to develop common guidance systems, common engines, and common nuclear warheads. Clements was trying to cut costs, win supporters in Congress, and carve a permanent niche for cruise missiles in the Pentagon's defense budget.

The requirement for subsystem commonality meant that the Air Force would have to use the same contractor the Navy chose to build the Tomahawk's guidance system (either McDonnell Douglas Astronautics or E-Systems) and that the Navy would have to rely on the Air Force's engine subcontractor, Williams Research. Not surprisingly subcontractors squeezed out of the running were unhappy. Selection of a common nuclear warhead attracted far less interest in the defense industry because all U.S. nuclear warheads were produced in two government-owned laboratories: Lawrence Livermore in California or Los Alamos in New Mexico. Ultimately Los Alamos was chosen as the supplier of warheads for both cruise missile programs.

Meanwhile, the Navy still had to choose between two contenders to build its Tomahawk. It turned out to be an easy choice. What began as a hotly contested race between GD and Vought for the full-scale development contract ended as a runaway. GD's prototype missile easily outperformed its Vought rival throughout the fly-off, culminating in a series of test launches in early 1976 from simulated torpedo tubes at the Naval Undersea Center at San Clemente, California. On one test flight GD's cruise missile burst from the submerged torpedo tube, "its booster engine spewing brilliant red-orange flame like a Roman candle," and flew gracefully over the test range for about two miles. "GD's tests were very successful," recalled Captain Locke. "Vought's tests were a failure."

To make matters worse for Vought, the cost of its faltering development program had run way over budget. Locke could have provided the Dallas-based aerospace firm with additional funds, but he chose to terminate Vought's effort instead.

Ten days later, in March 1976, GD was selected as the prime contractor to develop the Navy's Tomahawk. McDonnell Douglas Astronautics and Williams were subsequently chosen to provide the guidance systems and engines respectively. GD was awarded $34.8 million to "integrate" McDonnell Douglas's guidance system into its airframe so the missile could maneuver itself for the first time during a test flight the following month. That initial Tomahawk contract may have looked puny in GD's defense portfolio, compared with the company's F-16 and submarine orders, but it provided a toehold in what has grown into a multibillion-dollar market.

Jimmy Carter's electoral victory in November 1976 left Clements only a few months to secure the future of cruise missiles. He knew the Air Force and Navy still resented these weapons. Both services were trying to perfect their missiles as quickly as possible, but Clements knew they could just as easily cancel their programs once a new Democratic administration had taken over, and he sought to prevent this. He hoped to leave his mark at a final DSARC meeting on cruise missiles scheduled for January 6, 1977—two weeks before Carter's inauguration.

Both programs had been making progress. It was time for Clements to answer some critical questions: Was the Air Force's air-launched cruise missile ready to enter full-scale development? Should the ALCM or an air-launched version of the Navy's Tomahawk be deployed on B-52 and B-1 bombers? Over what range, and on what kinds of missions, should the ALCM be flown? Should a joint program office be established to consolidate both efforts?

The members of the DSARC, who were to wrestle with these questions, took their seats around the conference table in room 1E-801 No. 7. Each participant brought along his personal biases as well as the institutional interests of the Defense Department office he represented.

Malcolm Currie, the director of defense research and engineering (DDR&E), held the job of "Mr. Technology," the Pentagon's traditional link to the defense industry. DDR&E coordinates the development and production of weapons by the military services. It's the director's responsibility to say no to a service when one of its weapons fails technically. However, it's also his responsibility to prod new weapons off the drawing board and onto the battlefield. DDR&E usually has resolved this inherent conflict by acting more like an accelerator than a brake. Often a technical expert, with long experience in industry, the director is expected to be an innovative official whose Pentagon staff nurtures high-tech answers to military problems.

Also at the table was the chairman of the Cost Analysis Improvement Group, an influential OSD office that provides independent estimates of what it will cost to design, build, and operate a weapons system. Most cost estimates are provided to the OSD by the program manager responsible for the weapon on the basis of figures supplied by the company that will build it. Historically these estimates have been too low, partly because program managers and contractors have a vested interest in optimistic forecasts and partly because engineers, as a group, are usually confident "can-do" professionals who sincerely believe they can meet ambitious cost targets.

Cost Analysis Improvement Groups, known as CAIGs, were established in the OSD and the services to supply decision makers with alternative cost estimates. Because CAIGs aren't responsible for developing individual weapons, their cost estimates—which usually are higher than the program manager's—often are considered more objective. "Historically CAIGs were rather accurate in their estimates," says former Undersecretary William Perry, who valued their contribution at DSARC meetings. "I would take an input from the CAIG as being a better judgment of cost than the inputs I was getting from the service."

However, CAIGs are not infallible. They must rely on individual weapons program offices to provide the contractors' latest estimates of labor, material, and overhead costs, but these offices are notoriously reluctant to supply such information. As a result, CAIGs sometimes have no firm basis except their own experience on which they can calculate a weapon's future cost.

Clements's cruise missile decision paper was issued hastily a mere six days before Carter moved into the White House. In it he acknowledged that the council had again considered killing Boeing's ALCM in favor of a common airframe. "In spite of the acquisition cost savings which would accrue from such a course of action, I have decided that a common airframe for all applications may impose unnecessary and unwarranted performance compromises on both weapons systems," Clements concluded. Instead, he decided to stick with separate airframes produced by Boeing and General Dynamics. That was the good news for Boeing and the Air Force.

The bad news came next. Clements finally established a Joint Service Cruise Missiles Program Office to oversee all U.S. cruise missile efforts. The Navy was designated the lead service, and Captain Locke was named the first director of that office. Clements expected the new office to save money by merging two service test programs into one, by purchasing common components in larger quantities at cheaper prices, and by consolidating the overlapping Navy and Air Force management staffs. He knew that both services would find it more difficult to cancel the program if it were managed by a joint office.

Clements's final DSARC decision also permitted several variants of the missile to enter full-scale development. These included the ALCM-B, which could fly more than 1,500 nautical miles (a nautical mile is about 15 percent longer than a standard mile); the Tomahawk's land-attack version, which could be launched from subs or surface ships and boasted a similar range; and the Tomahawk's antiship variant, which could be fired from most combatant ships.

The decision to name Walter Locke, still only a Navy captain, as the joint office's first program manager immediately alienated the Air Force. Locke was generally considered the government's top cruise missile developer, but the Air Force was miffed that a mere captain, rather than a Navy admiral or an Air Force general, was handed the top job. The Air Force certainly wasn't going to assign its preferred candidate for the job, a general officer with considerable ALCM experience, to work as a subordinate to a Navy captain.

There was also the mundane issue of geography. The Air Force's cruise missile offices were located at Wright-Patterson Air Force Base in Dayton, Ohio. The Navy's were located in Washington, D.C. Initially joint program officials had to shuttle back and forth. To establish joint offices, dozens of employees would have to be relocated, but neither Air Force nor Navy personnel felt inclined to move. Bureaucratic foot dragging and inescapable red tape made progress excruciatingly slow for the newly established joint cruise missile office. An edict had been handed down by the deputy secretary of defense, but it seemed that neither service paid very much attention.

Cruise missiles, the weapon neither service originally wanted, had come a long way during the Nixon and Ford years. But it would be the Carter presidency that propelled these wonder weapons to the forefront of strategic thinking.

## (7)

Jimmy Carter's election had a profound impact on the development of cruise missiles. The President's defense advisers and cruise missiles seemed made for each other. The transition team that prepared the new administration to take over at the Pentagon was briefed by Captain Locke. "It was not only the first but one of the best briefings we got," recalled one member of the team.

The cruise missile, particularly the air-launched version, fitted the new President's political needs. During the 1976 campaign Carter had frequently criticized the B-1 bomber, then being developed by Rockwell International, as too costly and militarily unnecessary. Cruise missiles could provide the perfect rationale for canceling the B-1. As Commander in Chief, however, the former engineer vowed to set aside his campaign oratory and carefully weigh the pros and cons of the expensive new bomber.

The policy question confronting Carter in the spring of 1977 was familiar. How could the United States ensure the viability of the air-breathing leg of its strategic triad? The Air Force remained steadfast in its support of the B-1 bomber, but some cost-conscious analysts in the Pentagon supported an alternative stand-off bomber—such as Boeing's B-52 or GD's FB-111—that could fire air-launched cruise missiles from well outside Soviet airspace.

Cruise missiles were cheaper, safer, and more difficult for enemy radar to detect, these analysts argued, so why risk a human pilot and an expensive B-1 aircraft? The Air Force's retort was always the same: Manned bombers are flexible, they can be called back if the military situation suddenly changes, and, most important, they are piloted by men who can exercise human judgment.

To help Carter reach his decision, Defense Secretary Harold Brown provided him with reports, more than an inch thick, with diagrams, charts, and statistics that described what he considered the two "militarily sustainable" options. On Monday, June 27, three days before he went public with his decision, Carter told Brown he was leaning toward canceling production of the B-1, as Brown had recommended.

At 10:30 A.M., on Thursday, June 30, the President strode into room 450 of the Old Executive Office Building, next to the White House, for his tenth presidential news conference and told reporters that he had decided to cancel production of the B-1 bomber. The announcement stunned the journalists and most of the members of official Washington, who for weeks had assumed that Carter might prune the Air Force's request for 244 B-1 aircraft but wouldn't terminate the program altogether. The pundits reasoned that the prime contractor, Rockwell International, and such subcontractors as General Electric, Boeing, Goodrich, and Bendix had operations in forty-eight states. The B-1 had been the Air Force's top priority for years. And major weapons programs are virtually never canceled.

Carter's decision was particularly surprising because it had been kept so secret. Normally a presidential decision of this magnitude would have leaked to the press. Congress had been kept in the dark until Carter telephoned Speaker of the House Thomas "Tip" O'Neill an hour before his press conference. The military was kept guessing until just before the announcement, when Defense Secretary Harold Brown telephoned General George Brown, chairman of the Joint Chiefs, with the news.

President Carter's announcement was even more stunning because it placed a heavy emphasis on the strategic utility of the air-launched cruise missile, a relatively new weapon most people hadn't even heard of. The President had concluded that long-range air-launched cruise missiles mounted on existing B-52 bombers would be more cost-effective than new B-1 bombers at $100 million apiece. "I think that in toto the B-1, a very expensive weapons system basically conceived in the absence of the cruise missile factor, is not necessary," he told reporters. The President may have calculated that promoting cruise missiles at the same time that he was killing the B-1 would dissipate some of the political heat.

Carter's decision had all sorts of repercussions. At Rockwell International in California, where about 13,000 people were working on the B-1 program, company executives estimated that at least 8,000 employees would be laid off. Representative Robert Dornan, the Republican who represented the congressional district where the B-1's would have been built, reacted bitterly. "They are breaking open the vodka bottles in Moscow," complained the former TV talk show host.

Praise for Carter's decisiveness echoed through other corridors on Capitol Hill. "Three cheers for the President," said Senator Frank Church of Idaho. "We can now avoid squandering $100 billion on the 20th century version of the Spanish Armada." Senator George McGovern of South Dakota was equally pleased, hailing the President's announcement as "a historic event— a choice on a weapons system based not on momentum, Pentagon lobbying and contractor pressure, but upon a rational analysis of what our security requires."

In fact, Senator McGovern wasn't far off in his assessment. Carter made his decision only after he and Defense Secretary Brown had personally and thoroughly examined several strategic alternatives. As Brown saw it, the U.S. strategic posture needed improvement in several major areas. The sea-based leg of the strategic triad was in reasonably good shape. The Soviet Union couldn't locate submerged U.S. Poseidon submarines carrying SLBMs, Brown knew, but he was prudent enough not to place too much emphasis on that one delivery system. Existing U.S. land-based intercontinental ballistic missiles (Titans and Minutemen) were growing increasingly vulnerable to attack as Soviet ICBMs grew heavier and more accurate. Brown was most concerned about the bomber leg of the triad, which at that time consisted of 316 B-52's and 66 FB-111's.

The secretary's primary question was: Which of several options would be the most cost-effective way to bolster the air-breathing leg of the triad? The existing FB-111 bombers could be modernized with new engines, but he rejected that idea because the improved FB-111's would be no more cost-effective than the B-1. Even so, after Carter had canceled the B-1, the Air Force briefly resurrected the FB-111 idea, proposing to modify 65 existing FB-111's and build 100 new ones at a total cost of $7 billion—far less than the $24.8 billion price tag for the canceled B-1's. The Air Force's proposal garnered some support on Capitol Hill, but Representative Les Aspin of Wisconsin, then a former Pentagon analyst and congressional gadfly on defense issues and now the chairman of the House Armed Services Committee, scoffed at the idea. "This is an awfully expensive consolation for the Air Force's not getting the B-1 bomber," he remarked. The FB-111 proposal died a quiet death.

A second option was to upgrade SAC's B-52 bomber fleet, with new engines and larger bomb bays. This proposal also collapsed under its own weight. An improved B-52 bomber, dubbed a B-52X, would still present too large a cross section on enemy radar screens, Brown concluded, and the rebuilt B-52X's would be too expensive to operate. Also, the B-52X proposal was still at the paper study stage, and there was no guarantee the proposed improvements would be effective.

A third proposal was to develop an entirely new penetrating bomber that would cost less than the B-1 and fly at subsonic (slower than 700 miles per hour) rather than at the B-1's supersonic speeds. Brown concluded that development of any new plane would take too long to be practical and that the projected savings would probably prove illusory.

A fourth option was to install a large number of air-launched cruise missiles on wide-bodied cargo transport planes. These cargo planes, which would supposedly be cheaper than B-1 bombers, could stand off from enemy territory and safely launch their cruise missiles at distant enemy targets. Though the defense secretary was reluctant to put too many eggs in one basket by placing a large number of cruise missiles on only a few transport planes, he decided that this proposal warranted further study.

Ultimately Brown saw production of Rockwell B-1 bombers or installation of air-launched cruise missiles on updated B-52G's and B-52H's as the most promising alternatives.

The choice turned on Carter's assessment of what steps the Soviets might take to improve their air defenses during the coming two decades. In the summer of 1977 the Soviet air defense system included 10,000 surface-to-air missile launchers installed at more than 1,000 sites across the USSR that could fire both low-level and high-level missiles. In addition, the Soviets deployed more than 2,600 interceptor aircraft, including the MiG-25, that could fly at 80,000 feet and attack enemy aircraft below them with their advanced "look down, shoot down" radar.

Brown was impressed with the B-1's relatively small radar cross section, its electronic countermeasures equipment, and the way it handled at low altitudes. But he concluded that because cruise missiles could fly at even lower altitudes with even smaller radar cross sections, they were even more likely to penetrate Soviet air defenses.

"I have more confidence in our estimates of the effect that the low detectability of the cruise missiles will have on Soviet radars than in the effect that the B-1's radar countermeasures would have had," Brown later explained.

While the media focused most of their attention on the demise of the B-1 bomber, the Pentagon bureaucracy heard a different message: "Carter and Brown are serious about cruise missiles." Suddenly the lethargic effort to pull together a Navy-Air Force joint cruise missile project office took on a new urgency.

Carter's enthusiasm for air-launched cruise missiles suggested the existence of a well-organized weapons program, with an existing budget, a well-defined design, and an agreed-upon deployment date, known in the procurement community as the Initial Operational Capability (IOC) date. In fact, none of that existed. Boeing had already developed and flown a smaller, short-range cruise missile known as an ALCM-A, but the company hadn't designed an air-launched missile capable of flying intercontinental distances. No budget had been prepared, and no IOC date had been chosen.

Shortly after Carter's announcement the Air Force moved to rectify the situation. Lieutenant General Alton Slay, then head of the Air Force Systems Command, summoned a few cruise missile program officials from Wright-Patterson Air Force Base to his office for what they recalled as the "Night of the Knives." Pressed by General Slay, one of the Air Force's sternest taskmasters, the group worked around the clock for several days, creating the ALCM program from whole cloth. They analyzed cost estimates, drew up a budget, and translated SAC's performance requirements into technical specifications. "When we established the IOC of December of 1982, we did that in conjunction with the contractors," said retired Air Force Colonel Alan Chase, a former ALCM program manager. "We went back to them and said, 'All right, this is what we want. Can you develop it on this schedule?' They said, 'Yes.' "

By the time Carter announced the B-1's cancellation the Godfather of Cruise Missiles, Bill Clements, had left Washington to seek his political fortune in Texas. His role as the Pentagon's champion of cruise missiles was taken up by William Perry, the new undersecretary for research and engineering.

Brown and Perry worked together so closely for the next four years that it was often difficult for them to remember whose ideas were influencing whom. Both men were convinced the United States could enhance its strategic security as much by negotiating bilateral weapons reductions with the Soviet Union as it could by building new weapons. They also believed that true national security for the United States couldn't exist without a sturdy national economy, a belief that placed a ceiling on the amount of money the nation could reasonably allocate to its defense budget.

Both men believed there were better ways to strengthen U.S. defenses than simply to earmark more and more money for the Pentagon. "A very important way of doing that was getting leverage through technology," Perry explained a few years after leaving office. If the Defense Department couldn't spend the billions of dollars required to keep pace with the quantity of weapons the Soviet Union was producing, its next best option was to develop technologically superior weapons the quality of which could offset the Soviets' numerical advantage.

Perry considered the cruise missile a perfect example of a relatively inexpensive, technologically sophisticated weapon. He became its ardent, outspoken fan.

The undersecretary set out to organize the cruise missile program in a way that would reduce interservice rivalries, accelerate the development schedule, and cut costs. He reorganized the Joint Cruise Missiles Project Office that Clements had established. As already noted, Clements's decision to hand the leadership of the office to the Navy had raised the hackles of the Air Force. Perry took a different tack. He recognized that the Navy was more favorably disposed to cruise missiles than the Air Force and agreed that Navy Captain Locke was the right officer to head the joint effort. But to placate the Air Force, he reconstituted the office *without* any lead service.

Instead of reporting through the formal Navy chain of command, the reorganized office would report directly to a special executive committee within the OSD that was chaired by Perry himself. This extraordinarily simple arrangement totally bypassed the usual layers of military bureaucracy. Captain Locke would report directly to Perry rather than have to request money or technical guidance from his military superiors.

Perry established this unorthodox structure for a number of reasons. First, by establishing a joint program office that neither the Navy nor the Air Force controlled, he hoped to minimize the interservice rivalry that threatened the cruise missile program. Secondly, he figured it would be easier to transfer the air-launched cruise missile program back to the Air Force at some future date, as he had promised, if he set up the joint office with neither service in charge. Thirdly, Perry wanted to elevate the status of cruise missiles within the Pentagon bureaucracy. He knew that the influence any program manager can exert is directly related to the clout wielded by the person to whom he reports. A Navy captain, such as Walter Locke, traditionally exercises little influence in the inner councils of the Navy or the OSD, where admirals, generals, and political appointees hold sway. Wary of the lukewarm support for cruise missiles within the Navy and Air Force, Perry didn't want Locke reporting to either service's top officer. "It could either have been the chief of naval operations or the chief of staff of the Air Force, neither of whom I found acceptable," said Perry. "Or I could have Locke report to me, which is what I did."

By shortcutting the traditional chain of command, Perry increased the cruise missile program's visibility and prestige, but he also placed Captain Locke in a difficult position with the admirals who outranked him. The admirals were never sure what assignments Locke was accepting from Perry or what commitments he was making on behalf of the Navy.

As long as Perry was around to safeguard his cruise missile program and "protect" Captain Locke from predators within the Navy, everything proceeded smoothly. But when Perry left office with the rest of the Carter administration, Locke's days were numbered.

As history demonstrated, Carter's decision to cancel the B-1 was not the last word on Rockwell's bomber program. Carter had ordered a halt to the further *production* of bombers, but he hedged his bet by not cutting the Air Force's research and development funds for the B-1. So the wounded program limped along, waiting for a savior.

Carter's defeat in 1980 brought just such a savior, in Ronald Reagan. One of Reagan's first decisions on moving into the Oval Office in 1981 was to revive the production of the B-1 bomber.

*(8)*

Carter's interest in a long-range air-launched cruise missile spurred General Dynamics into action. GD sensed that the real money was now to be found in air-launched cruise missiles rather than in its Tomahawk version, so it sought permission to compete with Boeing for the Air Force's ALCM production contract. Naturally Boeing resisted the idea, arguing that it had already developed SCAD and ALCM and that competition at this stage was unnecessary. But Boeing soon discovered that it is difficult to lobby against competition.

GD offered compelling reasons for competition: It had already demonstrated much of the technology required for ALCM in successful demonstration flights of its Tomahawk, and a head-to-head competition between GD and Boeing might inspire more creativity and lower costs from both companies.

General Dynamics's final argument was, perhaps, its most persuasive. Shortly before he had announced his B-1 decision, President Carter screened a film in the White House that showed GD's Tomahawk going through a series of impressive test launches and terrain-hugging flights. Insiders are convinced the film helped sell Carter on cruise missiles. "That was our film President Carter saw," GD representatives argued as they prowled the Pentagon. "Besides, we already have a long-range cruise missile—the SLCM. We should be allowed to compete."

GD prevailed. In September 1977 Perry announced a competitive fly-off for the ALCM production contract. GD was awarded a full-scale development contract from the Air Force, so it could "catch up" to Boeing.

The fly-off was unusual in several respects. First, it was rare for a military service to award a full-scale development contract to more than one company. Generally contractors compete at the advanced development stage, and only the winner is funded for full-scale development. Secondly, it was unusual to have a Navy contractor try to modify a Navy weapon for an Air Force mission. To accommodate this unusual situation and minimize Air Force bias, Perry decided that half the military men who would help select the Air Force's ALCM contractor would be Navy officers. Finally, both companies had good reason to think their opponent enjoyed a tactical advantage. General Dynamics was concerned that the Strategic Air Command might automatically favor Boeing, which had already produced SAC's B-52 bombers, the existing ALCM prototype, and its predecessor SCAD. GD worried that Boeing also had far more experience catering to SAC's maintenance requirements.

Boeing, meanwhile, was worried that GD's Tomahawk might be farther along technically than its own ALCM. If GD could successfully adapt its sea-launched missile for launches from an aircraft, Boeing might have a tough battle on its hands. Furthermore, because GD had a larger cruise missile business than Boeing, thus a larger base across which to spread its overhead, GD might be able to price its air-launched missiles more cheaply. Boeing also worried that Walter Locke, a Navy captain, might favor his Navy Tomahawk's prime contractor, General Dynamics.

Perry spoke with an anxious senior manager from Boeing before the fly-off began. "We're being set up," the executive said fretfully. "How can we possibly compete in this program? General Dynamics has already built a full-range missile. They've already flown it a number of times. We're just being brought in to give the appearance of competition." Confident that the source selection would be fair, Perry told the manager to quit whining about Boeing's supposed disadvantages and get on with its development program.

At the outset, GD probably had more reason than Boeing to worry. Many Air Force officials were indeed leaning toward Boeing's candidate whether they admitted it or not. Many of the civilian engineers at the Aeronautical Systems Division in Dayton, who had worked with Boeing for years, were wary of GD's belated entry into the ALCM program. "For a long period of time, my most senior engineer was referring to GD and Boeing as 'them' and 'us,' " recalled Colonel Chase, the former ALCM program manager.

However, as the fly-off got under way and government officials began working closely with both companies, many of those early biases seemed to dissolve. When Boeing's first ALCM prototype crashed and GD's succeeded, Air Force officials sensed they might have a real horse race. "As we proceeded through flight tests, we could see that these guys were pretty much neck and neck," said Colonel Chase. During the fly-off each company launched ten prototypes and each suffered four crashes or system failures. "I wouldn't call it a public relations success," admitted Undersecretary Perry.

An elaborate source selection bureaucracy within the Air Force scored both missiles on several criteria before forwarding its recommendation to the source selection authority, Air Force Secretary Hans Mark. At stake was an Air Force production contract for about 3,400 ALCMs worth about $4 billion.

In March 1980 Mark took the podium in room 2E-781 of the Pentagon, the cramped hall used for Defense Department press briefings, and announced that Boeing had won. The final scores for the two cruise missile contenders had been very close. But as David Lewis had predicted when GD entered the fly-off, Boeing had an edge and was able to keep it. "We figured that if we did well and Boeing did well, we'd lose," Lewis recalled.

The reasons for Boeing's victory are difficult to pinpoint, in part because the Pentagon is usually so worried about legal protests from losing contractors that it makes very little information available about the rationale for its source selections. Nevertheless, a debriefing document that was read to GD representatives following their ALCM loss sheds some light on the decision.

Air Force officials told GD that its ALCM prototype had too large an infrared signature, which might allow the missile to be spotted by enemy sensors; that its computer software might be difficult to integrate into the nation's overall strategic battle plan, known as the Single Integrated Operation Plan (SIOP); that its quality assurance program was weak; and that SAC and other Air Force agencies were worried by GD's inadequate logistics planning.

The document didn't mention the most important reason for Boeing's triumph: cost realism. The cost proposals Boeing and GD had presented in the spring of 1979 were comparable, and both seemed reasonable. But when the two contractors submitted their best and final offers on October 22, 1979, Boeing's price rose slightly, while GD suddenly cut its price by more than 20 percent. The dramatic reduction was a red flag to the source selection officials, who were sensitive to the possibility that one or both contractors might try to buy in to the ALCM program with an unreasonably low bid.

Leonard Buchanan, the general manager of GD's Convair division, claimed his division could trim its missile production costs substantially by implementing several cost-cutting manufacturing techniques. But his explanation didn't wash with the source selection panels. "It was too late, and it wasn't believable," recalled Colonel Chase. Buchanan may have sensed that GD was about to lose the fly-off anyway and lunged for victory with a surprisingly low offer. If so, his strategy failed. Some Air Force officials considered GD's last ALCM bid a blatant buy-in attempt. Others thought it was simply a tactical error. "It was a mistake," said Chase. "It was a real mistake."

Generally the reasons one company beats out another for a major weapons contract are *very technical*—and not terribly interesting. Back room deals, in which political wheeler-dealers play a significant role, are extremely rare. The source selection process is designed to distribute authority widely, rather than concentrate it in a single individual. The final choice of a winning contractor is based on hundreds of separate evaluations that can't be inordinately influenced by a few people, whether they are high or low in the source selection hierarchy or outside it altogether.

In the ALCM source selection, for example, neither GD nor Boeing was able to exercise any undue leverage over the Air Force's final choice. "No doubt they were talking to everybody they could to try to influence the decision," recalled Perry. "But in fact, my estimate was that they had zero influence on the decision, other than the influence they had through the way they conducted their programs."

Once Boeing had been declared the winner, the question arose whether it would produce *all* the ALCMs or a second source contractor would be brought into the program to build some of the missiles from its designs. Naturally Boeing favored the former approach and GD the latter. Perry and other OSD officials who wanted to maintain continued competition between two prime contractors favored a leader-follower approach, in which Boeing would become the leader and a second contractor, presumably GD, would become the follower. "It is anticipated that the ALCM production quantity will be split approximately 65/35 percent *if* the leader-follower concept is chosen," said one internal OSD memo.

The Air Force acknowledged that awarding production contracts to two rival companies might hold down costs. "Leader-follower production in the out years could ensure continuing benefits of competition as each contractor would control costs to retain a share of the production," an internal memo observed. But the Air Force ultimately recommended that Boeing be awarded a sole source prime contract and that competition be ensured by awarding subcontracts to two different companies for each of the ALCM's major subsystems: the mainframe, the engine, and the guidance system. Perry resisted that recommendation, but the DSARC ultimately decided to accede to the wishes of the Air Force. Boeing would serve as prime contractor for the 3,418 ALCMs the Air Force planned to buy.

From its inception the Navy's procurement strategy for the Tomahawk cruise missile emphasized competition among contractors. This reflected Locke's conviction that defense contractors perform best—at the lowest possible price—when forced to compete with each other for as long as possible. As noted earlier, the initial field of twelve companies was narrowed then to five that received study contracts and finally to two finalists: General Dynamics and Vought. The two contractors were asked to develop and demonstrate working prototypes of their cruise missiles. The company that won the full-scale development contract, General Dynamics, was never guaranteed a sole source contract to produce *all* the sea-launched cruise missiles.

The procurement strategy laid out by the Navy (and adopted by the Joint Cruise Missiles Project Office) always entertained the possibility that a second source contractor might be added to share the production of SLCMs with General Dynamics. The possibility of a second source supplier (some contractors consider it a veiled threat) provides the government with useful leverage should it become displeased with its contractor's performance.

On the Tomahawk program, competition appeared to end with the selection of General Dynamics to enter full-scale development. GD confidently expected to remain the exclusive supplier for years to come. In fact, executives at GD's

Convair division seemed to take their Tomahawk contract for granted. Their cavalier attitude irritated officials in the Joint Cruise Missiles Project Office, who felt GD wasn't paying enough attention to their program. GD executives seemed to be spending most of their time peddling F-16 fighters at home and abroad. Perhaps that was understandable. As of 1980, the Carter administration wasn't planning to buy that many sea-launched cruise missiles, so GD stood to make a lot more money selling F-16's than Tomahawks.

The long-range outlook for cruise missiles began to change when Ronald Reagan became President in 1981. The Navy decided to increase its total Tomahawk purchase from 522 to 644 missiles soon after John Lehman took over as secretary, and it hinted that the total might grow much larger. As the profit potential for the Tomahawk grew, so did GD's interest in it. By the time the Navy decided to procure almost 4,000 GD had fallen in love with sea-launched cruise missiles.

Unfortunately its fondness manifested itself too late. Rear Admiral Locke —he was promoted from captain in 1978—recommended that a second source contractor share the production of the Tomahawk with GD. Locke calculated that the increased size of the Navy's Tomahawk purchase justified the extra cost of setting up a second production line. More important perhaps, Locke was dissatisfied with the quality control at GD's San Diego plant. He figured he could hold GD's feet to the fire by allowing a competitive contractor to build Tomahawks from GD's designs. His decision illustrates how the government can use competition when all else fails.

The transition from full-scale development to production is often troublesome for a defense contractor. In the advanced development phase, a handful of specialized designers and engineers collaborate closely to fashion the initial working prototypes. During full-scale development the company assembles its manufacturing equipment and prepares to produce the new weapon in large quantities but still builds just a few prototypes. It's only when the company begins production that it relies on thousands of factory workers to perform complex production operations. The transition from a few highly skilled specialists to factory employees requires close supervision if the quality of each finished weapon is to remain high. One misplaced wire, one loose screw, or one poorly fitted component can make a missile malfunction.

As GD made this transition on the Tomahawk, the Navy noticed a distressing drop in quality control. When this occurs, the government can take a prescribed series of steps to rectify the problem.

The first step is taken by on-site representatives of the Defense Contract Administration Service (DCAS), the agency of the Defense Department that administers current defense contracts. DCAS personnel monitor a contractor's work, help solve production bottlenecks, supply historical cost data to contracting officers negotiating new contracts with the same company, and generally serve as the Pentagon's eyes and ears in a contractor's plant.

DCAS officials at GD's Convair division believed that some of the technical problems plaguing the Tomahawk missiles were caused by employees who relied on the company's poorly written work instructions. As a result, at least one worker was assembling his part of the Tomahawk incorrectly.

DCAS officials were particularly annoyed by these problems because they sensed that nobody at GD was taking the quality assurance problem seriously. Convair's general manager, Leonard "Buck" Buchanan, listened to the government's complaints but took few positive steps to correct the problem. "Buchanan's mentality is technology, engineering, and marketing, and he's good at that," said GD's David Lewis. "He did not enjoy solving the problems of production."

Repeated failures delayed production of the missile. Finally, in June 1982, the DCAS issued a Method D action against GD, essentially suspending work under the Tomahawk contract until the company met certain government quality control standards. Few companies had ever been hit with a Method D, the toughest action the Pentagon can take short of canceling a contract.

GD suddenly woke up. A company "gold team," comprised of engineering and quality control specialists, was flown into San Diego to correct the production problems at Convair. David Lewis spent a week in San Diego, examining the operations at Convair and other GD divisions but paying closest attention to the Tomahawk program. GD acted too late.

Locke recommended that the Navy choose a second contractor to share production of the Tomahawk with GD. The Navy could run an open competition for a second source, but to save time, Locke instructed GD to turn its designs over to McDonnell Douglas, the firm that was already building the navigation and guidance systems for the Tomahawk and ALCM programs and was the prime contractor on the Navy's Harpoon missile.

The decision was a stab in the back to GD. Under the new arrangement McDonnell Douglas was given access to GD's designs and production techniques for the Tomahawk airframe and assembly and was guaranteed at least 30 percent of each year's production award. GD would be guaranteed another 30 percent of each year's contract. And the two firms would submit competitive price quotations each year for the remaining 40 percent.

At the same time GD was made a second source to McDonnell Douglas on the guidance and navigation systems. So competition on the Tomahawk, which seemed to have ended with the awarding of full-scale development contracts

10. A Tomahawk sea-launched cruise missile built by General Dynamics being
test-fired from the deck of the battleship *New Jersey* in 1983. GD's
development of the cruise missile began with the sea-launched version but
has since extended to ground-launched and air-launched models as well.
*Department of Defense*

years earlier, was restored after the missile had entered production.

For a while GD's role in the Pentagon's cruise missile program seemed to
be diminishing, but the company came roaring back. In 1983 the Air Force
decided to cut short its production of Boeing's air-launched cruise missile in
favor of a newer version with a reduced radar signature. Boeing, Lockheed,
and GD vied for the unexpected advanced cruise missile contract, and GD
won the competition. GD was already building ground-launched cruise missiles (GLCM, pronounced "glick-ems") for the Air Force, which were placed
in Western Europe in 1983 despite widespread protests. GD now has a piece
of all three cruise missile programs—a remarkable conclusion to the story of
a weapon that, at first, nobody wanted.

# Chapter Eight
## The Fighting Falcon

### (1)

General Dynamics's F-16 Fighting Falcon has become one of the most widely praised aircraft ever developed by the Air Force. Begun as little more than a "flying test bed" for emerging aircraft technologies, GD's YF-16 prototype was a lightweight, highly maneuverable aircraft viewed as a threat by the Air Force's senior generals, who preferred the more expensive, more capable F-15 Eagle. Defense Secretary James Schlesinger had to twist the Air Force's arm to get it to evaluate new lightweight fighters.

GD's YF-16 prototype won a fly-off against Northrop's YF-17 and was selected as the Air Force's new lightweight fighter in 1975. Five months later, in what was billed as the Deal of the Century, the Fighting Falcon triumphed again when it was chosen by four NATO allies over the rival French Mirage.

The sleek, supersonic strike fighter has become GD's most reliable money-maker in the past decade, adding more than $250 million to the company's profits in 1984 alone. The Air Force and GD signed a multiyear contract in 1982 for the purchase of 480 fighters over four years for about $3 billion—the first time the service committed itself for more than a single year to a major aircraft procurement. Another agreement, for an additional four years, has extended that multiyear program through 1989.

Soon after the first prototype was rolled out of GD's Fort Worth aircraft factory in December 1973, the plane was hailed as a fighter pilot's fighter.

"What you've got," said one enthusiastic pilot, "is the biggest best engine with as little as possible for it to carry." When it was introduced in the mid-1970's, the F-16 was just over forty-seven feet long, weighed about 22,800 pounds at takeoff, could exceed Mach 2 (twice the speed of sound), and could fly more than 2,000 miles without refueling. Neal Anderson, a GD test pilot who flew the original prototypes, described the sensation of sitting in the F-16's bubble-covered cockpit: "You feel like you're riding on top of the airplane . . . you feel it might run out from under you . . . it's like driving the world's fastest drag racer."

GD has sold more than 2,900 F-16's to the U.S. Air Force and eleven foreign countries and expects to sell at least another 1,100 in the years ahead. "The F-16 is in worldwide demand," noted T. R. Milton, a retired USAF general, "thanks in part to some expert showcasing by the Israelis." Highly skilled Israeli pilots used F-16's and F-15's to attack an Iraqi nuclear reactor in 1981 and to destroy numerous Syrian antiaircraft weapons in 1982. The company's Fort Worth division, which has built thousands of bombers and fighter-bombers since World War II, consistently leads every other division in sales and profits. With production continuing at peak levels and additional foreign orders expected, "the F-16 is living up to expectations as one of the most significant fighter programs of the decade," concluded DMS Inc., a defense market research firm.

The origin of the "world's fastest drag racer" and its selection by both the U.S. Air Force and a consortium of four European nations illustrate the unpredictable path a major weapons program can follow from the drawing board to the runway. The history of the F-16 demonstrates how an aircraft that began life as a technology demonstrator can evolve into a full-fledged production program, how competing defense contractors adopt different marketing strategies to sell their weapons, how the Air Force's choice of fighters was affected by the prospect of a multibillion-dollar sale in Europe, how the rivalry between the Air Force and Navy prevented the two services from agreeing on a common fighter, and how the original F-16 has been continually modified.

The plane emerged as the solution to several problems confronting the Air Force in the late 1960's. Cost overruns, schedule delays, and poor performance had hampered many of the service's aircraft programs during that decade, thwarting its efforts to keep pace with the Soviet Air Force. To counter Russia's most advanced fighters, the Air Force was developing the McDonnell Douglas F-15 Eagle, a Mach 2.5 aircraft, armed with heat-seeking and radar-guided missiles that could fight in darkness as well as daylight. The Eagle would be an impressive machine, but as its price tag escalated, Air Force officials recognized that they couldn't afford to deploy enough of the twin-engine planes to keep up with the relentless Soviet assembly lines.

Responding to the dilemma, a small group of weapons analysts, engineers, planners, and former fighter pilots within the Pentagon began promoting the concept of a less expensive, lightweight fighter as an affordable alternative, or "little brother," to the F-15. This group, which became known as the Fighter Mafia, envisioned a highly maneuverable fighter that could challenge Soviet aircraft during daylight hours in one-on-one aerial dogfights.

The concept of a lightweight fighter fitted into a broader procurement philosophy—the "high-low mix"—that was gaining support in defense circles during the late 1960's. The idea behind this philosophy was that the Air Force needed both *high*-performance fighters to compete against the most capable Soviet fighters and *low*-cost aircraft that could be procured in large quantities.

The members of the Fighter Mafia concerned themselves with more than the rising price of new fighters. They were also alarmed at what seemed an almost unstoppable trend: For decades U.S. fighters had been growing larger and heavier. Each new generation of aircraft required more interior space to house increasing quantities of electronic hardware. Extra space meant added weight, which meant bigger engines. Heavier fighters required more sophisticated mechanical systems to manipulate their aerodynamic control surfaces, which added yet more weight.

The McDonnell Douglas F-104G, for example, which entered service in the early 1960's, weighed about 29,000 pounds at takeoff. Later variants topped the scales at more than 50,000 pounds. And at the end of the 1960's General Dynamics's troubled F-111A fighter-bomber weighed in at about 70,000 pounds. The only exception to this trend toward heavier fighters was Northrop's F-5A fighter, a veritable pip-squeak at about 20,000 pounds—and it was developed primarily for foreign sales.

Soviet fighters were traditionally much lighter. MiG-15's and MiG-17's, which began flying in the late 1940's and early 1950's, weighed only about 15,000 pounds; the MiG-21 fighters of the late 1950's reached about 20,000 pounds.

In the 1950's and 1960's the U.S. Air Force relied largely on F-4 Phantom II and F-105 Thunderchief fighter-bombers, the tactical advantages of which over Soviet fighters were range and sophisticated electronics rather than maneuverability. Soviet fighters at the time were primarily defensive. They were relatively short-range aircraft built to outmaneuver U.S. fighters at close range. U.S. fighters, by contrast, could fly long distances and were able to strike far from their bases. "We were going for lower thruster weight in the aircraft and higher wing loading, so we could get better cruise efficiency," recalled Henry

Stachowski, a long-range planner at the Aeronautical Systems Division at Wright-Patterson Air Force Base. "The Soviets weren't worried about cruise efficiency," he added. "They were going for a higher thruster weight and lower wing loading."

The design of fighter aircraft flows from the military's conception of how the next war will be fought, and the Air Force's conception was undergoing dramatic changes in the late 1960's. Before the Vietnam War the Air Force had begun to deemphasize aerial dogfighting and rely more heavily on air-to-air missiles that could strike an enemy plane "over the horizon"—at long distances. "We felt we didn't need the maneuverability at the time," Stachowski explained.

But the Vietnam War experience changed that. The air-to-air missiles carried by U.S. fighters proved less useful than the Air Force had expected because pilots were generally required to identify North Vietnamese aircraft before firing at them. The need for eye contact inevitably led to close-in dogfighting, which placed a premium on the thrust of the aircraft's engine. "If a Soviet fighter ran into a five g turn at some altitude, it could keep up its speed," Stachowski explained, "whereas if we ran into a five g turn, we would lose speed and altitude." (One g equals the normal pull of gravity on a body at rest; 5 g's equals five times that force.)

The emerging concept that fighter aircraft should be able to outmaneuver their adversaries or sneak up on enemy ground targets and escape quickly was a departure from the U.S. fighter tactics that had developed since World War II. One man, Air Force Colonel John Boyd, played a major role in the formulation of the new tactics and the development of the F-16 to implement them.

Boyd was the father figure and chief theoretician of the Fighter Mafia. The blunt, hard-driving Air Force colonel had earned a reputation as one of America's hottest fighter pilots flying F-86 Sabres during the Korean War. He became known as Forty-second Boyd because of his audacious challenge to fellow pilots. "You could start on John Boyd's tail in a mock fight and he either would be on your tail in 40 seconds or he would pay $40," according to an account in *The Wall Street Journal.* There were apparently few takers.

After the Korean War Boyd taught pilots his innovative air combat strategies at Nellis Air Force Base in Nevada and wrote *Aerial Attack Study,* a widely used training manual that outlined his fighter tactics. The essence of Boyd's theory, based on his own success in shooting down MiG-15's, was that an aircraft's maneuverability was more important in a one-on-one dogfight than its top speed or acceleration. His notion was simple: Outwit, rather than overpower, the enemy.

In subsequent years Boyd translated his air combat theories into an overall strategy for modern combat, known as maneuver warfare. Tapping historical precedents back to the Battle of Marathon in 490 B.C., Boyd assembled a four-hour 160-chart briefing he called "Patterns of Conflict," which made the case for maneuver warfare. Colonel Boyd presented this *tour de force* to military and civilian audiences throughout the defense establishment for years.

He suggested that brigades, divisions, and whole armies should shift combat strategies frequently and flexibly in an effort to confuse the enemy—with such surprise tactics as lightning strikes, end runs, and feigned assaults—rather than wear the enemy down through traditional attrition warfare. A small group of combat theoreticians who shared Boyd's enthusiasm for maneuver warfare informally became the intellectual nucleus of today's military reform movement.

If Colonel Boyd was the theoretician of the Fighter Mafia, Pierre Sprey, a dogmatic weapons analyst and statistician, was the group's energizing ideologue. In 1967, while Boyd was still an instructor on Air Force tactics, he met Sprey, who had taken a job as a systems analyst in the OSD. The analyst was already causing a stir at the Pentagon by advocating the development of a lighter, simpler, less expensive fighter than the Air Force's F-15.

Sprey was a self-assured analyst who liked to flaunt his considerable technical knowledge. He had earned a bachelor's degree in mechanical engineering at Yale in 1958 and a master's degree in mathematical statistics and operations research at Cornell in 1961. Before arriving at the Pentagon in 1966, he had worked full time for only two years, as a research scientist for Grumman Aircraft, where he was involved in a variety of military, space, and commercial programs.

When Sprey landed his systems analysis job, he was initially assigned to study issues of strategic mobility. Before long he shifted his focus to fighter aircraft. Sprey sought to identify the technical characteristics common to the successful fighter planes of the past, and like Boyd, he was concerned by what he saw as the military's consuming passion for increasingly complex and costly weapons.

After poring over reams of historical data on various fighter planes as well as design data generated during the development of the Air Force's newest F-15 fighter, Sprey wrote a provocative paper in 1968 that spelled out his concept for a new fighter. He envisioned a plane that would weigh about 25,000 pounds and outperform the Air Force's F-4 Phantom II fighter. He called his conceptual lightweight fighter the FXX and vigorously began advocating it.

Boyd and Sprey reached similar conclusions from different starting points: Boyd as a fighter pilot and combat strategist; Sprey as a statistician, engineer, and weapons analyst. They found themselves ideological allies in a bitter struggle against the Pentagon's "technology advocates" (as Sprey called them), who pushed for ever more sophisticated weaponry. "They were attracted by each other's outlook and they shared the fear that the trend toward costly planes would leave the Air Force hopelessly outnumbered and outfought," wrote James Fallows in his provocative book *National Defense.*

Mind you, Sprey did not actually *design* a new airplane; he designed a concept for one. He made a complex series of calculations to determine how a new lightweight fighter might perform on the basis of hypothetical specifications and the performance records for existing aircraft. His FXX concept departed dramatically from prevailing wisdom. Most new fighter designs emphasized sophisticated radar, electronic warfare equipment, electronic countermeasures systems, and air-to-air missiles to help a USAF pilot detect and defeat an enemy aircraft at long range, if necessary. Sprey envisioned an aircraft with stripped-down electronics and armaments. While many new fighters were designed to perform a variety of missions (one-on-one dogfighting at close range, air-to-air battles at long range, or air-to-ground bombing) by day or by night, in good weather or bad, Sprey's "austere" fighter was designed primarily for daytime air-to-air dogfighting.

Sprey's analysis led him to believe in the technical feasibility of a 25,000-pound single-engine fighter that would exhibit 140 percent better maximum turning capability and a 110 percent better acceleration than its Phantom II predecessor, at two-thirds the cost. "Such a performance breakthrough has never been achieved previously in the history of fighter aviation . . ." Sprey immodestly told the Senate Armed Services Committee in 1971. "Most of this increase resulted from austere requirements, not from technological advances."

Of course, Sprey's improvements were *hypothetical.* His analysis hinged on several crucial assumptions about the proposed thrust-to-weight ratio of the FXX (that is, the power of the proposed engine in relation to the aircraft's weight), the configuration of its wing, the military value of its stripped-down electronics gear, and a variety of other factors.

Sprey's assumptions and calculations were challenged by most of the aircraft designers who reviewed his work. His FXX concept was closely examined by senior analysts in the Naval Air Systems Command, Air Force Systems Command, and OSD. All three rejected his conclusions. Among other things, the analysts believed Sprey's lightweight fighter would be no match for a Soviet MiG-25 Foxbat fighter. Furthermore, they concluded it wasn't possible to build a plane weighing only 25,000 pounds that could carry all the armaments Sprey envisioned and still provide the promised thrust-to-weight ratio.

"When we looked at his claim of what the airplane could carry and how far it could go, there was nothing about it that had any degree of rationality," recalled George Spangenberg, the Navy's top civilian aeronautical engineer at the time. Experienced aircraft designers scoffed and wondered if Sprey planned to construct his lightweight fighter from a new miracle material—*"baloney-um."*

Spangenberg and Frederick Gloeckler, another Navy tactical aircraft expert, were scorching in their criticism of Sprey's FXX concept paper. "In common with past papers by the same author, this study contains many fallacious assumptions, half truths, distortions and erroneous extrapolations," the two men wrote in a Navy memorandum. "Unsubstantiated opinions are presented as facts. Any rebuttals are given the appearance of arguments against the rudimentary virtues of simplicity, high performance and low cost."

Testifying on fighter aircraft designs before the Senate Armed Services Committee in 1971, Sprey acknowledged the icy reception his 1968 FXX analysis had received. "All they did was criticize the concepts, indirectly through the press and with internal memorandums that never reached me . . ." he said. He had clearly been hurt by the Navy's criticism and his critics' use of the media to discredit his ideas, but he wasn't about to throw in the towel.

## (2)

Sprey's push for a lightweight fighter was initially resisted by senior Air Force generals who preferred their all-weather top-of-the-line F-15 Eagles and by senior Navy admirals who were equally fond of their carrier-based F-14 Tomcats. Even so, the Fighter Mafia's campaign for lightweight fighters eventually led to the development of the Air Force's F-16 and the Navy's F-18.

By 1970 Air Force planners had begun to pay more attention to Sprey's fighter concepts and Colonel Boyd's air combat tactics. A year later the lightweight fighter idea had gathered enough support within the OSD and Air Force to warrant a development program.

Under ideal circumstances, the Air Force might have plunged ahead and committed itself to designing, developing, and producing such a plane even before the technical obstacles had been overcome. But the $79 billion defense budget was stretched thin, and the Pentagon had been burned recently by several costly weapons programs. To prevent similar problems with the lightweight fighter, Deputy Secretary of Defense David Packard pushed for a new approach to procurement.

Packard, former chairman of the Hewlett-Packard Company, the multi-

11. Deputy Secretary of Defense David Packard, a founder of the
Hewlett-Packard Company and a leading defense industrialist, visits in the
field with U.S. soldiers. As deputy secretary he championed the
commonsense "fly-before-you-buy" approach to weapons procurement which
supplanted the Pentagon's traditional reliance on computer models and paper
analyses. *U.S. Army*

billion-dollar computer and instrumentation manufacturer that he and William
Hewlett had founded in 1939 with $595, was a tall, relaxed, self-assured busi-
nessman known for his collegial style of corporate management and down-to-
earth common sense. He thought that the Pentagon awarded too many weapons
contracts on the basis of incomplete technical information or imprecise cost
estimates because the competing contractors hadn't actually built the weapons
they were trying to sell. He believed that in its attempts to save money, the
Pentagon too often relied on sophisticated computer models and paper analyses
of competing weapons systems to select its winning contractors.

To make matters worse, the Air Force had combined this paper approach
to picking its contractors with another equally misguided contracting theory
known as Total Package Procurement. Under Total Package Procurement, as
noted earlier, competing companies were asked to submit a single bid for the
design, development, and production of a complete weapons system, rather

than to bid separately on each successive phase of a new program. Theoretically that would reduce the opportunity for a contractor to buy in to a new program by underbidding on the initial development portion of the contract, with the expectation of recouping its losses on the later production run. Instead of bidding for various phases of development, the company would be asked to submit a bid for the complete job. The Air Force would hold the contractor to that price and demand a finished weapon that lived up to the promised performance specifications.

The Total Package Procurement idea, which looked reasonable on paper, proved less reasonable in real life. Lockheed's C-5A cargo transport aircraft, for example, which the Air Force purchased under a Total Package Procurement plan, was a fiasco. Lockheed signed a contract with the Air Force to design, develop, and produce cargo planes that were supposed to meet specific weight, takeoff, and performance characteristics.

When Lockheed built the C-5A prototype, it was heavier than planned and couldn't take off within the distance specified in its contract, Packard recalled. "It would have been desirable at that time for the Air Force to say, 'Well, we can get by with a couple hundred feet more than the specified takeoff distance. It isn't all that important because the number was arbitrary to begin with. Or we can go with a little more weight,' " said Packard. "But those goddamned specifications were both written into the contract, and there wasn't any give in them."

Lockheed was forced under its Total Package Procurement contract to shave weight off the C-5A. It removed a substantial portion of the wing's metal support system to trim the aircraft to the specified weight. The resulting wings proved too weak to last the required 30,000 hours and ultimately had to be rebuilt. "Lockheed made these compromises simply because they were written into the specifications," said Packard. "It would have been a hell of a lot better to have had some flexibility in adjusting that."

When the lightweight fighter was being planned, Packard rejected paper analyses and Total Package Procurement. Instead, he reached back to the days of the original Army Air Corps (AAC) and adopted some of the traditional procurement practices used in those days. The early contracting officers of the AAC, men like Reuben Fleet and Henry "Hap" Arnold, didn't award contracts based on computer models or slick "brochuremanship." They required aircraft companies to construct flying prototypes that competed with each other in realistic trials.

Packard pressed the Air Force to adopt a similar fly-before-you-buy approach. "My theory on this prototype program was that we would ask the contractor to develop a model that would have some general performance requirements at a *set* price," he explained years later. "The contractor would have complete freedom to use his ingenuity to come up with the best machine he could. Another contractor would do the same thing. Then you have a fly-off and test them against each other and pick the best one. That's a much more sensible way than to sit down and specify every nut, bolt, and screw in the plane to begin with," he concluded.

Not everyone agreed. Some critics pointed out that it takes longer to select a winning contractor by building and testing prototype aircraft than it does through paper analyses. That extra time adds to the program's cost without necessarily improving the performance of the finished aircraft, they argued.

Packard's fly-before-you-buy approach was also intended to inspire more realistic cost estimates from contractors. He knew from his experience at Hewlett-Packard that high-technology manufacturers have a difficult time estimating how much it will cost to build a product that hasn't yet been designed. For that reason, he wanted the competing aircraft contractors to develop a lightweight fighter that could be manufactured for a *given* price, a practice known in the defense industry as design-to-cost. After the Air Force had selected the better plane, the winning contractor could return to the drawing board to calculate its production costs more realistically.

When the lightweight fighter program began, it wasn't expected to lead directly to a production aircraft. "The F-16 did not start out as a weapons system," remembered Stachowski, a planner at Wright-Patterson. "It started out as a technology demonstrator." The Air Force wanted to build lightweight fighter prototypes that could experiment with emerging technologies that might prove useful in future fighters. Those design features and components that looked promising could be put "on the shelf," so the Air Force later on could adopt them quickly if it chose to.

The Aeronautical Systems Division is the unit within the Air Force Systems Command that develops and buys aircraft. (Other divisions develop electronics gear, armaments, and space equipment.) In 1971 it sent the aerospace industry a Request for Proposals (RFP) to develop a new lightweight fighter prototype. "The prototypes were intended to determine the viability of a small, light-weight, low-cost air superiority fighter, and to aid evaluation of the operational potential of such an aircraft as well as establishing [*sic*] its operational role," reported *Jane's* aircraft yearbook. In keeping with Packard's procurement philosophy, the RFP was remarkably short and flexible. In a mere twenty-one pages, the Air Force outlined the general performance characteristics it sought and the price it expected to pay for a new fighter prototype.

One defense contractor explained Packard's design-to-cost strategy this way: "It's like a man buying a new suit. No longer does he describe what he wants to his tailor, with lapels this wide, a belted back, and maybe change from cheviot to tweed if the first jacket doesn't please him. And just send the bill whatever it is. Now he goes to Macy's and asks the clerk, 'what can you give me for 75 bucks?' Aerospace companies are instructed to meet certain cost parameters and to design the best plane they can within existing technology." The Air Force's original target was a flyaway cost of $3 million per airplane (expressed in 1972 dollars), a price that compelled contractors to keep their proposals simple, straightforward, and cheap.

Five companies—General Dynamics, Northrop, Boeing, Lockheed, and LTV—responded to the Air Force's RFP. A few months later two became finalists: General Dynamics, which had proposed the YF-16, a single-engine fighter, and Northrop, which had recommended the YF-17, a twin-engine aircraft. They were chosen in part because they offered different technical approaches.

GD planned to wrap a newly designed fighter around the proved F100 engine that Pratt & Whitney was already supplying for the Air Force's twin-engine McDonnell Douglas F-15. Use of the same F100 model would minimize technical risks and cut the YF-16's maintenance and logistics costs.

Northrop planned to rely on a less powerful YJ101 turbojet engine it expected the General Electric Company to develop. The YF-17's use of two engines was considered safer for pilots, but the fact that GE had not yet perfected or tested its new engine added to Northrop's risks.

Both finalists desperately wanted the Air Force's lightweight fighter contract. GD's aircraft plant in Fort Worth was in serious trouble. With production of new F-111 fighter-bombers due to end in 1976, the facility was crying out for new business. GD hadn't produced a pure fighter aircraft since the late 1950's, when it had churned out F-106 Delta Darts. If the Fort Worth division were to remain viable, it had to win this award.

Northrop was just as hungry. It had built F-5 Tiger fighters for the export market for about two decades, but the F-5's had fallen behind the times. The company had designed a modern derivative of the F-5, the Cobra, but couldn't afford to build a flying model. If Northrop won the Air Force's lightweight fighter contract, it planned to build a Cobra prototype and market the plane in Europe. If it lost, it would virtually be out of the fighter business by the late 1970's.

Both companies began developing their technology demonstrators in earnest. Senior Air Force generals, still hoping the notion of a lightweight fighter would die quietly, hadn't committed themselves to producing either prototype.

But David Lewis figured the generals would eventually have to yield to OSD pressure. "When we started that fighter program, we said, 'This is going to be a weapons system,' " Lewis recalled. He ordered the Fort Worth division to build a YF-16 prototype that could fire its guns and missiles and carry its bombs and fuel tanks on external racks, as if it were an operational aircraft. If and when the Air Force gave the lightweight fighter program the green light to begin production, Lewis wanted to be ready.

GD rolled out its prototype YF-16 for the first time in December 1973, twenty-one months after it had received its initial $37.9 million development contract from the Air Force. Decorated with a bold red, white, and blue paint scheme Lewis had chosen, the prototype was small enough that an enemy would have a hard time detecting it visually or with radar. It was armed with a twenty-millimeter machine gun that could fire up to 6,000 rounds per minute and Sidewinder heat-seeking missiles, and it could carry about 15,000 pounds of bombs, electronics gear, and fuel tanks. "Not only does the craft give twice the combat radius, but when compared to other recent air superiority fighters, it does so at about half the weight and for less than half the cost," noted one enthusiastic aviation writer.

The YF-16 was a technological marvel. Its wings and body were joined in a way that increased its fuel and equipment capacity. Its fly-by-wire circuitry enabled the pilot to manipulate his control surfaces smoothly and precisely through electrical wires rather than with heavier cables, pulleys, mechanical linkages, and pushrods. The leading-edge maneuver flaps of the YF-16's wings adjusted themselves automatically to provide better lift and less drag whenever the aircraft's speed changed. The pilot's bubble-shaped cockpit canopy provided greater all-around visibility than other fighter cockpits, and his seat was tilted back thirty degrees, rather than the traditional thirteen degrees, to increase his tolerance of g forces. A unique side-stick controller, mounted next to the pilot's armrest, enabled him to manipulate the plane's control surfaces electronically, with only the slightest pressure from his hand.

To reduce production costs, GD designed its YF-16 to make minimum use of exotic construction materials. Only 2.2 percent of the aircraft structure was titanium, 4.2 percent advanced composites, and 4.7 percent steel. Less expensive aluminum accounted for 78 percent of the aircraft. By contrast, in proportion to its weight, the F-15 consisted of twelve times as much titanium and nine times as much composite material, but less than half as much aluminum.

The YF-16 would consume half the fuel of an F-4 Phantom II and 17 percent less than an F-104 Starfighter, when performing similar missions, GD predicted. The Pratt & Whitney engine, which generated eight pounds of thrust for every pound of its own weight, produced almost no smoke that an enemy could see.

"They are the highest-performance, most exclusive planes you could ever conceive of for a visual, close-in dogfight," noted an Air Force pilot. "They're not armed to shoot beyond visual range, like an F-15. They don't have the radar, and they don't have the weapons to do that. They're not F-14's, and they're not F-15's, but as close-in, turning dogfighters, the F-16 is the finest thing you can imagine."

General Dynamics was first to get its prototype lightweight fighter into the air, in January 1974. In fact, the YF-16's maiden flight occurred accidentally, a few weeks earlier than planned. The plane had been ferried inside a C-5A transport from Fort Worth to Edwards Air Force Base, home of the Air Force Flight Test Center, ninety miles northeast of Los Angeles. In that isolated facility, both prototypes were scheduled to undergo a rigorous 300-hour flight test program.

Philip Oestricher, a GD pilot, was putting the YF-16 through a high-speed taxi test when he realized that the aircraft's horizontal stabilizer wasn't working properly. Rather than bring his plane to a dangerous halt, Oestricher allowed it to lift off the runway for an unscheduled flight that lasted six minutes and ended uneventfully. The following month the YF-16 made its first official flight without a hitch. The Air Force still preferred its top-of-the-line F-15 to any lightweight fighter, but recent events were making acceptance of a stripped-down fighter almost inevitable.

For one thing, the Navy also had begun to toy with the notion of lightweight fighters. The Navy had relied on a twin-engine fighter known as the F-14 Tomcat built by the Grumman Aerospace Corporation since 1972. The F-14 was considered the finest modern fighter designed to operate off the deck of an aircraft carrier. Powered by Pratt & Whitney engines, it could achieve Mach 2.3 speeds. Unfortunately it had become extremely expensive. Though many admirals were emotionally wedded to the impressive Grumman fighter, others recognized that its price was becoming prohibitive. Pressure was building among some Navy weapons analysts and aircraft designers to find a lightweight alternative to the F-14. Though neither service had formally committed itself to buying lightweight fighters, the Navy's interest in such planes became an increasingly important factor in the Air Force's decision.

Western European interest in the lightweight fighter became another factor in Air Force decision making. Just as the U.S. Air Force's F-4's and F-105's were growing obsolete, so, too, were the Lockheed F-104 Starfighters that several NATO allies had been flying. Ever since the Starfighters had been chosen over France's Mirage III fighters in the 1960's, they had become the mainstay of fighter squadrons in Belgium, the Netherlands, Norway, and Denmark. Now these four countries wanted to replace their Starfighters with several hundred new aircraft.

12. James R. Schlesinger, President
Nixon's last defense secretary,
remained somewhat aloof from the
scramble for the NATO consortium's
multibillion-dollar fighter contract in
1975. A thoughtful geopolitical
strategist, he seemed more concerned
that the United States and its NATO
allies "standardize" their air forces by
buying a single aircraft. *Department of
Defense*

   The YF-16 and YF-17 fighter prototypes being tested at Edwards were likely
candidates to meet the requirements of the NATO countries. So by the spring
of 1974, GD and Northrop found themselves vying for possible sales to the
U.S. Air Force, the U.S. Navy, and four Western European allies. The stakes
in the lightweight fighter program had become enormous.
   A thoughtful international strategist, Defense Secretary James Schlesinger
had his own agenda. He was convinced that the United States and its NATO
allies had to increase their use of common weapons and logistical support
systems if they were to hold their own against the Warsaw Pact countries.
There was pressure during the 1970's for greater transatlantic cooperation, for
rationalization, standardization, and interoperability (RSI) of NATO weapons
systems. Schlesinger was a big fan of NATO RSI. The alternative, in his view,
was a disorganized array of weapons systems scattered across Western Europe
that allied troops could neither share nor maintain efficiently. Schlesinger saw
the U.S. lightweight fighter program not only as a low-cost domestic alternative for U.S. forces but also as a weapons system the United States and its
NATO allies could procure cooperatively.
   During the spring of 1974 Schlesinger, his deputy, William Clements, and

his director of defense research and engineering, Malcolm Currie, pressured the Air Force to transform the technology demonstration under way at Edwards into a full-fledged program to develop a new lightweight fighter. Schlesinger ran into stiff opposition from such senior officers as General George Brown, the Air Force chief of staff, who still favored the all-weather F-15, but the defense secretary persisted. The Air Force reluctantly capitulated in April 1974.

The Air Force decided to stage a competitive fly-off between the YF-16 and the YF-17 prototypes and procure the winning aircraft as a low-cost replacement for its F-4 Phantoms. "Schlesinger's decision showed his commitment to the lightweight fighter program," explained Frank Shrontz, assistant secretary of the air force for installations and logistics at the time, "but equally important was the fact that he was willing to stick his political neck out to push for his NATO standardization process in Europe."

Schlesinger hoped the air forces of the United States, Belgium, the Netherlands, Norway, and Denmark would pick a U.S.-built aircraft, but that didn't seem to be his principal concern. Apparently he took little interest in the commercial rivalry between GD and Northrop and the international rivalry between U.S. and European manufacturers. In fact, some observers thought Schlesinger didn't care who built the new fighters so long as all five air forces bought the same plane.

Luckily for GD and Northrop, Clements took a greater interest in the commercial aspects of the consortium's fighter purchase. While the remote, pipe-puffing defense secretary considered geopolitical strategy, his deputy focused on the more parochial task of peddling U.S. fighters to Europe.

The four European nations had formed a consortium to choose a common fighter and negotiate jointly for about 350 aircraft. Its choice had narrowed to France's Mirage F-1, Sweden's Viggen, or an American fighter when Schlesinger asked the Europeans to postpone their decision for several months while the Air Force chose between the YF-16 and the YF-17. He knew that if the consortium purchased any U.S. fighter, it would want to buy the plane selected by the U.S. Air Force. Schlesinger promised to move the source selection decision up from April 1975 to January 1975 and promised to submit all the performance data and cost figures the consortium would need to evaluate the American fighter candidate by January 1975. Finally, he invited the Europeans to observe the source selection process at Wright-Patterson so that they could get an early look at the competing American aircraft.

Schlesinger's moves increased the chances for an American fighter candidate to win the consortium's "Deal of the Century." But his actions put Northrop at a distinct disadvantage. GD's YF-16 was well into its flight test program at Edwards, while Northrop had not yet begun flying its first YF-17. Now that the Air Force had decided to produce one of the prototypes, and Schlesinger had accelerated the source selection timetable, Northrop was in serious trouble. "We caught Northrop flat-footed," GD's Lewis recalled, with a smile.

The flight test program at Edwards pitted two YF-16's against two YF-17's for about eleven months. Pilots for the fly-off were drawn from General Dynamics, Northrop, the Air Force Systems Command, which was developing the new fighters, and the Tactical Air Command, which eventually was to deploy them. By the time the tests were completed each model had flown more than 300 hours, during which ground technicians collected reams of data on their drag, stability, control, and maneuvering performance. The prototypes were put through high-energy climbs, turns, rolls, pull-ups, and simulated dogfights against F-4E Phantoms. They were flown at subsonic and supersonic speeds, loaded with Sidewinder air-to-air missiles and 2,000-pound bombs. They fired machine-gun rounds at towed targets, strafed the ground in simulated air-to-ground attacks, and dropped their bombs.

In addition, Air Force technicians studied the maintenance procedures and turnaround times required by each aircraft's support team between landings and takeoffs. On its best day the YF-16 made six separate flights, with its quickest turnaround time at twelve minutes.

The Air Force's choice between the GD and Northrop candidates was inextricably bound up with the Navy's quest for a fighter of its own. Pressure had been mounting from a cadre of vocal aircraft planners and defense analysts to develop the VFAX, a new lightweight fighter still in the conceptual stage. This aircraft was seen by its promoters as a low-cost alternative to the F-14A. The Navy would continue to rely on F-14's for long-range delivery of weapons, but a new VFAX could help F-14's defend the U.S. fleet at close range.

Despite increased discussion of the VFAX, most senior admirals preferred the more sophisticated Grumman aircraft. "These officers all had F-14 religion," explained one observer. "All they could see was the F-14. That was what the Navy needed, and they didn't want to hear about anything else. It didn't matter what it cost. They felt that Congress and the American people would give them only the best—what they said they needed."

Officials in the OSD began to wonder if the Navy and Air Force could use the same airplane. Would it be possible for the Navy to adapt either GD's YF-16 or Northrop's YF-17 for use off an aircraft carrier? Two schools of thought developed. Some cost-conscious OSD officials, congressmen, and Capitol Hill staffers wanted the two services to choose the same basic aircraft if in fact both decided to buy lightweight fighters. The military could save money by enlarging the production run of the chosen aircraft and eliminating duplication of maintenance, spare parts, and logistics expenses.

Others, particularly the Navy's allies in Congress, resisted the notion of a common aircraft. They pointed out that the Navy's fighter would have to make treacherous carrier takeoffs and landings and operate regularly at sea. Those perilous conditions justified a fighter designed specifically for the Navy, they argued.

Congress was sharply divided on the issue. The Senate, for the most part, backed the Navy. It supported the Navy's request for an upgraded version of the VFAX fighter that would outperform either of the Air Force prototypes. The House, meanwhile, resisted the Navy's plan for a separate fighter program, preferring that the two services save money by adopting variants of the same basic airplane. After a drawn-out battle Congress came up with a compromise: The Navy would be allowed to develop its own aircraft, renamed the Navy air combat fighter, but to cut costs, the plane would have to draw upon the technology and hardware demonstrated in the Air Force fighter program as much as possible.

## (3)

The admirals were flustered by the language of the legislative compromise. It appeared that Congress was permitting them to develop their own fighter as long as it was derived from one of the Air Force prototypes. The Navy wasn't satisfied. A group of admirals met with Clements to negotiate a compromise. They agreed to develop their new Navy air combat fighter from either prototype. In return, Clements agreed to support the admirals in their demand for higher performance specifications for the carrier-based fighter, a team of Navy-qualified contractors, and sufficient money to evaluate the fighters before the Air Force made its choice.

When the dust settled, the Navy had not won the stripped-down version of the F-14 Tomcat it had originally sought. But it had wrested permission from Congress and the OSD to develop a plane based on the YF-16 or YF-17 that was modified to its own performance standards and built by its own contractors. Despite all the political rhetoric on Capitol Hill about interservice commonality, it appeared as if the stubborn Navy would once again go its own way.

Once Clements had agreed to support the idea of Navy-qualified contractors for the Navy air combat fighter, it behooved General Dynamics and Northrop to team up with companies that had built carrier-based aircraft. In October 1974 they did so. Northrop chose McDonnell Douglas, the St. Louis-based aircraft builder that had produced the hugely successful F-4 Phantom fighter used by the Navy, Marine Corps, and Air Force. McDonnell Douglas teamed with Northrop, rather than GD, because Northrop offered better financial terms and its twin-engine YF-17 prototype seemed more suitable for adaptation to carrier operations.

GD's Fort Worth division joined with the LTV Aerospace Corporation, which was still building the Navy's A-7 Corsair attack plane in Dallas. The new Navy air combat fighter was expected to replace the A-7's, so cooperation with GD represented LTV's best hope of staying in the fighter-attack aircraft market.

The Navy sent its Request for Proposals for the Navy air combat fighter through the Air Force procurement bureaucracy to GD and Northrop. In theory, the Navy was looking for a derivative of the YF-16 and YF-17. In fact, the service's performance specifications were nearly identical to those it had circulated earlier for the proposed VFAX fighter, the aircraft that Congress deemed too sophisticated and costly.

The Navy had broken free from a fighter program dominated by the Air Force. It solicited proposals from both contractor teams and busied itself evaluating the more expensive carrier-based aircraft.

At the same time the Air Force was preparing to choose between the YF-16 and the YF-17 aircraft it had been testing in the skies over Edwards Air Force Base. It had requested formal proposals from GD and Northrop in September 1974 and had received them two months later. These included separate plans to build fighters in Europe in case the NATO consortium selected one of the American planes over the French and Swedish contenders.

Air Force officials planned to spend December evaluating the flight data they had amassed at Edwards, so they could announce their winner in January 1975, as Schlesinger had promised the consortium. The Air Force felt pressure from two sides. The Navy wanted the Air Force to postpone its decision until *after* the Navy made its fighter choice. The admirals feared that despite their agreement with Clements, they still might be forced to accept whichever plane the Air Force chose. If the European consortium selected the same fighter as the Air Force, pressure on the Navy to use the same plane would become even greater.

Schlesinger, meanwhile, was urging the Air Force to stick to its source selection timetable. He had always been less concerned with the rivalry between the Air Force and the Navy than he was with selling the Air Force's chosen plane to the Europeans.

Northrop executives were nervous. Fearing that their YF-17 was about to lose the Air Force sweepstakes, the California-based aircraft builder and General Electric, its Massachusetts-based engine maker, mounted an intense lobbying effort in Washington. Both contractors called upon their allies in Congress. The entire Massachusetts delegation, including such antiwar activists as Father Robert Drinan and Michael Harrington, sent a joint letter on Majority Leader Tip O'Neill's stationery to Schlesinger, urging the selection of the YF-17. The California delegation, with the exception of a few congressmen whose districts included sizable GD plants, sent a similar appeal. Schlesinger wasn't impressed.

As things turned out, it wasn't a tough call. When Air Force officials gathered at Wright-Patterson to compare the performance data and cost estimates, GD's YF-16 was the clear favorite. Beyond the political arguments, beyond the debates over single-engine versus twin-engine planes, joint Air Force-Navy programs, or NATO standardization, the YF-16 was simply the superior aircraft.

At supersonic speeds it outperformed the YF-17 in virtually every way. It could accelerate faster, turn more quickly, fly farther, and was more agile than its Northrop competitor. Pilots enjoyed greater visibility from the YF-16's cockpit and could withstand greater g forces in their tilt-back seats. At subsonic speeds, the Air Force concluded, the two planes were closer in performance, but GD's prototype had a definite edge.

In addition, the Air Force expected GD to have an easier time shifting from full-scale development to production because its YF-16 relied on a proved Pratt & Whitney engine already in service with the F-15.

The YF-16 easily outclassed the YF-17 in terms of projected costs. GD was fortunate to have opted for a single-engine fighter design, which consumed about 30 percent less fuel than a twin-engine plane, *before* the unexpected jump in oil prices during the mid-1970's. "The cost of owning a two-engine airplane over a one-engine airplane, based upon a fleet of 1,300 airplanes, was in excess of one billion dollars," recalled Harvey Gordon, then an Air Force procurement official involved in the source selection. "That was a billion-dollar delta [difference] that the Northrop people could never overcome."

Air Force Secretary John L. McLucas, a seasoned government and defense industry veteran who was to make the official source selection, flew out to Wright-Patterson for a final briefing on January 7, 1975. He conferred with the Air Force chief of staff, General David C. Jones, and other top generals. "All of us agreed that the YF-16 was the right choice for the Air Force," McLucas said later.

Before long, disappointed Northrop executives learned of the decision. They worried that the Air Force's choice of the YF-16 might put pressure on the

Navy to go along with the same plane. If so, the European consortium would probably follow suit. To prevent such a triple defeat, Northrop persuaded the Navy to seek a three-week postponement of the Air Force's formal announcement. Schlesinger considered the request at a review meeting on January 10, less than a week before the decision deadline he had promised the European consortium.

The defense secretary was concerned that the Navy still might try to kill the lightweight fighter program in favor of its beloved F-14's. "You want me to delay this program so that you can select a plane that you have no intention of buying?" he asked the admirals incredulously. Schlesinger rejected their plea and instructed the Air Force to announce its fighter choice on January 13. The Navy was free to choose whichever plane it wanted after that, Schlesinger declared. It was a split decision. The Air Force's announcement would proceed on schedule, but the Navy was given even greater latitude to develop its own fighter. "We were quite satisfied with the outcome," said one admiral who had attended the meeting, "once Schlesinger gave us a free hand to choose whichever plane we wanted."

Rumors of the YF-16's impending victory spread through Washington and Wall Street a few days before the official announcement, boosting the price of GD's stock and depressing Northrop's. Through it all, Northrop maintained an optimistic façade. NORTHROP CONFIDENT ITS PLANE WILL WIN, declared the front-page headline of the *Los Angeles Times,* Northrop's hometown newspaper, the morning of the Air Force's press conference.

The first words out of Secretary McLucas's mouth disabused Northrop of that notion. "Ladies and gentlemen," he began, "I am here today to announce the selection of General Dynamics Corporation as winner of the competition which we conducted for our Air Combat Fighter." GD had just won what promised to be the most lucrative fighter program of all time.

As an immediate down payment the Air Force awarded GD a $418 million contract to build fifteen full-scale development F-16's (the *Y* was dropped from the plane's designation when it was no longer considered an experimental aircraft). It also handed Pratt & Whitney a $55 million contract to produce F100 engines.

McLucas said the Air Force planned to buy for its own use 650 F-16 fighters, the total R&D and production costs of which were expected to total $4.3 billion. F-16 sales to the NATO consortium, other foreign countries, and perhaps the U.S. Navy could boost the total production run to more than 3,000 planes, McLucas predicted.

He saw the F-16 as a real bargain. Its estimated flyaway cost (hardware alone) was $4.6 million per plane, about 8 percent cheaper than Northrop's entry. When spare parts, training, and logistical support were included, the F-16's program cost was calculated at $6.7 million per plane, or about $1 million less than the YF-17.

General Dynamics was jubilant. After enduring years of criticism for its costly F-111 fighter-bombers, the Fort Worth division could once again stand tall in the defense industry. The bars along Bomber Road, outside the Texas plant, filled with GD employees celebrating McLucas's announcement. GD said it expected to hire 3,700 new employees immediately and about 7,000 altogether within two years. Almost a third of the money the Air Force planned to spend on F-16's was destined for the Fort Worth area, where GD would assemble the planes, and for Connecticut and Florida, where Pratt & Whitney would build the engines.

Back in the nation's capital, GD celebrated within sight of the Pentagon, at the Marriott Twin Bridges Hotel, where enthusiastic revelers watched promotional films of the sleek single-engine fighters on the screen dropping their bombs in slow motion to a stirring sound track of inspirational music.

The night before the Air Force announced its selection of GD's fighter, sixteen U.S. officials flew from Washington to Brussels to brief their Belgian, Dutch, Norwegian, and Danish counterparts in the NATO multinational fighter consortium. The delegation was led by Frank Shrontz, the assistant secretary of the air force for installations and logistics, who acted as chief negotiator for the U.S. side. If the Americans could sell the F-16 to all four European air forces, it would mean billions of dollars in additional orders for General Dynamics, lower unit costs for the U.S. Air Force, and a common frontline fighter for NATO.

As noted earlier, the four countries had already announced plans to replace their F-104 Starfighters. They were shopping for a multimission airplane that could intercept enemy aircraft at high altitudes, provide close-in support to friendly troops on the ground, and attack enemy warships close to their shores. "The consortium's purchase, involving an investment of at least $1.7 billion, is only the tip of a lucrative iceberg: a worldwide market for thousands of jets, spare parts and maintenance contracts worth more than $20 billion over the next decade," *Time* magazine predicted.

At Schlesinger's request, the consortium had delayed its decision to allow the U.S. Air Force to choose its fighter first. Now that the Air Force had picked the F-16, it was widely assumed that the Europeans would follow suit *if* they wanted an American plane. For months consortium officials had assured the Air Force that either prototype competing at Edwards would be acceptable to them. "They say, 'If we buy an American airplane, we would buy the airplane the U.S. Air Force buys,'" explained General David Jones, the Air Force chief of staff.

But that was a big if. The Northrop YF-17 was apparently out of the running, the British-French Jaguar had been eliminated because the consortium considered it too slow, and the Swedish Viggen was deemed a long shot because Sweden's neutrality might make deliveries during wartime less reliable. But the F-16 faced stiff competition from France's Mirage F-1, an agile, single-engine fighter built by Dassault-Breguet Aviation and capable of Mach 2.2 speeds.

Unlike the spanking new F-16, which incorporated the latest advances in aerodynamic technology, the Mirage and the Viggen had entered service in the mid-1960's. Their electronics had been upgraded, but their basic structural designs had remained largely unchanged.

The F-16 could outperform its European competition, but the consortium countries were looking for more than performance alone. They were concerned that despite Schlesinger's assurances, the U.S. Air Force might eventually turn its back on the lightweight F-16 in favor of the more advanced F-15. They were equally concerned with the political and economic rewards that could be gained from their fighter decision.

In the political atmosphere of Western Europe in the mid-1970's, which emphasized the development of indigenous industries, the consortium was under some pressure to buy a European, rather than an American, fighter. For years NATO members had grumbled that the United States sold far more arms to Western Europe than it purchased from them. To many Europeans, the upcoming "Deal of the Century" provided an ideal opportunity for Europeans to rectify the imbalance in cross-Atlantic arms trade.

The French in particular argued that a purchase of F-16 aircraft by the consortium would stunt the growth of the European aerospace industry. French government officials warned darkly that a Dassault aircraft factory in Belgium might have to close if the F-16 were chosen over the Mirage. Belgian companies of all kinds were quietly informed that they might lose French orders if their government didn't push for the French fighter.

France promised to boost its purchase of Dutch food products and help clean up the polluted Rhine River if the Netherlands backed the Mirage. In fact, France's anti-American rhetoric at times became so blatant that one Dutch newspaper accused Paris of trying to sell Western Europe not only French fighters but also French foreign policy.

The United States flexed its political muscles as well. Pentagon officials openly discussed the possibility of reducing the number of U.S. troops stationed in Europe. Others in Washington spoke of reviewing the landing rights at U.S. airports of European commercial airlines that competed head-on with American carriers. U.S. trade officials mentioned the possibility of European merchant ships' carrying a larger proportion of American-bound oil if business conditions permitted.

## (4)

While France and the United States continued their carrot-and-stick pressure tactics, insiders knew the key issue would probably be one of industrial offsets. Air Force Secretary McLucas said of the consortium's decision making, "I suspect that the cost will not be the main factor. I would think that offset arrangements, etc., are more dominant."

French and American officials offered all four consortium nations the chance to build a significant proportion of the fighters they agreed to buy. Such subcontracts would create thousands of jobs that would help offset a large part of the price each consortium member would pay for its new fighters. Belgium, the Netherlands, Norway, and Denmark would pay full price for their planes, but much of that cash would be spent within their own economies, boosting local employment and strengthening their indigenous aerospace industries. Such offset arrangements would ease each buyer's balance of payments problem by reducing the amount of money it had to send beyond its borders.

Offset deals had become familiar during the 1970's as a device for sweetening major international arms transactions. Indeed, by 1975 offsets had become an essential element in many major weapons sales. When France sold Atlantic antisubmarine warfare aircraft to the Netherlands and Alpha-Jet trainers and Mirage V fighters to Belgium, both buyers were offered roles in Dassault's military and civilian aircraft production.

The consortium became involved in the U.S. Air Force's fighter selection soon after Schlesinger had agreed to speed up that decision-making process. In June 1974, long before the fly-off was completed at Edwards, a group of consortium officials met with Schlesinger in the Pentagon to discuss the GD and Northrop contenders. The Europeans seemed to be leaning toward the Mirage because they still didn't believe the U.S. Air Force would procure the lightweight F-16, recalled Frank Shrontz, who participated in the meetings.

In September, as the war of words between France and the United States grew hotter, the defense ministers of the consortium set off on a three-stop shopping expedition. They first visited Paris at the invitation of their French counterpart, Jacques Soufflet. During that visit the French Air Force indicated that it would buy for its own use forty of the same Mirage fighters that it hoped to sell to the consortium.

The four defense ministers flew to Edwards Air Force Base in California a few days later to see the YF-16 and YF-17 in action and then to Washington for another session with Schlesinger. Offsets came up early in the talks. The first U.S. proposal covered production work only for the planes the Europeans planned to buy. The American negotiators were reluctant to allow the consortium countries to take on more offset work than their aerospace industries could handle. They feared the subcontractors might fall behind schedule or incur huge cost overruns. If that happened, the U.S. prime contractor—either GD or Northrop—would suffer financially. Unlike the U.S. Air Force, which negotiated annual production contracts with its aircraft manufacturers, the European consortium expected to negotiate one fixed price for all 348 planes it planned to buy. Under such an arrangement the U.S. prime contractor would receive a fixed amount of money from the consortium and absorb any cost overruns experienced by its European subcontractors out of its own pocket.

The Europeans weren't satisfied with the Americans' first offset package, said Shrontz. They wanted more production work in Europe. The United States, however, was reluctant to give them a larger portion of the work on the planes they would be buying. Instead, negotiators offered the Europeans a smaller piece of the work on a larger number of planes. The United States would ask European companies to build parts for the fighters sold to the U.S. Air Force and other foreign countries. "The Air Force wasn't particularly enamored with the idea that the Europeans would be building part of the planes its pilots would be flying," recalled Shrontz. But eventually it agreed, and a three-tier offset package was formulated.

The highlight of the defense ministers' visit to the Pentagon was Schlesinger's presentation of this new offer. The United States would invite the four consortium members to manufacture 40 percent of the parts used to construct the 348 fighters the Europeans planned to procure. In addition, their fighters could be assembled in aircraft factories in the Netherlands and Belgium, and the engines could be built in Belgium. The Americans would also allow the consortium countries to produce and ship back to the United States 10 percent of the parts used in the U.S. Air Force's fighters. Finally, the consortium would be asked to build 15 percent of any fighters the United States sold to other foreign countries.

Under this 40-10-15 percent offset arrangement, the Pentagon estimated that the consortium would receive subcontracts worth about 80 percent of the purchase price for its fighters, assuming that the U.S. Air Force bought 650 fighters, the consortium ordered 350, and other countries purchased an additional 500. If this 1,500-plane forecast grew to 2,000, the consortium would receive approximately 100 percent of its purchase price in subcontracts. "Taken together the United States offset proposals could result in the placement of orders and work worth nearly $2 billion with European aerospace industries," the Pentagon announced.

France, meanwhile, was dangling an attractive offset package of its own. Each consortium country would be awarded contracts for about 70 percent of the available production work, generating enough employment to keep 3,000 workers busy for ten years. Sweden, which hadn't conceded defeat yet, not only offered subcontracts to the consortium's aerospace industries but promised to build Swedish *automobile* plants in countries that bought its Viggen.

Consortium officials sat with their U.S. Air Force counterparts at Wright-Patterson throughout the source selection process but didn't actively influence the Air Force's choice between GD and Northrop. Similarly, Schlesinger took a keen interest in the consortium's deliberations but didn't interfere with the Air Force's decision makers at Wright-Patterson. "He was very instrumental in convincing the consortium to consider an American airplane and to hold off their decision until we made our decision," recalled procurement specialist Harvey Gordon. "But he did not influence us on which airplane we bought."

In May, as the consortium approached its decision, the U.S. Navy grabbed the attention of the aerospace industry by announcing that it had selected the fighter developed by McDonnell Douglas and Northrop rather than the carrier-based version of the YF-16 proposed by General Dynamics and LTV Aerospace. The Navy knew its decision would anger many in Congress who had voiced their opposition to two separate fighter programs. In the 1975 defense appropriations bill, House and Senate conferees had ordered the Navy to ensure that its Navy air combat fighter was an adaptation of the fighter the Air Force picked. If that message wasn't clear enough, the conferees warned, "Future funding is to be contingent upon the capability of the Navy to produce a derivative of the selected Air Force air combat design."

Despite these congressional guidelines, the Navy opted for a carrier-based version of the YF-17, which it called the F-18. The Navy said the twin-engine F-18 could operate more effectively off a carrier than the less powerful F-16 could. In the months after the YF-17 had lost to GD's YF-16, General Electric had modified its turbojet engine to increase its thrust by about 17 percent to compensate for the heavier aircraft. "This has made all the difference in the world," explained Malcolm Currie, the OSD's director of defense research and engineering.

Advocates of a common fighter grumbled about the Navy's stubborn insistence on selecting its own fighter, but in the end the Navy got its way. To some observers, the OSD had been indecisive about this issue. When the Pentagon was trying to sell Congress on the F-16, OSD officials talked enthusiastically about the money that could be saved by buying a common aircraft for the Air Force and Navy. Now that the Navy had resisted the idea of common fighters, they began talking about the unique requirements of a carrier-based aircraft.

Rumors that the consortium might opt for the twin-engine F-18, now that it was being procured by at least one U.S. military service, circulated in Washington. Before long, however, it became clear that a land-based version of the F-18 would cost the Europeans more than the F-16 or the Mirage and that it wouldn't be available as soon as either of its rivals. The U.S. Navy was pleased to have its own plane. And the consortium seemed content to choose between the F-16 and the Mirage.

By late May it looked as if the Netherlands, Norway, and Denmark were ready to accept the latest American offset package and pick the F-16. The only holdout was Belgium, which traditionally maintains strong commercial ties with France. France was urging Belgium to buy the Mirage, while the other consortium members were pleading for a united negotiating front.

Last-minute concessions won Belgium over. The United States agreed to establish a Military Assistance Command complex and a currency exchange facility in that country that would create local jobs. Also, Schlesinger allegedly agreed to a quid pro quo with the Belgian government by which the U.S. Army would buy about $30 million worth of machine guns from a Belgian ordnance firm, Fabrique Nationale, in exchange for Belgium's purchase of F-16 aircraft. The Maremont Corporation, an American machine-gun manufacturer which had expected the Army contract, loudly objected to Schlesinger's reported agreement, which the defense secretary publicly denied.

In June 1975 the four-nation consortium announced that it, too, had chosen General Dynamics's F-16 as its next frontline fighter. GD's David Lewis hailed the decision. "The competition from the builders of foreign aircraft, and indeed from their governments, was intense," he recalled a year later. "The financial, emotional and national stakes were high—but we were able to win those contracts by having the right product in the right market at the right price and at the right time. And I can assure you we won without the extra help and special influence we read so much about these days."

Together the consortium planned to purchase 348 planes, for just over $6 million apiece. Belgium wanted 116, the Netherlands 102, Norway 72, and Denmark 58, at a total cost of about $2.2 billion.

It appeared to many aerospace officials on both sides of the Atlantic that the United States and France had proposed offset packages so generous that they virtually nullified each other. "Looking back, there seems little doubt that technology had won once again," observed *Flight International* magazine.

"The customer wanted the shiniest new aeroplane, as had happened before with the F-104."

General Dynamics captured the Deal of the Century. Now it had to produce this stunning aircraft on time and on budget.

## (5)

The Fighter Mafia celebrated its greatest success when the Air Force announced in January 1975 that it would buy lightweight fighters based on GD's prototype. That aircraft was essentially what Boyd, Sprey, and their colleagues had been recommending—a stripped-down aircraft that would carry a twenty-millimeter gun and two Sidewinder air-to-air missiles and could outmaneuver almost any fighter in the sky.

However, as the F-16 progressed from the prototype phase through full-scale development to production, the Fighter Mafia was no longer able to influence its design. Over the years new electronic equipment was added, the aircraft gained weight, and its cost increased. Its mission was expanded to include ground attack as well as aerial dogfighting. The plane that eventually rolled off the General Dynamics production line in Fort Worth, Texas, was not the lean, agile fighter Sprey, Boyd, and their allies had so vigorously fought for.

That's not surprising.

Winning a major new fighter program changes an aircraft manufacturer's outlook dramatically. With production workers busy and the assembly line operating at full tilt, a defense contractor typically begins to think less about initiating new weapons programs and more about models that can be derived from current programs. An active aircraft program can fill a factory; its absence can be financially ruinous.

Companies that are out in the cold spend a lot of time hustling after new business. Companies with active aircraft programs devote most of their energy to updating their aircraft's designs to extend the life of the programs.

GD's Fort Worth division, for example, is working on at least five variants of its original F-16: a phased-in program to upgrade the aircraft's electronics, a less powerful export version for third world countries, an "adversary aircraft" for Navy training exercises, a flying test bed to demonstrate a series of innovative aerodynamic technologies, and a high-performance F-16E model, featuring a redesigned delta-shaped wing and a stretched fuselage, that can fly farther and carry a bigger weapons payload.

Under what's known as a Multinational Staged Improvement Program, the company is modifying its original single-seat F-16A's and tandem F-16B's into

13. GD's most profitable weapons system, the F-16 fighter aircraft, carries
Sidewinder air-to-air missiles and MK-84 bombs on a flight over Nellis Air
Force Base, Nevada. Having beaten out Northrop for the Air Force's
multibillion-dollar fighter contract in January 1975 and defeated France's
Mirage fighter for NATO's "deal of the century" a few months later, GD
currently expects to sell more than 4,000 F-16's to the United States and at
least eleven foreign nations. *U.S. Air Force*

F-16C and F-16D versions designed to counter Soviet improvements into the
late 1980's and the 1990's. In the initial stage of this improvement program,
the fighters will have their wiring redesigned and their internal storage space
enlarged to accommodate the improved radar, "head-up" display panels for
pilots, jammers, electronics, and navigation systems planned for future years.
In later stages the F-16 will be armed with a radar-guided AMRAAM missile
that enables a pilot to shoot at an enemy plane before he sees it, a night-attack
bombing navigation system called LANTIRN, and other advanced electronics
gear.

Some critics complain that such planned improvements not only add weight
and cost but actually reduce the F-16's capabilities. They blast the modifications as unnecessary frills that satisfy only ambitious program managers and
the military brass. "They'll wreck the airplane," warned Colonel Boyd, who

helped design the original F-16 and now argued that the costly modifications would turn the Fighting Falcon into a gold-plated monster.

F-16 program officials, the Air Force, and the OSD don't see it that way. They want a fighter that can detect the latest Soviet aircraft at long range and defeat them with air-to-air missiles. Harvey Gordon, the procurement expert, defended the concept of planned improvements. "There's no reason why you should continue to build an airplane which is obsolete—because of your strict adherence to the original concept—when you're faced with a completely changing scenario and enemy threat," he argued. As the Soviet Union develops aircraft with the capability to fight at night, in bad weather, and at long range, most Air Force officials believe U.S. fighters must keep abreast technologically.

The original F-16, which began life at the low end of a "high-low mix" of fighter aircraft, has attracted a large group of devoted Air Force supporters. "I think it's one of the great planes of the 20th Century," said Air Force General Delbert Jacobs. "But the low end of the mix has to rise with time, as the threat increases."

Similarly, Alton G. Keel, Jr., the Air Force's assistant secretary for research, development, and logistics, argued that modifying an existing aircraft is often the *cheaper* option. "One cannot—and dare not—presume that the F-16 design of the early 1970s would meet the threat of the late 1980s, the 1990s and beyond without some change," he asserted. "The options are: Design a new aircraft or improve one that is in production. We have chosen the latter, which, coincidentally, is significantly less costly."

The Fort Worth division has developed a downgraded version of the F-16 for sale to less developed countries. This model is known as the F-16/79 because it uses a General Electric J79 engine with less thrust than the standard Pratt & Whitney power plant. It was developed after President Carter had made it clear that his administration would frown upon the sale of top-of-the-line fighters to financially pressed countries. Northrop developed a competing export fighter, since dubbed the F-20, by adding a more powerful engine to its best-selling F-5. Because the Reagan administration has largely abandoned Carter's restrictions on peddling top-of-the-line fighters overseas, neither the F-16/79 nor the F-20 has been purchased by any foreign country.

Northrop's F-20 aircraft took a severe beating in 1985 when the Navy instead chose GD's F-16N derivative as an adversary aircraft that could play the role of Soviet fighters during the Navy's air combat training. Since then, Northrop has mounted an aggressive campaign to sell its F-20 to the Air Force as a low-cost alternative to the F-16. Its intensive lobbying campaign was picking up momentum when one of its two prototype aircraft crashed over Canada in May 1985 during a practice session for the Paris Air Show.

A fourth derivative of GD's F-16, known as the Advanced Fighter Technology Integrator (AFTI/F-16), is a flying test bed reminiscent of the early days of the lightweight fighter. The program experiments with a series of unprecedented in-flight maneuvers that enable a plane to ascend or descend, like an elevator, without raising or lowering its nose, to slide sideways without banking, and to point from side to side or up and down while flying straight ahead. The AFTI/F-16 isn't intended to become a production fighter; it is expected to explore a variety of emerging technologies that might be adapted on future aircraft.

General Dynamics has also spent millions of dollars designing a souped-up derivative of its F-16A model that boasts longer range, larger bomb loads, shorter takeoff and landing distances, and better maneuverability than its predecessor. This model, which GD calls the F-16XL and the Air Force designated the F-16E, was tested at Edwards Air Force Base alongside a derivative of the McDonnell Douglas fighter known as the F-15E Strike Eagle. In February 1984, after a thorough examination of both derivatives, the Air Force chose the McDonnell Douglas F-15E to become its premier fighter-bomber. At the same time the Air Force said it was pleased with the F-16E's new cranked-arrow wing design and also would buy GD's derivative aircraft, which has subsequently been designated the F-16F.

It's easier for a defense contractor to sell a derivative of an existing aircraft to the Pentagon and Congress than it is to start with a completely new plane. Modifying an existing aircraft cuts down on the number of technical surprises. "Rather than make a quantum leap in technology—with all the attendant risks and uncertainties—we do it in measured steps," noted Harvey Gordon. Many components of the F-16E, for example, had been tested on the original F-16A for years.

"We've got proven hydraulic pumps on the F-16E," said Major Edwin Thomas, an Air Force pilot who served as deputy director of the F-16E test program at Edwards. "We've got proven fuel pumps. We've got proven avionics. All of them are flight-rated. We've got years and years and years of experience with those things. . . . Thousands of problems that you'd have to solve if you started from scratch are already solved because of the experience with the F-16As and Bs."

Derivatives are also easier to peddle politically. "It was no mistake that this airplane is called an F-16E, instead of an F-18, F-20 or F-21," Major Thomas pointed out. The F-16E shares 80 percent of its components with the F-16A, but it is sufficiently different from its predecessor to justify giving it a completely new designation, said Thomas. "But if you call it an F-20," he explained, "you've got to go back to Congress and procure a new weapons system. You don't have to do that this way.

"We have made a weapons system acquisition process that is so cumbersome, so lengthy, and so difficult that it's far easier to sell a modification or an evolution of an existing system than it is to get Congress to commit a huge amount of money to start from Square Zero to develop a new follow-on aircraft," he added.

The flight test program is one of the most critical phases in an aircraft's development. It is usually divided into two parts: development, test, and evaluation (DT&E), in which the prototype aircraft tries simply to meet the Air Force's predetermined performance specifications, and operational test and evaluation (OT&E), in which one or more aircraft compete in simulated combat scenarios. Development testing measures the performance of the machine. Operational testing determines how effectively real-life pilots will be able to operate the aircraft.

The shirt-sleeved technicians who gather data in the flight test control center at Edwards play an increasingly important role in a modern test program, but the central figure is still the pilot. He's the person who has to jockey an unproved airplane to the limits of its endurance, translating his physical reactions inside the cockpit into a language that's useful to the engineers on the ground. "No longer are they called upon to expand the envelope, as they say, of speed and altitude, to fly planes faster and higher than ever before," wrote John Noble Wilford in *The New York Times.* "An earlier generation did that, creating a lasting image of test pilots as fearless flying jocks, cool in the cockpit and devil-may-care the night before and after."

Today's pilots are a new breed; half pilot and half engineer, riding the cusp between guts and technology. "They are courageous and cool as ever," wrote Wilford, "but they also are more analytical and sober-sided, generally older and better educated and more likely to be expanding the rather prosaic envelopes of maneuverability, fuel efficiency and safety."

Major Thomas is part of this new breed. "It's no small trick to find a pilot who can speak engineering with the guys that sit at the other end of this hall," he has suggested. If the test plane displays an unusual pitching motion, for example, the engineers will want an accurate description of that motion immediately after the flight.

"Engineers talk in terms of frequency, damping, and amplitude to make a complete technical description of the airplane's motion," Thomas pointed out. A typical pilot, describing the same pitching motion, might say, "The damn nose is bouncing up and down so hard I couldn't read the instruments," or, "It bounced just a little bit and it was a nuisance," or, "I couldn't land the airplane." The challenge for the modern test pilot is to bridge the communications gap. "You're trying to observe those things well enough to quantify them:

The amplitude was about two degrees, plus or minus; the frequency was about three cycles per second," Thomas explained.

The first task for any test pilot is to "expand the envelope" in which his aircraft can operate safely. Beginning with relatively slow speeds, low altitudes, and easy maneuvers, he gradually pushes his plane faster, higher, and through more demanding twists and turns, enlarging the envelope outward from the center. "The early work we do with the airplane is to get the speed, the altitude, and the g-level envelope expanded to the point where we can come back and do the performance-type stuff," said Thomas, who was an operational fighter pilot for years before becoming a test pilot.

The pilot flies the plane as slowly as possible, just short of the point where it stalls or spins. He flies it as swiftly as possible, beyond which a control surface might flutter or blow off, causing the aircraft to career out of control. "There are lots of times I'm flying the airplane when I'm up there gritting my teeth," Thomas admitted. Is the plane going to hang together? Is the engine going to keep running? Is the airplane going to remain controllable? "If the thing comes apart supersonic, you're not going to tell anybody about it. That's going to be the end of you."

Test pilots at Edwards usually don't talk much about the dangers of their work. They don't need any reminders of the perils they face. Edwards Air Force Base took its name from Glenn W. Edwards, a pilot who died in 1948 while testing a craft called the Flying Wing. "It's a bad idea to forget that airplanes can kill you," Stephen Ishmael, another test pilot, told *The New York Times.* "But you shouldn't be flinching every time a light goes on."

After the flight envelope has been expanded sufficiently, the pilot begins the real work of the test program: putting his aircraft through thousands of individual test points, various maneuvers and structural stresses at different altitudes, speeds, and g forces that enable the technicians on the ground to collect data on the plane's performance.

On a typical morning the test pilot starts the engine, taxis to the runway, and shifts his controls back and forth to allow the engineers in the test center to determine if their instruments are functioning. He consults a small card on which the morning mission is outlined and sees, for example, that he is expected to take off with his throttle at the maximum power position. As his plane rises above the arid Mojave Desert, dozens of engineers in the test center peer at tiny needles recording data on paper strip charts, monitoring the aircraft's speed, power, temperature, vibration, and other flight characteristics.

Although this is an Air Force development test program, General Dynamics, the prime contractor, clearly dominates the process. Seventy of the engineers at the site work for GD; ten work for the Air Force. The test director, who runs the test center and maintains constant two-way radio communications with Thomas, is employed by GD. An Air Force officer stands alongside GD's test director during each flight with the authority to call it off if trouble develops. Air Force personnel sit next to GD engineers and monitor the same instruments. But the contractor, not the Air Force, generally supplies the driving force behind a development test program.

Contractors are always eager to push their test programs as quickly as possible. "They want to do everything as soon as they can, as fast as they can, in the most spectacular way that they can," said Major Thomas. "Our role in the Air Force is to pull back on the reins, making the judgment that this is, or isn't, reasonable to do at this point. . . . Contractors look at us as if we're conservative and stodgy and have no interest in ever seeing the airplane go into production. . . . We look at them and say, 'God, you guys are crazy. You'd do anything for money or publicity.' Contractors will say, 'Let's add this onto the aircraft. We'll go out and do it this afternoon. Let's do another test point. Let's go faster.' "

GD asked Air Force pilots to fly the F-16E at supersonic speeds the *first* time it lifted off a runway. "We turned them down," said Thomas. "We did it on the second flight." Northrop, which developed the F-20 export fighter with its own money, didn't have to ask the Air Force's permission. The F-20 hit supersonic speeds on its maiden flight, a dramatic achievement Northrop frequently highlighted in its promotional material.

The F-16E's spectacular ripple release of a dozen 500-pound bombs, with only a fifteen-millisecond interval between each bomb, was another example of contractor showmanship. "My personal feeling is that the major motivation to do it was to let General Dynamics take pictures of twelve bombs raining off that airplane for publicity purposes," Thomas suggested. Indeed, the risky test was performed successfully in August 1982, and impressive photos appeared the following month in *Aviation Week & Space Technology* and other publications. "It was the cleanest separation from external carriages that I have ever seen," declared GD vice-president Harry Hillaker, but Thomas was less impressed. He thought the ripple release was performed before the F-16E was ready, primarily as a publicity gesture. "There was no *technical* reason to do it at that point whatsoever," he said.

As the pilot ticks off one test point after another, the GD and Air Force technicians compare the data they receive with the results they expected. If the actual data deviate significantly from their predictions, the pilot will generally cut short his mission and return to the ground. Such an incident occurred in January 1981, when an F-16 test pilot noticed his engine was consuming too much fuel. Technicians on the ground observed the same problem. The pilot shut off his engine and made a successful dead stick landing back at Edwards. An investigation later identified the trouble as a fuel leak, which was corrected before the test program was allowed to continue.

For Thomas, as for many test pilots, a successful flight is one in which he flies his plane precisely as requested and hits each of the planned test points. "A really good day for me is when I go up and get some solid test data on the airplane that supports the derivative fighter comparison and tells us something about the airplane that we didn't know," he said.

The contractor, General Dynamics, has different goals, according to Thomas. "A good day for GD is when they get some marketing fodder for that airplane. If it goes faster than it has ever gone before or cruises from here to Fort Worth without refueling, or . . . if they get a really good comment out of the mouths of one of the pilots testing that airplane," he told me.

GD executives would hear those comments at the debriefing session held after each test flight. Despite mountains of data collected every time the F-16E goes aloft, more than forty engineers and flight test officials, including GD personnel, assemble in a large briefing room at Edwards to hear the pilot describe what he saw and felt. "There are many things about the airplane that will never show up on the strip charts," said Thomas. "It's a feeling, or it's a sensation . . . 'the airplane was on the verge of this,' or 'the airplane wasn't moving, but if I'd persisted, I know it would have done that' . . . those kinds of things."

GD employees eagerly pounce on any complimentary remark the pilot may make about their aircraft. These remarks, often lifted out of context like a single glowing sentence from a lukewarm movie review, are rushed to GD offices in Fort Worth, St. Louis, and Washington, where they're incorporated into comments GD executives make in briefings on Capitol Hill and at the Pentagon.

In addition to these debriefing sessions, test pilots jot down one-paragraph reports that summarize their impressions after each flight. These form the basis for a final report written months later, after the entire test program has been completed. Contractor personnel have access to the daily flight reports, but they are not supposed to see the pilots' final evaluation.

However, because it's understood within the flight test community that the pilots' daily reports are circulated widely, the Air Force encourages its pilots to be upbeat and positive. "Our basic guidance is: 'If you can't say anything nice, don't say anything at all about the airplane,'" explained Thomas. Even so, some contractors are very touchy when they read comments in the flight reports that they fear might be used to bad-mouth their aircraft. "Gee, you guys really don't understand the impact these comments have on our program," a contractor might whine, said Thomas. "We have to assume that all the bad comments you pilots are making about the F-16XL will get to the 'Mac Air' [McDonnell Douglas] people. That's going to kill us because they're going to announce this on the floor of the House."

Despite pressure from contractors, most Air Force test pilots aren't reluctant to criticize the planes they fly. "I get enthusiastic when I see good performance out of the airplane," Thomas said. "On the other hand, I am scrupulous about coming back and talking about a problem I have seen. The spectrum runs from 'This is unusual; take note of it because we might run into it later,' to 'This was disagreeable,' to 'This is completely unacceptable,' to 'You tried to kill me today!' "

Air Force test pilots inevitably find themselves at odds with the Systems Program Office (SPO) at Wright-Patterson, which is responsible for the aircraft's overall development. "The best news the SPO would ever get from me is that the aircraft works just like the contractor promised," explained Thomas. But technical glitches are inevitable. "What normally happens is, we say, 'This doesn't work right. We can't do that as fast as we expected. We've got problems here,' " he added. "They always get bad news from us."

# Chapter Nine

## Tanks for Everything

*(1)*

In February 1982 brief newspaper articles reported that the Chrysler Corporation had agreed to sell its profitable defense division to General Dynamics. GD would pay nearly $350 million for the automaker's subsidiary, known as Chrysler Defense, Inc. (CDI), which held Army contracts to build the newest M-1 Abrams tank. Chrysler's pugnacious chairman, Lee A. Iacocca, confidently declared that the injection of cash from the tank sale would enable his hard-pressed company to ride out the auto industry's worst recession in decades.

Most of the news stories about the sale of CDI that day focused on the transaction's salutary effect on Chrysler. But the transaction could be viewed quite differently. GD had just become America's most important defense contractor, the only company to hold major, long-running, multibillion-dollar weapons contracts with *each* of the three military services. It was already selling F-16 fighter planes and ground-launched cruise missiles to the Air Force. It was selling nuclear-powered submarines and sea-launched cruise missiles to the Navy. Now it was to sell M-1 tanks to the Army.

This unprecedented situation brought several questions to mind: Would the Army, the Defense Department, and the U.S. government benefit from this extraordinary concentration of defense business in the hands of a single contractor? Would anyone in government object to GD's purchase? How did this deal take shape? What motives and strategies drove Chrysler's Iacocca and GD's chairman, David Lewis, as the M-1 tank sale was conceived and consummated?

As it turned out, Chrysler desperately needed to raise cash, GD was initially reluctant to get involved with the much criticized M-1 tank program, and the Army quietly insisted that Chrysler sell its tank unit *only* to a solvent, top-notch defense contractor. What emerges is not a story of heroes and villains, rip-offs and financial chicanery. Rather, it is an inside look at how two huge corporations managed to strike a private business deal that benefited each of them, without upsetting the Army, the Defense Department, or the public interest. The deal took shape in Detroit.

Lee Iacocca, the burly, bristling fifty-seven-year-old chairman of the Chrysler Corporation, pushed aside his quarterly cash projections in the autumn of 1981 and groaned. If he didn't do something quickly to increase his company's cushion of cash, the nation's third-largest car maker could careen into bankruptcy by December. For three long years the American automobile industry in general—and Chrysler in particular—had been squeezed mercilessly by inflation, high interest rates, Japanese competition, and stiff federal requirements for better pollution controls and fuel efficiency.

Chrysler had watched its auto sales drop steadily for five years: from 2.4 million units in 1976 to a disastrous 1.2 million units in 1980. Detroit motorists could monitor the sorry state of the nation's auto industry by watching two famous Goodyear tire billboards that stand alongside I-94 and I-75 and continually flash the latest figures on U.S. car production, measuring the Motor City's blood pressure in effect. The symptoms weren't encouraging. Sales for the four major auto companies (General Motors, Ford, Chrysler, and American Motors) had plummeted from 10.6 million units in 1979 to 8.5 million in 1981.

Faced with possible bankruptcy at Chrysler, Iacocca turned to the Carter administration for help in 1979. The cocky car salesman cajoled the administration and Congress into guaranteeing loans of as much as $1.5 billion that Chrysler might have to borrow from private lenders to stay alive. Critics hollered, "Bailout!" Defenders hollered, "Jobs!" And Iacocca exuded confidence.

In June 1980 Chrysler "drew down" the first $500 million in its federal guarantees with the permission of the newly created Loan Guarantee Board. By the spring of 1981 Iacocca had tapped $1.2 billion of the $1.5 billion in federal guarantees that *might* be available. Despite the injections of cash, his company was still showing losses. The situation was grim, but Iacocca refused to surrender. He needed a plan to pull Chrysler out of its tailspin by the fourth quarter of 1981, or the company, its 87,000 workers, and the hard-earned reputation of Lido Anthony Iacocca might crash.

Chrysler's balance sheet boasted one oasis of profitability: Chrysler Defense, Inc., a wholly owned subsidiary that manufactured the Army's M-60 and M-1 main battle tanks. In 1981 CDI earned about $81 million in pretax profits on sales of $852 million, not a spectacular performance but healthier than that of the rest of the company. Ironically, most of the buildings and production machinery Chrysler used to manufacture the tanks were owned by the federal government, *not* by Chrysler. CDI's most valuable assets were the contracts it held to build M-1's for the U.S. Army and M-60's for overseas customers.

Chrysler began producing tanks in 1941. Its defense operation was broken off as a separate division thirteen years later. In four decades the corporation had manufactured more than 48,000 tanks and other combat vehicles for the United States and its allies. During World War II alone, 22,234 medium tanks —enough to equip more than 100 armored divisions—rolled off the assembly line at Chrysler's 113-acre Detroit tank plant (actually located just north of Detroit in Warren, Michigan). The company modified another 1,610 tanks for the British.

Tanks weren't all that Chrysler churned out for the war effort. Converted factories contributed everything from ambulances, troop carriers, and swamp buggies to air-raid sirens, landing gears, pontoon bridges, and aircraft wings. In the years since World War II the defense division enhanced its reputation with the production of M-47 and M-48 tanks, both known as Pattons, and more than 13,800 M-60's. For two generations, military and industry leaders had come to view Chrysler and battle tanks as virtually synonymous. By 1981, 7,000 CDI employees were building M-60 and M-1 tanks in five separate locations in Michigan, Ohio, and Pennsylvania.

Unlike its auto-producing parent, CDI earned profits consistently through the years. In many ways the tank subsidiary served as the company's "money cow," generating cash for Chrysler's strapped automobile operations. CDI pumped money into the corporate coffers, but very little ever flowed back to pay for in-house R&D work on future tank designs. Historically the defense division had been run as a separate business at Chrysler, with little day-to-day involvement by the automobile men at corporate headquarters and little interchange of personnel—people were either in automotive or in defense.

"The people in 'corporate' did not really understand the defense business, and because it never really represented a serious problem to them, they didn't get involved," explained one Chrysler insider. One year, when a CDI executive was droning through a fact-filled annual briefing on the tank plant's operation,

Iacocca interrupted him to ask, "Jesus Christ, I've got to listen to all of this again? I don't know what the hell you're talking about."

About the only time the tank division heard from corporate headquarters was when it received a memo discussing leased cars for company employees or other such peripheral subjects. The men who ran the defense operation liked to convey the idea that selling to the Pentagon was a mysterious art with its own magic language, which only they understood. The automobile executives tolerated the defense division's independent ways as long as it delivered profits, but they never considered it a very important part of their business.

Lynn Townsend, a former chairman of Chrysler, was once explaining to a group of businessmen that the company's defense division represented only a small part of the corporation's total sales when Thomas Morrow, who then ran the division, pointed out that it nevertheless generated a lot of profit. Townsend wasn't above humiliating his top executives. He reached into his pocket, pulled out a small handful of coins, extended his open palm, and sneered, "Yeah, this much!"

The possibility of Chrysler's bankruptcy worried the Army. As early as July 1981 an attorney in the Army general counsel's office in the Pentagon telephoned his counterpart at the Army's Matériel Development and Readiness Command, the weapons development agency in nearby Alexandria, Virginia, known as DARCOM. Generals in Army headquarters wanted to know if Chrysler's production of M-1 tanks would be affected if the giant automaker went under. Four days later a DARCOM lawyer had assembled a reassuring answer: Tank production at CDI could probably survive the demise of its corporate parent.

The government had already taken steps to insulate the tank division from any financial calamity that might cripple the parent Chrysler Corporation. When Iacocca sought help from the Carter administration in 1979, the new Loan Guarantee Board had required Chrysler to set up its defense division as a distinct corporate entity, one that could legally survive the collapse of Chrysler itself. The company complied by incorporating CDI in Delaware in June 1980 and swapping 10,000 shares of common stock in the new corporation for the assets and contractual obligations of its former defense division.

The following month Chrysler, CDI, and the Army signed an important novation agreement that recognized this transfer of assets and obligations. The agreement also required CDI to obtain the Army's written approval before it could sell its tank contracts to any other defense contractor. Once the novation agreement had been signed, the Army effectively held veto power over any proposed sale of CDI.

In the autumn of 1981, at the time Chrysler was thinking of selling CDI, General Dynamics was actively looking for a high-technology commercial business to acquire—especially a computer or telecommunications company. For years David Lewis had been assuring Wall Street financial analysts and his stockholders that GD was going to increase its civilian business, as a hedge against fluctuations in the defense market. "We have had a goal of trying to get fifty percent, commercial or non-governmental, and fifty percent, government business," he had told a group of stock analysts a few years earlier. At the time 60 percent of GD's sales came from the government, mostly from the Defense Department. Since then the proportion of GD's sales to the Pentagon had steadily *increased* rather than decreased, so that by 1981 government sales accounted for 84 percent of the company's revenues. (The figure rose to 86 percent in 1984.)

If GD were to purchase Chrysler's tank-building operation or any other defense firm, the proportion of its government sales would climb even higher. For that and other reasons, Lewis wasn't eager to acquire another defense unit. GD wasn't enjoying a good year in 1981. Its net income was down from the year before. Electric Boat was embroiled in an acrimonious contract dispute with the Navy. And its telecommunications business had lost money. Lewis might consider buying CDI if Chrysler put it up for sale, but he wouldn't be very eager.

As Iacocca's cash outlook grew bleaker, his options narrowed. He could try to sell off a portion of Chrysler's profitable car and truck operation in Mexico, but he hated to part with Chrysler de México, which had been the sales leader among U.S. auto companies in that country for eight straight years. He could try to sell off Chrysler's 15 percent interest in Peugeot of France, but Chrysler had already borrowed $100 million against its Peugeot stock. He could try to unload the company's 15 percent interest in the Mitsubishi Motors Corporation of Japan, but such a move might disappoint many Chrysler dealers across the United States who wanted to continue selling Mitsubishi autos in their showrooms.

That left Iacocca with one other option: Sell CDI. Though never an ardent fan of his tank-building operation, he was reluctant to cut into Chrysler's financial muscle by relinquishing one of its few profit-earning divisions. To do so might jeopardize his long-range plans for the corporation. Iacocca had pointed proudly to CDI's annual profits of about $80 million while lobbying for Chrysler's federal loan guarantees. He hesitated to sell the asset now.

Iacocca devoted little of his time to the defense division, but he occasionally got a kick out of driving the tanks around the Army's proving grounds. "I think he visualizes himself a bit like General Patton," observed one Chrysler executive. "He certainly has the same cigar-chomping style of General Creighton Abrams," the admired tank commander and former Army chief of staff after whom the M-1 tank was named.

The question Iacocca wrestled with was this: Which of Chrysler's assets—Peugeot, Mitsubishi, or CDI—best fitted into his long-term goal of selling automobiles in North America? The issue was debated along "Mahogany Row," the corridor of executive suites on the fifth floor of Chrysler's corporate headquarters in Highland Park, Michigan. It boiled down to automobiles versus tanks. To nobody's surprise, Iacocca, who had grown up in the car business and sometimes seemed to have motor oil coursing through his veins, stuck with automobiles.

Before he would resort to selling CDI to raise cash, however, Chrysler's chairman turned once again to the Loan Guarantee Board. In theory, Chrysler was still entitled to draw down the remaining $300 million in loan guarantees. The company had borrowed only $1.2 billion of the $1.5 billion in federally backed private loans. Unfortunately for Chrysler, the sympathetic Carter administration had been turned out of office, and the new Reagan administration might take a different view of the controversial bailout plan. The Loan Guarantee Board, the three voting members of which were the secretary of the treasury, the comptroller general, and the chairman of the Federal Reserve System, could decide not to approve any further drawdowns by the shaky Chrysler Corporation. Chrysler asked William Timmons, a leading Republican lobbyist in Washington, about the prospects for a further drawdown of $300 million. Timmons sensed the new administration would balk at additional loan guarantees but suggested that Iacocca test the water anyway with Treasury Secretary Donald Regan.

Chrysler's chairman flew to Washington, D.C., in mid-October 1981 on the pretext of testifying before Congress on legislation of interest to the automobile industry. Actually he had come to ask Secretary Regan if Chrysler would be allowed to tap its remaining $300 million in loan guarantees. Having declared publicly that he *wouldn't* ask for further loan guarantees, Iacocca did his best to conceal the true purpose of his visit. He didn't want the automotive trade press or the financial community to learn how desperate for cash Chrysler had become. Iacocca expected a cool reaction from Regan, and that's exactly what he got. The treasury secretary suggested that Iacocca not even ask for the remaining $300 million in guarantees because Regan didn't want the Loan Guarantee Board to have to reject Chrysler's request publicly.

In one sense Iacocca was disappointed. A final drawdown of the remaining $300 million would have provided the cash cushion he thought he needed. He was also relieved. Drawing down the first $1.2 billion had been a painful—and costly—experience for Chrysler. To make matters worse, the critical press Chrysler received during the well-publicized loan guarantee hearings made potential car buyers jittery. "Our sales went to hell during all the hearings and every drawdown," Iacocca complained later. He flew back to Detroit determined to sell CDI, the free world's leading tank manufacturer.

The man he chose to engineer the transaction was John W. Day, then president of CDI and an executive vice-president of the parent corporation. Day had worked for Chrysler since 1957 and spent his first five years in the defense division. This was his second stint as president of CDI. He had left that post during the negotiations for the federal loan guarantees to become corporate comptroller. A former Marine Corps rifle company commander, Day had more affection for Chrysler's tanks than most of his automotive-minded colleagues had. He was different in other ways as well. Having spent eighteen years running Chrysler operations overseas, he had developed a more subtle, indirect European management style than most of the hard-driving Detroit-trained Chrysler executives had. Ironically, the peddling of CDI would not be the first time Day would see a Chrysler operation sold out from under him. He had headed Chrysler's European automotive operations before they were unloaded.

Despite his history with the defense unit, Day urged Iacocca to put CDI on the block. "It was a desperation move," he recalled. "My recommendation was to sell it." He predicted that the tank-building subsidiary might sell for more than $250 million, an optimistic estimate that surprised Iacocca.

Peddling CDI was more urgent and would require far more diplomacy than the earlier sales of other Chrysler assets. The company was on the brink of bankruptcy and needed cash quickly. Iacocca and Day hoped to complete the tank division sale by the end of 1981, and Chrysler needed the approval of the Army before it could sell its tank contracts to any other company. Unless the Army was satisfied that the new buyer could build M-1 tanks as well as, or better than, Chrysler, it could nix any proposed sale.

## (2)

To many observers, a company would have to be foolish or masochistic or both to take over the embattled M-1 tank program. Having suffered through years of technical snags and accompanying negative news accounts, the tank had become a shorthand symbol to many Americans of what they sensed was wrong with the Pentagon's weapons procurement system.

Here was a tank that supposedly had taken decades to develop, broke down too frequently, guzzled nearly four gallons of fuel for every mile it traveled (that's *gallons per mile,* not miles per gallon), was vulnerable to the latest Soviet antitank shells, and had skyrocketed in cost. Surely no defense contractor would want to take on such a headache.

In fact, by 1981, insiders in the Army, Congress, and defense industry were not that troubled by the tarnished reputation of the Abrams tank. They knew that its nagging image problem was caused as much by the critical press coverage as by any inherent or unsolvable flaws in the weapon itself. By the time Chrysler was ready to sell CDI, M-1 tanks were deployed with the U.S. Army's 3d Infantry Division, stationed in Würzburg, West Germany, and praised enthusiastically by the commanders who operated them. Some defense contractors may have been wary about getting involved with such a controversial weapon, but most realized that the Army and Congress were unlikely to cancel a high-priority program in which so much time and money had been invested.

The M-1 tank, the most expensive peacetime procurement in Army history, traces its roots to 1963, when the United States began a cooperative tank development program with West Germany. Both that joint venture and a subsequent all-U.S. tank program died for lack of congressional support. A third American effort, the XM-1 tank, began in 1971. That program took on a greater urgency following the Arab-Israeli war two years later as weapons analysts studied the damage inflicted on Israel's M-60 tanks by relatively inexpensive enemy rockets and missiles. The XM-1 was designed to be an improved battle tank that could survive in such a "missile-rich environment" and protect its crew at the same time.

The XM-1's strengthened armor, top speed of forty-five miles per hour, unprecedented quietness, and ability to fire its 105-millimeter main cannon while on the move made it vastly superior to the M-60. "Its special armor, its hypervelocity main-gun ammunition, its revolutionary power plant, its cryogenic (supercold) night-vision system, its computerized aiming, its laser sensing devices, and its unique crew protection, among other innovations, stretch technology to its present limits," *Discover* magazine reported in 1982.

To reap the benefits of competition, the Army awarded development contracts in 1973 to two U.S. firms with experience building combat vehicles: General Motors and Chrysler. They were handed performance goals and a cost target of $507,000 per tank. Within that unit cost ceiling, the contractors were allowed to design any prototype tank that could meet the Army's performance criteria. After testing the Chrysler and GM prototypes and examining their manufacturing plans, the Army was to have two key decisions to make in 1976:

Which contractor should build the tanks and where should they be built?

Unlike some defense contracts, which are carried out in plants owned and operated by the winning company, this tank contract was destined for a government-owned contractor-operated facility (known in the defense industry as a GOCO plant). The Army planned to outfit the plant with government-owned machinery and turn the installation over to Chrysler or GM to operate. Under such an arrangement the government could put some of its idle factory space back to work. In theory, a GOCO plant would also cut the tank's cost by minimizing the capital investment the winning contractor would have to make.

The intense competition that erupted among a trio of midwestern cities to become the site of the Army's M-1 production plant demonstrates how attractive a major weapons system can be to a region racked by unemployment. Warren, Michigan, and Brook Park, Ohio, a Cleveland suburb, appeared to be the strongest contenders for the production plant. Each boasted a giant government-owned manufacturing facility that could accommodate the M-1 assembly line. (Chrysler was already building M-60's in the Warren plant.) And each desperately needed blue-collar jobs.

Plagued by the migration of manufacturing companies to the South and West, beleaguered mayors and municipal officials throughout the Midwest were trying to lure new employers to their cities any way they could. Thus, when the phone rang on the desk of Mayor Harry Moyer, of Lima, Ohio, and the unfamiliar caller refused to give his name, the city's top elected official was more than a little curious.

The anonymous caller said he was a native Ohioan, working in Washington, D.C. He hinted that he was a senior official at the Pentagon or a member of President Ford's White House staff, someone "in a position to know." The caller had a tip for the graying, small-town Mayor Moyer: The Army was still looking for a site to locate its new M-1 tank plant. It was considering Warren, once the rhubarb capital of Michigan, and Brook Park. But the city fathers of Lima might be able to persuade the Army to use the former Lima Ordnance Depot five miles south of town, which had lain virtually dormant since 1959.

Mayor Moyer was intrigued but nervous. The cautious leather goods merchant was still savoring his first election as Lima's mayor. Perhaps his political opponents were out to embarrass him with this anonymous tip.

"My God, I'm being set up," Moyer thought. "I can be blamed for *losing* the tank plant." He needed to fortify his position politically.

"Can you call me back at two o'clock?" he asked his caller. "I'll have the financial people, the Chamber of Commerce, and the 'movers' in my office. You repeat what you said. Then, we'll see what happens from there."

At 2:00 P.M., the nameless informant obliged, repeating his tip on a speaker phone to the bankers, retailers, and assorted "movers" assembled in the mayor's cluttered city hall office. With the prospect of thousands of new jobs dancing before their eyes, the movers and shakers of Lima, Ohio, committed themselves to winning the Army's new tank contract.

The economy of Lima, a city of 50,000 people located midway between Toledo and Dayton, was probably no better and no worse than many other hard-pressed midwestern cities in the mid-1970's. A blue-collar town of German, English, Italian, Irish, and Slavic workers, Lima (pronounced like the bean, not the capital of Peru) was the economic hub for about half a million people. Much of its population had recently fled the city itself to the surrounding counties. And many of the downtown shops and department stores, following the same pattern, had relocated to the new shopping malls sprouting on the outskirts of town. "Our downtown was a disaster," recalled the mayor, "just a wasteland."

Lima was home to several large corporate employers, including Procter & Gamble, Continental Can, Westinghouse, and Standard Oil, but other companies, like Ford, Clark Equipment, Ex-Cell-O, Dana, and Teledyne Steel, had already cut back their payrolls or closed their local operations. "We were out looking for industry," Moyer recalled later, "so this tank plant was just what we needed."

An Army GOCO facility would help in several ways. The city government couldn't levy property taxes on any federally owned buildings and acreage, but it could charge the tank manufacturer water and sewerage fees. In addition, it could collect a 1 percent city income tax from any plant employees who lived within the city limits. More important was the money that would be pumped into the local economy. "It takes three vendor support people to keep one hourly employee on that production line," the mayor figured. "The man in the sandwich shop, the tailor, the hardware store man. Your multiplier is at least three to one."

At times it wasn't clear whether Lima was courting Chrysler and GM or the rival contractors were courting the city. Locked in a fiercely competitive weapons development program, both tank manufacturers wanted Lima to support their pitches to the Army. Executives from Chrysler and GM toured Lima's empty ordnance depot and lunched with the city's bigwigs at the local country club. Chrysler officials came on particularly strong. Unlike GM, which planned to manufacture most of its tank parts itself, Chrysler said it expected to boost the Lima economy by purchasing many of its tank parts from small local businesses.

Despite the pleas, Lima officials never sided with either company. They were too busy touting their city's advantages over Warren and Brook Park. The Lima area offered an abundant supply of skilled factory workers, many of whom were hardworking part-time farmers, a pretty countryside instead of the urban congestion of Cleveland or Warren, and the wholehearted support of the community. Best of all, the plant site itself offered unencumbered access to cars, trucks, and railroads.

The history of the ordnance depot mirrored America's wartime surges and postwar demobilizations. An undeveloped 169-acre tract south of the city was first put to use by the Army in May 1941, seven months before the attack on Pearl Harbor. GM won a contract to operate the bustling GOCO plant during the war, employing more than 4,000 workers by late 1943 and eventually shipping some 100,000 vehicles.

The Lima Ordnance Depot was reactivated briefly as a modification facility where about 2,700 employees prepared tanks for shipment to Korea. But with the Korean truce, Lima's payroll shrank again. In March 1959 the installation, renamed the Lima Ordnance Modification Center, was placed on inactive status. Four years later it became an Army records warehouse.

When news spread that the Army was looking for a home for its new M-1 tank plant, many old-timers figured the Lima depot might hit the jackpot once again. The city's politicians and business leaders enlisted Ohio Governor James Rhodes, Senators Robert Taft, Jr., and John Glenn, and their local Republican congressman, Tennyson Guyer, to push Lima's case with the Army. They cornered President Ford during two 1976 campaign swings through Ohio and reminded him of their town's industrial assets. "We got enough out of the President to know that he knew Lima *existed,*" said Mayor Moyer.

The hard work paid off. In August 1976 the Army chose Lima over Warren and Brook Park as the initial production site for its M-1 tank. Lima was to build M-1 tanks for the first few years; then the Warren plant would be added to the production program. The Army may have selected Lima because it wanted a second tank plant to complement the one already turning out M-60's in Warren. Or it may have been impressed with Lima's obvious desire for an Army contract. Whatever the reason, the Lima community, with the exception of a few local preachers who publicly objected to residents building military weapons, rejoiced at the heartening news.

After extensive testing of both prototypes, the Army selected Chrysler over GM in November 1976 to develop the XM-1 tank. Chrysler's prototype had outclassed its GM rival in nearly every technical category. Despite some misgivings about Chrysler's commitment to quality control, the Army awarded the corporation $196 million to begin building eleven full-scale development tanks.

The XM-1 program attracted negative press from the start for two reasons. The development program was plagued with technical and cost problems. And it was actively opposed by a small, influential cadre of defense analysts who argued that the M-1 tank, like many other sophisticated weapons, was more expensive but no more effective than the weapon it was designed to replace.

It was true, as the media had reported, that there had been numerous malfunctions and technical glitches during the XM-1's development program. The steel tracks on the sixty-ton tank had an embarrassing habit of breaking. The tank's power train—its engine, transmission, and front drive—failed too frequently, causing the XM-1 to grind to a halt. The engine subcontractor, Avco Lycoming of Stratford, Connecticut, couldn't meet the delivery schedule for its 1,500-horsepower gas-turbine engines, the first such engines used on a battle tank. When the engines finally arrived, they had a tendency to suck up too much dust and often broke down prematurely. Gas consumption was alarmingly high (3.86 gallons per mile, according to one set of tests), raising the specter of an expensive brigade of fuel trucks accompanying the tanks onto the battlefield.

The absence of bulldozer blades on the front of the XM-1 tanks raised the additional possibility of a fleet of costly superbulldozers having to be driven alongside the tanks to help them burrow into protective positions during combat. The hydraulic fluid used inside the tank was said to be so flammable it could cause internal fires. And the heat from the turbine engine would make it difficult for the XM-1 to hide from enemy infrared detectors. The list of supposed deficiencies reported by the media during the tank's development phase went on and on.

Some of these technical snags showed up because the Army chose to accelerate the tank program by conducting the development testing (DT) and operational testing (OT) concurrently rather than consecutively. "This succeeded in saving time, but tended to exaggerate the teething pains uncovered in the trials, since engineering shortcomings found in the DT often cropped up in the OT trials as well," explained DMS Inc., a defense market research firm, in its analysis of the M-1 program.

The M-1 tank was widely criticized during its development phase for another reason: It had become the chief target of an orchestrated campaign mounted by weapons analysts and defense critics, inside and outside the Pentagon, who were convinced that the tank was a waste of money. Through a series of well-timed leaks to the media, the group was able to generate many newspaper articles and news broadcasts that seriously challenged the tank's value.

14. General Dynamics bought the U.S. Army's contract to build M-1
Abrams tanks, shown above at a NATO training exercise in West Germany,
from the Chrysler Corporation in 1982. With that $336 million acquisition
GD became the country's most important defense contractor, supplying
battle tanks to the Army, nuclear-powered submarines and sea-launched
cruise missiles to the Navy, and fighter aircraft and cruise missiles to the Air
Force. *Department of Defense*

Organized efforts to criticize an expensive weapons system during its development phase had become a familiar part of the Pentagon's procurement process.

"Whenever a new weapons system reaches the testing stage, a predictable
pattern emerges," observed former Secretary of Defense Harold Brown. "Test
failures occur and are highly publicized. No one explains that tests would not
be necessary if it were not expected that some of them would result in failures
or that these failures illuminate the changes that need to be made in the
system's design."

The Project on Military Procurement, a tiny advocacy organization established in Washington in 1981, criticized the M-1 tank more aggressively than
any group in town. The project was set up by a young woman named Dina
Rasor, at the suggestion of A. Ernest Fitzgerald, the Pentagon's most famous
whistle blower. It was designed to serve as a protective shield for Pentagon
employees who wanted to disseminate information that was critical of the

development, testing, or cost of individual weapons systems. Rasor served as a conduit between these employees, who had access to internal memorandums and test reports that discussed flaws in various weapons, and the Washington-based defense reporters, who were eager to see such information.

Rasor began her efforts by concentrating on the Abrams tank, rather than on fighter aircraft or exotic electronic gear, because the difficulties the M-1 was experiencing with its power train would be familiar to the average American. "It was something the public could understand," she recalled. She obtained test reports on the M-1 tank from sources inside the Army Tank-Automotive Command and additional material from the Pentagon through the Freedom of Information Act. She supplied a group of reporters with the information, which became the grist for a slew of articles criticizing the M-1 tank that appeared in *The Wall Street Journal, Christian Science Monitor, Chicago Sun-Times,* and other newspapers in April 1981. Rasor recalled the episode as "Holocaust Week" for the M-1 tank. By the time the media's first wave of interest had passed more than three dozen newspaper and magazine articles had blasted the tank.

The negative press coverage precipitated a furious and detailed rebuttal by the Army. "They put out these slick brochures, and it did the opposite of what they wanted," Rasor remembered. "It naturally made all the other journalists say, 'Man, they must really have something here because the Army is over-reacting.' "

Throughout the M-1's development and testing program, the Project on Military Procurement provided leaked memorandums and test reports to the sympathetic journalists Rasor called her "killer reporters." Each distribution of documents produced another wave of critical articles and news broadcasts. "I'm sure that for everything that I do, there's a great deal of activity in the Pentagon trying to undo it," she said.

In the M-1's case, press coverage turned sour even before the Project on Military Procurement got into the act. Trouble began shortly after November 1980, when the M-1 program manager, Major General Duard Ball, publicly announced that the estimated cost for all 7,058 tanks the Army planned to buy had risen dramatically. The total program acquisition cost, General Ball said, was expected to jump from approximately $13 billion to $18 billion—a 38 percent hike.

The press pounced on that new $18 billion figure, compared it with the earlier unit cost figure that had been associated with the XM-1 program, and reported an outrageous cost overrun. In the ensuing whirlwind of media criticism, the Army had little chance to explain what its newly released cost figures actually meant. "People took that eighteen-billion-dollar number, and they divided seven thousand fifty-eight tanks into those dollars, and said, 'My God, that adds up to two point six million dollars per tank,' " General Ball explained later. Then they found another cost estimate from eight years earlier that said the Army expected its contractor to build the tanks for $507,000 apiece. It looked as if the price per tank had increased fivefold since 1972. "Both numbers are accurate," the general continued. "But one is a projection of total program acquisition costs. The other is an estimate of the unit hardware costs." They are *not* the same thing.

The confusion is understandable. The procurement community uses four separate terms to describe four categories of weapons-related expenses. Comparing one category of costs to another makes little sense. It would be like comparing the cost of buying a single apple in a supermarket to the cost of growing and maintaining an apple orchard for twenty years.

Recurring unit production cost, often referred to simply as unit cost, is the price of manufacturing the weapon itself. If the Air Force pays General Dynamics $200 million to supply ten fighter aircraft, for example, the unit cost is said to be $20 million—that is, $200 million divided by ten aircraft. The unit cost does *not* include the cost of any extra equipment, such as the engine or electronic warfare equipment that the Air Force buys directly from other contractors and supplies to the prime contractor as Government Furnished Material (GFM).

Flyaway cost equals the unit cost of the weapon plus the cost of any GFM. If the same fighter aircraft, with a unit cost of $20 million, is equipped with a $2 million engine and $1 million worth of electronics, all supplied to General Dynamics by the Air Force, the flyaway cost of the plane will amount to $23 million.

Program acquisition cost includes the flyaway cost plus all the costs incurred to design, develop, and test the weapon prior to the beginning of its production. This broad category encompasses conceptual studies, think tank analyses, engineering and design work, construction of models and prototype weapons, simulations, and laboratory and field testing. A fighter aircraft with a flyaway cost of $23 million may have cost $900 million to design, develop, and test *before* production began. If the Air Force ultimately purchases 300 of those fighters, the program acquisition cost would equal approximately $26 million —the $23 million flyaway cost plus $3 million in development costs attributable to each of 300 planes.

Life-cycle cost is the broadest category used in the procurement community and the one most difficult to define. Basically, it includes all the expenses associated with developing, building, and *operating* a weapons system during its lifetime. For our hypothetical 300 fighter aircraft purchase, life-cycle costs would include all program acquisition costs plus the costs of recruiting and training the required pilots, maintenance crews, and support personnel; the fuel to operate the aircraft; the facilities and equipment to store, diagnose, and repair the planes; the spare parts; and a host of other expenses for a lifetime of perhaps twenty years. If the program acquisition cost of an aircraft is $26 million, its life-cycle cost could be 50 percent higher or more.

From this brief rundown, it's easy to see how confusion occurred in the media when the unit cost of the M-1 tank, as of 1972, was compared with the program acquisition cost, as calculated eight years later. The earlier figure covered only the price of building each vehicle, while the 1980 figure included the vehicle, all Government Furnished Material, all design, development, and testing expenses plus eight years of inflation.

Many journalists—and many of their readers—find these arcane distinctions between weapons costs incredibly boring. As a result, cost estimates from the early days of a program are sometimes mistakenly compared to later estimates. The fact that the two figures might measure entirely different categories of expenses can get lost in the shuffle. Unfortunately it's easier and quicker to keep it simple—a cost is a cost is a cost.

By 1981, when the development phase ended, most of the M-1 tank's technical shortcomings had been corrected. Despite the continuing criticism—some of it justified, much of it ill-informed—Chrysler's program survived. When the XM-1 tank dropped the $X$ (for "experimental") from its name and entered full-scale production, the vehicle was one of the fastest, safest, most maneuverable and hard-hitting tanks ever built. Critics might quarrel with the tank's escalating price tag and debate whether defense dollars could be better allocated, but the technical merits of the Abrams tank had been largely demonstrated.

Defense Secretary Caspar Weinberger's decision in September 1981 to authorize full-scale production marked the last formal hurdle the M-1 tank had to clear. Once it had entered production, there was virtually no stopping it.

Ironically, the M-1 tank passed its final milestone at about the same time that Lee Iacocca was deciding to sell CDI.

*(3)*

By pressing his dealers to sell cars, Iacocca had begun to build a cash cushion by the fall of 1981, but he wasn't satisfied. He needed at least $150 million on hand at all times just to cover his daily expenses. The sale of CDI looked like Chrysler's best bet. If Iacocca could raise $300 million to $350 million through the sale of his tank subsidiary, Chrysler could earn nearly as much *in interest* on that money as CDI had been earning by manufacturing tanks. With the prime interest rate hovering between 15 and 20 percent during the second half of 1981, the impulse among many American businessmen was simply to turn their capital assets into cash.

In October 1981 CDI president John Day decided it was time to notify the Army of Chrysler's intentions. On a visit to Washington he called Undersecretary of the Army James Ambrose, a former engineer and technical troubleshooter at the Ford Aerospace and Communication Corporation, who was then closely monitoring the controversial M-1 tank program for the Army. Ambrose is a tough-minded public official who knows the defense industry inside and out. "He can go through a four-drawer file cabinet and absorb it faster than any man on earth," said John "Jack" Guthrie, a retired Army general who once commanded DARCOM. Day considered Ambrose "an absolute workaholic"—often difficult to deal with, but always straightforward and fair.

Ambrose was too busy to see the CDI president that afternoon but suggested the two men meet later that evening in his apartment near the Pentagon. Soon after he had arrived, Day came promptly to the point. "I'm going to sell our defense business," he announced. Ambrose wasn't surprised. "We suspected that something might be happening," he said. Day assured the Army undersecretary that Chrysler understood its obligations under its novation agreement, intended to abide by those restrictions, and planned to offer CDI only to "reputable" companies. By "reputable," he meant large, financially stable *U.S.* companies.

Ambrose made it clear the Army expected nothing less from Chrysler. The Army held all the cards on this transaction, and Ambrose knew it. The conversation took less than an hour. As he headed back across the Potomac River to his hotel, Day realized it had been one of his more pleasant encounters with the no-nonsense Army official.

Chrysler executives assumed that the Army would welcome their proposed sale of CDI, and they were right. The Army realized that almost any defense contractor would be in better financial shape than Chrysler. Replacing the ailing automaker would lessen the chances of an interruption in the M-1 production. In addition, Army officials were dissatisfied with Chrysler's quality control. Too many "finished" M-1 tanks required extensive rework after rolling off CDI's assembly line. They also considered CDI's top managers stodgy, unimaginative, and timid, enjoying too little support from their corporate parent.

The Army's low regard for Chrysler wasn't new. It predated Chrysler's victory over GM for the M-1 development contract in 1976. Shortly after that source selection had been announced, a Chrysler employee bumped into a friend on the Army headquarters staff who candidly acknowledged the service's distaste for Chrysler. "We'd rather buy our new tank from the Soviets than buy it 'sole source' from Chrysler," the blunt officer admitted. Nevertheless, the Army had reluctantly awarded its M-1 program to Chrysler, which undeniably had designed the superior prototype.

Even though he sensed the Army was pleased that Chrysler wanted to sell its tank contracts, John Day wasn't taking any chances. He hired at least three different firms to help him orchestrate this delicate transaction. The most visible of the three was the prestigious New York investment banking firm of Lehman Brothers Kuhn Loeb, Inc. Day turned to Lehman Brothers for two compelling reasons. First, Roger Altman, a Democrat who had been deeply involved in Chrysler's loan guarantee negotiations as an assistant secretary of the treasury during the Carter administration, had returned to Lehman Brothers as a partner. Altman knew the workings of the Loan Guarantee Board from the inside. Second, Peter Peterson, chairman of Lehman Brothers, was an influential Republican who had served as Nixon's secretary of commerce. Peterson was respected by Wall Street executives and Republicans throughout the Reagan administration. Between Altman and Peterson, Lehman Brothers could cover the political waterfront.

Chrysler wanted to avoid the impression that the sale of CDI was a desperation move. "There was some thinking that this was a fire sale," acknowledged Chrysler's treasurer, Robert Miller. "Some companies thought they could get it cheaply." To avoid such notions, Chrysler authorized Lehman Brothers to organize what amounted to a sealed-bid auction. Lehman Brothers hoped that at least two companies would remain interested right up to the end. "We didn't want the bidders to be buying the subsidiary from Chrysler," said Stephen Schwarzman, the managing director of Lehman Brothers who actually peddled CDI. "We wanted them to be buying the subsidiary from each other." Schwarzman, a savvy deal maker, came highly recommended. He had helped Pan American raise cash quickly by selling the airline's Intercontinental Hotels Corporation subsidiary for $500 million in September 1981.

In late November 1981 Lehman Brothers contacted the chairmen of about thirty major U.S. defense contractors from a list Chrysler and Schwarzman had compiled. The roster included all the obvious giants in the defense industry and some smaller firms that might have been interested in getting involved in government contracting. Schwarzman sent a sales brochure to each chairman, asking if he'd be interested in acquiring the nation's only active tank manufacturer. Eight serious bidders stepped forward: General Dynamics, Litton, LTV, Martin Marietta, Paccar, Rockwell International, Teledyne, and United Technologies.

Day and Lehman Brothers recognized that Chrysler's dubious financial condition might dampen the prices offered for CDI. But they sensed the Reagan administration's vigorous defense buildup then getting under way would have the opposite effect. The President's initial Five-Year Defense Plan (FYDP, pronounced "fid-ip") for fiscal years 1982 through 1986 called for $181 billion more for defense spending than Jimmy Carter had envisioned. This overall jump in military spending made CDI an attractive business opportunity, even though the Army hadn't increased its planned purchase of 7,058 M-1 tanks.

In addition to Lehman Brothers, Chrysler retained Joseph Califano, Jr., the quintessential Democratic insider, who sat on its board of directors and had opened a law firm in Washington shortly after President Carter had axed him as secretary of health, education, and welfare in 1979. Chrysler turned to the fledgling firm of Califano, Ross & Heineman to sort out any problems that concerned the Army, the Federal Trade Commission, or the Justice Department, all of which had to approve any sale of CDI.

"We weren't looking for a lobbyist," Day recalled. "We were looking for a guy who was a lawyer, who understood the workings of the *bureaucracy,* as opposed to the legislative side of the business." Califano spent much of his time talking with Army officials and attorneys with Jones, Day, Reavis & Pogue, the firm the Army retained to provide additional legal advice.

Chrysler also retained the services of a lawyer-consultant named Francis McKenna, who operated with an even lower profile than Califano's. McKenna had just retired as the top civilian lawyer at DARCOM, the Army's weapons development command that oversees the M-1 tank program. As command counsel he had been involved in drawing up the novation agreement that now required Chrysler to seek the Army's permission before it could sell its tank operation. Having left the government, McKenna was a handy person to advise Day on steps Chrysler should take to win the Army's approval. He knew the people to see and the levers to pull.

There was nothing illegal about McKenna's sudden switch of loyalties. As long as he refrained from directly *representing* Chrysler in any of the automaker's dealings with the Army, he was legally allowed to advise Chrysler behind the scenes in any way he wished. Even so, Day and McKenna were extremely reluctant to discuss with me McKenna's involvement in the CDI transaction.

Perhaps it was that his consulting role with Chrysler, beginning only months after he had left DARCOM, might present the *appearance* of a conflict of interest even when none technically existed. Or perhaps it was that one of McKenna's business associates, Paul Cyr, with whom he shared a small office overlooking Washington's Maine Avenue marina, had been the subject of controversy in the past.

Once a DARCOM "legislative liaison" officer (a Washington euphemism for lobbyist), Cyr pleaded guilty in July 1982 to accepting a bribe of several thousand dollars from Edwin P. Wilson, former CIA agent and convicted arms merchant to Libya. In the close-knit community of defense contractors and Washington lawyer-consultants in which McKenna operated even the appearance of a conflict of interest or an informal relationship with a convicted bribe taker could raise uncomfortable questions.

GD's David Lewis was hesitant to get involved with the embattled M-1 tank program, but two of his subordinates had other, more personal reasons to take a strong interest in CDI. Taki Veliotis, who had been pulled out of the Electric Boat shipyard after clashing repeatedly with Admiral Rickover, had been appointed GD's executive vice-president for marine and international operations. Lewis asked him to head the first task force of GD employees dispatched to look over the Chrysler tank operation.

Oliver Boileau, GD's president, soon took over Veliotis's role. A relative newcomer at GD, Boileau may have felt the need to prove himself to Lewis. He had been lured away from a high-paying job as president of the Boeing Company's aerospace division in January 1980, with the tacit understanding that he might assume the chairman's position upon Lewis's retirement. However, Boileau's first eighteen months on the job had not been particularly impressive. His tenure as president began on a sour note when GD's air-launched cruise missile candidate lost a $4 billion Air Force fly-off to Boeing Aerospace, the company Boileau had just left.

Boileau had difficulty adjusting to GD and David Lewis. Lewis's firm but courteous manner contrasted sharply with Boileau's charismatic, tough, even explosive decision-making style, punctuated frequently with street-level vulgarities. "Boileau is crude," observed one admiring subordinate, "but crude as a tool. He uses vulgarity like a surgeon uses a scalpel. He uses it for effect, to shake a person out of his lethargy." Lewis is reserved and more indirect about calling a subordinate's bluff; Boileau slams the table in disgust and starts screaming. Both men get results, but their styles are completely different.

Meanwhile, Veliotis felt the GD chairmanship had been promised to him. He recalled having had a conversation with Lewis, soon after Boileau was named GD's new president, in which he was again assured of the top job. "It was understood that Boileau was only a figurehead," Veliotis said years later.

Lewis set up an unannounced horse race between Boileau and Veliotis for the chairman's position. Boileau would be forced to prove himself in a head-to-head competition with the hard-charging, egotistical Veliotis in a corporate "duel of the titans" designed to wring 110 percent effort from both executives. It was never clear whether Lewis had adopted this idea because he was disappointed with Boileau's performance or had planned it all along.

Boileau and Veliotis never got along. Competing with each other in a tacit succession contest only added to their ill will. Boileau was made to feel unwelcome at launching ceremonies at the Electric Boat and Quincy shipyards as long as they remained under Veliotis's control. And when Boileau was away from St. Louis headquarters on temporary assignments, Veliotis did his best to place his own people in critical corporate staff slots. The competition was intense.

Acquiring the M-1 tank operation and ensuring its financial success could be just the kind of bold business decision Boileau needed to demonstrate his value to Lewis. Boileau listened to Chrysler's sales pitch attentively. CDI executives pointed out that M-60 and M-1 tank production took place in Army-owned GOCO plants, not in company-owned facilities, just as GD's highly profitable F-16 fighters were built in an Air Force-owned GOCO plant in Fort Worth, Texas. Like many defense contractors, General Dynamics preferred to use government factories and equipment rather than spend its own money erecting expensive production facilities. In addition, Chrysler emphasized that the media attacks on the M-1 tank were no worse than the press criticism that had been aimed at Electric Boat's submarine programs, criticism GD had learned to endure.

Chrysler made a persuasive case. Boileau concluded that CDI's tanks would complement the rest of GD's product line and instantly turn GD into the Army's principal contractor. It looked like a good deal. And if he could convince Lewis and GD's board of directors to purchase CDI, his chances of landing the top slot at GD someday might be improved.

The acquisition of Chrysler's defense subsidiary made sense for General Dynamics. The tank contracts were already generating about $80 million annually in pretax profits. As assembly-line workers gained experience and GD managers adopted some advanced metalworking techniques the company was already using at Electric Boat's Quonset Point shipyard, those profits might be increased. Most important, the purchase of the M-1 tank contract would catapult GD into an unprecedented position as the major supplier of weapons to all three services.

The other seven companies that expressed an interest in Chrysler's defense unit shared many of GD's concerns about the controversial Abrams tank. To allay these concerns, Lehman Brothers set up a series of meetings for the eight potential bidders with top managers at CDI, executives at the Avco Lycoming engine plant, and various Army and Defense Department officials. Ostensibly these meetings allowed each company to gather information about CDI, but Chrysler and Lehman Brothers knew the sessions would also generate a competitive atmosphere and push the bids higher. This selling tactic had its drawbacks. Some companies resented the auctionlike atmosphere Lehman Brothers had orchestrated and withdrew from the bidding.

Preliminary offers were solicited in December 1981, and final bids were due the following month. After the first round three top bidders emerged: LTV, Teledyne, and General Dynamics. LTV was parent to such well-known companies as Jones & Laughlin steel, Lykes Brothers shipping, and Vought, a defense subsidiary that had been building weapons since World War II, including the A-7 attack plane and the Lance battlefield missile. LTV was headed by Paul Thayer, a seasoned defense industry executive who later served as President Reagan's deputy secretary of defense for one year before resigning to defend himself against allegations of insider stock trading.

Teledyne was the Defense Department's thirty-fifth-largest prime contractor in 1981, largely on the strength of its engines, remotely piloted vehicles, and navigation equipment. The Los Angeles-based company built the diesel engines for the Army's M-60 tanks. If Teledyne bought Chrysler's tank operation, it could remain in the tank business—even after production of the M-60 had stopped—and gain valuable experience in the turbine engine field.

## *(4)*

Once the field had been winnowed to three bidders, the Army invited each to a separate meeting at the Tank-Automotive Command headquarters in Warren at which its officials would outline their concerns and size up the prospective buyers. Above all else, the Army wanted to ensure that any new buyer would be able to deliver completed M-1 tanks on schedule. In addition, it expected the new contractor to cut costs and improve the quality of the M-1 tanks.

Chrysler's production techniques were considered inefficient by many observers. On one tour through the tank plant, Army Undersecretary Ambrose had been disappointed to see a lot more hand grinding of metal than he had anticipated. He also saw Chrysler workers machining tank turrets in one piece, an inefficient process that required too many man-hours.

Army officials cited several conditions that LTV, Teledyne, or General Dynamics would have to meet in order to purchase CDI. The buyer would have to: (1) sign an agreement with the Army, similar to the existing novation agreement, that would obligate it to continue all of Chrysler's current contracts; (2) carry out CDI's foreign military obligations, including a possible sale of the M-1 tank to the Swiss Army; (3) assist South Korea in developing its own tank-manufacturing operation; (4) cover all of Chrysler's pension obligations so that none of CDI's 7,000 employees would be hurt financially as a result of the sale; (5) put a ceiling on the *extra* payroll costs that could be passed along to the Army after the company had signed a new labor contract with the United Auto Workers (UAW), the union that represented about two-thirds of CDI's workers. Finally, any proposed transaction would require approval from the Loan Guarantee Board (which was primarily concerned with Chrysler's financial viability), the Federal Trade Commission, and the Justice Department (which would examine the deal's antitrust implications).

Boileau headed GD's contingent during its meeting at the Army Tank-Automotive Command. He stressed that although GD was a far-flung enterprise with 84,000 employees, its lean corporate staff of 250 people became intimately involved with every GD weapons program. St. Louis would always know what its divisions were doing, Boileau promised.

The company took pride in its role as a systems manager on the Air Force's F-16 fighter program, he added, a role he considered far broader than that of a traditional prime contractor. As a systems manager GD concerned itself with the quality and delivery problems that plagued *all* suppliers to the F-16 program, those that were subcontractors to GD as well as those that sold components directly to the Air Force. Boileau promised that GD would apply the same corporate philosophy in its management of the Army's M-1 tank program.

Major General Oscar Decker, head of the Tank-Automotive Command, was impressed with Boileau's masterful presentation and GD's strong management team. In fact, the general was a bit worried that the controversy surrounding the embattled M-1 tank program might scare GD off. "I am concerned that the company possibly is overrating the risks of taking over ownership and, therefore, may submit a bid too conservative to be competitive," General Decker wrote in an internal memo after the meeting. He reached this conclusion when Boileau asked pointedly if the Army might persuade Chrysler to accept other than the highest offer for its tank contracts. General Ball, the M-1 program manager, was also impressed, particularly with GD's management of its F-16 program and Boileau's pledge to dispatch immediately a "tiger team" of financial and production experts to recommend improvements at the tank plants.

Compared to its long-standing work for the Air Force and Navy, GD's defense contracts with the Army were minuscule. The company was developing the Viper, a portable antitank weapon (which has since been canceled), and building Stinger antiaircraft missiles. The two Army programs brought GD about $100 million in revenues in 1981. The addition of the M-1 contract would increase GD's sales to the Army tenfold, to more than $1 billion.

The Defense Department was satisfied with GD as a potential buyer of CDI. The Defense Logistics Agency, a procurement organization that buys common items for all the services, prepared a background fact sheet that gave GD a clean bill of health, saying it was in "excellent financial condition."

David Lewis thought the Defense Department might hesitate before permitting GD to purchase the M-1 tank operation—not because GD would be able to wield too much power but because there might be a *political perception* that it was receiving special treatment from the Pentagon. "The Defense Department worries about the political situation," explained Lewis, who could imagine GD's rivals wailing, "They're giving all that damned business to General Dynamics." In fact, GD hasn't been able to exercise inordinate influence over Pentagon decision makers, even with its many defense contracts. Lewis said that's because each of GD's contracts exists in an "isolated pigeonhole" and the military services operate independently. "We don't feel like we've got much clout," he added.

That fact became clearer to Lewis when he was unable to set up an appointment to meet in the Pentagon with Defense Secretary Weinberger. Despite the concerted efforts of GD executives in St. Louis and Washington, Weinberger still hasn't met face-to-face with Lewis as of this writing.

The final decision to approve or disapprove the proposed sale of CDI would be made by the Army, not by the OSD, but Weinberger was briefed on the status of the transaction before the final bids were received. Army officials told him that Chrysler had been allowed to search throughout U.S. industry for a qualified buyer. At the same time the Army had protected its interests by notifying prospective bidders of the strict obligations under which they would operate if they bought the tank contracts.

The Army told Weinberger that Chrysler's top executives hadn't been paying enough attention to their tank subsidiary. "Chrysler was consumed with keeping Chrysler alive as a corporation," General Ball recalled. "Tank production did not have a high priority." Even worse, the Army expected no improvements if CDI remained in charge of the M-1 program because the parent company obviously had no money to invest in tank production.

For months the Army had been hammering at Chrysler about late deliveries and the poor quality of its M-1 tanks. At first the Army program manager complained to his Chrysler counterpart, the president of CDI. The complaints produced few visible improvements on the factory floor. The Army's unresolved problems were elevated to General John Guthrie, the commander of DARCOM, who corresponded directly with Chrysler's chairman. Iacocca simply referred the general's letter back to John Day and disinterestedly told the CDI president to "handle it."

General Guthrie met privately several times with Iacocca, who invariably assured the general of his renewed commitment to the M-1 tank. Guthrie was temporarily pacified, but hearing Iacocca's promises and witnessing their results were two different things. "When you don't see quality come onto the floor, and you don't see the vice-president for quality given a little clout, and you don't see the proper inspections established, but you do see a continuing high number of deficiencies at the end of the line, you know quality is not there," General Ball declared.

After the Army had completed its briefing, Weinberger wondered aloud why Chrysler was able to sell its M-1 tank contracts for hundreds of millions of dollars. "How can anyone expect to sell *our* contract for that kind of money?" he asked. "Explain that to me." The Army officers told him that Chrysler was selling not only its Army contracts but also the technical expertise of its designers, engineers, manufacturing specialists, and production workers who constituted the nation's only active tank-building team. Virtually all of CDI's employees would move onto the buyer's payroll after the sale was consummated. That expertise and experience were worth a lot of money, they explained.

GD, LTV, and Teledyne, the three top bidders, were offered sales contracts and access to CDI's books. They submitted their final bids in January 1982. Officially the Army didn't indicate its preference among the three companies. Because it deemed each company financially and technically qualified, the Army left the final choice to Chrysler.

Unofficially many officers hoped that Teledyne wouldn't win. Teledyne had built the diesel engine that GM had used in its losing XM-1 prototype. Ever since, Teledyne marketing representatives and public relations executives had mounted a quiet campaign in Washington to discredit the rival Avco Lycoming turbine engine. Teledyne employees had leaked several Army documents critical of the Avco engine, which served as the grist for numerous negative newspaper stories about the turbine engine and the tank itself. Guerrilla public relations campaigns of this sort are not uncommon among defense contractors in Washington, but the Teledyne effort was bolder than most. "Teledyne are tough marketers, and do everything they can to promote their cause," said

General Ball. "I get a little ticked-off with them once in a while because they do overrepresent their case."

The marketing strategy mapped out by Chrysler and Lehman Brothers to boost the price of CDI apparently worked. GD made a generous bid that was almost 40 percent *higher* than John Day had optimistically predicted a few months earlier. The fact that the offer included a large chunk of cash up front made it even more attractive. It appeared Chrysler would get its badly needed money and GD instantly would become the Army's most important contractor.

During a month of final negotiations Chrysler and GD continued to haggle over the employee pension obligations GD would have to assume. At one point Chrysler tried to fatten up GD's offer by negotiating through the press. "If the price is right, we'll consider selling any of our assets, including divisions, plants and operations," a spokesman for Chrysler coyly told a Reuter's reporter ten days after the final bids had been submitted but before the possible sale of CDI had been acknowledged publicly. "But it must be a very tempting offer."

John Day recalled GD's bargaining tactics as the deadline approached: "They wanted to keep negotiating this, that, and the other thing, and it was getting down to the hairy last minute. We were just about to tell them to go fly a kite; we would go back and start negotiating with Teledyne." As the bargaining came down to the wire, David Lewis played a personal role in the negotiations for the first time. He spoke with Iacocca, insisting on one contract concession after another. The chairman of Chrysler yielded again and again but finally sensed his company was getting too close a haircut. "You just cut enough hair, Dave," Iacocca barked into the phone. "If you want a deal, the deal is here now, and that's it." Lewis took the deal.

On February 16, at a union conference in Detroit, UAW president Douglas Fraser leaked word of the impending sale before either Chrysler or GD was ready to announce it. Fraser, who sat on Chrysler's board of directors, predicted the sale would hurt the automaker over the long haul because the company would be parting with an assured source of profits. Three days later Iacocca and Lewis, at their respective headquarters, unveiled the $348.5 million deal. Iacocca was enormously pleased, saying the sale of CDI would bring in about $350 million and allow Chrysler to focus its attention on its car and truck operations without having to rely on auto rebate gimmicks to generate cash.

Wall Street reacted calmly to the announcement, recalled Arvid Jouppi, a longtime auto industry analyst. Chrysler's decision could have been criticized,

15. Lee Iacocca, Chrysler's chairman, wasn't eager to sell his profit-making tank operation, Chrysler Defense, Inc., but the auto company's financial predicament in late 1981 left him few alternatives. *Chrysler Corporation*

but it was generally greeted sympathetically in investment circles, perhaps because so many banks and financial institutions stood to lose a lot of money if the company went under.

In a characteristically restrained public statement, Lewis said the tank division had the potential for higher sales and earnings in the future and would fit in well with the rest of GD's other defense business.

The deal was hailed in the press. "Given the likelihood that the sale will be approved by the Army and the Pentagon," the *Chicago Sun-Times* declared dramatically, "General Dynamics stands to become the military-industrial complex's supercontractor of the decade, dwarfing McDonnell Douglas Corporation, United Technologies Corporation, Boeing Company, General Electric Company, and Lockheed Company." In somewhat more measured tones, *The Wall Street Journal* predicted, "The sale will make the Pentagon as dependent upon General Dynamics as ever it has been on a single supplier."

A month later, after GD had audited CDI's inventory, both companies agreed to lower the final selling price by $12.4 million to $336.1 million. Chrysler's lawyers and lobbyists had cleared the path for the transaction in Washington, where it was approved without objection by the Loan Guarantee Board, the Federal Trade Commission, and the Justice Department's antitrust division.

Chrysler got its money. GD got the nation's largest tank production contract. Oliver Boileau was assigned to oversee the integration of the tank plant into the GD management system. And the Army got General Dynamics as its major supplier. Everyone was pleased.

## (5)

The decision to part with CDI may have been difficult for Iacocca to make, but it came as welcome news to the UAW. The union had feared a bankrupt Chrysler would throw thousands of tank plant employees out of work. Union members at the company's profitable tank plants were still bitter that along with workers at the unprofitable automotive division, they had been forced to make wage concessions in 1980 as a condition of the federal government's loan guarantee. The UAW had accepted wage and cost of living concessions worth about $880 million, leaving Chrysler workers earning between $2 and $3 less per hour than their counterparts at GM and Ford. "We're paying for the automobile division being in trouble," grumbled one employee at the Lima tank plant.

With GD as the new owner, the union expected to win back those wage concessions when its contract expired in September 1982. "We're in a booming industry now with defense," added James Coakley, president of the UAW local at the Warren tank plant, "and we expect to be compensated accordingly." David Lewis and Oliver Boileau, however, were not about to bow to the auto workers' wage demands.

GD drew up plans to resist any strike the UAW might call. The plan, which was outlined in a confidential memorandum, called for hiring nonunion, or scab, labor, employing extra security guards, and reassigning supervisory employees to the tank production lines to avoid any interruptions. This "get tough" memorandum was left—either accidentally or intentionally—on a desk where union negotiators could see it. The union intercepted the memo and quickly provided copies to Detroit's newspapers, according to Marc Stepp, a UAW vice-president. The union realized that negotiating with a healthy GD might be just as difficult as it had been with an ailing Chrysler. "The unions are discovering that David Lewis is no shrinking violet," observed Wolfgang Demisch, a prominent defense industry analyst.

Signs quickly went up at the facilities in Ohio, Michigan, and Pennsylvania announcing that Chrysler Defense, Inc., had been renamed the Land Systems division of General Dynamics. The M-1 tank, the subcontractors, the GOCO plants, and the work force remained the same; only the prime contractor had changed.

As Boileau had promised, GD dispatched a tiger team of about twenty purchasing, quality control, financial, industrial relations, and production troubleshooters to oversee the transition from Chrysler to GD. The team consisted of employees gathered from other GD divisions on short-term assignment and a group of private management consultants. Every Sunday evening tiger team members would fly into Columbus, Ohio, and drive the seventy-five miles to Lima for the week's work.

The team quickly established a conservative, button-down image. At the Davis Plaza Motel they rose punctually at 5:30 A.M. and regularly ate breakfast together. "You'll know 'em," said one motel employee, "they're the *only* ones around here who wear business suits." The tiger team had originally taken rooms across I-75 at the Regency Inn, but the female "distractions" and late-night noise from the motel's Sly Fox Lounge soon sent them packing. "We're all family men," confided one tiger who requested anonymity, "and we want to stay that way."

GD moved swiftly to spruce up its plants and embrace its new work force, concrete steps that buoyed the spirits of employees who had worried for years that the next paychecks from Chrysler might be their last. "They were now part of a living, thriving organization, rather than the hind leg of a dinosaur," said one former Chrysler employee who asked not to be identified.

GD also moved quickly to try to win a key prize: an Army production contract worth more than $2 billion to build 54,973 one-and-a-quarter-ton High Mobility Multi-Purpose Wheeled Vehicles (HMMWV), known more commonly by their nickname, Humvees. These versatile vehicles would replace old Marine Corps and Army Jeeps, serving such diverse roles as troop carrier, ambulance, and antitank missile launcher.

Boileau hastily tried to pull together an attractive proposal for the Army by tapping some of GD's best technical brains. He personally briefed the Army's program office in what one participant called a charismatic, virtuoso performance. He oversaw every detail of the presentation, down to the color of the business suits he permitted his GD subordinates to wear. (He banned brown because he believed that color conveys insincerity.) Despite a valiant, catch-up effort, GD lost its bid for the Humvee contract one month after it had bought CDI. "GD missed the brass ring of the century," mused one knowledgeable insider.

The Army awarded the contract to AM General, the division of American Motors that builds the Jeep. Critics at the time accused AM General of buying in by offering the Army an unusually low price to build the Humvees. Suspicions were aroused further when the financially strapped American Motors Corporation announced four months later it was selling its AM General subsidiary to LTV for about $190 million.

Since GD took over Chrysler's tank operation, it has showered the Land Systems division with technical brainpower drawn from other divisions of the company. It has invested large sums of money on new equipment to improve worker productivity. And it has listened to suggestions from its own employees. "They loosened the corset around the whole corporation," noted one former CDI employee. But GD has not yet revealed any grand vision of the future. The Land Systems division, like its predecessor, CDI, remains virtually dependent for its future revenues on the sixty-ton M-1 main battle tank or its various "heavy" derivatives. Until recently, GD had expended relatively little R&D effort exploring smaller, lighter tanks that might meet changing military requirements in the future.

Shortly after General Dynamics had acquired CDI, Lewis announced that Oliver Boileau was moving to Detroit for several months to ensure that the Land Systems division would be melded into the GD management structure without a hitch. To some industry analysts, Boileau's temporary assignment looked like the kiss of death—a calculated move by Lewis to banish his number two man from the inner sanctum of corporate headquarters. Why else would Lewis send the president of the corporation to run one division? Boileau had already "punched that ticket" at Boeing Aerospace, cynical analysts pointed out. Perhaps Boileau wasn't Lewis's heir apparent after all.

Those defense industry pundits had missed the significance of Boileau's new assignment. Just as James McDonnell, Jr., had dispatched forty-nine-year-old David Lewis to California in 1967 to integrate the newly acquired Douglas Aircraft into the McDonnell Douglas Corporation, Lewis may have devised a similar rite of passage for Boileau. If GD's president avoided any serious missteps in Detroit, his chances of succeeding Lewis would be greatly enhanced.

Before long Land Systems was able to eliminate the production backlog that had plagued Chrysler. GD actually lost money on the initial M-1 tanks that rolled off its assembly line because the company had to make good on warranty work required on earlier Chrysler-built tanks. Within a few months, however, Land Systems was turning a small profit on each new tank. When Lewis originally examined the CDI deal, he hadn't counted on a large profit in the short run from the tank contracts. His plan was to cut costs and streamline the manufacturing process so that the tank plants eventually resembled GD's smoothly functioning F-16 assembly line in Fort Worth.

It took Boileau about twelve months to establish his management team at Land Systems, somewhat longer than Lewis had expected. The key was the appointment of Robert Truxell, a former executive with GM's truck and bus division, as general manager of the tank operation and a corporate vice-president. With Truxell in place, Boileau returned to GD headquarters in St. Louis.

*    *    *

The management philosophies at Chrysler and GD could not have been more different. Under Chrysler's laissez-faire attitude, CDI executives rarely heard from their corporate headquarters. Under GD's ownership, the same executives suddenly discovered they couldn't make a move without feeling David Lewis's breath on their collars. "This is an absolute dictatorship," said one former CDI employee who weathered the transition. "There's nothing wrong with a benevolent dictatorship, but it's still a dictatorship."

Under Chrysler, tank division executives never drew up formal business plans that detailed their future marketing strategies. They simply sat back and waited passively for tank orders to arrive from the Army. By contrast, a telex from GD headquarters arrived at the Land Systems division within a few days of GD's takeover outlining specific requirements for a strategic plan: Each GD division was required to complete lengthy work sheets that described its existing weapons programs, current and future funding levels, any anticipated technical or budgetary problems, and the long-range profit projections. These annual plans enabled corporate staff members to spot trouble, identify new marketing opportunities, or redirect a division's efforts.

Each division's strategic plan would be presented formally to David Lewis, but it would be "scrubbed" by experts at headquarters several times before it reached the chairman's office. Soon after Land Systems had been established, a small team of specialists flew in from St. Louis to help the tank executives translate vague plans from their CDI days into GD's structured format. A second team followed to review the first draft. "You can't fail to dot an *i* without someone telling you," explained one employee who endured the rigorous planning process. Finally, in July 1982, a "murder board" of fourteen strategic planning experts from corporate headquarters flew to Detroit to be briefed on Land Systems's annual plan.

By the time it reached David Lewis the plan had been challenged, criticized, and probed by three layers of GD's corporate management. Technical problems with individual weapons programs had been confronted. Profit projections had been questioned. Excessive cost optimism had been expunged. The plan was ready for the scrutiny of a very demanding chairman.

Such conscientious preparation of each division's annual strategic plan is only one indication of GD's tightly centralized management style. Every month a team of financial experts from corporate headquarters visits each division to monitor its performance. Every quarter top divisional managers meet, usually in St. Louis, for exhausting two- or three-day operational reviews with Lewis, during which they bare their souls about problems, personnel, and objectives. Lewis demands to know *everything*. "He is not a management-by-exception guy," explained James Beggs, a former GD executive who became the head of NASA. "He doesn't wait for things to happen. The division managers are always amazed by what Lewis knows about what's going on in their divisions."

A team of lawyers and accountants at corporate headquarters oversees the preparation of cost estimates and contract prices for all GD weapons programs. These decisions are made in St. Louis, rather than at the divisional level, because Lewis believes they are crucial to success in the defense industry. "In government business cost estimating, contract administration, and financial controls are probably as important, if not more so, as the satisfactory performance of the operating division," Lewis has contended. GD succeeds because it bids conservatively, negotiates its contract prices cautiously, and controls its production costs.

# Chapter Ten

# The Fraud Fighters

## (1)

When General Dynamics and the Navy settled their attack submarine claims dispute in June 1978, one of the most unpleasant eras in Navy shipbuilding history finally appeared to come to a close. The opposite was true. Outraged by Assistant Navy Secretary Hidalgo's financial compromise with GD, Admiral Rickover badgered the Navy to investigate the way Electric Boat had prepared its $544 million claim. He suspected fraud.

At the admiral's insistence the Navy eventually referred his allegations to the Justice Department, which launched a two-year grand jury probe in Hartford, Connecticut, to determine whether any GD employees had defrauded the Navy by intentionally submitting false, misleading, or padded contract claims. Federal prosecutors tried to identify someone working for GD who knew that Electric Boat had sought reimbursements for shipbuilding costs it hadn't actually incurred. After an exhaustive probe, in which more than forty witnesses testified before the grand jury, prosecutors announced in January 1982 that they would *not* seek indictments against General Dynamics or any of its employees. The case was officially closed.

Predictably Rickover blasted the Justice Department and implied that the prosecutors had whitewashed the investigation. In a letter to Attorney General William French Smith, written the week after the GD probe had been dropped, the admiral criticized Justice for its efforts on the GD case as well as on pending fraud investigations involving claims submitted by two other naval shipbuilders, Litton and Newport News. "Today, after years of effort," Rickover wrote, "it appears that the Justice Department is systematically closing down these investigations—either overtly or by inaction—even though the claims are demonstrably false and those who have investigated them have, I believe, recommended to their superiors that indictments be sought."

As usual, Rickover's criticism made snappy newspaper headlines, but on this occasion his assessment of the GD probe was fundamentally inaccurate. Prosecutors had dropped their investigation of General Dynamics not because they wanted to go easy on a powerful defense contractor but because they couldn't put together a strong enough case.

The outcome of the investigation illustrates the difficulties the Pentagon and Justice Department often confront when they try to convict a major defense contractor of fraud. In some cases prosecutors discover that actions they initially suspected to be fraudulent turn out to be innocent instances of corporate mismanagement, wishful thinking, or incompetence. In other cases, when they *know* a defense contractor has submitted a fraudulent claim to the government, they have a hard time dissecting the company's management hierarchy and identifying the proper individuals to blame. As Rickover lamented, "finding individuals to hold accountable is far more difficult than proving the claim is false."

The GD probe also illustrates how a well-intentioned team of Justice Department prosecutors, FBI agents, and naval investigators can vigorously pursue a defense contractor and then legitimately conclude that it shouldn't indict anyone. It demonstrates how prosecutors conduct themselves during a grand jury investigation and how they decide to drop a case. In the end this incident underscores one immutable fact: It is a lot easier to allege contract fraud than to prove it.

The seeds of the fraud investigation were sown in 1977 when Charles Masalin, a little-known Navy captain, prepared an internal memorandum for the commander of the Naval Sea Systems Command (NAVSEA) that outlined irregularities he saw in GD's pending contract claim. The Masalin Memo, as it came to be known, identified what he considered misleading information or grossly inaccurate statements in the mammoth claim.

Though written for the NAVSEA commander, the Masalin Memo was welcomed enthusiastically by Admiral Rickover, who had long believed that Electric Boat, and many other naval shipbuilders, regularly gouged the Navy with inflated and fraudulent claims. Rickover surprised Masalin by using the memo repeatedly to bolster his call for an investigation of General Dynamics for fraud. "He certainly got a lot more mileage out of it than I ever expected," Masalin acknowledged years later.

In December 1977 Rickover referred what he called "specific examples of apparent fraud," largely drawn from the Masalin Memo, to his superiors. Those senior admirals, familiar with Rickover's distrust of shipbuilders, weren't particularly eager to pursue a criminal investigation against GD. In late 1977 the Navy was still embroiled in bitter claims disputes with its three largest shipbuilders, Electric Boat, Newport News, and Litton. A fraud investigation stemming from Electric Boat's attack submarine claim would only increase the acrimony.

But Rickover was too powerful for the Navy to ignore. Once his allegations had made their way to Capitol Hill, it became politically impossible for the Navy general counsel's office to stifle a criminal investigation of GD. The Navy reluctantly referred the allegations to the Justice Department then headed by Jimmy Carter's attorney general, Griffin Bell.

Like their counterparts in the Navy, senior officials at Justice were accustomed to Rickover's vehement insistence that most, if not all, defense contractors were cheats and scoundrels. Nevertheless, after reviewing the Navy's file, Justice prosecutors decided to investigate further. They referred the file to the department's criminal division, which in turn assigned the case to its fraud section. It assembled a prosecution task force that consisted of one, and later two, Justice Department attorneys, a handful of FBI agents, and a representative from the Naval Investigative Service.

Merely by accepting the case and establishing a prosecution team, Justice went farther with the GD fraud allegation than it goes with hundreds of cases referred to it by agencies and departments in the executive branch. Many of these agencies and departments have investigative units to detect crimes against their personnel and property, but none of them can prosecute suspected criminals under federal law without the cooperation of the Justice Department. Investigators throughout the government are thus forced to "sell" their cases to a Justice prosecutor—either a U.S. attorney working in the field or a prosecutor based at the Justice Department's headquarters in Washington.

This selling process has often been a problem for the Pentagon. Investigators working for the OSD or the three military services (in the Army's Criminal Investigation Command, the Naval Investigative Service, or the Air Force's Office of Special Investigations) historically have had a hard time convincing U.S. attorneys to prosecute their cases. Justice declines many of these cases because they lack an elusive quality known as jury appeal. Prosecutors hesitate to take on cases they think they won't win.

For example, individuals accused of defrauding the gargantuan Defense

Department out of health benefits or pension payments sometimes appear too sympathetic to prosecute successfully. Cases involving corporate fraud, even when the dollar value is high enough to warrant prosecution, might be rejected if the documentary evidence would inevitably put a jury to sleep. Other cases are declined because they simply aren't strong enough.

It's impossible to pin down the amount of money the Pentagon loses each year to contract fraud. Joseph Sherick, the Defense Department's first inspector general, has estimated that fraud costs the Pentagon roughly $1 billion a year. "The opportunity is there to steal one percent to three percent of the procurement budget," he has said, while acknowledging that no one really knows.

Contract fraud, compared to other felonies, isn't easy to prove, because its victims aren't obvious. Unlike murder, contract fraud leaves no dead body on the carpet. Unlike robbery, it involves no obvious theft of goods or property. Unlike rape, it produces no immediately apparent victim. In murder, rape, assault, and theft cases, investigators usually ask, "Who committed the crime?" In white-collar contract fraud cases, they generally begin by asking, "Was a crime committed?"

## (2)

Government contract fraud—the intentional deception of the government by a contractor or would-be contractor for its own financial benefit—takes many forms. A company may promise to sell the government goods of a specified quality and instead supply cheap, substandard merchandise. An Illinois firm and two of its former officers, for example, were convicted of fraud in 1983 for selling more than 1,000 miles of substandard parachute cord to the Pentagon. An assistant U.S. attorney who happened to be a Vietnam War veteran and a former parachutist prosecuted the case.

A firm's bid for a government contract may fraudulently specify its average labor costs at $12 per hour when in fact it knows its labor costs are only $9 per hour. Another company may blame the government for costly production delays in a weapons program when it knows its own management failures have caused the problem.

A firm may try to include under a cost-reimbursement contract lavish expenses and unrelated perks for its executives which it knows aren't legally reimbursable under that contract. GD was accused of this form of fraud at a congressional hearing in February 1985 for allegedly charging the government $18,000 for an executive's country club initiation fee, $800 for liquor for the Air Force Association, $155 to board an executive's dog at a fancy kennel, and thousands of dollars for David Lewis's flights in GD corporate aircraft to and from his family farm in Georgia, among other questionable expenses. GD officials admitted that a few of the dubious expenses had been submitted improperly but generally maintained that its overhead charges conformed to explicit government acquisition regulations. A company may try to shift some of its costs from a fixed-price contract to an unrelated cost-plus contract so the government picks up the tab. Another company may alter the invoices it has received from a subcontractor and charge the government $100 for a component it bought for only $5.

In each of these examples the company *knowingly* tries to cheat the government. When a company acts inadvertently, federal prosecutors treat the matter much more leniently. "If we see evidence of an intent to defraud, it's a criminal case," Jo Ann Harris, a veteran prosecutor, once warned an audience of private contract lawyers. "If we see only mistakes of judgment made in good faith, it's a matter for the administrative and civil process."

In its war on fraud the federal government draws upon an arsenal of legal weapons, including statutes prohibiting conspiracy, false claims, false statements, mail fraud, and kickbacks. These laws have been available to prosecutors for years. The challenge for prosecutors is not identification of which statute a contractor has violated but the finding of specific individuals who have violated the law and the proving beyond a reasonable doubt that they intended to deceive the government.

This becomes especially difficult in complex investigations involving multibillion-dollar defense contracts that are hundreds, or thousands, of pages long. These deals are often negotiated by dozens of people, many of whom rotate to new jobs before the company's performance under the contract has been finished. (This is particularly true in the military services, where program managers and contracting officers frequently are reassigned before the contracts they've negotiated have been completed.) Prosecutors have a hard time reconstructing the negotiations and identifying instances in which company representatives may have committed fraud.

In large companies, responsibilities for bid and proposal preparation, cost estimates, production schedules, engineering, quality assurance, and other areas susceptible to fraud are usually dispersed among several senior executives. Thus, pinning a particular act on a single individual, when the business decision cuts across several areas of responsibility, is almost impossible. By denying any firsthand knowledge of those decisions, senior executives can easily insulate themselves from the fraudulent actions of their subordinates. Sometimes their denials are valid; at other times they are merely shields to protect the executives from criminal prosecution.

One experienced prosecutor supplied this hypothetical example. Suppose the general manager of a shipyard calls in one of his subordinates, a cost estimator responsible for preparing the bid on a new ship, and flatly declares, "Our estimated costs are *not* going to go over the Navy's budget for that ship." In a sense the boss is implicitly telling his subordinate to do whatever is necessary to ensure that the shipyard's bid is less than the Navy's budget, including submitting a fraudulent, unrealistically low estimate. However, if the general manager were ever confronted by criminal prosecutors and accused of fraud, he could simply deny that his stern instructions to his subordinate constituted an order to commit fraud.

"Hell, no," he could say. "I'm hired to be a tough manager. I never expected my subordinate to *lie* to the Navy. But I know that ship can be built for less than its budgeted cost. If that employee can't do it, I might fire him. But I never intended for him to defraud the government."

How is the Justice Department supposed to prove to a jury that the general manager is lying?

Prosecutors usually don't try to indict first- or second-level employees, such as supervisors or project managers, in a major contract fraud case. Their targets generally are chief executive officers, chief financial officers, or other top-level executives. Thus, prosecutors try to identify an intentional misstatement or false claim made by a mid-level employee and then "bust" their way up the corporate ladder to the senior executives. In a tightly managed company, the employees of which are unwilling to turn on their bosses (and jeopardize their own jobs and pensions), this investigative technique often produces nothing. One prosecutor with long experience interrogating such mid-level employees has encountered a remarkable number of memory lapses among this group.

Convincing a jury that a defense contractor has defrauded the government gets harder and harder with the passage of time. Facts grow stale. Witnesses' memories fade. The urgency of the alleged crime seems to diminish. In January 1983, for example, a federal judge in Mississippi dismissed criminal fraud charges that had been filed more than five years earlier against the Ingalls shipyard. It had been accused of defrauding the Navy of $37 million during construction of three submarines. The shipyard's attorneys successfully argued that the long-standing indictments should be dismissed because of "inexcusable and prejudicial delays," demonstrated in part by the death of seven potential witnesses and the government's supposed loss of several boxes of documents.

The military services usually refer potentially fraudulent bids or claims to the Justice Department only after they have failed to negotiate financial compromises with contractors. By that point the government's ability to prosecute the contractors for fraud has been severely compromised by the fact that the military has already tried to negotiate with the companies. If the services referred suspicious bids or claims to Justice as soon as they were received, prosecutors would have a much better chance of winning convictions. But such a policy would make it harder for the services and their contractors to reach amicable settlements. Which approach is preferable? It's a tough call.

Richard Sauber, the energetic young Justice Department prosecutor assigned to the Electric Boat fraud case, knew a challenge when he saw one. He sat in his Washington office in 1981 staring at the mountain of documents in front of him. On his desk was a Navy contract as thick as a telephone book, obligating GD's Electric Boat division to build a second flight of eleven SSN-688-class attack submarines. On a bookshelf sat a row of volumes as long as his arm, which documented EB's $544 million claim against the Navy. The tomes contained thousands of shipyard records justifying the shipyard's request to the Navy for a price increase.

"I must have read the claim four hundred times before I realized it was really simple," Sauber explained later. Essentially Electric Boat claimed that the vast majority of the cost overruns it had experienced were caused by explicit or implicit Navy actions, not by its own mismanagement.

It was up to Sauber and his fellow prosecutor, Donald McCaffrey, to determine whether executives at either Electric Boat or GD corporate headquarters had defrauded the Navy by submitting a claim that they knew was padded. If Sauber and McCaffrey concluded that GD executives had indeed tried to cheat the Navy, they would then have to persuade their superiors at Justice that they could win convictions against GD in court.

The issue turned on one critical question: When Electric Boat executives submitted their bid back in 1973 to build the second flight of eleven attack subs, did they know that their bid was unrealistically low? If so, the executives could more easily be prosecuted for fraud when they submitted their $544 million claim three years later to recoup those anticipated losses. However, if they honestly didn't know that their second flight bid was too low, they were much less likely to be convicted of fraud.

EB executives said their bid in 1973 was based on calculations they had made two years earlier for the first flight contract. The Navy disagreed, arguing that Electric Boat had already begun building the *Philadelphia*, its first submarine in the new SSN-688 class, by the time it prepared its second flight bid and knew, or should have known, that its earlier cost estimates had been overoptimistic.

EB acknowledged that it had begun working on the first flight before its cost estimators completed the second flight bid. But the shipyard insisted its estimators hadn't used any "real world" data from the *Philadelphia* project to help recalculate its costs. Instead, the shipyard said it relied on the traditional cost estimating technique used in the shipbuilding industry known as parametric forecasting. Under this procedure a shipyard estimates the weight of each portion of the proposed submarine and then figures its labor costs by multiplying an appropriate number of man-hours per ton of work, based on its experience, for each portion of the vessel. EB had begun to receive detailed designs for the SSN-688-class sub from Newport News, but because these designs weren't anywhere near complete, it chose to stick with its earlier parametric estimates. Had it based its calculations on a complete set of designs from Newport News, Electric Boat might have realized that its construction costs would be a lot higher than normal.

EB maintained that none of its employees who had access to actual cost data from the *Philadelphia* construction program helped prepare the second flight bid. It said one group of its engineers reviewed the Newport News designs while a separate group of engineers and cost estimators prepared its second bid.

That narrow issue became the focus of Sauber and McCaffrey's probe. Did one part of the shipyard know what the other part was doing? Did the individuals preparing EB's second bid realize that the early SSN-688-class subs were costing more than expected? If so, why hadn't the shipyard adjusted its second bid accordingly?

The two prosecutors concentrated their search on that small facet of the case. They had to find a participant in the bid preparation who would admit he had also reviewed the Newport News designs. With such an admission they might be able to nail GD for fraud.

Sauber guessed that Electric Boat executives originally had expected their building costs to decline over time, as their workers' productivity improved. However, when the shipyard's costs increased dramatically, he speculated that some EB officials might have become alarmed by the soaring costs and concerned about the optimism reflected in their second bid. He could envision the executives' yielding to pressures from corporate headquarters to shave its second bid to be more competitive with Newport News.

Sauber's scenario was plausible, perhaps, but he had no hard proof. Years later GD's David Lewis dismissed the suggestion that he or anyone else in St. Louis had pressured Electric Boat to submit a fraudulent bid. "At that time with the material we had in hand . . . we did not think we were buying in," Lewis recalled. "We thought that we were putting in a competitive bid, and we *were* competitive."

*(3)*

In order to mount a successful case against General Dynamics, Sauber and McCaffrey had to reconstruct the process through which EB had prepared its second flight bid. Then they had to find someone who knew it would cost the shipyard more to build the next eleven submarines than EB had proposed. To do that, the prosecutors had to locate either incriminating documents or a GD employee who had helped prepare the bid, thought it was fraudulent, and was willing to testify against his employer.

In their search for documents and cooperative witnesses, prosecutors often rely on their most potent legal tool, the grand jury. These twenty-three men and women are impaneled to hear testimony, receive evidence, and determine whether an individual should be brought to trial on felony charges. They operate as independent panels under the auspices of a U.S. district court and in theory can investigate any matter they choose and subpoena any witness they want to question. Grand juries are supposed to act not as an arm of the Justice Department but rather as the embodiment of the public interest.

In practice it doesn't work that way. Grand juries usually take their marching orders from the local U.S. attorney and essentially serve as tools of the prosecutor's office. "The contemporary grand jury investigates only those whom the prosecutor asks to be investigated, and by and large indicts those whom the prosecutor wants to be indicted," observed Marvin E. Frankel and Gary P. Naftalis, the authors of *The Grand Jury: An Institution on Trial.*

Grand juries are expected to operate in complete secrecy. Testimony and documentary evidence brought before a grand jury are sealed from the public. Even the names of its members are never announced. The few government officials allowed access to grand jury records under the Federal Rules of Criminal Procedure are prohibited from discussing the case with anyone else. This confidentiality is designed to protect the privacy and reputation of targets of a grand jury investigation who are never charged with a crime. It also enables witnesses to testify anonymously and more candidly than they might in open court. "Open and unlimited probing is possible, in part, because most rules of evidence that normally protect a defendant in a criminal trial, such as the barring of hearsay or irrelevant evidence, need not be observed in the grand jury proceeding," wrote Leroy Clark in *The Grand Jury: The Use and Abuse of Political Power.*

A grand jury can issue a nationwide subpoena that requires the prompt appearance of virtually any witness. It then can exercise one of its most intimidating powers: forcing a witness to testify without a lawyer, *alone,* behind closed doors. Even Judah Best, a former federal prosecutor and highly regarded defense attorney in Washington, D.C., was shaken by his solo appearance before a grand jury. "It scared hell out of me," he admitted. "There is nothing more efficient, more awesome or more sweeping than a grand jury request for information."

In the hands of an aggressive U.S. attorney, a grand jury can act as a vacuum cleaner, sucking up all relevant documents and witnesses that might help prosecutors flesh out their case before it goes to trial. Prosecutors can use a witness's testimony before a grand jury as evidence at a subsequent trial. In this way prosecutors sometimes use a grand jury to "freeze" the testimony of a hostile witness who might otherwise respond unpredictably in open court.

After a grand jury has received all the evidence and heard the U.S. attorney interrogate a parade of witnesses, one of three things may happen. If the U.S. attorney requests that certain targets be formally indicted on specific charges, the grand jury may approve that request and the accused individuals will be brought to trial. Alternatively, if the U.S. attorney seeks indictments, the grand jury may disapprove that request, and the probe will probably be dropped. Thirdly, the Justice Department may decide that it didn't have a strong enough case to warrant asking the grand jury to indict anyone. In that instance the investigation will probably be closed.

Even before a grand jury had been impaneled in the Electric Boat investigation, word that Justice was looking into fraud allegations leveled against the shipyard leaked to the press. Reporters peppered Attorney General Bell with questions about the case at a press conference in New Haven, Connecticut, in the spring of 1978.

"Can you tell us whether those discussions are about to lead to the meeting of the grand jury to look into those charges?" asked one journalist. Bell declined to answer, citing the Justice Department's secrecy rules.

"Well, tell us what you think personally," demanded a persistent reporter.

"I won't say anything," Bell insisted. "I wouldn't admit there's an investigation."

The following year, hoping to ferret out a friendly witness or an incriminating piece of evidence, federal prosecutors took their fraud investigation before a Hartford, Connecticut, grand jury. All memos, letters, and documents related to the disputed submarine contracts were requested from Electric Boat. More than forty GD employees and Navy personnel, whose names appeared on those records, were served with subpoenas. The prosecutors kept a particularly sharp eye out for any shipyard employee who might have benefited personally from his involvement in the submarine contracts, whether through financial bonuses, stock ownership plans, or promotions. While such personal aggrandizement wouldn't necessarily prove any wrongdoing, it might suggest a motive that the prosecutors could offer to a jury.

Sauber and McCaffrey tried to piece together a giant jigsaw puzzle—the labyrinthine method by which Electric Boat personnel had prepared the bid and subsequent claim for its SSN-688-class submarines. After the prosecutors had reconstructed that process, perhaps they could discover a weak spot in GD's defense.

During interviews that preceded the actual grand jury interrogation, Sauber would show a document to a GD employee. "Did you prepare this document?" he'd ask.

Normally the witness would answer, "Yes," and little more.

Each time Sauber and McCaffrey hoped the witness would continue talking. Perhaps he'd go on to say, "Yes, I prepared that document . . . but I knew it wasn't realistic when I finished it. I took it to my supervisor and told him I couldn't justify a bid that low when I knew our actual construction costs were running much higher."

If the prosecutors found such a talkative witness, they'd nod their heads earnestly. Perhaps the witness would continue: "My supervisor wasn't satisfied. 'That's not good enough,' he said. 'Go back and find some way to justify our bid at that price.' " Sauber and McCaffrey searched for such a cooperative witness, but they never found one.

Early in the investigation they focused their attention on a few senior executives, whose names have not been disclosed. They tried to flush out information about those executives by questioning mid-level employees in front of the grand jury about any pressure they'd felt from their bosses to fudge or falsify EB's bid or claim. In theory such employees might be more willing to speak freely inside a grand jury room, where they weren't accompanied by GD's lawyers or any top executives. But Sauber and McCaffrey weren't that lucky.

"We could never find an individual who had input on the second estimate and who had seen the detailed drawings," Sauber acknowledged. As in most grand jury probes, the prosecutors made many false starts and watched several promising leads fizzle out. Try as they might, they couldn't identify any irregularities in Electric Boat's bid preparation process. "I could never find anyone to say that the way Electric Boat went about bidding on that contract was unnatural," Sauber admitted.

Without such witnesses or incriminating evidence, the government had very little basis on which it could pursue criminal charges against GD. In a criminal fraud case, as opposed to a civil suit, the government usually seeks to indict individuals as well as the corporation itself. In this case the prosecutors had no individuals they could name. It's tough to win a criminal conviction. In a civil case a jury can reach a guilty verdict if the "preponderance of the evidence" supports such a decision, but in a criminal case the accused must be found guilty beyond a reasonable doubt—a higher standard of certainty. Furthermore, jury members typically are reluctant to put real-life white-collar businessmen behind bars.

## (4)

General Dynamics considered the fraud investigation unwarranted from the beginning. Even so, it cooperated with the Hartford grand jury probe by supplying the requested documents and producing the subpoenaed witnesses.

To supplement the advice of Jenner & Block, its long-standing Chicago law firm, GD sought specialized counsel from Thomas Edwards, a criminal defense attorney based in Boston. Edwards came highly praised, not only because of his undergraduate and law school diplomas from Harvard but also because he had served as chief of the criminal division in the U.S. attorney's office in New York City in the mid-1970's. His background as a federal prosecutor and familiarity with white-collar crimes helped him formulate GD's defense during the grand jury proceeding.

Hoping for a breakthrough, Sauber and McCaffrey continued to subpoena GD employees and Navy personnel to appear before the grand jury. The original jury, impaneled in 1979, expired in August 1980. A second jury was organized to pick up where the first left off.

Legal costs mounted on both sides. David Lewis became frustrated and angry as the prolonged investigation dragged on. At one stage he dispatched a few GD representatives to urge Justice to decide whether it was going to prosecute GD or not. Those meetings apparently ended inconclusively. In January 1981 Jimmy Carter yielded the White House to Ronald Reagan. Witnesses continued to troop before the Hartford grand jury. Finally, officials at Justice recognized that they needed to resolve the GD fraud probe—one way or the other.

The department made that decision in its usual manner, on the basis of a written document, known as a prosecution memo, prepared in mid-1981 by Sauber and McCaffrey. The memo, which hasn't been released, outlined their proposed case against Electric Boat. In a fraud case a prosecution memo typically lists the proposed indictments, outlines the contention the prosecutors intend to prove, describes the legal strategy they plan to follow and the defense arguments they expect to face, and explains why they expect to win. It is generally circulated among supervisors in the fraud section and other experienced attorneys throughout the Justice Department, who assess the plan's strengths and weaknesses. Often, at a brainstorming session veteran attorneys try to poke holes in the prosecutors' proposed litigation strategy. They may question the wisdom of indicting a certain individual, or suggest ways to develop additional corroborative evidence, or challenge a particular allegation.

Eventually, after the prosecution memo has been thoroughly examined and the attorneys in charge of the case have defended their recommendations, the director and deputy director of the fraud section decide whether or not to seek indictments from the grand jury. In a highly visible case, like the GD fraud investigation, their decision is usually referred for approval up the bureaucratic hierarchy to the assistant attorney general in charge of the criminal division and, perhaps, to the attorney general himself. In rare instances a decision by the fraud section is reversed at higher levels; in most cases it is merely reviewed and approved.

In their prosecution memo Sauber and McCaffrey acknowledged that they hadn't identified any star witness or uncovered any crucial piece of evidence that enabled them to indict any individual GD employee for fraud. But using a novel theory of collective corporate guilt, they recommended that General Dynamics, as a corporate entity, be indicted for fraud because the corporation knew, or should have known, that its contract claims were grossly exaggerated. Sauber and McCaffrey had spent more than a year gathering evidence against GD. They wanted the chance to present that evidence to a jury. In addition, in November 1981 the FBI submitted a report to Justice recommending that GD and two individuals (whose names have not been released) be indicted.

The chief of the fraud section, Jo Ann Harris, and her deputy, James Graham, disagreed. After weighing the evidence, they concluded that the prosecution team hadn't put together a strong enough case. Harris and Graham were concerned that a decision *not* to seek indictments against GD might send the wrong signal to the defense industry and the public, but they were more reluctant to launch a criminal prosecution that they thought they wouldn't win. In December 1981 they decided to drop the case. At GD's request, Justice announced publicly in January 1982 that it had dropped the probe. In a brief statement issued in St. Louis, the company expressed its corporate relief: "We weren't surprised and are pleased that this decision puts this long and expensive exercise behind us."

On the face of it, Justice's decision not to seek any indictments from the grand jury appeared to be a complete exoneration of General Dynamics. That is not necessarily so. Harris and Graham may have believed that GD executives were indeed guilty of defrauding the Navy but concluded that Justice simply couldn't *prove* it. In any case the grand jury in Hartford was dismissed.

Within a few days Rickover had fired off a letter to Attorney General Smith, criticizing the Justice Department's "poor record" in prosecuting fraudulent contract claims. "In investigating these claims, the Justice Department has tended to focus its efforts on finding the so-called 'smoking gun'—forged or altered documents, fraudulent invoices, and the like," the admiral wrote. "While such evidence makes conviction easier, today's sophisticated claims lawyers rarely leave incriminating evidence of this sort. However, this should not excuse the crime."

The following month Rickover's staunch ally on Capitol Hill, Senator Proxmire, sent a follow-up letter to the attorney general demanding a status report on the GD probe and three other fraud investigations, plus "the names of each of the attorneys assigned principal responsibilities together with the present addresses of those no longer with the Justice Department."

Rumors that the decision to drop the GD investigation was made not in the fraud section but at much higher levels in the Justice Department or perhaps the White House inevitably circulated around Washington. Political considerations were said to be paramount. These assertions were untrue.

As with any significant criminal case, the fraud section's decision on the GD case was forwarded through the criminal division to the attorney general. But William French Smith never took an active interest in the matter. He might legitimately have wondered what his prosecutors had been doing for two years if they came up empty-handed, but Smith was still a newcomer to Washington and the Justice Department, and he paid little attention to the day-to-day activities of the criminal division.

The probe was dropped, despite what cynics believed, because Justice couldn't build a strong enough case against GD. If Justice was guilty of anything in its handling of the initial GD probe, it was in not supporting the investigation with enough manpower. During most of the four-year investigation the department assigned only one full-time attorney to the case. GD took advantage of Justice's thin staffing by trying to overwhelm the prosecution team with mountains of documents, Veliotis said years later. GD also obtained a copy of the prosecution brief from a Justice Department lawyer and tailored its defense strategy accordingly, Veliotis added.

However, prosecutors point out it is often good public policy *not* to seek indictments if the government doesn't think it can win in court. Trials are costly to the taxpayer and agonizing to those accused. It might be emotionally satisfying to an individual prosecutor to pursue his prey, but cooler heads at Justice are often more objective.

"Prosecutors are a cautious lot," one experienced prosecutor observed.

"They like to win. But when you reach the conclusion, after exhausting all reasonable avenues, that you don't have enough evidence to convict somebody, you shouldn't seek indictments."

Even Sauber, who wanted to prosecute GD, acknowledged that the arguments against taking such a step made sense. "I was unhappy that the case was dropped," he said, "but it was a case in which there could be a reasonable difference of opinion."

For the second time in four years it looked as if Electric Boat's claims dispute would fade into history. But the controversy continues to haunt General Dynamics.

# Chapter Eleven

## "Taki"—Fugitive from Justice

### (1)

The dramatic rise and dishonorable fall of Panagiotis Takis Veliotis has fascinated the shipbuilding industry for years. When he arrived at General Dynamics in 1973, as noted, Veliotis took over the unprofitable Quincy shipyard and whipped it into shape in very short order. A supremely confident manager, he rose to national prominence in the early 1980's when he clashed publicly with the crusty Admiral Rickover, restored order at the Electric Boat submarine yard, and defended EB from a horde of angry critics in the Navy, Congress, and the media. At six feet three inches Taki Veliotis was an arrogant giant of a man.

Between his Greek family's shipping business and his own American investments, he was also extremely wealthy. At one time he had been the second-largest individual shareholder in a company that controlled six banks, including the South Shore Bank in Quincy, Massachusetts. He wore elegantly tailored clothes, drank expensive scotch, and sailed his yacht, *Paulette II* (named after his second wife), as frequently as possible.

In 1980 he became an executive vice-president of General Dynamics and landed a seat on the board of directors. Two years later, in June 1982, he stunned many colleagues by resigning from GD and returning to Greece. Word spread that his mother had died and that he had returned to protect his family's shipping fortune from avaricious Greek tax collectors, but his hasty departure still raised eyebrows.

Not long after Veliotis had dropped from public view, a federal grand jury in New York yanked him back into the spotlight. The fifty-seven-year-old former executive was formally charged with awarding one of GD's marine equipment suppliers $45 million in subcontracts in exchange for $1.35 million in illegal kickbacks. The self-assured executive who had launched his career at GD by saving the Quincy shipyard ended it as a fugitive from justice.

In the two years since his indictment Veliotis has waged a one-man war against his former employer. He has provided Justice Department attorneys, congressional investigators, and journalists with tapes and documents from his days at Electric Boat which, he contends, prove that GD tried to defraud the Navy out of billions of dollars. Almost single-handedly Veliotis has transformed GD into the most reviled defense contractor of the 1980's. The odyssey of this Greek shipbuilder is surely one of the strangest in the annals of the defense industry.

Veliotis had taken over at the hopelessly overburdened Electric Boat submarine yard in October 1977 with a clear mandate from David Lewis. He was to build Trident- and SSN-688-class submarines with fewer workers, in less time, for less money. Few doubted he could do it. "He knows how to chop overhead faster than a farmer can chop lettuce," declared one of his former subordinates. Veliotis cut EB's staff mercilessly yet promised to build his subs on time, with an air of certainty that impressed the whole shipbuilding industry.

The settlement of the $544 million claims dispute between GD and the Navy, eight months after Veliotis had taken the helm at EB, was painful for GD to accept, but it allowed Veliotis to get on with business. As Senator Abraham Ribicoff of Connecticut described it, "A huge cloud which hung over the Thames River [in Groton, Connecticut] and darkened relations between the Navy and the shipyard had been pushed out to sea by this settlement." The shipyard was finally able to concentrate on getting its Trident- and SSN-688-class submarine programs back on schedule.

Three months after Veliotis had taken over, he submitted revised construction schedules which he considered realistic. He pried more than $250 million out of GD corporate headquarters to build new production facilities at Groton and Quonset Point.

These initial efforts were largely successful. "For nearly two years, Electric Boat consistently beat the new schedules and consistently underran the new budgets," Veliotis later boasted. The shipyard's next three attack subs—the *Omaha,* the *Groton,* and the *New York City*—were delivered sooner than the Navy expected. The Trident program was back on schedule. By mid-1979 the problems that had plagued Electric Boat for half a decade finally seemed to be disappearing. GD and the Navy breathed a collective sigh of relief. Then the bottom fell out.

Suddenly one problem after another befell the shipyard. First, it was nonconforming steel. During a routine audit of EB's raw material inventory, shipyard employees discovered piles of carbon steel bars and angles that didn't meet Navy standards or match the yard's own purchase orders. For about nine years steel suppliers had delivered unmarked substandard material, and the shipyard's employees had overlooked the shipping labels that described the metal's incorrect chemical content. Now EB had tons of unacceptable carbon steel on hand.

The bars and angles weren't intended for use in the pressure hull or other critical parts of the submarine. They were to be used to build foundations for small pieces of equipment or to hang pipes and wires. Even so, the Navy was alarmed by EB's discovery.

The shipyard eventually determined that about 12 percent of the 6,126 tons of carbon steel it had received between 1970 and 1979 were substandard. That sounded serious, although in fact, nonconforming steel was fairly common in the shipbuilding industry. One of the Navy's chief quality assurance officials acknowledged in 1980 that 30 percent of the carbon steel bar stock in the Navy's own shipyards and supply system was also nonconforming.

When journalists learned of EB's problem, articles criticizing unsafe submarines began to appear. Then the Navy disclosed that the nonconforming steel could have been installed in 126,000 locations in a Trident submarine. The shipyard established more rigorous inspection procedures, construction on some of the attack subs was delayed, and Veliotis's delivery schedules began to slip. Relations between the Navy and General Dynamics were once again strained. Shipyard employees found themselves at odds with Navy inspectors based in Groton and officials visiting from the Naval Sea Systems Command (NAVSEA) in Washington.

In November 1979 a routine inspection of the *Bremerton* attack sub uncovered serious defects in EB's welding operations. Further inspections revealed that improper welding and incomplete or missing inspection reports had frequently gone unnoticed during EB's chaotic expansion in the mid-1970's. Welding errors that had occurred before Veliotis's arrival in 1977 evoked criticism from the Navy and the press that reinforced the company's developing image as an incompetent shipbuilder.

The welding problem, like the substandard steel problem, looked worse than it was. Of the more than thirty-five miles of welds that required magnetic particle inspection on the *Bremerton,* for instance, Electric Boat had to repair or replace only about one-quarter of a mile, or seven-tenths of 1 percent. Moreover, the unsatisfactory welds didn't jeopardize the sub's safety. They affected only less critical areas of the submarine, such as pipe hangers, foundations, and support systems.

Although Veliotis took steps to correct the welding foul-ups, his deteriorating relations with the Navy were now exacerbated by an exchange of mean-spirited letters among Veliotis, the supervisor of shipbuilding (SUPSHIP) in Groton, and officials at NAVSEA headquarters in Washington. In the summer of 1980 a union paint steward at Electric Boat had walked into the SUPSHIP's office and informed the Navy that EB workers were coating the *Bremerton*'s bilges with oil-based paint instead of the required epoxy paint. The worker offered this unsolicited revelation without first informing his superiors at the shipyard.

Twelve days later, when the Navy told EB about its paint problem, Veliotis hit the roof. In a heated letter to Navy Captain Joseph F. Yurso, the supervisor of shipbuilding, Veliotis had the temerity to scold Yurso for waiting twelve days before alerting him to EB's own error. If the Navy's delay disrupted his submarine delivery schedule, Veliotis wrote, "or if it results in additional costs because we continued to use the wrong paint in other applications during that 12-day period, we will hold the Government liable for those consequences."

Threats of this sort from private shipbuilders didn't sit well with Navy ship procurement officials, many of whom still resented the omnibus claims settlement of 1978. Captain Yurso's response to Veliotis's intemperate letter fairly bristled with indignation. "I recognize inaccuracies, innuendoes, and implied threats contained in your letter," he wrote. "By choosing not to address them individually, I am not acquiescing in their validity, but am suppressing the emotionalism they apparently were intended to evoke."

Tempers flared on both sides. Within the Navy several people became involved. Captain Yurso argued with EB about day-to-day shipbuilding procedures. Vice Admiral Earl Fowler, the commander of NAVSEA, dealt with the broader submarine scheduling and cost controversies. Admiral Rickover fumed about many things. The new secretary of the navy, John Lehman, Jr., entered the fray when the multibillion-dollar question of future Trident and attack submarine contracts came up.

Veliotis served as General Dynamics's front man on virtually every submarine issue and suffered all of the Navy's abuse. His relations with Rickover were terrible from the beginning. Though officially responsible only for the propulsion system of a nuclear-powered submarine, Rickover had traditionally wielded vast influence at Electric Boat, often dictating which employees the private shipbuilder should hire and fire. "I told Rickover to go to hell," Veliotis

16. P. Takis Veliotis, an arrogant Greek-born shipbuilder who headed the Electric Boat submarine yard during its most contentious period, frequently clashed with Admiral Rickover. He resigned unexpectedly from GD in 1982, returned to Greece, and was indicted in New York the following year for allegedly pocketing more than $1.3 million in kickbacks from a marine subcontractor. Since then, as a fugitive from justice, he has leveled accusations of contract fraud against his former employers at General Dynamics. *General Dynamics*

recalled. "I am running the shipyard, not him." The Navy's chief curmudgeon wasn't used to such resistance. He would shout and pound on his desk, expecting EB executives to kowtow to his demands, but Veliotis wasn't easily intimidated. "Admiral," he'd say, "if it comes to shouting and pounding, I can outshout you and I can pound harder on the desk than you."

Rickover repeatedly accused Veliotis of bidding too low on new submarine contracts, submitting unreasonable claims, and building shoddy vessels. In 1980, for example, Rickover met with Dr. Seymour Zeiberg, an OSD official in charge of strategic weapons, to criticize EB's faulty workmanship on the Trident program. "Admiral Rickover again alluded to welding and quality assurance problems at Electric Boat and reiterated his position that he did not want the [*Ohio*] delivered unless it was absolutely complete and letter perfect, apparently without recognition of the fact that SSBN 726 is the lead ship of a new class," Veliotis complained in a letter to Admiral Fowler. It was impossible to stop Rickover from meddling in areas outside his own responsibility.

The Veliotis-Rickover battles became famous throughout the defense industry. "They clashed pretty hard," acknowledged David Lewis, recalling the admiral's frequent insults to Veliotis. "They had nothing to do with each other the last year or two."

In the meantime, Veliotis accused the Navy of supplying defective equipment and requiring far too many design changes in its submarines. He was particularly frustrated by the Navy's insistence that construction at EB shouldn't be delayed by the constant stream of what the Navy considered *minor* design changes. "Electric Boat has no intention of being bludgeoned into accepting a Navy position which it considers to be invalid and unrealistic," Veliotis informed Fowler with characteristic abrasiveness.

As the dispute between the shipyard and the Navy grew more contentious, the construction of Trident and attack subs fell farther behind schedule. Eventually Navy Secretary Lehman was drawn into the battle.

Young, brash, and politically savvy when he took over the Navy, Lehman was unique among the service secretaries. President Reagan had selected Verne Orr, a Pasadena car salesman, to head the Air Force and John O. Marsh, Jr., a former Virginia congressman, presidential counselor, and American history buff, to head the Army. Neither had lobbied aggressively for his job or displayed outstanding qualifications to hold it. Lehman was different. A well-informed veteran of the defense policymaking scene in Washington, he had actively sought his post. Indeed, he later said it was the only job he wanted. After taking a Ph.D. in international relations at the University of Pennsylvania, he had served on the staff of Henry Kissinger's National Security Council, as a delegate to the U.S.-Soviet troop reduction talks in Vienna, and as deputy director of President Ford's Arms Control and Disarmament Agency.

The Abington Corporation, a management consulting firm Lehman founded in 1977, helped U.S. and foreign defense contractors peddle aircraft and other weapons to the Pentagon. That defense consulting work, which paid him $180,000 in 1980, the year before he had joined the Reagan administration, cost him a few political points two years later. *The New York Times* reported that he had sold his firm to a British businessman shortly after becoming navy secretary, with an implied option to buy it back after he left public office. Such an arrangement, *The Times* suggested, could represent a conflict of interest because Lehman might profit indirectly from decisions he made while heading the Navy. Lehman steadfastly denied any such conflict and refused to rule out the possibility that he'd resume his consulting work after he left the

17. Navy Secretary John F. Lehman, Jr., who regularly dons the flight gear of a bombardier-navigator in the Naval Reserve, publicly blasted Electric Boat in 1981 for what he deemed excessive costs and schedule delays in GD's submarine construction program. *U.S. Navy*

government. With characteristic moxie, he was able to weather the brief political storm without much long-term damage.

His role as a commander in the Naval Reserve was well publicized. Once a year the cocky secretary would don his flight uniform and report for two weeks of active duty as a bombardier-navigator with an A-6 Intruder attack wing in Oceana, Virginia. "I want to be treated like any other commander," he would tell his fellow reservists, *The New York Times* reported. "A simple genuflection and a kissing of the ring will do."

Lehman's sense of humor was nowhere in evidence during his prolonged clash with Electric Boat in 1981. The Navy was anxious to sign contracts for four SSN-688-class attack subs that Congress had already approved for fiscal years 1980 and 1981. Electric Boat and Newport News had submitted competitive bids. The question was whether or not Lehman would award any of those subs to Electric Boat.

Dissatisfied with the construction delays and production problems on the SSN-688 and Trident programs at Groton and Quonset Point, Lehman was reluctant to hand additional contracts to Electric Boat. "If you have a 'gridlock' situation you don't want to keep feeding cars through [Manhattan's] Holland Tunnel until you are sure they can get out the other end," he observed.

Lehman wanted to spur Electric Boat to greater productivity. To accomplish that, he decided to beat up on General Dynamics with the help of the media. In a series of one-on-one interviews and a group session with the

Pentagon press corps, Lehman openly speculated about how the Navy might accelerate the delivery of submarines. He mentioned the possibility of equipping the Navy's shipyard at Mare Island, California, so that it could build nuclear submarines. And he alluded to the possibility of awarding submarine contracts to shipyards in Canada, Great Britain, and other countries.

Veliotis didn't appreciate Lehman's heavy-handed tactics. "I could save him a consultant's fee and tell him where he could get good delivery on the Trident —from the Soviet Union," said EB's general manager.

In March 1981 the issue came to a head at congressional hearings before the Seapower Subcommittee of the House Armed Services Committee on the controversial submarine construction program. Admiral Fowler spoke for the Navy on March 12. Veliotis was slated to defend Electric Boat two weeks later. Industry lobbyists, journalists, and defense analysts braced for a showdown.

Fowler came on strong. His criticism of General Dynamics was heavily reported in the press. It left the impression that Electric Boat was totally inept, incapable of welding properly, applying the right paint, or recognizing nonconforming steel.

After Fowler's scorching testimony Veliotis was supposed to meet for lunch with Lehman, Admiral Thomas Hayward, the chief of naval operations, and the head of the Naval Material Command. The luncheon meeting never took place. Reacting to Fowler's congressional testimony and the media's coverage of it, Lehman invited David Lewis to Washington on March 17 and told him that the Navy had canceled its competitive procurement of attack submarines. Lehman had decided to negotiate with Newport News, on a sole-source basis, for three of the four submarines. Electric Boat would not be awarded any additional subs.

Lehman also chose not to exercise the Navy's option for the ninth Trident before it expired on March 31, even though its price had already been negotiated with EB as part of the eighth Trident contract. Lehman knew the price of the ninth missile-firing submarine would inevitably rise by millions of dollars if the Navy had to renegotiate that contract with EB because the shipyard would be forced to let its own options with its subcontractors expire. But Lehman wanted to put General Dynamics under as much pressure as possible.

David Lewis was shaken. At Veliotis's urging, EB had invested hundreds of millions of dollars in new machinery and buildings in Connecticut and Rhode Island to improve productivity. If Electric Boat landed none of the upcoming submarine contracts, General Dynamics would suffer a devastating financial blow.

Lewis felt Lehman's impulsive decision was based on inaccurate, outdated information, and he didn't mind saying so. "We talked for quite a while and I told him in words of one syllable that he didn't know what he was doing," said Lewis. "I've been in this damn business an awful long time and I've never known anyone to take such drastic action without making an effort to find out the whole story."

Lewis felt that most of the production problems at EB that worried the Navy had already been solved. Furthermore, GD had proposed a lower price for the new SSN-688-class subs than Newport News.

Lehman maintained that the awards to the Virginia shipyard were based on the nation's need for two strong submarine builders. Newport News, which hadn't received a submarine contract for almost four years, was in danger of losing many of its skilled workers. Additional submarine orders could hold those workers together. Lehman's argument made sense, but few observers doubted that his principal motive was to squeeze Electric Boat.

In his congressional testimony a week later Veliotis didn't yield an inch. For each of Fowler's accusations, Veliotis offered an explanation, pointed to a chart, or presented a set of statistics to rebut the Navy's position. He confidently declared that Electric Boat had cured its problems and could deliver one Trident and twice as many attack subs by the end of the year as Admiral Fowler had predicted. "Given the support and cooperation of the Navy," Veliotis promised, "we will prove it during 1981 by delivering six new 688 class submarines and the lead Trident, *Ohio.*"

Veliotis's brash style was unfamiliar to the legislators in room 2118 of the Rayburn House Office Building, before whom congressional witnesses customarily adopt an obsequious manner. Fowler's criticism had riled Veliotis, and he let his Greek temper flare. It was a masterful performance.

At one point, to dramatize the insignificance of EB's nonconforming steel problem, Veliotis spilled on the witness table a wrench and forty small steel fittings, which he said weighed a total of fifty pounds. "Do you know how much steel we bought for construction of the *Ohio?*" he asked the subcommittee. "23,600,000 pounds." Pointing to the meager pile of steel parts in front of him, he announced triumphantly, "*This* was the extent of the problem."

## (2)

The acrimony that had developed between the Navy and Electric Boat escalated sharply when GD announced its intention to recoup its most recent financial losses from the Navy. Under the 1978 claims settlement GD had agreed not to submit any additional contract claims to the Navy for work it had already performed on the SSN-688-class or Trident submarines. Because some of the recently discovered nonconforming steel and welding problems occurred before the 1978 agreement, GD officials felt they needed something other than a contract claim to try to recoup those extra costs, which internal estimates showed would run between $100 million and $200 million. They had to devise a legal argument to support such a request.

Jenner & Block, GD's longtime Chicago law firm, consulted with government contract lawyers in Washington. Together they came up with an innovative premise. GD could argue that the Navy, in its role as the shipyard's insurer, was liable for the extra shipbuilding costs Electric Boat had incurred as a result of its own employees' faulty workmanship. GD would submit not claims, in the traditional sense of that word, but insurance reimbursement requests.

Since 1942 the Navy had prohibited private shipyards from purchasing marine builder's risk insurance from commercial underwriters and adding the cost of those premiums to the prices of their ships. Instead, the Navy had decided to act as its own insurer. It promised its private shipbuilders the same coverage offered in the standard insurance policy used in the commercial shipbuilding world, the Marine Builder's Risk—Navy Form—Syndicate. "In short, in order to save the premium costs of commercial insurance—and the Navy has in fact saved hundreds of millions of dollars in such premiums since 1942—the Navy went into the marine insurance business," Veliotis explained. The Navy, as insurer, was obliged to reimburse a shipyard for such unexpected accidents as a dockyard explosion or the collapse of a construction crane. Whether it was also liable for extra expenses brought on by a shipyard's mistakes and negligence wasn't clear.

GD thought the Navy was liable. The company's lawyers argued that a commercial insurance policy would cover *all* unforeseen production costs, even those attributable to the shipyard's workers—through improper welding, for example. Veliotis translated GD's legal theory into everyday terms. "If you have collision insurance on your new car and you get involved in an accident, the insurance company will pay, regardless of whether or not the accident was your fault," he explained. "Similarly, if you fall asleep while smoking in bed and as a result your house catches fire and burns down, your homeowners insurance will pay, even though in this example it is obvious that you were at fault." In the same way, Veliotis argued, the Navy should cover EB's unexpected costs even if the latter was at fault.

When GD's lawyers first suggested the insurance reimbursement idea, Lewis was dubious. "I was incredulous," he recalled. He wasn't aware that the Navy had frequently settled insurance claims from private shipbuilders, sometimes for as much as $1 million. His Washington attorneys argued that the law was on GD's side. "It just didn't seem right to me," said Lewis, "but what's right in your mind, as an exercise in logic, is not necessarily right under the law."

GD's chairman sat on the provocative insurance claims, unable to bring himself to submit them to the Navy. Then Avondale Shipyards, Inc., of New Orleans, was awarded about $300 million by its commercial underwriters as reimbursement for insulation that cracked during its construction of liquefied natural gas tankers. "They got some enormous settlement from the Lloyd's group," Lewis recalled. "*That* was the inspiration that made me recognize that these insurance claims were an asset I couldn't throw out the window."

In 1979, when GD first raised the idea that the government insurance should cover the costs of replacing EB's substandard steel, the Navy said no. It insisted that its insurance coverage was not intended to reimburse a shipyard for its own negligence or defective workmanship. It objected again the following year, when GD said that it also considered its defective welding difficulties to be covered. By February 1981 the Navy was concerned that EB might be accumulating a mountain of insurance "requests" that it would ultimately have to honor. Navy officials asked EB either to submit their insurance claims or to drop the matter.

By the time Veliotis appeared before the House Seapower Subcommittee, the prospect of a huge insurance claim from GD had already hit the newspapers and caused a stir on Capitol Hill. Veliotis tried to sidestep the issue by telling the panel that GD hadn't finished preparing its insurance reimbursement requests, so he couldn't predict their total value. He knew that GD's $484 million claims settlement with the Navy in 1978 still irked many congressmen. One such legislator, Representative Charles F. Dougherty, an aggressive Republican from Philadelphia, badgered Veliotis for a specific dollar figure for GD's forthcoming insurance requests.

"I think that this committee has to know from you at least a ballpark figure today as to how much you are talking about," Dougherty demanded. "Are you talking about another $500 million? Are you talking $300 million?"

Finally, Veliotis relented. "I do not have a ballpark figure, but I can tell you it will be less than $100 million," he offered. "But let me tell you I am not asking the Navy to pay me in its capacity as my customer. . . . They went into the insurance business in competition with free enterprise. They pocketed the premiums, and now they say when it comes time to pay, we are not going to pay."

Congressman Dougherty wasn't buying. He envisioned a worst-case scenario that troubled him. "The Navy has indicated it is not going to pay," Dougherty told Veliotis. "You have indicated you are going to force them to pay. If it follows what has happened in the past, there will be an out-of-court settlement. The Navy will come up with millions of dollars to pay. You will acknowledge a loss of some million dollars, but in the meanwhile, money that could have been used in other areas, in the area of national defense, is going to be lost."

Clearly the issue didn't lend itself to calm debate. No matter how solid GD's legal argument might be (and it was never very convincing), the Navy concluded that it couldn't honor such insurance claims for political reasons. Congress and the public simply wouldn't tolerate the Navy's reimbursing a negligent defense contractor for its own construction errors—especially not General Dynamics.

Despite resistance from the Navy and Congress, Lewis submitted EB's insurance claims in June 1981. Navy Secretary Lehman discussed the issue with his assistant secretary for shipbuilding, George Sawyer, and Deputy Defense Secretary Frank Carlucci III. "This was a massive challenge to the Navy because it was a massive claim," Lewis recognized. "The precedent [it would set] made it intolerable." Angry meetings took place throughout the Pentagon. "They couldn't accept this," recalled Lewis. "They went berserk."

GD's chairman was concerned that Defense Secretary Weinberger and Lehman had reacted so strongly to his insurance claims. He tried to meet with the defense secretary face-to-face, but Weinberger steadfastly refused to see him.

Instead, Lewis took his case to Edwin Meese III, then President Reagan's White House counselor, on August 7, 1981. Although Meese refused to become personally involved in the dispute between GD and the Navy, he agreed to contact Weinberger and try to set up a meeting for Lewis. Meese may also have called Lehman after his conversation with GD's chairman.

Lehman was angered by both GD's claim and Lewis's back-door approach to the White House.

He vented some of his outrage when he spoke at the National Press Club in Washington a few days later. "For a corporation to pursue, as a policy, the principle that the taxpayers should pay for the mistakes, the negligence, the poor workmanship or the inadequate management of the company in carrying out a contract with the government is preposterous," he insisted. The rock-jawed secretary didn't doubt that GD could hire platoons of corporate lawyers to devise supporting legal arguments, but he pointedly warned Lewis that his insurance claim provided a clear indication of GD's attitude toward the Navy. "The Department of Defense will *not tolerate* such corporate attitudes," Lehman continued. "They are unacceptable. We will *not* subscribe to the notion that the government always pays, and we intend to respond in two ways."

First, he warned, the Navy would carefully evaluate GD's claims as it planned its future submarine program. Secondly, the Navy would consider filing counterclaims against GD, not only for any direct damages caused by the shipyard's construction delays but also for any consequential damages its lawyers could identify.

Publicly Lehman was playing hardball. He had already suspended competitive bidding on the next four attack submarines authorized for 1980 and 1981 and had handed three of those subs to Newport News. Now he was threatening to cut off Electric Boat altogether until it withdrew its insurance claims and brought its construction program back on schedule.

Privately Lehman was only slightly more flexible. He met with Lewis and GD's chief Washington lobbyist, Edward J. LeFevre, in the Pentagon on August 25, 1981. In a heated session that lasted two hours and ten minutes, Lewis and Lehman argued about the validity of GD's insurance claims and the Navy's refusal to award Electric Boat a new contract for attack submarines.

Lehman was still fuming over Lewis's meeting in the White House with Meese, but GD's chairman refused to back down. "You bet . . . we went around to Meese," he told the navy secretary. "We were not getting any satisfaction. We had to go up there. We had to go."

Later, in a phone conversation with Veliotis (which the latter secretly recorded and subsequently made public), Lewis described GD's bargaining posture with Lehman and Sawyer. "We didn't back down one iota and neither did they," Lewis recalled, "but it's obvious to me that someone told him [Lehman] to settle." (Lehman later denied that anyone had pressured him to come to terms with GD.)

Lewis was in a predicament. "The company was faced with the problem of obtaining something of value for the assets represented by the insurance claims," he later said. As the men talked in the Pentagon, the outline of a horse trade began to take shape. GD might withdraw its insurance claims if the Navy awarded Electric Boat a generous new attack submarine contract.

One sticking point seemed to be the rate of profit that the Navy would be willing to write into such a contract. Lewis and Veliotis sought about 18 percent, the rate they figured Newport News was earning under its latest SSN-688 submarine contracts.

Lewis indirectly asked Lehman for the same profit margin. "You've given those guys eighteen percent earnings," he told Lehman, according to his tape-recorded conversation with Veliotis. "Hell, you know, that's terrible, and if you [Lehman] want to do that with us, that's fine, too." Lewis stressed that Lehman ought to be willing to give up something to get rid of GD's insurance claims.

Although the navy secretary wasn't ready to agree with Lewis's proposals, he was apparently looking for some kind of compromise. "We don't need a settlement where anybody loses," Lehman said as the tense meeting drew to a close. "Let's keep working."

As Lewis and LeFevre got into their car in the Pentagon parking lot, Sawyer ran out and asked for a ride to nearby Crystal City, Virginia. The assistant navy secretary seemed eager to settle the dispute, Lewis later told Veliotis.

"This is just between us," Sawyer assured Lewis and LeFevre. "We've got to figure out a way to sit down here and negotiate some contracts, give you some stuff that maybe we can do to find a solution."

"Fine, that's what we're asking you to do," Lewis recalled saying. A tough negotiator, GD's chief executive seemed to be making progress. "We're not giving this stuff up," Lewis added, "without something in return."

As GD and the Navy edged closer to a settlement, a new factor appeared. James E. Ashton, the assistant general manager for engineering at Electric Boat, had become convinced that GD's insurance claim was spurious and that the shipyard's SSN-688-class sub program was confronting a cost overrun far larger than the $90 million GD's top officers had forecast among themselves.

Ashton already had shared his pessimistic "cost-to-complete" estimate with Lewis, Oliver Boileau, GD's president, and Gorden MacDonald, the company's chief financial officer. Each had told him to sit tight. Now it looked as if Ashton might take his dire cost estimates to the Navy or to Arthur Anderson & Company, GD's outside auditing firm.

Lewis and Veliotis knew they were at a delicate point in their negotiations with Lehman. They were close to landing a contract for one new attack submarine and perhaps options for several more. They feared their talks with the Navy might collapse if Ashton suddenly disclosed his ominous cost projections or openly questioned the merits of GD's insurance claims. "I was more concerned about the Ashton efforts to undermine the validity of our insurance claims, which were our principal bargaining chips in negotiating a settlement of our outstanding differences with the Navy," Lewis said later.

It's unclear whether Lewis and Veliotis believed Ashton's cost estimate was accurate and deceitfully tried to keep him quiet, as Veliotis now maintains, or whether they truly thought his cost estimate was inaccurate and sought to muzzle an employee they considered ill-informed, as Lewis insists. What is clear is that Lewis and Veliotis schemed together, during a phone conversation on October 7, 1981 (which Veliotis recorded and later made public), to discourage Ashton from talking to the Navy, Arthur Anderson, or the newspapers.

"What really scared us about this," Lewis told Veliotis, "if this silly bastard [Ashton] starts popping off . . . , if he starts talking that we've got a big loss on the [submarine program], then we bring Arthur Anderson in, immediately, saying, well, now, look, if this is the true story, we've got to record a loss, you know. We didn't want that issue to even arise."

Lewis had telephoned Veliotis to prevent him from firing Ashton, figuring such a dismissal might trigger precisely the reaction neither of them wanted. "My real concern here is if we give him the gate today, which I think would be a good idea except for this one factor, he is very likely to run, A, to the Navy and, B, the newspapers or both . . ." said Lewis.

Instead, GD's chairman suggested that Veliotis attempt to pacify Ashton by dangling in front of him the prospect of being promoted to the general manager's position at Electric Boat (which would soon be vacated when Veliotis was named a corporate executive vice-president).

"I don't think it's the honest thing to do," said Veliotis, who recommended that he simply say nothing to Ashton.

"It isn't the honest thing to do . . ." Lewis acknowledged, "[but] we ought to talk about it, consider it."

As it happened, Lewis and Veliotis said nothing to Ashton and the assistant general manager didn't take his alarming cost estimate to the Navy or GD's outside auditors. Closed-door negotiations continued in the Pentagon without disruption.

Lewis eventually concluded that if he continued to press his insurance claims, he might permanently poison GD's relations with the Navy. The advice he got from veterans in the shipbuilding industry was pessimistic. "You are absolutely right," he remembered their saying, "but you will never win. The Navy will fight you to the bitter end."

Lewis knew GD could take the insurance dispute to court, but he had no taste for that. "We agonized at great length," he remembered. "We knew we would probably win eight years down the road, but we'd destroy ourselves in the process." He reluctantly accepted the idea of withdrawing the claims if the Navy agreed to resume negotiations on a new contract. "I decided life was too short," he later explained, with a simple shrug of his shoulders.

A week after the tape-recorded phone call the Navy announced it had rejected GD's controversial insurance claim. A few days later, on October 22, Lewis and Lehman surprised many defense industry observers by appearing together at a Pentagon press conference to declare that the dispute between GD and the Navy had been resolved.

GD agreed to withdraw its claim, and the Navy announced it would resume negotiations with Electric Boat on a new attack submarine contract. When those negotiations were completed in February 1982, the Navy awarded GD a $231.5 million contract for one SSN-688 submarine—the first submarine awarded to the shipyard in three years—plus options for three more attack subs. The profit rate included in that contract has not been made public, but Lehman has insisted repeatedly that no negotiated shipbuilding contract signed since he became navy secretary has included a profit rate as high as 18 percent.

Lewis has since been accused by Veliotis and others of trying to withhold from GD's auditors, the SEC, and the public vital information that might have affected the company's earnings. Lewis has contended that Ashton was professionally unqualified to develop reliable estimates of the cost overruns at Electric Boat. Although Ashton held a master's degree from Harvard business school and a doctorate in engineering from the Massachusetts Institute of Technology, he had never worked in a shipyard before transferring to EB from the company's Fort Worth aircraft division the year before.

Lewis also argued that it was top management's responsibility—not Ashton's—to determine if a major cost overrun was likely to occur. Lewis said top GD officials and Arthur Anderson auditors were confident that the company's pending insurance claim would bring in enough money to offset the looming cost overrun at Electric Boat. Thus, said Lewis, he didn't think it was necessary to pass along to his auditors or stockholders Ashton's more pessimistic figures.


Lewis's willingness to drop the claims alleviated the strains between GD and the Navy. Another peace gesture was his decision in October 1981 to remove the quarrelsome Veliotis from day-to-day operations at Electric Boat. Veliotis relinquished his position as general manager at the submarine yard and took on broader responsibilities, overseeing not only GD's overall marine operations but also its expanding international arms sales. His headquarters shifted from Groton to Quincy, Massachusetts, where he was less likely to cross swords with Admiral Rickover.

Veliotis had loyally taken the heat for Electric Boat during the spring of 1981, but his continued presence at the submarine yard had exacerbated tensions between GD and the Navy. "Veliotis had just burned too many bridges," Lewis decided. "He did a good job at EB, except the problems of confrontation sometimes were overdone with the Navy. He could never understand that sometimes customers are more equal than suppliers." Some people who have dealt with Veliotis in recent years suggest that his bitterness toward GD stems, in part, from the shabby treatment he was afforded by Lewis during this tense period.

Secretary Lehman claimed he demanded the removal of Veliotis. "We insisted—and this is the first time I've ever made this public—that before [GD] got another contract they commit to get him out of running Electric Boat," Lehman said three years later. "We didn't trust him. . . . We felt he was a poor manager and that he was constantly picking fights with the Navy and the yard."

GD and the Navy reached an understanding that Veliotis and Rickover would be withdrawn from their respective "front lines." As Lewis described the arrangement, "There was an awareness that we had to do our part or we were never going to get the working levels back together."

Most Electric Boat executives hoped that the eighty-two-year-old admiral, whose active duty had already been extended twenty years beyond normal, would be forced to retire. But GD made no moves to encourage that outcome, said Lewis. "We thought it was too dangerous to take any position."

Nevertheless, Lehman did what no secretary of the navy had done before him: He recommended that the President resist the inevitable pressure from the admiral's allies in Congress and *not* extend Rickover's active duty. President Reagan followed Lehman's recommendation. In February 1982 the father of the nuclear Navy officially retired. A grateful and much relieved Navy provided Rickover with office space at the Washington Naval Yard, safely separated from the ongoing power struggles in the Pentagon by the Potomac River.

*(3)*

Veliotis appeared to have settled in as one of five GD executive vice-presidents and an assertive member of the board of directors. Insiders considered him one of a handful of contenders for David Lewis's job if and when the much respected chairman ever stepped down. Veliotis occasionally talked about the possibility of leaving his job and returning to Greece to care for his ailing mother and safeguard his family's sizable shipping fortune, but few of his colleagues took such talk seriously. At one point he visited Greece for several weeks to attend to family business. When he returned, friends concluded that his frequent talk of resigning was just that, talk.

In May 1982, a month before an important board of directors meeting, Veliotis again confronted Lewis on his retirement plans. "I wanted to know if Lewis would be stepping down," Veliotis recalled years later. Veliotis hoped to be named chairman, with the full board's approval, at the upcoming June meeting, as he claims Lewis had promised five years earlier.

Lewis balked. "What am I going to do if I retire?" Veliotis remembered him asking. Lewis simply wasn't ready to step down. Veliotis refused to wait and, instead, submitted his resignation in early May. He left for a brief trip to Italy

18. GD chairman David S. Lewis (at podium) and Navy Secretary John F. Lehman, Jr., appear together at a Pentagon press conference in 1981 after the two settled their differences on the future of the Navy's submarine program. GD withdrew its controversial insurance reimbursement claim, and the Navy awarded Electric Boat a $232 million contract for one attack submarine. *U.S. Navy*

to visit friends, during which time Lewis declined to accept his resignation and saw to it that Veliotis was reelected to GD's board.

Shortly after his reelection and several months after his mother had died, Veliotis formally resigned from General Dynamics. He told Lewis that he wasn't feeling well and was returning to Greece. It certainly made more sense for him to protect the Veliotis estate, said to be worth hundreds of millions of dollars, than to continue toiling at General Dynamics, earning a salary of $150,000 a year, plus perks and stock options worth another $100,000. Although he departed the United States suddenly, few suspected he had other motives to leave.

Many people in the defense industry considered Veliotis a hero, so it came as a shock when the combative shipbuilder was charged in September 1983 with racketeering, conspiracy, false and fraudulent claims against the government, bankruptcy fraud, perjury, and obstruction of justice. He faced maximum penalties of more than ninety years in prison and more than $150,000 in fines. Veliotis and another General Dynamics executive were accused of splitting some $2.7 million in kickbacks secretly paid by one of GD's shipbuilding subcontractors. Veliotis was also accused of lying about the kickbacks when he had testified three years earlier at bankruptcy proceedings for the same subcontractor.

"Veliotis was a controversial character," said an EB employee who knew him well. "People liked him, or they hated him." While his allies were saddened by his indictment, his enemies wondered aloud why it had taken the Justice Department so long to catch up with him. "This has been a horrifyingly, terribly disappointing thing to happen to a person we felt highly of," Lewis said initially. "He did a good job for the company the whole time he was there. We made money on the shipyard." Many acquaintances couldn't understand why he would allegedly commit such a crime. "It doesn't make any sense to me," said Vice Admiral Williams, who worked briefly under Veliotis at Electric Boat after retiring from the Navy. "He didn't need the money."

Federal prosecutors were more interested in how than in why. Working from a collection of telex messages, credit memos, company checks, and records of wire transfers and phone calls, they pieced together an elaborate embezzlement and kickback scheme that allegedly involved four men: Veliotis; James Gilliland, his longtime assistant and a vice-president at the Quincy shipyard; and two former officers of the defunct Frigitemp Corporation, George Davis, a senior vice-president in the firm's marine division, and Gerald Lee, the chairman and chief executive officer.

Federal prosecutors contended in a forty-eight-page indictment that an illegal conspiracy began in 1973, when Davis and Lee tried to win a lucrative subcontract from the Quincy shipyard, then headed by Veliotis. Quincy was building the country's first commercial tanker ships designed to transport liquefied natural gas (LNG) at sub-zero temperatures in huge superinsulated spherical tanks. Frigitemp, which had grown from a small restaurant-refrigeration firm in Brooklyn to an $85 million marine shipfitting and insulation company, wanted a piece of the LNG business. Davis and Lee concluded that their marine division could land subcontracts to supply insulation material and install interior fixtures for Quincy's tankers if they agreed to kick back a portion of those contracts to Veliotis and Gilliland, the government charged.

According to the indictment, Veliotis and Gilliland awarded Frigitemp subcontracts altogether worth more than $44 million between 1974 and 1977, sometimes against objections from their own employees at Quincy. For example, in 1974 Veliotis and Gilliland approved a $4.6 million subcontract to Frigitemp for the installation of interior fixtures, known in the shipbuilding business as joiner work, despite the fact that Quincy's purchasing department had recommended another bidder, according to the indictment. The following year they approved a $10.7 million subcontract to Frigitemp to supply insulation material, even though the shipyard's bidding period for potential suppliers hadn't officially expired. In October 1977, three days before Veliotis left Quincy to become general manager at Electric Boat, he presented Frigitemp with a going-away present: subcontracts for insulation and joiner work worth another $12.4 million, the government charged.

According to the indictment, after Veliotis's transfer to EB, the kickback scheme was expanded to include GD's submarine building operations. Frigitemp already had won subcontracts to supply galley equipment for Trident missile-firing submarines and sound-deadening insulation for attack submarines worth a total of $1.7 million. It had begun selling to Electric Boat even before Veliotis took over the submarine yard, but the new general manager would be able to direct even more work its way.

However, Frigitemp ran into severe cash flow problems in 1977 and 1978. Bankruptcy was imminent, and the kickback scheme was imperiled. According to the indictment, the four executives agreed that Davis would set up a new company, Intersystems Design and Technology Corporation (later called the IDT Corporation), which would take over the endangered subcontracts. In February 1978 Frigitemp transferred all of its LNG and submarine subcontracts to the newly formed IDT Corporation, receiving *nothing* in return. The next month David Lewis sent a routine memo to Veliotis and Gilliland authorizing them to terminate GD's subcontracts with Frigitemp and award its subcontracts to IDT. In return for the IDT subcontracts, the indictment charged, Veliotis and Gilliland continued to receive their kickbacks. And as expected, Frigitemp was declared bankrupt in 1979.

Steering GD subcontracts to Frigitemp was only part of the alleged plot. Davis and Lee also had to devise a scheme to embezzle about $5 million from Frigitemp's treasury to pay the kickbacks to Veliotis and Gilliland, according to the indictment. First, they acquired a dormant company, Fintracon International Ltd., which had been incorporated in 1973 in the Cayman Islands, British West Indies, the government charged. Then they set up other dummy corporations, with such exotic names as the Cryginic Insulation Company, Ltd., Zucon Machinery and Supply Company, Ltd., Polychem Corporation, and Typhont Machinery and Supply Company, Ltd. These fictitious companies submitted invoices to Frigitemp for consulting services that were never actually performed or materials that were never actually delivered. As officers of Frigitemp, Davis and Lee authorized payment of these bogus invoices, the indictment said. They then instructed their dummy companies to divert the ill-gotten funds to their personal use, the indictment charged.

To top it all off, Frigitemp recovered part of this embezzled money by including the fraudulent expenses in the invoices it submitted to General Dynamics. Thus, U.S. taxpayers, who thought their tax dollars were buying submarines, were actually subsidizing the kickbacks allegedly paid to Veliotis and Gilliland.

Davis and Lee were accused of paying Veliotis and Gilliland about $1.35 million each between 1974 and 1979. Every few months the Frigitemp executives wired kickbacks, ranging from $50,000 to $225,000, to account number 33910 at the Union Bank of Switzerland in Lausanne, a secret account controlled by Veliotis and his wife, Paulette, the indictment charged. The prosecutors said that similar payments were made to Gilliland's secret account at the same bank. The rest of the $5 million was "laundered" through banks in Montreal, New York, and Grand Cayman Island before winding up in Davis's Swiss account, the indictment charged.

The kickback amounts listed in the indictment are probably conservative. According to one attorney involved in the case, Veliotis may have actually received more than $3 million in illegal payments, at least double what he was charged with, but the statute of limitations had expired on some of the earliest kickbacks, so they weren't included in the indictment.

In addition, Veliotis might have used similar shakedown tactics with other GD subcontractors, David Lewis believes. "Now that this has all come out," said Lewis, "we are getting rumors—they are rumors—from other potential suppliers that maybe the same thing was happening in their case, which is why they didn't get any business."

The Justice Department had to pursue the four accused businessmen. Three of them were outside the United States when the indictments were issued.

Veliotis was in Greece, where he holds Greek citizenship. His New York lawyer, John Gross, issued a statement after the indictments had been announced, denying that his client was guilty, but Veliotis refused to return to the United States to face the charges. Because of his dual citizenship, Veliotis has been able to resist U.S. attempts to extradite him.

Gilliland fled but was arrested by police in England in November 1983. He was expected to be returned to the United States. Lee was living in Ireland when the indictments were issued, but he returned to the United States after a Dublin judge had ordered him jailed for contempt of court in a related legal matter. Davis was arrested in the United States and subsequently freed on a $5 million bond.

Three months after the indictments had been issued, federal prosecutors won their first conviction. Lee, the former Frigitemp chairman, testified in court that he had written checks for about $5 million to obtain the subcontracts from GD and pleaded guilty to two counts of conspiracy. The other fifteen counts he had faced were dropped in exchange for his cooperation with the prosecutors.

In July 1984 Davis was convicted in a Manhattan court of wiring illegal payoffs to secret Swiss bank accounts controlled by Veliotis and Gilliland.

In addition to the criminal case against the four alleged conspirators, a civil suit has been filed in Delaware by Lawson Bernstein, the bankruptcy trustee who represents the defunct Frigitemp Corporation. That civil suit not only names the same four individuals but also accuses the General Dynamics Corporation itself of indirect participation in the alleged kickback conspiracy. Bernstein has sued General Dynamics for $50 million, charging that it knew about Veliotis's involvement in the alleged kickback scheme and tried to cover it up by promoting him three times and offering him a seat on the board of directors. GD removed Veliotis from day-to-day contact with Quincy and Electric Boat, Bernstein maintained, in an effort to prevent the kickback scheme from exploding into a scandal that could endanger its defense contracts. A GD spokesman vigorously denied those charges, claiming, "The company knew nothing of [Veliotis's] involvement in a kickback scheme while he worked for General Dynamics."

In fact, it's difficult to determine precisely what Lewis and GD's directors knew about Veliotis's alleged kickback activities and when they first learned it. Frigitemp filed for bankruptcy in 1978 and was declared officially bankrupt the following year. Lewis admitted having heard rumors of a kickback scheme involving Frigitemp at Quincy as early as 1979 but said the three top-to-bottom audits he ordered at the shipyard turned up nothing suspicious.

In February 1980 Bernstein conducted sworn depositions in Boston with Veliotis and Gilliland, who were accompanied by a GD attorney.

Q. Mr. Veliotis, did Mr. Davis ever give or transfer any sums of money to you?
A. No, sir.

Q. Did you ever receive any money personally from any company owned or controlled by George Davis?
A. No, sir.

Q. Did you ever receive any money from Frigitemp Corporation personally?
A. No, sir.

Q. Did you ever receive any money from any officer or former officer of Frigitemp?
A. No, sir.

Veliotis was later indicted for perjury on the basis of these eight words. It would seem that Bernstein's pointed questions should have alerted GD's top management to the fact that Veliotis and Gilliland were under suspicion of receiving kickbacks. But an Electric Boat executive familiar with the controversy says it's just as likely that GD's top management assumed that the abrasive shipbuilder was being framed.

By early 1982 the U.S. attorney's office in New York City had begun a criminal investigation of the alleged embezzlement and kickback racket. Veliotis was asked to testify before a New York grand jury. "Our first question was: 'Are you going to testify?,' " recalled Lewis. "And he said, 'Absolutely, I am eager to testify.' " Despite his "eagerness," Veliotis never voluntarily testified. He was later subpoenaed but still didn't appear. He fled to Europe in May 1982. Within a few weeks he had abruptly resigned from GD and sent word that he wouldn't appear before the grand jury but would plead the Fifth Amendment instead. "That, of course, was a devastating blow to us," recalled Lewis, who said he hasn't spoken to Veliotis since.

For several months after the indictments, Veliotis seemed to be thumbing his nose at the Justice Department. He took up residence in a handsome private house near the American Embassy in Athens and dined in some of the city's finer hotels. "He may miss the 20-room mansion in Massachusetts or the waterside condo in Florida, or wife Paulette, or Kilo the killer German shepherd," *Forbes* magazine observed wryly. "It might be lonely out there, sailing his 58-foot Hatteras on the Mediterranean, or hiding in Greece with only the millions—some guess $100 million, but people exaggerate—in Swiss banks to keep him warm. But such are the penalties for stepping over the line."

Apparently Veliotis knew he was in serious trouble before the indictments were released. During one fifteen-day period in the spring of 1983, before he was charged, he sold 35,000 shares of his General Dynamics stock. Through intermediaries he still controlled nearly 70,000 additional shares. Two days after the U.S. District Court for the Southern District of New York had issued the kickback indictments, it slapped a restraining order on General Dynamics prohibiting Veliotis from disposing of his remaining GD stock. The court didn't want Veliotis selling off his "allegedly tainted property." In Greece, Veliotis, in turn, sued GD for about $142 million for allegedly freezing his financial assets, said to total about $6 million, and preventing him from pursuing other business interests.

For a while it appeared that Veliotis was content to avoid U.S. prosecution by remaining a fugitive from justice in Greece. Then he apparently changed his mind. "Unless he can strike some kind of bargain, he will be forced to stay in Greece for the rest of his life," suggested one former colleague. In January 1984 an unnamed "source close to Veliotis" told *The Washington Post* that Veliotis was willing to meet with Justice Department officials in Greece to work out a deal. It appeared he was ready to turn on General Dynamics.

The former general manager at Electric Boat was reportedly willing to describe how in the early 1970's General Dynamics had deliberately underbid on the contracts it had won to build eighteen SSN-688-class attack subs. Veliotis was also ready to explain how GD had allegedly cheated the Navy out of hundreds of millions of dollars by submitting fraudulent claims under those controversial contracts. "He intends to tell the government why General Dynamics should not have gotten one penny and why its claim was false," the source told the *Post,* in an extraordinary example of front-page plea bargaining. Veliotis wanted immunity from the kickback charges and any indictments that grew out of his disclosures about GD's claims fraud.

General Dynamics seemed stunned by Veliotis's public accusations. A spokesman at the St. Louis headquarters "categorically denied" the allegations. He pointed out that Veliotis hadn't begun working for GD at the time Electric Boat bid for the original SSN-688-class submarine contracts.

Justice Department prosecutors suddenly found themselves in an awkward situation. They had indicted Veliotis and three others on fraud, conspiracy, and kickback charges but were unable to extradite the most famous of the four defendants. Anxious to bargain for his own immunity, Veliotis dangled in front of the prosecutors tape-recorded conversations and confidential documents that might enable them to reopen their unsuccessful fraud investigation of GD. As noted, they had dropped that investigation in December 1981, after they acknowledged that they hadn't found enough solid evidence to convict anyone. Afterward Admiral Rickover and others had accused Justice of whitewashing a major fraud investigation against a leading defense contractor. That criticism had stung the prosecutors. Veliotis's offer might provide them with a chance to redeem themselves.

But there were risks. First, Veliotis might not have the tapes and documents he had promised to turn over. Justice prosecutors had paraded more than forty witnesses before a Connecticut grand jury and combed through thousands of shipyard documents. Reluctantly they had concluded that they couldn't prove that any GD employee had *intentionally* defrauded the Navy. Oral testimony or new evidence from Veliotis might not make enough difference. Even if he swore that he had participated in meetings in which GD executives had conspired to submit fraudulent claims to the Navy, his testimony might not be very persuasive. After all, how convincing would a jury find a witness who had agreed to testify only when he faced ninety years in prison on separate kickback charges?

Secondly, Justice was negotiating in the dark. Ordinarily prosecutors don't like to plea-bargain with a defendant in a criminal case until they know what evidence that person has to offer. In this case Veliotis's lawyer was unwilling to say. He insisted that Justice Department prosecutors negotiate face-to-face with Veliotis in Greece. That didn't appeal to the prosecutors, but they felt compelled to act. Soon after Veliotis's plea bargaining hit the newspapers, Senator Proxmire began pressuring Justice to negotiate with Veliotis in Greece and reopen its fraud investigation of Electric Boat. "I am greatly concerned now that the offer of information from Mr. Veliotis not be turned down because of fears within the Justice Department that the information may prove an embarrassment in light of the dropping of the original investigation," he wrote in a letter to Attorney General Smith.

Despite such pressures, Justice attorneys were wary. They didn't want to travel to Greece and then feel compelled to strike a deal with Veliotis even if he had nothing of value to trade. How would it look to the public if government attorneys returned from Greece empty-handed and chose for a second time not to indict anyone at General Dynamics?

Eventually, after much hand wringing, the Justice Department sent a team of prosecutors to Greece in May 1984 to interview Veliotis. The information he provided prompted Justice to open yet another grand jury investigation in Connecticut of GD's alleged claims fraud.

For several months Veliotis's alleged lack of moral scruples was overshadowed by the threat he could pose to U.S. military security. He probably knows as much about building top secret Trident missile-firing nuclear submarines as anyone alive. That knowledge, if it fell into the wrong hands, could compromise U.S. submarine tactics for decades.

It wouldn't be the first time questions of national security arose in connection with GD executives placed in charge of the Electric Boat submarine yard. Veliotis was replaced as general manager at Electric Boat by Fritz Tovar, a mild-mannered German-born engineer who had run the Quonset Point submarine yard for the previous four years.

Tovar's low-key, conciliatory style was markedly different from that of his predecessor. Veliotis, at six feet three inches, is a domineering figure; the balding Tovar is physically unimposing. The cold, imperious Veliotis barks orders; Tovar speaks softly, with a clipped German accent. Veliotis is expansive, almost explosive; Tovar is subdued.

Tovar's background is extraordinary in two ways: As a teenager he was a member of the Hitler youth organization, and during World War II he was a sergeant in the Luftwaffe, the German air force.

Tovar isn't the only German who served the Third Reich and went on to become an American citizen. Wernher von Braun, the engineer who helped develop the German V-2 rocket and later became a leading figure in the U.S. space program, was another. But Tovar is certainly the only veteran of the Nazi youth movement and the Luftwaffe to run a top secret American submarine yard.

Friedrich Gerhard Tovar was born in 1923 in Westphalia, in northwestern Germany, the son of a wealthy manufacturer of steel and porcelain pots and pans. Like many German teenagers in the late 1930's, he joined a Hitler youth group. He has since told American friends that he wasn't an enthusiastic supporter of the Nazi regime. To illustrate the point, he relates how during World War II, when officials demanded that his parents donate the iron fence surrounding their property to the war effort, the Tovars resisted, arguing that Hitler should have thought about his resource requirements before entering the war. (Their iron fence was dismantled and seized nonetheless.)

Tovar was eighteen years old when the United States declared war on Germany, and he joined the Luftwaffe. He spent most of the war in German-occupied Holland as a telegraph operator in the offices of the German high command, according to an Electric Boat spokesman.

After the war Tovar applied for admission to seven countries. He emigrated to Canada in 1951 and worked in Quebec as a draftsman and manager at Davie Shipbuilding Ltd., in the same engineering division that later hired Veliotis. Tovar moved across the U.S.-Canadian border several years later and held a series of engineering jobs with American manufacturers before joining General Dynamics in 1975. For the next seven years he worked under Veliotis, first as general manager of Quincy's shipbuilding facility in Charleston, South Carolina, then as head of EB's submarine yard in Quonset Point.

Tovar's wartime service in Hitler's air force apparently didn't alarm U.S. immigration authorities. The U.S. government granted him American citizenship in November 1974, four months after he had submitted his petition for naturalization. Similarly the Defense Department apparently was satisfied with its investigation of Tovar's background because he was granted a top secret security clearance in the early 1980's.

Tovar doesn't speak about World War II very often, say his friends. "He occasionally got upset with the TV show *Hogan's Heroes,*" recalled George Gaston, a former co-worker, "because it depicted Germans as not being very intelligent." Tovar resented the situation comedy's portrayal of German military officers as buffoons. Apart from such casual remarks, however, his German heritage rarely comes up in conversation.

In Veliotis's case, the dilemma facing the Justice Department seemed minor compared with the dilemma facing the U.S. intelligence community. The experts had to contend with the fact that Veliotis, a fugitive from justice living outside the United States, is an experienced shipbuilder who knows a great deal about the sonar, communications, countermeasures, and sound-deadening systems in American submarines. Soviet intelligence agents were probably eager to speak with Veliotis about such submarine technology, according to U.S. officials.

If such a meeting occurred, it wouldn't be the first time Veliotis had spoken with Soviet officials about building submarines. While he was general manager at Electric Boat, Veliotis often conferred with shipbuilding experts in foreign countries, including the USSR. "They didn't let me see their shipyards in the Soviet Union," Veliotis told a Senate subcommittee, "but I spoke to the Minister of Shipbuilding." Though Veliotis has gone out of his way to emphasize that he is *not* a security risk, the U.S. government probably wouldn't want Veliotis to talk with the Russians again.

One government insider, familiar with the Veliotis case, speculated that the Office of Naval Intelligence or the CIA might someday play a covert role in the Veliotis affair. In addition, there are rumors that Veliotis has been followed and harassed since he moved to Athens and that his property has been broken into. Veliotis said there have been three attempts to kill him since he returned to Greece. One has to wonder what the future holds for P. Takis Veliotis.

Initially prosecutors in the Justice Department's fraud section doubted that Veliotis possessed the kind of hard evidence they would need to justify reopening the GD investigation they had closed in 1981. That four-year probe had run through two grand juries in Connecticut and come up empty-handed.

But Veliotis insisted, through his New York lawyer John Gross, that he had a cache of secretly recorded tapes of telephone conversations he'd had with Lewis, MacDonald, and other top GD officers which would make very incriminating evidence. Their curiosity piqued, three wary Justice prosecutors visited Veliotis in Athens for the first time in May 1984.

At first Veliotis was equally suspicious. He was concerned that the prosecutors would take copies of his tapes but not pursue a second investigation of GD very seriously. During their first face-to-face encounter Veliotis reneged on his promise to turn over some of the tapes.

Patrick E. Tyler, a reporter for *The Washington Post* who was following the story and had already gained Veliotis's confidence, helped convince the former GD executive to cooperate with the prosecutors, according to one source close to the probe. After two or three more sessions in Athens the tone between Veliotis and the Justice lawyers began to change, and he handed over some of his tapes. The attorneys from Washington immediately recognized that there was substance behind his sensational allegations.

As each month passed and several of his allegations were partially confirmed by other sources, Veliotis began to cooperate more confidently. By the spring of 1985 he claimed to be in touch with the prosecutors "on a daily basis."

Meanwhile, Veliotis was providing tapes to *The Washington Post,* which in September and October 1984 ran front-page stories that featured excerpts from the tapes along with Veliotis's interpretation of the events being discussed.

A parade of journalists from the national media followed the *Post*'s lead. Reporters soon queued up at Veliotis's lavish villa, a handsome home with bulletproof windows and elaborate security systems, in the affluent Athens suburb of Ekali. The journalists made their trips to hear Veliotis's tapes, listen to his explanations, and soak up some local color in Athens for profile pieces on the renegade defense contractor.

This was an unusual story, indeed. A former top executive of the world's leading defense contractor flees the United States to avoid prosecution on kickback charges and then spins a tale of defense contractor fraud that, if true, would confirm anyone's worst fears of corruption in the military-industrial complex.

Dramatic "Veliotis versus GD" stories hit official Washington like bombshells, setting off a chain reaction on Capitol Hill. With so much of the congressional debate focused on the inviolability of Reagan's fiscal year 1986 defense budget, GD's dilemma provided some Pentagon critics with a perfect tool with which to chip away at the Defense Department's spending program. Several congressional committees jumped into the act, launching investigations and scheduling hearings of their own.

The House Energy and Commerce Committee, headed by Michigan Democrat John D. Dingell, delved into the ever-widening GD scandal most aggressively. Technically this committee's only entrée into the GD controversy was its responsibility to oversee the Securities and Exchange Commission. But before long Dingell's committee became a hotbed of GD investigators. Staffers looked into GD's alleged gifts to Admiral Rickover, its questionable overhead charges, its apparent use of corporate aircraft for personal travel, its alleged withholding of Trident information to manipulate its stock price, its questionable role in the Lester Crown affair, its supposed failure to supply adequate documentation with its expense vouchers, and several other allegations.

When Lewis and MacDonald first testified before Dingell's Subcommittee on Oversight and Investigations at a tense "showdown" hearing in February 1985, they wound up answering a wide range of charges that had little or nothing to do with the subcommittee's actual jurisdiction.

Senator William Proxmire, a veteran in the battle against defense contract fraud, instructed the International Trade, Finance, and Security Economics Subcommittee of the Joint Economic Committee to reexamine GD's 1978 claims settlement with the Navy (which he had opposed at the time) and Justice's decision in 1981 to close its first probe at Electric Boat without seeking any indictments.

Senator Charles Grassley, a conservative Republican from Iowa and a relative newcomer to the defense fraud arena, badgered Justice to supply his Judiciary subcommittee with complete documentation of its 1981 Electric Boat investigation. Some observers took Grassley's cordial meeting in March 1985 with newly confirmed Attorney General Edwin Meese III as a sign that Justice might become more receptive to Congress's keen interest in the GD case.

The House Armed Services Committee, which also reexamined the controversial 1978 claims settlement, announced that Veliotis had agreed to testify before its members on television, via communications satellite from Greece.

Weinberger wasn't in Washington the day of Congressman Dingell's first GD hearing. But the defense secretary huddled with his deputy, William H. Taft IV, soon after returning to the capital to map out the Pentagon's response. Apparently neither Weinberger nor Taft had read GD's lengthy prepared statement or seen tapes of Lewis's testimony, but both of them were hopping mad at what they understood to be Lewis's unapologetic arrogance. (In fact, Lewis's complete statement and testimony were far more conciliatory than was widely reported.)

Weinberger and Taft promptly decided to suspend GD's overhead payments for one month. The decision caught most OSD staff members by surprise, but even more stunning was the defense secretary's hasty decision to require all defense contractors to certify in writing, under penalty of perjury, the accuracy of their overhead expense submissions. Few on the OSD staff had ever heard this idea mentioned before it appeared in a hastily revised speech Weinberger delivered a few days after Lewis's first Capitol Hill appearance. Weinberger seemed to be slapping GD's wrist, but his action was widely viewed as a theatrical gesture to help defend the Pentagon's much-maligned $314 billion budget request.

A month later, at a second hearing of the House Energy and Commerce subcommittee, Lewis announced that GD would withdraw $23 million in overhead charges it had submitted to the government between 1979 and 1982. That represented about one-third of the overhead charges challenged by the Pentagon's auditors and about one-eighth of GD's entire overhead submission for those four years.

Lewis recognized that an overhead charge questioned by the Defense Contract Audit Agency was not necessarily improper or invalid, as is widely believed. Auditors are expected to issue nonbinding "advisory" reports, which identify costs they consider questionable. But it is the program's contracting officer who ultimately decides which costs will be reimbursed. A responsible contracting officer will make that decision after evaluating his auditor's advice, the company's rebuttal, and any additional information he can gather.

"Although we believe the vast majority of the questioned items are probably allowable under the applicable regulations, we have now looked at those questioned items in light of today's environment," said Lewis. Representative Dingell welcomed GD's first sign of capitulation by calling Lewis's decision "a useful beginning in correcting these problems."

Lewis also defended himself against allegations that he had discussed job possibilities with George Sawyer for about three months in the spring of 1983 before the assistant secretary of the navy left his government job to join GD as an executive vice-president. Lewis acknowledged having had "exploratory" talks with Sawyer while the assistant secretary was still overseeing GD shipbuilding contracts. But Lewis said he hadn't engaged in any formal negotiations until after the assistant navy secretary had disqualified himself on May 5 from further official dealings with GD. Justice prosecutors scrutinized the documents Sawyer had signed as assistant navy secretary before and after he began negotiating his job with GD. And the grand jury in Connecticut opened an investigation into whether or not Sawyer's actions had violated any conflict of interest laws.

By the spring of 1985 some observers assumed that Veliotis had exhausted his supply of damaging revelations. However, the former GD executive insisted that the best was yet to come. He said he had turned over 60 percent of his tapes to *The Washington Post* and 90 percent of the same collection to Justice prosecutors. He also claimed to have saved about five hours of recordings, with particularly damaging evidence against GD, which he planned to release if Justice "doesn't play it straight." In addition, presumably for his own personal safety, he told reporters he had instructed his lawyers to remove any undisclosed tapes from a bank vault in Athens and release them upon his death.

Prosecutors in Washington consider the tapes a rare find. They're not accustomed to having such compelling evidence when they deal with alleged white-collar crimes. Although the tapes may not represent ironclad proof that any GD employee has engaged in fraud or conspiracy, they are just the sort of flesh-and-blood evidence trial attorneys dream about.

Mounting a successful fraud prosecution would require Justice attorneys to develop a plausible scenario of the alleged crime and then to demonstrate to a jury how all the available evidence supported that scenario. Excerpts of the tapes could be used to fill in some of the gaps that were left unexplained by other documentary evidence.

The tapes might also help prosecutors puncture any façade of respectability that a defendant would inevitably try to present to the jury. The impression left by the tape-recorded voices of Lewis, MacDonald, and other GD executives would certainly differ from the impression those men could create in a courtroom, should they be indicted. If played before a jury, the tapes might rattle some GD executive and pry loose revelations that nobody anticipated.

During the first year of their discussions with Veliotis Justice prosecutors offered him immunity only from any *new* fraud indictments that might arise from his own testimony. They refused to grant him blanket immunity that would also shield him from the kickback charges he already faces in the Frigitemp case. These charges represent the only leverage Justice still maintains over Veliotis to gain his continuing cooperation.

After the prosecutors determine the strength of their case and identify any GD officials they may want to indict, the Justice Department will have to determine what kind of deal it's willing to strike with Veliotis. The aristocratic, imperious Greek shipbuilder has said he would be willing to return to the United States to testify before congressional committees or in open court if his freedom were protected. But it's possible that Justice will choose not to let him off the hook that easily, insisting instead that he stand trial on the kickback charges and, perhaps, serve some time in prison. "It would just gall them at Justice that a guy who took three million dollars would go free," said one observer familiar with the prosecutors' thinking.

On the other hand, if the prosecutors become convinced that Veliotis's testimony is crucial for them to mount a strong case against GD, they may decide to meet his terms.

Thus far prosecutors have moved cautiously, despite mounting pressure in Washington to indict GD executives for *something*. Prosecutors recognize better than anyone that the day after any indictments were announced, and the immediate publicity had subsided, the arduous task of building the case would fall to them. That would entail mountains of documents, months of depositions, and years of hard work. Furthermore, they realize that any GD executive they might indict would be defended by a well-financed, first-class legal team.

While the Justice Department was pursuing its investigation, political pressure mounted in Washington to punish GD for its alleged transgressions. Lewis and MacDonald vigorously denied that any GD employee was guilty of contract fraud at Electric Boat, but they were forced to acknowledge that the company had an embarrassing record of improperly charging the Pentagon for unallowable overhead expenses. They also admitted that GD had given Admiral Rickover gifts and gratuities over the years.

Based largely on evidence that surfaced during Representative Dingell's congressional hearings, the Pentagon's Inspector General Joseph Sherick recommended that the Navy debar from future government contracting three of GD's top officers: Lewis, MacDonald, and George Sawyer.

Navy Secretary Lehman rejected Sherick's recommendation. In what some observers initially considered a relatively mild slap on the wrist, Lehman decided not to debar any individuals. Instead, citing GD's "pervasive" climate of business misconduct, Lehman canceled two of GD's Navy contracts totaling $22.5 million, temporarily suspended two GD divisions from any new Navy business, and fined the company $676,283 (ten times the amount of its alleged gifts to Rickover). Before it could resume business with the Navy, GD had to adopt a rigorous code of ethics for its employees and settle about $75 million in disputed overhead charges.

At first GD appeared to breathe a sigh of relief, pledging to work constructively to resolve its outstanding problems with the Navy. The next day, May 22, 1985, the missing element in Lehman's surprisingly mild punishment became clearer.

In what was perhaps the culmination of his long-distance duel with Veliotis, the embattled sixty-seven-year-old Lewis announced his plan to retire from GD by the end of the year. At the same time, Lewis named as his successor Stanley C. Pace, sixty-three, the former president and current vice-chairman of TRW, Inc., a leading defense contractor. Pace was scheduled to join GD as vice-chairman on June 1, 1985, and ascend to the chairman and chief executive officer positions when Lewis stepped down.

Lewis insisted publicly that he had been planning his retirement since 1983 (probably true) and that his decision had nothing to do with Lehman's punitive action against GD the day before or his company's continuing troubles (probably false). It seems far more likely that the Navy agreed to go easy on GD only after Lewis threw in the towel and agreed to retire.

The outcome of the current assault on General Dynamics is by no means certain. While its sales, profits, funded backlog of orders, and financial prospects are strong, GD's reputation in the court of public opinion has never been worse and several of its top officers still face the worrisome prospect of criminal indictments. The company that John Holland and Isaac Rice helped found, Reuben Fleet and John Hopkins helped build, and Henry Crown and David Lewis helped climb to the pinnacle of the defense industry still faces the struggle of its life.

# Epilogue

*The great enemy of truth is very often not the lie—deliberate, contrived and dishonest—but the myth—persistent, persuasive and unrealistic.*

—*President John F. Kennedy,*
*Commencement address at Yale University,*
*June 1962*

At 8:29 P.M. on January 17, 1961, the last images of the television program *Father Knows Best* flickered across many of the 55.5 million TV sets in the United States. The extraordinary television event that was about to take place could have been called "*Grand*father Knows Best." The oldest President to have occupied the White House was preparing to bid farewell to the nation. The seventy-year-old Dwight David Eisenhower had served his country for half a century: as supreme allied commander during World War II, as president of Columbia University, as NATO commander, and as the nation's thirty-fourth President. Having retained an unusual measure of personal popularity throughout his eight years in office, the grandfatherly "Ike" was now about to alert his fellow citizens to the darkening storm clouds he saw on America's horizon. Eisenhower's somber warning caught most of Washington by surprise.

With a phalanx of cameramen, technicians, and aides crowded into his

White House office, Eisenhower spoke earnestly and somewhat nervously. "We face a hostile ideology—global in scope, atheistic in character, ruthless in purpose and insidious in method," he declared, referring to the Soviet Union. The way to meet that Communist threat, he advised, was not through emotional or transitory sacrifices but through a steady and prolonged struggle.

More dangerous than an *external* threat, Eisenhower warned, was an *internal* threat to the nation's liberty. "A vital element in keeping the peace is our military establishment. Our arms must be mighty, ready for instant action, so that no potential aggressor may be tempted to risk his own destruction."

He understood that a military establishment was necessary. But in the past decade the U.S. military establishment he had known all his life had changed in dramatic, unprecedented ways. Until World War II the United States had never maintained a *permanent* defense industry; companies had not existed primarily to build weapons. In the past, whenever a military crisis threatened the peace, manufacturers of steel and automobiles, commercial airplanes, and a thousand other consumer products had harnessed their skills and manpower to build the requisite warships, tanks, guns, or aircraft. "But we can no longer risk emergency improvisation of national defense," the President maintained as he approached his central point. "We have been compelled to create a permanent armaments industry of vast proportions."

In the final years of his presidency Eisenhower had witnessed a sea change in the country's attitude toward national defense. Ike knew that the United States had historically maintained a minimal defense establishment, relying instead on the protection of two oceans and the innate civility of the rest of the world. Most Americans believed that if war were to come, a competent soldier could be trained within days or weeks, so that there was little need for a garrison state. Even after devastating wars America's traditional impulse had been to demobilize its forces as quickly as possible, in the belief that armed strife was unlikely to recur.

When the Korean War ended in 1953, however, the recently inaugurated Eisenhower decided that a sizable, permanent defense establishment—funded by a substantial military budget—was the best way to deter further aggression by America's enemies. U.S. defenses were not dismantled after the Korean armistice had been signed. In fact, national defense spending, which accounted for 29 percent of the federal budget in 1950, swelled to 58 percent of the budget by 1955.

The creation of a permanent defense industry altered the landscape of the American economy during the 1950's. Individual cities and entire geographic regions grew dependent on the employment provided by major weapons manufacturers. Local, state, and national politicians vied for defense contracts and military installations that would funnel dollars to their constituents. Scientists, technicians, and academics looked to Washington, especially to the Defense Department, for financial support.

These by-products of a permanent defense establishment came as no surprise to Eisenhower, nor could he wash his hands of responsibility. As Army chief of staff in 1946 he had been instrumental in promoting the marriage of America's civilian resources—its technicians, scholars, and industrialists—to the country's defense apparatus. "The future security of the nation," Eisenhower wrote in an Army memorandum, "demands that all those civilian resources which by conversion or redirection constitute our main support in time of emergency be associated closely with the activities of the Army in time of peace." Now, as his presidency drew to a close, Eisenhower sensed that the risks inherent in this marriage between civilian and military interests had become too great to ignore.

"The total influence—economic, political, even spiritual—is felt in every city, every state house, every office of the Federal Government. We recognize the imperative need for this development. Yet we must not fail to comprehend its grave implications. Our toil, resources and livelihood are all involved; so is the very structure of our society."

Eisenhower had tried for eight years to balance the need for a strong national defense with the need for an independent political and economic system. If the scales now teetered to one side, he wanted desperately to alert the nation to that imbalance.

"In the councils of Government," Eisenhower warned, in the most memorable passage of his farewell address, "we must guard against the acquisition of unwarranted influence, whether sought or unsought, by the military-industrial complex. The *potential* for the disastrous rise of misplaced power exists and will persist."

The *potential* for a disastrous rise of misplaced power that Eisenhower recognized has not been fully realized. His warning was valid and timely, but unfortunately it helped create a distorted view of the defense industry that persists.

Since that night in 1961 commentators, journalists, and the general public have come to believe in a nefarious network of greedy, influence-peddling arms manufacturers, incompetent and tradition-bound military officers, self-serving political appointees in the Pentagon, and corruptible members of Congress. Actually the conception of a venal military-industrial complex is largely a myth.

Certainly nobody would deny the existence of an enormous American defense establishment. A permanent arms industry has developed since World War II in the United States as well as in most other industrialized nations in the world. This industry of some 25,000 companies absorbs a substantial part of the federal budget each year (about 11 percent in fiscal year 1984) and accounts for a significant portion of the country's gross national product (about 3 percent in 1984). The defense industry plays a crucial role in thousands of communities and countless aspects of American life.

Nor would anyone deny that the defense industry has suffered its share of cost overruns, technical failures, and management blunders, illustrated throughout this book.

Defense contractors too often underestimate their costs to develop and build new weapons systems, as General Dynamics did with its SSN-688-class attack submarines. Companies sometimes run into technical snags while trying to design a weapon with advanced capabilities, as Chrysler did with its turbine-driven M-1 tank. Contractors sometimes place too little emphasis on quality control when they shift from the development phase to full-scale production of a new weapon, as GD's Convair division did with its initial Tomahawk cruise missiles.

In recent years contractors have been loudly criticized for charging the Pentagon seemingly outrageous prices for such low-cost spare parts as screws, hammers, light bulbs, and Allen wrenches. On a grander scale, defense industry giants are sometimes accused of fraudulently overcharging their military customers or building weapons that don't work. General Dynamics currently faces a daunting array of allegations.

With such a long list of indictments, it isn't surprising that much of the public is ready to condemn the defense industry outright. I think such a sweeping condemnation is unfair. With all its faults, the defense industry isn't the inept or malevolent institution that some observers suggest. It is peopled not by scoundrels and fools but by ordinary human beings who generally try their best to produce high-quality weapons, often with remarkable success. Like companies in every industry, defense contractors continually attempt to correct their imperfections.

General Dynamics emerged as the dominant contractor in recent years because it had the foresight in the 1950's to diversify into every facet of the arms business and because it learned to develop high-quality weapons at competitive prices. The notion that GD succeeds by cheating its Pentagon customers or exerting undue influence over Congress is simplistic and inaccurate.

GD, like many of its competitors, has tried to harness the best technical brains in the country. It spends millions of dollars forecasting future military requirements and "selling" the armed services on the need to upgrade their military equipment. Ultimately GD and its industry competitors win defense contracts and earn profits because they know how to produce sophisticated weapons, not because they submit padded overhead charges or because they give gifts to cantankerous admirals.

Shiny new weapons aren't automatically embraced by the Pentagon. Contrary to the popular conception of a military officer drooling for new "gold-plated" weapons, the armed forces have demonstrated a conservative approach to major technological advances. As was shown in the histories of the first submarine, the cruise missile, and the lightweight fighter, the military bureaucracy can be exceedingly slow to accept new weapons.

The weapons procurement system in the United States is unquestionably cumbersome and costly. Too many bureaucrats become involved in every weapons decision. The designs for new weapons systems are changed too frequently, adding to their costs. Congress, for its own self-serving political reasons, becomes too involved in the management of the Pentagon and budget allocations for individual weapons programs. Contractors operate under too much pressure (from the military services, Congress, and their industry competitors) to be realistic in their cost estimates and proposed delivery schedules. The military has made insufficient use of multiyear contracts which could cut costs by making prime contracts and subcontracts more stable. And too little effort has been made by contractors and the military services to ensure that companies seek reimbursements from the government *only* for their legitimate expenses.

The weapons acquisition system in the United States unquestionably has its problems. Still, on balance, it functions more admirably than is commonly believed.

# General Dynamics: Chronology

**1841:** John P. Holland, father of the modern submarine, born in Liscannor, Ireland.

**1873:** Holland emigrates to United States, settles in New Jersey, and continues to design his submarine.

**1887:** Reuben Hollis Fleet, founder of Consolidated Aircraft Corporation, born in Washington Territory.

**1893:** Holland and business associates incorporate John P. Holland Torpedo Boat Company and enter his submarine designs in a Navy competition.

**1899:** Professor Isaac L. Rice incorporates Electric Boat Company and absorbs Holland Torpedo Boat Company as a major subsidiary.

**1900:** U.S. Navy purchases its first workable submarine, *Holland VI*, from Electric Boat.

**1918:** Major Fleet heads Army program to provide nation's first airmail service, connecting Washington, D.C., Philadelphia, and New York.

By conclusion of World War I prosperous Electric Boat has constructed more than 200 submarines and cargo ships for U.S. Navy.

**1923:** As a civilian Fleet incorporates Consolidated Aircraft Corporation and begins manufacturing planes in a leased factory in Rhode Island.

**1924:** Consolidated relocates to Buffalo, New York.

**1935:** Consolidated wins a $6 million production contract for sixty PBY-1 long-range patrol bombers, the largest defense contract awarded since World War I.

Consolidated relocates to San Diego, where it quickly becomes the city's largest employer.

**1941:** At the urging of government officials dissatisfied with his one-man management style, Major Fleet sells his interest in Consolidated.

**1943:** Consolidated merges with Vultee Aircraft, Inc., forming Consolidated Vultee, or Convair, and becomes the leading manufacturer of B-24 Liberator bombers and PBY Catalina patrol planes during World War II.

**1947:** John J. Hopkins becomes president of Electric Boat and promptly engineers the acquisition of Canadair, Ltd., Canada's largest aircraft manufacturer.

**1950:** Electric Boat accepts Navy Captain Hyman G. Rickover's invitation to develop the world's first nuclear-powered submarine, *Nautilus*.

**1952:** Recognizing that the name Electric Boat no longer describes his company's diversified activities, Hopkins changes its name to the General Dynamics Corporation. The submarine division continues to be called Electric Boat.

**1954:** Consolidated Vultee and General Dynamics merge, with Convair becoming another division of GD.

**1957:** Hopkins dies of cancer, and GD chairmanship passes to Frank Pace, Jr., a former federal budget director and secretary of the army.

GD acquires Material Service Corporation from multimillionaire Henry Crown, who becomes an influential member of GD's board of directors.

**1962:** After GD's financially disastrous attempt to enter commercial jetliner market, Pace yields chairmanship to Pan American World Airways executive Roger Lewis.

**1963:** GD embroiled in controversy over Defense Secretary Robert McNamara's selection of its TFX fighter-bomber rather than the Boeing entrant preferred by most top military officers.

**1966:** Power struggle at GD between chairman Roger Lewis and largest stockholder Henry Crown culminates in Crown's decision to sell out and leave board.

**1970:** Crown and business associates quietly accumulate stock, reclaim effective control of GD, force Roger Lewis to step down, and lure David S. Lewis, Jr., president of McDonnell Douglas Corporation, to become GD's new chairman.

**1971:** Navy awards Electric Boat a fixed-price contract to build seven SSN-688-class nuclear-powered attack submarines.

**1973:** Electric Boat wins contract to construct another eleven SSN-688-class subs, which begin to overload shipyard's labor force.

**1974:** Navy awards Electric Boat contract to build first Trident nuclear-powered ballistic missile submarine, which further taxes shipyard's management, work force, and inventory system.

**1975:** After a hotly contested fly-off U.S. Air Force selects GD's YF-16 prototype over Northrop's YF-17 as its new lightweight fighter. Five months later, in the Deal of the Century, Norway, the Netherlands, Belgium, and Denmark also choose GD's F-16, rather than France's Mirage, to modernize their air forces.

**1976:** GD's Convair division wins Navy contract to develop Tomahawk sea-launched cruise missile, first of a family of sea-, ground-, and air-launched cruise missiles that GD eventually dominates.

GD submits a contract claim for half a billion dollars, arguing that the Navy was primarily responsible for the cost overruns and construction delays it has suffered on its attack submarine program.

**1978:** Faced with crippling financial losses, GD threatens to stop work on remaining attack subs unless Navy settles its outstanding claim. Three months later the Navy agrees to controversial claims settlements with GD as well as with Litton and Newport News shipyards.

**1981:** Following revelations of nonconforming steel, faulty welding, and improper paint at Electric Boat, GD submits "insurance reimbursement claims" to Navy to recoup its cost overruns. Navy Secretary John Lehman calls insurance claims outrageous and refuses to award GD additional submarine contracts. GD reluctantly withdraws insurance claims, and Navy awards it contract for one new sub.

**1982:** Following a lengthy grand jury investigation of alleged contract fraud at Electric Boat, Justice Department announces it has collected insufficient evidence to indict anyone for fraud.

GD pays Chrysler Corporation $336 million for its Army contracts to build

M-1 and M-60 battle tanks and becomes the leading weapons supplier to all three military services.

Combative P. Takis Veliotis, executive vice-president and former head of Electric Boat, suddenly resigns from GD and returns to his native Greece.

Quality-control problems GD suffers while shifting from full-scale development to production of Tomahawk cruise missiles lead frustrated Navy officials to hand portion of the production contract to McDonnell Douglas.

**1983:** Veliotis indicted in New York City for allegedly accepting $1.35 million in illegal kickbacks from a subcontractor to GD's Quincy and Electric Boat shipyards.

**1984:** Veliotis tells Department of Justice prosecutors and journalists that EB submitted fraudulent claims to the Navy during 1970's but refuses to return to United States to testify. He provides tapes and documents that lead to congressional hearings, further allegations, and another grand jury investigation of EB's alleged fraud.

**1985:** Following highly publicized appearances by David Lewis and GD's chief financial officer Gorden MacDonald before an aggressive House Energy and Commerce subcommittee, Defense Secretary Weinberger moves to recoup $244 million in disputed overhead charges by withholding progress payments from the company.

The Pentagon's Inspector General Joseph Sherick recommends that the Navy debar Lewis, MacDonald, and other top GD executive from doing business with the government, but Navy Secretary John Lehman, Jr., rejects that advice.

Instead, on May 21, Lehman cancels two existing Navy contracts with GD, suspends any new contracts with two of the company's largest divisions, and fines GD $676,283 (ten times the amount of its alleged gratuities to Admiral Rickover). Lehman calls upon GD to establish a rigorous code of ethics for its employees and to settle $75 million in disputed overhead charges.

The following day, Lewis, sixty-seven, announces his plan to retire by the end of the year. He names as his successor Stanley C. Pace, sixty-three, vice-chairman of TRW, Inc., a leading defense contractor based in Cleveland.

# Glossary

**ABM:** Antiballistic missile
**AFSC:** Air Force Systems Command
**ALCM:** Air-launched cruise missile
**AMRAAM:** Advanced Medium-Range Air-to-Air Missile
**ASD:** Aeronautical Systems Division
**ASW:** Antisubmarine warfare
**B&P:** Bid and proposal
**CAIG:** Cost Analysis Improvement Group
**CDI:** Chrysler Defense, Inc.
**CNO:** Chief of naval operations
**DARCOM:** Army Matériel Development and Readiness Command
**DARPA:** Defense Advanced Research Projects Agency
**DCAA:** Defense Contract Audit Agency
**DCAS:** Defense Contract Administration Service
**DDR&E:** Director of Defense Research and Engineering
**DLA:** Defense Logistics Agency
**DOD:** Department of Defense
**DSARC:** Defense Systems Acquisition Review Council
**DT&E:** Development, test, and evaluation
**EB:** Electric Boat division of General Dynamics
**FY:** Fiscal year
**FYDP:** Five-Year Defense Plan

**GAO:** General Accounting Office
**GD:** General Dynamics Corporation
**GE:** General Electric Company
**GFI:** Government Furnished Information
**GFM:** Government Furnished Material
**GLCM:** Ground-launched cruise missile
**GOCO:** Government-owned contractor-operated
**HAC:** House Appropriations Committee
**HASC:** House Armed Services Committee
**HMMWV:** High Mobility Multi-Purpose Wheeled Vehicle
**ICBM:** Intercontinental ballistic missile
**IG:** Inspector General
**IOC:** Initial Operational Capability
**IR&D:** Independent Research and Development
**JCMPO:** Joint Cruise Missiles Project Office
**JCS:** Joint Chiefs of Staff
**LANTIRN:** Low-Altitude Navigation and Targeting Infrared System for Night
**MAC:** Military Airlift Command
**MILSPECS:** Military specifications
**NATO:** North Atlantic Treaty Organization
**NAVAIR:** Naval Air Systems Command
**NAVMAT:** Naval Material Command
**NAVSEA:** Naval Sea Systems Command
**NSC:** National Security Council
**O&M:** Operations and maintenance
**OMB:** Office of Management and Budget
**OPNAV:** Office of the Chief of Naval Operations
**OSD:** Office of the Secretary of Defense
**OT&E:** Operational test and evaluation
**PA&E:** Office of Program Analysis and Evaluation
**PPBS:** Planning, Programming, and Budgeting System
**R&D:** Research and development
**RDT&E:** Research, development, test, and evaluation
**RFP:** Request for Proposals
**RSI:** Rationalization, Standardization, and Interoperability
**SAC:** Senate Appropriations Committee
**SAC:** Strategic Air Command
**SALT:** Strategic Arms Limitation Talks
**SASC:** Senate Armed Services Committee

**SCAD:** Subsonic Armed Cruise Decoy
**SIOP:** Single Integrated Operation Plan
**SLBM:** Submarine-launched ballistic missile
**SLCM:** Sea-launched cruise missile
**SPO:** Systems Program Office
**SSBN:** Nuclear-powered ballistic missile submarine
**SSN:** Nuclear-powered submarine
**SUBROC:** Submarine Rocket
**SUPSHIP:** Supervisor of Shipbuilding
**TAC:** Tactical Air Command
**TACOM:** Army Tank-Automotive Command
**TERCOM:** Terrain contour matching
**USDRE:** Undersecretary of defense for research and engineering

# Notes

In a sense my research for this book started in 1976, when I began writing about the defense industry. Since then I have observed the weapons business as a journalist, market researcher, and consultant in the Office of the Secretary of Defense. I have spoken with thousands of people connected with the industry in private companies, the government, the military, trade associations, law firms, and related organizations. These conversations helped lay the foundation for this project.

During the three years I spent researching and writing this book, I interviewed another group of more than 100 people with expertise in the arms business. Their names are cited throughout this section, followed by their relevant position *as of the time we spoke* and the dates on which those conversations took place. Some individuals agreed to speak with me only if I guaranteed them anonymity, a request I have honored.

## Introduction

**Page xi**
"$2,400 for every family": This figure was derived by dividing the Defense Department's fiscal year 1986 budget request of $146.1 billion for the development and procurement of weapons by 61.4 million, the number of families in the United States, according to the 1985 *Information Please Almanac*, p. 772.

**Page xii**
"third largest contractor": "100 Companies Receiving the Largest Dollar
Volume of Prime Contract Awards, Fiscal Year 1984," Department of Defense, Directorate for Information, Operations and Reports, The Pentagon,
Washington, D.C., p. 9.

## Chapter One
## General Dynamics and the Defense Industry

**Page 4**
"Electric Boat had suffered losses": Letter from P. Takis Veliotis to Vice
Admiral Clarence R. Bryan, March 13, 1978, declaring Electric Boat's inten-
tion to halt construction on SSN-688-class submarines.

**Page 4**
" 'the Navy was blackmailing us' ": Author interview with David S. Lewis,
chairman of the General Dynamics Corporation, May 4, 1983; hereafter referred to as Lewis interview.

**Page 4**
"GD had ranked eighth in sales": "100 Companies Receiving the Largest
Dollar Volume of Military Prime Contract Awards, Fiscal Year 1978," De-
partment of Defense, Washington Headquarters Services.

**Page 4**
" 'It was culturally difficult' ": Lewis interview.

**Page 5**
" 'there's no deck to strut on' ": John Niven, Cortland Canby, and Vernon
Welsh, eds., *Dynamic America: A History of General Dynamics Corporation
and Its Predecessor Companies* (New York: General Dynamics Corp. and
Doubleday & Co., 1960), p. 59; hereafter referred to as *Dynamic America.*

**Page 5**
"Consolidated Aircraft Corporation": A detailed history of this company is
presented in William Wagner, *Reuben Fleet and the Story of Consolidated
Aircraft* (Fallbrook, Calif.: Aero Publishers, 1976), which was the source for
all direct quotations of Reuben Fleet contained in this book, except where
otherwise indicated. I am indebted to Wagner for the thoroughness of his
research.

**Page 5**

" 'The genius of American inventors' ": *Dynamic America,* p. 115.

**Page 6**

"Hopkins usually managed to get his way": Author interview with Dorothy Young, Hopkins's longtime personal secretary, January 15, 1983; hereafter called Young interview.

**Page 6**

" 'Grow or die' ": *Dynamic America,* p. 337.

**Page 6**

"a new General Motors": Young interview.

**Page 6**

" 'Jonah has swallowed his *second* whale' ": *Dynamic America,* p. 338.

**Page 6**

" 'We are moving swiftly' ": *The New York Times,* March 2, 1954.

**Page 7**

" '*Nautilus* did not mark the end' ": Admiral Hyman G. Rickover, quoted in Joseph M. Dukert, *Nuclear Ships of the World* (New York: Coward, McCann & Geoghegan, 1973), p. 13, cited in report prepared by James W. Sheire, Division of History, National Park Service, U.S. Department of Interior, which recommended that the *Nautilus* be registered as a national historic place, dated February 12, 1982, p. 11.

**Page 7**

"the commercial jetliner market": Author interview with Phillip Prophett, former Convair executive and test pilot, November 22, 1982.

**Page 8**

"acquiring a commercial shipyard": *Forbes,* December 8, 1980.

**Page 8**

"Crown . . . lost confidence in Lewis": Author interview with Nathan Cummings, a member of GD's board of directors, September 20, 1982; hereafter called Cummings interview. Cummings died on February 19, 1985.

**Page 8**
"Lewis deserved much of the credit": Author interview with Wallace R. Persons, former GD director, May 5, 1983; hereafter called Persons interview.

**Page 9**
"more than 5 percent of all Pentagon prime contracts": "100 Companies Receiving the Largest Dollar Volume of Prime Contract Awards, Fiscal Year 1983," *loc. cit.,* p. 9.

**Page 9**
"Altogether, GD's future seems bright": Author interviews with defense industry analysts Andrew S. Adelson, of Sanford C. Bernstein & Company, August 25, 1982; Paul H. Nisbet, of Bache, Halsey Stuart Shields (now Prudential-Bache), August 25, 1982; and Donald T. Spindel, of A. G. Edwards & Sons, May 5, 1983.

**Page 9**
"a backlog of funded weapons orders": GD's 1984 Annual Report, p. 1.

**Page 9**
"Its profits have almost doubled": *Business Week* cover story (March 25, 1985), p. 72.

**Page 11**
" 'I am not here to say that our company is perfect' ": Testimony by GD chairman David S. Lewis at a hearing of the Subcommittee on Oversight and Investigations of the House Energy and Commerce Committee, February 28, 1985, distributed copy of statement; hereafter called Lewis testimony.

**Page 12**
"Boeing, Northrop, Grumman, and Lockheed": An article in *The New York Times* on February 1, 1985, with the headline DYNAMICS' DEFERRAL OF U.S. INCOME TAX, focuses primarily on GD's avoidance of taxes, though it is accompanied by a chart indicating that between 1981 and 1983 Boeing and Northrop, like GD, received multimillion-dollar tax refunds and that Grumman and Lockheed paid no taxes during the same period.

**Page 12**
"60 percent of Americans": A poll of 1,254 adults conducted between March 8 and March 11, 1985, by Louis Harris & Associates, Inc., claiming an accu-

racy within three percentage points, reported in *Business Week* (March 25, 1985), p. 73.

**Page 15**

". . . David Packard, established the DSARC system": Memorandum signed by Deputy Secretary of Defense David Packard, May 30, 1969, creating the DSARC, and author interview with David Packard, November 15, 1982; hereafter called Packard interview.

**Page 16**

"technical ideas are passed back and forth": Author interview with Vice Admiral Jon Boyes (USN-Ret.), president of Armed Forces Communications and Electronics Association, August 3, 1982.

**Page 16**

" 'It becomes sort of a ground swell' ": Author interview with Gerald Estepp, aircraft planner in the Air Force's Aeronautical Systems Division, July 29, 1982.

**Page 16**

" 'Contractors will always stand taller' ": *Ibid.*

**Page 17**

" ' "A one-year delay won't hurt you" ' ": Author interview with Henry Stachowski, aircraft planner in the Air Force's Aeronautical Systems Division, July 29, 1982; hereafter referred to as Stachowski interview.

**Pages 17–18**

" 'They give presentations . . . all the way up the line' ": *Ibid.*

**Page 19**

"Congressional representatives weigh in": Author interview with Senator Alan Cranston, then a candidate for the Democratic nomination for President, July 12, 1983.

**Page 20**

"In private negotiations": Author interview with former Assistant Secretary of the Navy Edward Hidalgo, October 27, 1982 (hereafter called Hidalgo interview), and Lewis interview.

**Page 20**
" ' "If you think this threat" ' ": Lewis interview.

## Chapter Two
## The Saltwater Enterprise

**Page 21**
"As children Holland and his two brothers": Richard K. Morris, *John P. Holland—1841–1914: Inventor of the Modern Submarine* (Annapolis, Md.: United States Naval Institute, 1966). I am indebted to Morris, a grandson of Charles A. Morris, the superintending engineer of the Holland Torpedo Boat Company and a friend of John Holland, for his exhaustively researched, cogent, and comprehensive biography, hereafter referred to as Morris. It served as the principal source of information for this chapter. In addition, an informal history of Holland's submarine work is presented in Robert F. Burgess, *Ships Beneath the Sea* (New York: McGraw-Hill, 1975), pp. 79–106.

**Page 21**
"A blight on the potato": Details on the disease, starvation, and death that resulted from the potato blight may be found in Reverend John O'Rourke, *The History of the Great Irish Famine of 1847* (Dublin, Ireland: James Duffy and Co., 1902), pp. 151–53 and 480–83. Also see Thomas A. Jackson, *Ireland Her Own* (New York: International Publishers, 1947), pp. 229–31 and 247–51.

**Page 22**
" 'He had imbibed a deep hostility' ": Frank T. Cable, *The Birth and Development of the American Submarine* (New York: Harper & Brothers, 1924), p. 36.

**Page 23**
"warships protected with iron armor": A vivid description of the duel between the *Monitor* and the *Merrimack* is presented in Allan Nevins, *The War for the Union,* volume II (New York: Charles Scribner's Sons, 1960), pp. 50–55.

**Page 23**
" 'the man . . . in a wooden ship is a fool' ": Bernard and Fawn Brodie, *From Crossbow to H-Bomb* (New York: Dell, 1962), p. 159.

**Page 24**
"Earlier attempts to develop naval submarines": For an overview of the early

history of underwater warfare, see Paul Cohen, *The Realm of the Submarine* (London: Macmillan Company, Collier-Macmillan Ltd., 1969).

**Page 24**
" 'tyrannic principles of Bonaparte' ": William Barclay Parsons, *Robert Fulton and the Submarine* (New York: Columbia University Press, 1922), pp. 32, 81, and 86.

**Page 24**
"the persistent Fulton": Robert Fulton, *Torpedo War, and Submarine Explosions, by Robert Fulton* (1810, reproduction published Chicago: Swallow Press, 1971), p. 4.

**Page 25**
" 'Thirty-nine men were drowned' ": Edwin P. Hoyt, *Submarines at War* (New York: Stein and Day, 1983), p. 14.

**Page 25**
" 'He was regarded as a second Jules Verne' ": Simon Lake, *The Submarine in War and Peace: Its Development and Its Possibilities* (Philadelphia and London: Lippincott, 1918), p. 90. Ironically, although Verne's science-fiction classic *Twenty Thousand Leagues Under the Sea* appeared in book form three years before Holland emigrated to the United States, Holland never read it. He considered fiction a waste of time. *Dynamic America*, p. 51.

**Page 26**
" 'to put anything through in Washington' ": Morris, *op. cit.*, p. 22.

**Page 26**
" 'death traps' ": *Dynamic America*, p. 59.

**Page 27**
"its American counterpart, the Fenian Brotherhood": For a description of the organization and goals of the Fenian Brotherhood, see Joseph Denieffe, *A Personal Narrative of the Irish Revolutionary Brotherhood* (Shannon, Ireland: Irish University Press, 1969), pp. 198–201 and 273–77.

**Page 27**
" 'His most spectacular fight' ": Desmond Ryan, *The Phoenix Flame: A Study of Fenianism and John Devoy* (London: Arthur Barker, 1937), p. 204.

**Page 28**
" 'He was cool, good-tempered' ": John Devoy, quoted in Morris, *op. cit.,* p. 25.

**Page 28**
" 'The place to strike John Bull' ": *Ibid.*

**Page 30**
DOWN AMONG THE FISHES: *Paterson* (New Jersey) *Daily Guardian* and *Daily Press,* May and June 1878, quoted *ibid.,* p. 28.

**Page 30**
" 'The bow went down first' ": Lake, *op. cit.,* p. 93.

**Page 30**
"anxious to safeguard his design": Holland's first submarine lay rusting and all but forgotten in the Passaic River for nearly half a century. Then, in 1927, seven enterprising engineering students unearthed the craft from beneath six feet of ground near the riverbank. "For three months the young men, who are employed in the daytime, had spent two nights a week and Saturday afternoons seeking the model, and when they finally uncovered a large portion of it about 8:45 o'clock they showed their joy by dancing and waving shovels in the air," reported *The New York Times* on August 14, 1927.

**Page 31**
" 'our boat was tight' ": Morris, *op. cit.,* p. 41.

**Page 32**
" 'I'll let her rot on their hands' ": *Ibid.,* p. 47.

**Page 32**
" 'I never bothered again with my backers' ": Lake, pp. 107–08, quoted *ibid.*

**Page 33**
" 'the best submarine man' ": Cable, *op. cit.,* p. 318.

**Page 33**
" 'a floating gun carriage' ": Article by Edmund Zalinski in the *Forum* (1886), cited in Morris, *op. cit.,* p. 53.

**Page 35**

" 'the most cretaceous of organizations' ": Henry D. Levine, "Some Things to All Men: The Politics of Cruise Missile Development," *Public Policy* (Winter 1977), p. 147.

**Page 35**

" 'punching a feather bed' ": M. S. Eccles, *Beckoning Frontiers* (New York: Knopf, 1951), p. 336, quoted in Levine, *op. cit.,* p. 147.

**Page 35**

" 'I know I can win the competition' ": Morris, *op. cit.,* p. 65.

**Page 36**

" 'I suppose you are here on the same errand' ": Lake, *op. cit.,* pp. 120–21.

**Page 38**

" 'I think I should be pardoned' ": Morris, *op. cit.,* p. 69.

**Page 39**

" 'The rabbit and the dove were dead' ": Cable, *op. cit.,* p. 101.

**Page 41**

" 'the feet of a duck' ": Franklin Matthews, "Under Water in the Holland," *McClure's Magazine* (February 1899), p. 293.

**Page 41**

" 'I don't think I can improve on the arrangement' ": *Dynamic America,* p. 66.

**Page 42**

" 'fully proved her ability' ": Morris, *op. cit.,* p. 86.

**Page 42**

"*Maine* was sunk": An unknown man raised his glass in a Broadway bar shortly after the sinking and solemnly said, "Gentlemen, remember the *Maine!,*" thereby furnishing an expression that became famous around the world, according to Burton Stevenson, *The Home Book of Quotations* (New York: Dodd, Mead & Co., 1967).

**Page 42**

"voices . . . clamoring for war": For a discussion of the events leading up to the Spanish-American War, see Joseph E. Wisan, *The Cuban Crisis as Reflected in the New York Press (1895–1898)* (New York: Columbia University Press, 1934), pp. 400–01; Lewis L. Gould, *The Presidency of William McKinley* (Lawrence, Kan.: Regents Press of Kansas, 1980); and Edward T. Heald, *The William McKinley Story* (Canton, Ohio: The Stark County Historical Society, 1964).

**Page 42**
" 'Evidently she has great possibilities' ": Morris, *op. cit.,* p. 87.

**Page 43**
" 'the job of sinking the Spanish fleet' ": *Ibid.,* p. 90.

**Page 43**
" 'What? Me worry?' ": Actually even the creators of *Mad* magazine aren't sure of the origin of the expression "What? Me worry?" The Alfred E. Neuman character, who often utters it, is based on an earlier drawing of Painless Romain, "the original optimist," a cartoon character who announced after his front tooth had been pulled by a dentist, "It didn't hurt a bit." Bill Gaines, *Mad* magazine's editor, told me that the precise genesis of the expression "What? Me worry?" has been lost to history; telephone interview, January 10, 1984.

**Page 44**
" 'the tone of pure aesthetic feeling' ": *The New York Times,* May 18, 1875.

**Page 44**
"never considered a true chess master": Brief references to Rice's chess prowess can be found in Reuben Fine, *The Middle Game of Chess* (New York: David McKay, 1952), p. 191, and Anne Sunnucks, comp., *The Encyclopedia of Chess* (New York: St. Martin's Press, 1970), p. 404.

**Page 45**
" 'Mr. R—— played a game of chess with you' ": Dr. Emanuel Lasker, *The Rice Gambit* (New York: Press of Dr. Emanuel Lasker, 1910), pp. 41–42.

**Page 45**
" 'Nothing could stop their natural exuberance' ": *Dynamic America,* p. 13.

**Page 45**

" 'absorbing almost every possible competitor' ": Unidentified article published in 1895, quoted *ibid.,* p. 27.

## Chapter Three
## Airborne—the Genesis of Convair

**Page 48**

"at the height of World War II": For a detailed look at how Consolidated cooperated with the Ford Motor Company in the construction of B-24 bombers during World War II, see Allan Nevins and Frank Ernest Hill, *Ford: Decline and Rebirth, 1933–1962* (New York: Charles Scribner's Sons, 1962).

**Page 48**

"B-24 Liberators": *The New York Times* described the Army Air Corps's newest bomber on February 18, 1940.

**Page 49**

"Consolidated built about 33,000 planes": *Fiftieth Anniversary Book* (San Diego: General Dynamics, Convair Aerospace Division, San Diego Chapter of the National Management Association, 1973), p. 48. Another source of information on Convair's corporate roots is *The History of Convair—1908–1966,* a compilation of articles that originally appeared in the division's house organ *Convariety.*

**Page 49**

"the merger of Consolidated Vultee and General Dynamics": Author interview with Gordon Jackson, former GD employee and unofficial historian of Convair division, November 20, 1982.

**Page 49**

"an imposing man with a nonstop mouth": Fleet's business success and larger-than-life personality landed him on the cover of *Time* on November 17, 1941, along with his favorite aphorism: "Nothing short of right is right."

**Page 49**

"Senate committee investigating": Some of the results of Truman's effort were contained in a report issued by the U.S. Senate Special Committee Investigating the National Defense Program, Report No. 480, part 5, January 15, 1942.

**Page 49**
" 'I want to see your books, Fleet' ": Wagner, *op. cit.,* p. 219.

**Page 51**
" 'are you really the head of the Aviation Section' ": *Ibid.,* pp. 102–03.

**Page 53**
" 'Burleson went into a rage' ": Reuben H. Fleet, *Fifty Years of Air Mail,* brochure of reminiscences published by the National Aeronautic Association, honoring airmail pioneers on their fiftieth anniversary, May 15, 1968, p. 4.

**Page 55**
" 'The weather was so frightful' ": *Ibid.,* p. 6.

**Page 55**
" 'Tomorrow I want to extend the service' ": Wagner, *op. cit.,* p. 55.

**Page 58**
" 'Every company employing a staff' ": *The New York Times,* October 22, 1933.

**Page 59**
" 'It was nobody's business' ": *Ibid.,* February 10, 1934.

**Page 60**
"The average profit of companies": *Ibid.*

**Page 60**
" 'the Navy Department is not in a position' ": Wagner, *op. cit.,* p. 33.

**Page 61**
" 'This boy is not our usual type of hero' ": Will Rogers's syndicated column, May 25, 1927, as quoted in Richard Kenin and Justin Wintle, eds., *Dictionary of Biographical Quotation* (New York: Alfred A. Knopf, 1978), p. 492.

**Page 61**
"The world had a new hero": Fleet's repeated attempts to woo Lindbergh onto Consolidated's payroll are described in Charles A. Lindbergh, *The Wartime Journals of Charles A. Lindbergh* (New York: Harcourt Brace Jovanovich, Inc., 1970).

**Page 63**
"New York, Rio & Buenos Aires Line": For a detailed history of this international carrier, see Ralph O'Neill (NYRBA's founder) and Joseph F. Hood, *A Dream of Eagles* (Boston: Houghton Mifflin, 1973); Carl Solberg, *Conquest of the Skies: A History of Commercial Aviation in America* (Boston: Little, Brown, 1979), p. 86; and Robert Daley, *An American Saga: Juan Trippe and His Pan American Empire* (New York: Random House, 1980).

**Page 63**
"Lauretta Golem's niece, Dorothy Mitchell": A more informal look at Fleet's life, from his second wife's perspective, may be found in Dorothy Fleet, *Our Flight to Destiny* (New York: Vantage Press, 1964).

**Page 64**
" 'The plane struck some obstruction' ": *The New York Times,* September 14, 1929.

**Page 66**
"San Diego . . . a city of aviation firsts": *Fiftieth Anniversary Book, loc. cit.,* p. 23.

**Page 68**
"FDR sent his congratulations": *Ibid.,* p. 20.

**Page 68**
"San Diego promised to charge less for electricity": Author interview with David Fleet, November 19, 1982.

**Page 68**
" 'I prefer to live here' ": Dorothy Fleet, *op. cit.,* p. 106.

**Page 70**
"The company paid moving expenses": Fleet's obituary in the *San Diego Union,* October 30, 1975, includes an interesting description of Consolidated's move to San Diego.

**Page 70**
" 'No holding company owns or controls us' ": Wagner, *op. cit.,* p. 182.

**Page 71**
" 'We made 168 flights' ": *Ibid.,* p. 193.

**Page 71**

"Catalinas helped sink the . . . *Bismarck*": Ludovic Kennedy, *Pursuit: The Chase and Sinking of the Bismarck* (New York: Viking Press, 1974), pp. 153–55.

**Page 72**

"Fleet was eased out": Declassified records from the War Production Board, Policy Documentation File 313.01—Aircraft Administration, at the National Archives in Washington, D.C., make clear the federal government's dissatisfaction with Fleet's management of Consolidated as World War II approached. "Frankly, you have a one-man show and you are the man," George J. Mead, of the National Defense Advisory Commission, said in a blunt letter to Fleet, dated October 21, 1940. "Capable as you are, you cannot possibly keep your fingers on everything in an operation as large as you now have." By December 1, 1941, Vultee Aircraft had struck a deal with Fleet to buy him out. "The contract is all signed, sealed and delivered," the president of Vultee told the head of the government's aviation production section. "We have the benefit of his advice if we want it. If we don't ask for it it isn't to be proffered."

**Page 72**

"Consolidated was merged with Vultee Aircraft": An account of Consolidated's board meetings from 1923 through its merger with Vultee in 1943 is contained in typewritten Digest of Minutes, CAC and VA, Inc., Vol. 1, provided to the author.

## Chapter Four
## The Dynamic Duo

**Page 73**

" 'full-time, national-scale arms industry' ": *Business Week* (September 27, 1952).

**Page 74**

"a company with wide-ranging activities": Hopkins explained the corporation's name change in GD's 1952 Annual Report, p. 6.

**Page 74**

"Hopkins, a husky, square-faced executive": *Newsweek* cover story (October 18, 1952) profiled Hopkins and General Dynamics.

**Page 74**
" 'switching from guns to gadgets' ": *Newsweek* (May 13, 1957).

**Page 74**
"Hopkins had become a wealthy lawyer": For an interesting glimpse of Hopkins as a friend and business associate of oil magnate J. Paul Getty, see J. Paul Getty, *My Life and Fortunes* (New York: Duell, Sloan and Pearce, 1963), pp. 166–68, and J. Paul Getty, *As I See It* (Englewood Cliffs, N.J.: Prentice-Hall, 1976), pp. 44–45.

**Page 74**
"Hopkins led a comfortable life": Additional biographical details are presented in an obituary and two other articles in *The New York Times,* May 4, 5, and 7, 1957, and in *Time* (May 13, 1957).

**Page 75**
"Fifth Avenue Presbyterian Church": Young interview.

**Page 75**
" 'happy to repair hair curlers' ": *Dynamic America,* p. 187.

**Page 75**
"Five men and four women": The account of the foiled attempt to kidnap Henry Crown was drawn from news articles in the *Chicago Tribune* on December 7, 1980, and the *Chicago Sun-Times* on December 7, 8, and 14, 1980.

**Page 76**
" 'If they had kidnapped him' ": Author interview with newspaper reporter Charles Neubauer, July 12, 1983.

**Page 76**
" 'my security people knew about it' ": *Chicago Tribune,* December 7, 1980.

**Page 77**
"he controls more than 23 percent": General Dynamics Proxy Statement, dated March 26, 1984, p. 3.

**Page 77**
" 'When the colonel says something' ": Cummings interview.

**Page 77**
" 'he knows the size of your underwear' ": *The New York Times,* December 12, 1976.

**Page 77**
" 'Henry is a real wizard' ": Persons interview.

**Page 77**
"a grudge against A. N. Pritzker": *Forbes* (December 8, 1980).

**Page 78**
"fire spread to the warehouse": *Chicago Tribune,* April 15, 1980.

**Page 78**
"he bungled a customer's order": *The New York Times,* December 12, 1976.

**Page 79**
" 'I started my mythical company' ": *Ibid.,* February 21, 1960.

**Page 79**
" 'kid, you've got all the answers' ": *Chicago Tribune,* April 15, 1980.

**Page 79**
" 'come up with the back taxes' ": *Forbes* (December 8, 1980).

**Page 80**
" 'you're either going to be worth twice as much' ": Cummings interview.

**Page 80**
"business allies ever since": *Forbes* (December 8, 1980).

**Page 80**
"selling out and retiring comfortably": *The New York Times,* February 21, 1960.

**Page 81**
"the target of widespread suspicions": For a lengthy catalogue of allegations that have been leveled against Henry Crown over the years, see Ovid Demaris, *Captive City* (New York: L. Stuart, 1969). More recently, in 1974 Crown's son Lester and several other construction industry executives were involved in a grand jury investigation of alleged payoffs to Illinois state legislators in ex-

change for relaxed road construction regulations; see *Chicago Tribune,* October 23 and December 5, 1974. (GD was later criticized for allegedly failing to notify its stockholders, the SEC, and the Department of Defense of Lester Crown's involvement in the bribery scheme at the time Crown joined GD's board and applied for a top secret security clearance.)

**Page 81**
" 'Mr. Crown's reputation' ": *The New York Times,* December 12, 1976.

**Page 81**
" 'We know we're clean' ": Cummings interview.

**Page 82**
" 'not that I *mind* owning it' ": *The New York Times,* December 12, 1976.

**Page 82**
" 'Just out of curiosity' ": *Ibid.,* February 21, 1960.

**Page 82**
" 'swallow or be swallowed' ": *Ibid.,* December 12, 1976.

**Page 83**
" 'as a director, not as an officer' ": *Ibid.,* February 21, 1960.

**Page 83**
"the worst debacle": *Ibid.,* December 12, 1976.

**Page 83**
" 'Roger Lewis was fit to be an office boy' ": Cummings interview.

**Page 84**
"Crown would convert his preferred shares": For an explanation of this complex stock arrangement, see *The New York Times,* April 9, 1965.

**Page 84**
" 'I warned Roger [Lewis] we'd take cash' ": *Ibid.,* December 12, 1976.

**Page 85**
"One Friday afternoon in Paris": The episode at the Hôtel Athénée is drawn from the Cummings interview.

**Page 85**
"they met with André Meyer": *Ibid.*

**Page 86**
"Meyer negotiated": For a glimpse at André Meyer's strong-willed, theatrical negotiating style, see Cary Reich, *Financier: The Biography of André Meyer* (New York: William Morrow, 1983), p. 217.

**Page 86**
"Crown's successful tactics": *The New York Times,* February 26, 1970.

**Page 87**
" 'we'd run *him* out of gas' ": Lewis interview.

**Page 87**
"Lewis does his homework": For an in-depth look at David Lewis's management style, see the cover story of *Business Week* (May 3, 1982), pp. 102–06.

**Page 87**
" 'McDonnell got into enormous detail' ": *St. Louis Post-Dispatch,* January 16, 1977.

**Page 87**
"Lewis brings out the best": Lewis observed that a company takes on the "personality" of its chief executive officer in a speech at GD's annual meeting in St. Louis, May 1, 1974, excerpted in *GD World* (May 1974), p. 3.

**Page 87**
" 'traces of magnolia and mint julep' ": Karol White, "David S. Lewis," *Sky* (April 1981), p. 27.

**Page 87**
"the broad and sluggish Savannah River": *St. Louis Globe-Democrat,* February 22, 1975.

**Page 87**
"His father": Details about David Lewis's family and childhood in South Carolina were provided by his uncle, Robert Walton, in an interview with the author, August 19, 1982; hereafter referred to as Walton interview.

**Page 88**

"St. Cecilia Society": Founded in 1762, the St. Cecilia Society was originally America's pioneer musical organization. "Members and guests are selected according to rigid rules and to attend a St. Cecilia ball is an honor as greatly coveted in South Carolina as to be presented at court," wrote the authors of the Works Progress Administration book *South Carolina: A Guide to the Palmetto State* (New York: Oxford University Press, 1941), p. 4.

**Page 88**

"The Great Depression . . . spared the Lewis family": Author interview on August 18, 1982, with Dr. William M. Bryan, Jr., a college fraternity brother of David Lewis who became a physician in Columbia, South Carolina.

**Page 88**

"The stadium needed a huge new scoreboard": Author interview on August 19, 1982, with J. Willis Cantey, a college fraternity brother and longtime friend of David Lewis who became chairman of one of the largest banks in South Carolina; hereafter referred to as Cantey interview.

**Page 89**

"His years at USC": Lewis's academic transcript at the University of South Carolina indicates he was a solid but unexceptional student who concentrated on science and technical subjects.

**Page 89**

" 'Huey Long is on the line' ": Author interview on August 19, 1982, with Dr. George Brunson, a college fraternity brother of David Lewis who became a radiologist in Columbia, South Carolina.

**Page 89**

"the Flying Dude": Jeanne Gray, "Naval Aviation Hall of Honor—Glenn L. Martin," *Naval Aviation News* (October 1982), p. 36.

**Page 89**

"his mother's unending enthusiasm": *The New York Times,* December 5, 1955.

**Page 90**

"the Pentagon's 1983 list": "100 Companies Receiving the Largest Dollar Volume of Prime Contract Awards, Fiscal Year 1983," *loc. cit.,* p. 4.

**Page 90**
"takeover battle": For a behind-the-scenes look at the Bendix versus Martin Marietta showdown, see Hope Lampert, *Til Death Do Us Part: Bendix vs. Martin Marietta* (San Diego: Harcourt Brace Jovanovich, 1983); Allan Sloan, *Three Plus One Equals Billions: The Bendix-Martin Marietta War* (New York: Arbor House, 1983); and Mary Cunningham, *Powerplay: What Really Happened at Bendix* (New York: Linden Press/Simon & Schuster, 1984).

**Page 90**
" 'Eligible for Rehire' ": *St. Louis Globe-Democrat,* February 22, 1975.

**Page 91**
"McDonnell was no newcomer to aviation": Several biographical details about James McDonnell were found in Roland Turner, ed., *The Annual Obituary 1980* (New York: St. Martin's Press, 1981), p. 483, and in his obituary in *The New York Times,* August 23, 1980.

**Page 91**
"The first twelve months": The early history of McDonnell Aircraft is presented fully in Rene J. Francillon, *McDonnell Douglas Aircraft Since 1920* (London: Putnam, 1979).

**Page 91**
"two and one-quarter drinks": Author interview with Ted Schafers, senior editor of *St. Louis Globe-Democrat* and longtime observer of McDonnell Aircraft, May 4, 1983; hereafter called Schafers interview.

**Page 92**
" 'Mr. Mac has something in mind for you' ": Walton interview.

**Page 92**
"his baby-faced assassin": Author interview on August 18, 1982, with Lewis's college fraternity brother John Lumpkin, a lawyer and former bank chairman, and Cantey interview.

**Page 92**
"Lewis's rise . . . was meteoric": Lewis's advancement at McDonnell Aircraft was outlined in a biographical information sheet supplied by the company, dated March 10, 1966.

**Page 92**
" 'The most successful military airplane' ": *St. Louis Globe-Democrat,* January 28, 1967.

**Page 93**
" 'You would read a lot about old Mac' ": Persons interview.

**Page 94**
"$27.5 million": *The New York Times,* January 26, 1967.

**Page 94**
"plagued with financial problems": For a fascinating look at the commercial aircraft business, see John Newhouse, *The Sporty Game* (New York: Knopf, 1982).

**Page 94**
" 'unable to make their DC-9 machines pay' ": John Godson, *The Rise and Fall of the DC-10* (New York: New English Library, 1975), p. 20.

**Page 94**
"sales and profits had tripled": *St. Louis Globe-Democrat,* January 26, 1967.

**Page 95**
"the takeover . . . proceeded smoothly": Newhouse, *op. cit.,* p. 135.

**Page 95**
"announced they would merge": *The New York Times,* January 14, 1967.

**Page 95**
"where the real power would reside": *St. Louis Globe-Democrat,* January 26, 1967.

**Page 95**
"Douglas's . . . pay was cut from $116,700 to $50,000": *The New York Times,* April 4, 1967.

**Page 95**
" 'living high on the hog' ": Schafers interview.

**Page 95**
"cuts were made in Douglas's . . . staffs": Charles D. Bright, *The Jet Makers* (Lawrence, Kan.: Regents Press of Kansas, 1978), p. 160.

**Page 95**
" 'he rose to the occasion' ": *Business Week* (May 3, 1976).

**Page 96**
"He wasn't happy": Lewis interview.

**Page 96**
" 'It was a destructive competition' ": Newhouse, *op. cit.*, p. 22.

**Page 96**
" 'I had time to make some kind of a mark' ": Lewis interview.

**Page 96**
" 'I wanted to be the chief executive officer' ": *St. Louis Globe-Democrat*, February 22, 1975.

**Page 96**
" 'no one is going to ruin the company' ": *St. Louis Post-Dispatch,* January 16, 1977.

**Page 97**
"Crown offered Lewis the presidency": Lewis interview.

**Page 97**
"Lewis would join GD as chairman": *The New York Times,* October 22, 1970.

## Chapter Five
## Tug-of-War—Electric Boat Versus the Navy

**Page 99**
" 'an adversary attitude' ": "A Discussion of Navy-Shipbuilding Industry Business Relationships," a report published by the Shipbuilders Council of America, Washington, D.C., October 22, 1974, p. 7.

**Page 99**
" 'the most dysfunctional element' ": Assistant Secretary of the Navy Edward

Hidalgo's testimony on October 4, 1977, before the Task Force on National Security and International Affairs of House Budget Committee, committee report, p. 56.

**Page 99**

" 'the whole future relationship' ": Deputy Secretary of Defense Charles Duncan's testimony before the Senate Armed Services Committee, August 24, 1978, committee report, p. 21.

**Page 99**

" 'The current shipyard owners' ": Brady M. Cole, "Procurement of Naval Ships—It Is Time for the U.S. Navy to Acknowledge Its Shipbuilders May Be Holding a Winning Hand," National Defense University, Research Directorate, National Security Affairs Monograph Series 79-5, September 1975, p. 36.

**Page 100**

"Shipbuilders Council of America": The description of the lobbying effort mounted by the private shipbuilding industry was drawn from the author's interview with Edwin M. Hood, then the president and chairman of the board of the Shipbuilders Council of America, March 25, 1983. Hood has since retired from those positions.

**Page 101**

"twenty-seven private shipyards in the United States": Cole, *op. cit.,* p. 6.

**Page 101**

"the General Dynamics division had logged Navy orders of $7 billion": The past accomplishments and sales figures for the Navy's principal shipbuilders were presented in "Naval Ship Procurement Process Study," a detailed report prepared by Edward Hidalgo, assistant secretary of the navy for manpower, reserve affairs, and logistics, July 1978, p. 9.

**Page 103**

" 'drop them in the water' ": Author interview with Herbert Fenster, a partner in McKenna, Conner & Cuneo law firm, of Washington, D.C., and GD's principal ship claims attorney, on September 24, 1982; hereafter referred to as Fenster interview.

**Page 103**

"Rickover . . . held positions in two separate agencies": Sheire, *op. cit.,* p. 6.

**Page 104**
" 'a master at blurring the line' ": Elmo R. Zumwalt, Jr., *On Watch* (New York: Times Books, 1976), p. 97.

**Page 104**
" 'Rick doffed his admiral's suit' ": *Ibid.*

**Page 105**
" 'Rickover can cause some problems' ": Author interview with William P. Clements, former deputy secretary of defense, September 9, 1983; hereafter referred to as Clements interview.

**Page 105**
" 'I've always been crotchety' ": Author interview with Admiral Hyman G. Rickover (USN-Ret.), by telephone, February 18, 1983; hereafter called Rickover interview.

**Page 105**
"acquired by conglomerates": Cole, *op. cit.,* p. 13.

**Page 105**
"sell the Navy a cow turd": Rickover interview.

**Page 106**
" 'The admiral was a unique person' ": Testimony by David Lewis before Subcommittee on Oversight and Investigations of the House Energy and Commerce Committee, February 28, 1985, distributed copy of statement, p. 29.

**Page 106**
" 'the United States considered itself so . . . advanced' ": Report on U.S. submarine program issued by the Senate Armed Services Preparedness Investigating Subcommittee, chaired by Senator John Stennis, September 23, 1968, p. 3.

**Page 107**
"travel underwater at about forty knots": An excellent source of technical information about a naval ship's specifications and capabilities is *Jane's Fighting Ships.* The description of the SSN-688-class attack submarine was drawn from Raymond V. B. Blackman, ed., *Jane's Fighting Ships* (London: Haymarket Publishing Group, 1969–1970), pp. 439 and 441.

**Page 120**

" 'Maybe there were only five thousand changes' ": Lewis interview.

**Page 121**

" 'it is the change orders that kill you' ": Senator John Chafee, testifying before Senate Armed Services Committee, August 24, 1978, committee report, p. 13.

**Page 123**

" 'Some shipbuilders are trying to turn' ": Admiral Rickover, testifying before Defense Subcommittee of House Appropriations Committee, March 24, 1977, committee report, p. 583.

**Page 123**

" 'The firms create claims' ": James J. Cramer, in an Op-Ed piece in *The New York Times,* drawn from his longer article, "The Bar That Beats the Navy," *The American Lawyer* (March 1981), pp. 29–33.

**Page 124**

" ' "claim" is not a four letter word' ": Robert Martin and Fred W. Geldon, "Planning for the Negotiated Settlement of Claims," in *Federal Contracts Report* (Washington, D.C.: Bureau of National Affairs, Inc., May 31, 1982), p. K-1.

**Page 124**

" 'the corporate equivalent of a nervous breakdown' ": Louis Kraar, "Electric Boat's Whale of a Mess: The Trident Sub," *Fortune* (July 31, 1978).

**Page 124**

" 'hard-drinking, clannish men' ": Patrick J. Sloyan, "Showcase Fleet Sunk by Scandal," *Newsday,* June 28, 1978.

**Page 124**

"The average weekly paycheck": "Naval Ship Procurement Process Study," *loc. cit.,* p. 26.

**Page 126**

"The percentage of skilled workers": Senator William Proxmire, testifying before Senate Armed Services Committee, August 24, 1978, committee report, p. 35.

**Page 126**

" 'we lost a good welder' ": P. Takis Veliotis, quoted in *The Wall Street Journal,* October 6, 1981.

**Page 126**

"the high turnover rate": "Naval Ship Procurement Process Study," *loc. cit.,* p. 27.

**Page 126**

" 'Marijuana and pills were introduced' ": Sloyan, *op. cit.*

**Page 126**

" 'work only three or four days a week' ": *The Wall Street Journal,* October 6, 1981.

**Page 126**

" 'When women walked by bra-less' ": Kraar, *op. cit.*

**Page 128**

" 'resulting in mammoth delays' ": Letter from Veliotis to Bryan, March 13, 1978, *op. cit.,* p. 5.

**Page 129**

" 'he was a good shipbuilder' ": Williams interview.

**Page 129**

" 'I chose to cut clean' ": *Business Week* (November 14, 1977), p. 44.

**Page 129**

"newly employed workers . . . were sent home": *New London* (Connecticut) *Day,* which closely follows activities at the nearby Electric Boat shipyard, October 25, 1977.

**Page 129**

" 'a Prince Charming he isn't' ": *The Wall Street Journal,* March 30, 1983.

**Page 129**

" 'I am going to maintain my delivery schedules' ": *Business Week* (November 14, 1977), p. 44.

**Page 129**
" 'making their own organizational charts' ": *New London Day,* October 25, 1977.

**Page 130**
" 'he wanted to go ahead anyway' ": Excerpts of a telephone conversation on November 30, 1977, between Gorden MacDonald and Takis Veliotis, secretly recorded by Veliotis, were played at a House Energy and Commerce subcommittee hearing on February 28, 1985. My account of this alleged stock manipulation was drawn from that hearing, *The Washington Post*'s report on March 1, 1985, and the Lewis testimony.

**Page 131**
"Lewis turned to Veliotis": *Newsweek* (February 20, 1984), pp. 58, 59, and 61.

**Page 131**
" 'I was the fella' ": Author interview with P. Takis Veliotis, former GD executive and a fugitive from justice in Athens, Greece, by telephone March 12, 1985; hereafter called Veliotis interview.

**Page 131**
" 'We never discussed the matter' ": *Business Week* (June 25, 1984), p. 115.

**Page 131**
" 'I believe in controls' ": *Business Week* (November 14, 1977), p. 44.

**Page 131**
" ' "Where are you supposed to be?" ' ": Williams interview.

**Page 131**
"the classic turnaround executive": Author interview with Joseph Kehoe, a management consultant with Coopers & Lybrand accounting firm, April 3, 1984, hereafter called Kehoe interview.

**Page 132**
" 'arm wrestling with the government' ": Williams interview.

**Page 132**
" 'an adamant set-in-concrete attitude' ": Clements interview.

## Chapter Six
## Tough Bargaining

**Page 134**

" 'One of the dreariest problems' ": Edward Hidalgo's initial conversations
with W. Graham Claytor, Jr., about ship claims and the assistant secretary of
the navy's position, were drawn from Hidalgo interview.

**Page 134**

" 'an unbridgeable chasm' ": Hidalgo reviewed the salient points of the ship
claims negotiations in an interesting article, Edward Hidalgo, "An After-look
at History," *Sea Power* (April 1982), p. 45.

**Page 135**

" 'This was a highly charged environment' ": Kehoe interview.

**Page 136**

"EB had already lost more than $300 million": The origins of the claims
dispute, from GD's perspective, are outlined in a comprehensive letter from
Veliotis to Bryan, March 13, 1978, *op. cit.*

**Page 136**

" 'The amount of income a company books' ": Cramer, *op. cit.,* p. 32.

**Page 137**

"the SEC initiated just such an investigation": An excellent description of the
Navy-GD claims dispute, as well as other instances of contractors seeking
"extraordinary contractual relief" from their military customers under Public
Law 85-804, was contained in "The Use of Public Law 85-804 (Extraordinary
Contractual Relief): Essential Aid or Bailout?," a 100-page report published
in March 1983 by the Better Government Association, based in Chicago, p.
69. (The SEC has reportedly initiated a new investigation of GD's alleged
failure to disclose to its stockholders relevant information about the cost and
delivery schedule of its Trident submarine program and the bribery involvement of board member Lester Crown.)

**Page 137**

" 'Defense contractors are remarkably patriotic' ": Fenster interview.

**Page 138**

"Ingalls's corporate parent, Litton Industries": For a description of Litton's claims dispute with the Navy, see the Better Government Association report on "extraordinary contractual relief," *op. cit.,* and the Memorandum of Decision issued jointly by the Navy and Litton, June 22, 1978.

**Page 139**
"Bell agreed to set aside . . . litigation against Litton": Hidalgo interview.

**Page 139**
" 'coaxing, cajoling, bullying, and arm-twisting' ": John P. Diesel testifying before Seapower Subcommittee of House Armed Services Committee, quoted by Cole, *op. cit.,* p. 3.

**Page 140**
" 'You're going to undress financially for me' ": Hidalgo interview.

**Page 140**
*"Lo cortez no quita lo valiente":* Hidalgo, *op. cit.,* p. 55.

**Page 140**
" 'My first job is to change things' ": David Lewis's description of his first meeting with Edward Hidalgo provides an interesting contrast with Hidalgo's recollections, in Lewis interview.

**Page 140**
" 'We'll sit around here for a year' ": *Ibid.*

**Page 141**
"the Navy's five-year shipbuilding plan": U.S. Navy five-year shipbuilding program, by ship type and number of hulls, fiscal years 1979–1983, submitted to Congress by President Carter in March 1978, cited in "Naval Ship Procurement Process Study," *loc. cit.,* p. 13.

**Page 141**
" 'I am an old trial lawyer' ": W. Graham Claytor, Jr., testifying before Senate Armed Services Committee, August 24, 1978, committee report, p. 91.

**Page 142**
" 'We regret most sincerely' ": Letter from Veliotis to Bryan, *op. cit.,* p. 21.

**Page 142**
"it ranked fortieth in size": U.S. Industrial Outlook, U.S. Department of

Commerce, Industry and Trade Administration, January 1979, p. 310, quoted in Irwin M. Heine, *The U.S. Maritime Industry* (Washington, D.C.: National Maritime Council, 1980).

**Page 142**
" 'come hell or high water' ": Senator Abraham Ribicoff recalled Claytor's assurances while testifying before the Senate Armed Services Committee, August 24, 1978, committee report, p. 3.

**Page 143**
" 'In *no* way . . . could this thing fail' ": *Ibid.,* p. 3.

**Page 143**
"The government forecasts the rate of inflation": Author interview with L. Douglas Lee, senior economist and manager of the defense economic service at Date Resources, Inc., July 6, 1982.

**Page 143**
"the apparent size of GD's *projected* loss": Navy-GD Memorandum of Decision, *loc. cit.,* p. 65.

**Page 144**
"GD had spurned the offer": Letter from Veliotis to Bryan, *op. cit.,* pp. 3 and 12.

**Page 144**
"Lewis was reluctant to accept": Lewis interview.

**Page 144**
" 'Come on . . . we've offered you twenty-five million dollars' ": Hidalgo interview.

**Page 144**
"U.S. shipyards had paid 83 percent more": "Naval Ship Procurement Process Study," *loc. cit.,* p. 37.

**Page 145**
" 'I always felt there was a wall there' ": Hidalgo interview.

**Page 147**
" 'This is one party's determination' ": Claytor testimony before Senate Armed Services Committee, *loc. cit.,* p. 91.

**Page 147**
" 'Rickover talking to the President' ": Hidalgo interview.

**Page 147**
"his father, James Earl Carter, Sr.": For an intriguing study of President Carter's relationship to his father and Admiral Rickover, see Bruce Mazlish and Edwin Diamond, *Jimmy Carter: A Character Portrait* (New York: Simon & Schuster, 1979), pp. 114–15.

**Page 147**
" 'I break out in a cold sweat' ": Georgia Governor Jimmy Carter, in a speech delivered June 13, 1972, to Georgia Association of Broadcasters, quoted in Betty Glad, *Jimmy Carter: In Search of the Great White House* (New York: W. W. Norton, 1980), p. 154.

**Page 148**
" 'They were not negotiating honestly and fairly' ": Lewis interview.

**Page 148**
" 'I urge you to find a solution' ": *Ibid.*

**Page 149**
" 'We won't even think of it' ": Hidalgo interview.

**Page 149**
" 'Graham, I've got a wonderful pretext' ": *Ibid.*

**Page 150**
"GD was already carrying losses": Letter from Veliotis to Bryan, *op. cit.,* p. 2.

**Page 150**
"wipe out all the gross profits": Navy-GD Memorandum of Decision, quoted in Hidalgo, *op. cit.,* p. 52.

**Page 150**
" 'this is something I'll report to my board' ": Hidalgo interview.

**Page 151**
" 'plunge General Dynamics far into the red' ": Kraar, *op. cit.,* p. 105.

**Page 151**
" 'I will defend those settlements' ": *The Washington Post,* May 5, 1984. For further information on Hidalgo's role in the negotiations with GD, see Jack Anderson's columns in *The Washington Post* on July 26, 1984, and August 23, 1984. (Hidalgo's role in the settlement negotiation and his subsequent work for GD are under investigation by the Department of Justice.)

**Page 151**
"terms of the 1978 ship claims agreement": Navy-GD Memorandum of Decision, *loc. cit.,* pp. 61–62.

**Page 151**
" 'That is unrecovered costs' ": Deputy Defense Secretary Duncan testimony before Senate Armed Services Committee, *loc. cit.,* p. 22.

**Page 152**
" 'I would have liked a deal like that' ": Rickover interview.

**Page 153**
"critics of PL 85-804": For an excellent study of the application of PL 85-804 in the settlement of defense contract claims, see the Better Government Association's report, *loc. cit.*

**Page 153**
" 'Hidalgo was personally driving the 85-804 wagon' ": Lewis interview.

**Page 153**
" 'With all deference to the Navy' ": Senator John Stennis, during a hearing of the Senate Armed Services Committee, August 24, 1978, committee report, p. 5.

**Page 154**
" 'a bailout for General Dynamics' ": Senator Ribicoff, testifying before Senate Armed Services Committee, *loc. cit.,* p. 4.

**Page 154**
" 'No sane contractor' ": Senator Claiborne Pell, testifying before Senate Armed Services Committee, *op. cit.,* p. 17.

**Page 154**
" 'The message the Navy is sending out' ": Senator Proxmire, testifying before the Senate Armed Services Committee, *loc. cit.,* p. 25.

**Page 154**
"the Navy hammered out similar agreements": Report on PL 85-804 by Better Government Association, *loc. cit.*

## Chapter Seven
## The Weapon Nobody Wanted

**Page 155**
" '*dog who walks on his hind legs*' ": Quoted from an insightful article, Henry D. Levine, "Some Things to All Men: The Politics of Cruise Missile Development," *Public Policy,* vol. 25, No. 1 (Winter 1977), p. 165.

**Page 156**
" ' "You're going to kill our B-1" ' ": Clements interview.

**Page 158**
"More than 10,000 were fired at the United Kingdom": James F. McMullen, "The Cruise Comes of Age," *Defense 81* (November 1981), p. 3.

**Page 158**
"efforts to develop an unmanned flying missile": "Cruise Missiles—From 'Bugs' to Buzz Bombs to the B-52 Bomb Bay," background fact sheet released by Boeing Aerospace Company, Seattle, Washington, March 1979.

**Page 159**
" 'the Gorgon program gave us a guided missile' ": Rear Admiral Delmar S. Fahrney (USN-Ret.), "The Genesis of the Cruise Missile," *Astronautics & Aeronautics* (January 1982), p. 53.

**Page 160**
" 'When my U-2 was shot down' ": Francis Gary Powers with Curt Gentry, *Operation Overflight* (New York: Holt, Rinehart & Winston, 1970), p. 371.

**Page 160**
" 'cruise missiles shared a number of handicaps' ": Robert L. Pfaltzgraff, Jr., and Jacquelyn K. Davis, *The Cruise Missile: Bargaining Chip or Defense*

*Bargain?* (Cambridge, Mass.: Institute for Foreign Policy Analysis, Inc., 1977), p. 6.

**Page 161**
" 'We learned that we need proper tools' ": Commodore Shlomo Erel, commander of the Israeli Navy, quoted in *The New York Times,* October 23, 1967. The account of the Egyptian attack on the *Elath* was drawn from articles in *The New York Times* from October 22 to October 28, 1967.

**Page 162**
" ' "See, *this* is what we're talking about" ' ": Williams interview.

**Page 162**
"cruise missiles won little support": Author interviews with Rear Admiral Walter M. Locke (USN-Ret.), the first director of the Joint Cruise Missiles Project Office, December 20, 1982, and January 4 and 13, 1983; hereafter referred to as Locke interview.

**Page 162**
" 'the theory that our carriers were so effective' ": Zumwalt, *op. cit.,* p. 81.

**Page 164**
" 'they feel it's *their* solution' ": Locke interview, December 20, 1982.

**Page 164**
" 'Their pitch typically will be a technical pitch' ": Author interview with Colonel Alan C. Chase (USAF-Ret.), staff member of the House Armed Services Committee and former air-launched cruise missile program manager, April 15, 1983; hereafter referred to as Chase interview.

**Page 165**
"They rarely bought weapons abroad": For a discussion of the obstacles foreign suppliers of weapons confront when they try to sell to the U.S. government, see Jacob Goodwin, "Cracking the US Defense Market," *Armed Forces Journal* (December 1981), p. 50.

**Page 168**
" 'the integrity of the source selection process' ": Author interview with William J. Perry, former undersecretary of defense for research and engineering, November 12, 1982; hereafter referred to as Perry interview.

**Page 168**
"Legislators, lobbyists, and public officeholders": Author interview with Representative Norman D. Dicks (Democrat of Washington), a member of the Defense Subcommittee of the House Appropriations Committee, August 10, 1982.

**Page 170**
" 'a replacement to the manned bomber' ": Chase interview.

**Page 170**
" 'by God, they were going to have a manned bomber' ": *Ibid.*

**Page 171**
" 'single most important tactical development' ": Admiral Hyman Rickover, testifying before the Defense Subcommittee of the House Appropriations Committee on the fiscal year 1972 appropriations bill, part 8 of committee report, p. 22.

**Page 171**
" 'I was a little bit biased' ": Williams interview.

**Page 171**
" 'Zumwalt didn't want Rickover's big missile' ": Locke interview, January 4, 1983.

**Page 172**
"campaigning *in his Navy uniform*": Transcript of tape-recorded interview with Melvin R. Laird by Charles T. Morrissey, for Former Members of Congress, Inc., April 18, 1979, available in manuscripts division of Library of Congress.

**Page 172**
" 'Laird's position is that the Trident submarine' ": *The Washington Post,* June 22, 1972.

**Page 172**
"Laird's strategic cruise missile didn't exist": See testimony from various witnesses before Research and Development Subcommittee of Senate Armed Services Committee, March 27, 1973.

BROTHERHOOD OF ARMS

**Page 173**

" 'Those geniuses think the goddamn thing' ": Henry Kissinger, quoted in Strobe Talbott, *Endgame* (New York: Harper & Row, 1979), p. 35.

**Page 173**

" 'Scientists and economists invented new techniques' ": Arthur M. Schlesinger, Jr., *A Thousand Days* (New York: Fawcett World Library, 1967), p. 293.

**Page 174**

" 'manure separator for the defense secretary' ": Defense reporter George Wilson, in *The Washington Post.*

**Page 174**

" 'Laird had his new program' ": Levine, *op. cit.,* p. 155.

**Page 175**

" ' "Start that cruise missile program" ' ": Williams interview.

**Page 176**

" 'More than 90 percent of the IR&D projects' ": Richard DeLauer, in testimony before Defense Subcommittee of House Appropriations Committee, April 28, 1982.

**Page 176**

"The amount of IR&D money available": Author interview with Richard B. Lewis II, technical director of the Army Aviation Research and Development Command, May 4, 1983.

**Page 176**

" 'studying fruit flies' ": Admiral Hyman Rickover, testifying before a combined meeting of the Senate Armed Services Committee and the Joint Economic Committee, September 29, 1975, from Part 1 of a series of volumes, *Economics of Defense Policy,* p. 168.

**Page 176**

"the Pentagon gains some influence": DeLauer testimony, *loc. cit.*

**Page 177**

"Lewis wasn't certain": Lewis interview.

**Page 177**
" 'It had to fly like an airplane' ": Locke interview, December 20, 1982.

**Page 177**
"The list read like a Who's Who": The historic significance of several of these missiles was drawn from a background information sheet produced by Boeing Aerospace, *loc. cit.*

**Page 179**
"Boeing reasoned that the OSD was interested": Locke interview, January 4, 1983.

**Page 180**
"Clements, a millionaire oil driller": *Business Week* (January 27, 1973).

**Page 180**
"He cut $50 million from SCAD's $72 million budget": A. A. Tinajero, "Cruise Missiles (Subsonic): U.S. Program," Issue Brief No. IB76018, Foreign Affairs and National Defense Division, Congressional Research Service, Library of Congress, updated January 18, 1978, p. 20.

**Page 180**
" 'we're the only game in town' ": Locke interview, January 4, 1983.

**Page 180**
" 'a Navy-sponsored family of missiles' ": *Aviation Week & Space Technology,* July 16, 1973, p. 22.

**Page 181**
" 'I argued to Clements' ": Henry Kissinger, *Years of Upheaval* (Boston: Little, Brown and Co., 1982), p. 273.

**Page 182**
" 'We would have *commonality*' ": Clements interview.

**Page 182**
" 'We'll let you play in our backyard' ": Locke interview, January 4, 1983.

**Page 182**
" 'This was a joke in the eyes of the Navy' ": Lewis interview.

**Page 184**

" 'Davey Jones fought the program' ": Clements interview.

**Page 184**

"a group of bereaved mourners": Locke interview, January 13, 1983.

**Page 186**

"an abandoned YMCA camp in the Catskills": Gerald Ford, *A Time to Heal* (New York: Harper & Row Publishers, Reader's Digest Association, 1979), p. 24.

**Page 186**

"It was agreed at Vladivostok": *The New York Times,* June 22, 1975.

**Page 187**

" 'red-orange flame like a Roman candle' ": *GD World* (March 1976).

**Page 187**

" 'Vought's tests were a failure' ": Locke interview, January 13, 1983.

**Pages 187–88**

"Should the ALCM . . . be deployed on B-52 and B-1 bombers?": For a technical description of the capabilities and mission of the ALCM, see J. Philip Leddes, "The Air Launched Cruise Missile," *Interavia* (June 1976), p. 580.

**Page 188**

" 'I would take an input from the CAIG' ": Perry interview.

**Page 189**

" 'In spite of the acquisition cost savings' ": DSARC II decision memorandum for the air force and navy secretaries, the chairman of the Joint Chiefs of Staff, and the director of defense research and engineering, signed by Deputy Secretary of Defense William P. Clements, January 14, 1977, obtained by author under Freedom of Information Act.

**Page 189**

"the Air Force was miffed": Author interviews with Robert Holsapple, director of public affairs for Joint Cruise Missiles Project Office, Washington, D.C., February 1 and 8, 1983; hereafter called Holsapple interviews.

**Page 190**

" 'one of the best briefings we got' ": *Government Executive* (January 1980).

**Page 191**

"Carter telephoned Speaker of the House": *The New York Times,* July 3, 1977.

**Page 191**

" 'I think that in toto the B-1' ": *Ibid.,* July 1, 1977.

**Page 191**

" 'breaking open the vodka bottles in Moscow' ": Representative Robert Dornan's reaction to Carter's B-1 cancellation and the comments of Senators Frank Church and George McGovern were reported *ibid.,* July 1, 1977.

**Page 192**

"As Brown saw it, the U.S. strategic posture": For an interesting look at how the Carter administration wrestled with its policy alternatives, see Harold Brown, "The B-1 Cruise Missile Decision," *Commander's Digest* (September 15, 1977).

**Page 192**

" 'This is an awfully expensive consolation' ": *The New York Times,* September 20, 1977.

**Page 193**

" 'I have more confidence in our estimates' ": Harold Brown, *op. cit.,* p. 10.

**Page 193**

" 'Night of the Knives' ": General Slay's pressure to formulate an air-launched cruise missile program in a few days was recalled in Chase interview.

**Page 194**

" 'getting leverage through technology' ": Perry interview.

**Page 195**

" 'I could have Locke report to me' ": *Ibid.*

**Page 196**

" 'That was our film President Carter saw' ": General Dynamics's Washington representatives, quoted in Holsapple interviews.

**Page 197**
" 'We're being set up' ": Perry interview.

**Page 197**
" 'my most senior engineer' ": Chase interview.

**Page 197**
" 'I wouldn't call it a public relations success' ": *Aerospace Intelligence,* published by DMS Inc., Greenwich, Connecticut, February 25, 1980, p. 4.

**Page 197**
" 'if we did well and Boeing did well' ": Lewis interview.

**Page 198**
"a debriefing document": Eleven-page document, entitled "ALCM Source Selection Debriefing," obtained by author under Freedom of Information Act.

**Page 198**
" 'It was a mistake' ": Chase interview.

**Page 198**
" 'they had zero influence on the decision' ": Perry interview.

**Page 199**
"a second source contractor": Author interview with James A. Schaeffer, contracting specialist with Aeronautical Systems Division, July 29, 1982.

**Page 199**
" 'the ALCM production quantity will be split' ": Internal memorandum assessing the ALCM's readiness for production, prepared by Dale W. Church, deputy undersecretary of defense for research and engineering (acquisition policy), April 10, 1980.

**Page 199**
" 'Leader-follower production in the out years' ": Undated decision coordinating paper to support DSARC III review of air-launched cruise missile program, April 17, 1980, p. 14, obtained under Freedom of Information Act.

**Page 199**
"Perry resisted that recommendation": Perry interview.

**Page 200**

"Their cavalier attitude irritated": Holsapple interview, February 1, 1983.

**Page 201**

"eyes and ears in a contractor's plant": Author interview with Major Daryl Hoppe, commander of the Defense Contract Administration Service Plant Representative Office (DCASPRO) at the Singer Company's Link division in Binghamton, New York, October 12, 1982.

**Page 201**

"DCAS officials were particularly annoyed": Author interview with Navy Captain John J. McKechnie, commander of DCASPRO at GD's Convair division in San Diego, November 22, 1982.

**Page 201**

" 'Buchanan's mentality is technology' ": Lewis interview.

**Page 201**

"the DCAS issued a Method D action against GD": Statement issued by the Joint Cruise Missiles Project Office (JCMPO), July 15, 1982. After GD had tightened its quality assurance program, the Method D was revoked on December 17, 1982. See also the transcript of a press briefing on the status of the Tomahawk program by Assistant Secretary of the Navy Melvyn Paisley and Director of the JCMPO Rear Admiral Stephen J. Hostettler, January 6, 1983.

**Page 201**

"McDonnell Douglas was given access to GD's designs": Department of Defense news release, issued April 2, 1982.

**Page 202**

"the Air Force decided to cut short": For an interesting analysis of the origin of the advanced cruise missile, see Michael R. Gordon, "Pentagon's Shift on Cruise Missiles Leaves Big Contractors Scrambling," *National Journal* (March 26, 1983), pp. 644–47.

## Chapter Eight
## The Fighting Falcon

**Page 203**

"the company's profits in 1984": GD's 1984 Annual Report, inside cover.

**Page 204**
" 'the biggest best engine' ": *Washington Star-News,* January 26, 1975.

**Page 204**
" 'it's like driving the world's fastest drag racer' ": *Ibid.*

**Page 204**
"GD has sold more than 2,900 F-16's": GD's 1984 Annual Report, p. 6.

**Page 204**
" 'some expert showcasing by the Israelis' ": T. R. Milton, *Colorado Springs Sun,* July 12, 1982, p. 5.

**Page 204**
" 'the F-16 is living up to expectations' ": Analysis of F-16 fighter in *Military Aircraft,* a market research report published by DMS Inc., Greenwich, Connecticut, p. 8.

**Page 205**
" 'We were going for lower thruster weight' ": Stachowski interview.

**Page 206**
"Boyd was the father figure": For interesting profiles of Colonel John Boyd and Pierre Sprey, see James Fallows, *National Defense* (New York: Vintage Books, 1981), pp. 27–31, 95–106.

**Page 206**
" 'You could start on John Boyd's tail' ": *The Wall Street Journal,* April 13, 1982.

**Page 208**
" 'They were attracted by each other's outlook' ": Fallows, *op. cit.,* p. 102.

**Page 208**
" 'Such a performance breakthrough' ": Testimony by Pierre Sprey on weapons acquisition process before Senate Armed Services Committee, December 8, 1971, committee report, p. 255.

**Page 209**
" 'When we looked at his claim' ": Author interview with George Spangen-

berg, former weapons analyst with the Naval Air Systems Command, August 19, 1983.

**Page 209**
" 'this study contains many fallacious assumptions' ": Analysis of Sprey's FXX study by Naval Air Systems Command analysts George Spangenberg and Frederick Gloeckler, excerpted in report of Senate Armed Services Committee's hearing on December 8, 1971, pp. 276–77.

**Page 209**
" 'All they did was criticize the concepts' ": Sprey, *loc. cit.*, p. 275.

**Page 211**
" 'It would have been desirable' ": Packard interview.

**Page 211**
" 'Lockheed made these compromises' ": *Ibid.*

**Page 212**
" 'The F-16 did not start out as a weapons system' ": Stachowski interview.

**Page 212**
" 'The prototypes were intended' ": John W. R. Taylor, ed., *Jane's All the World's Aircraft,* 1976–1977 edition (New York: Franklin Watts, 1976), pp. 287–88.

**Page 213**
" 'It's like a man buying a new suit' ": David A. Loehwing, "Arms Deal of the Century," *Barron's,* January 20, 1975.

**Page 213**
"Northrop was just as hungry": For an inside look at congressional politics and the weapons procurement process, see G. Philip Hughes, "The Congress and Lightweight Fighter Commonality," a case study prepared in 1979 for use at the John F. Kennedy School of Government at Harvard University. Northrop's business outlook is described on page 19.

**Page 214**
" 'When we started that fighter program' ": Lewis interview.

**Page 214**
" 'Not only does the craft give twice the combat radius' ": William G. Holder
and William D. Siuru, Jr., *General Dynamics F-16* (Fallbrook, Calif.: Aero
Publishers, 1976), p. 41.

**Page 215**
" 'They're not F-14's' ": Author interview with Air Force Major Edwin
Thomas, F-16XL test pilot at Edwards Air Force Base, California, November
18, 1982; hereafter called Thomas interview.

**Page 217**
" 'Schlesinger's decision showed his commitment' ": Author interview with
Frank A. Shrontz, former assistant secretary of the air force for installations
and logistics, February 24, 1984; hereafter called Shrontz interview.

**Page 218**
" 'We caught Northrop flat-footed' ": Lewis interview.

**Page 218**
"its quickest turnaround time at twelve minutes": Holder and Siuru, *op. cit.,*
p. 70.

**Page 218**
"a new VFAX could help F-14's": For a technical description of the proposed
VFAX aircraft, see *Aviation Week & Space Technology* (September 9, 1974),
p. 38.

**Page 218**
" 'These officers all had F-14 religion' ": Hughes, *op. cit.,* p. 3.

**Page 221**
" 'That was a billion-dollar delta' ": Author interview with Harvey Gordon,
acquisition management specialist in office of the undersecretary of defense for
research and engineering, formerly with the U.S. Air Force, July 21, 1983;
hereafter called Gordon interview. Gordon has since left the OSD for a job
with the Martin Marietta Corporation.

**Page 221**
" 'All of us agreed' ": Transcript of Air Force Secretary John L. McLucas's
press conference announcing selection of the F-16, January 13, 1975.

**Page 222**

" 'You want me to delay this program' ": Defense Secretary James Schlesinger, quoted in Hughes, *op. cit.,* p. 16.

**Page 222**

" 'We were quite satisfied with the outcome' ": *Ibid.,* p. 16.

**Page 222**

" 'I am here today to announce' ": Transcript of McLucas's press conference, *op. cit.*

**Page 222**

"$55 million contract to produce F100 engines": Department of Defense news release, No. 16-75, January 13, 1975.

**Page 223**

"The bars along Bomber Road": *Time* (January 27, 1975).

**Page 223**

"enthusiastic revelers watched promotional films": *Washington Star-News,* January 26, 1975.

**Page 223**

" 'The consortium's purchase' ": *Time* (September 23, 1974).

**Pages 223–24**

" ' "we would buy the airplane the U.S. Air Force buys" ' ": General David C. Jones, quoted in *The Wall Street Journal,* January 6, 1975.

**Page 224**

"the U.S. Air Force might eventually turn its back": Shrontz interview.

**Page 224**

"Belgian companies of all kinds": Associated Press story by Fred Hoffman, carried in *Washington Star-News,* September 3, 1974.

**Page 225**

" 'I suspect that the cost will not be the main factor' ": Transcript of McLucas's press conference, *loc. cit.*

**Page 225**
"When France sold Atlantic antisubmarine warfare aircraft": *Manchester Guardian,* October 19, 1975.

**Page 225**
"The Europeans seemed to be leaning": Shrontz interview.

**Page 226**
"Offsets came up early in the talks": The description of the bargaining with the European consortium was drawn largely from Shrontz interview.

**Page 226**
"If this 1,500-plane forecast grew to 2,000": Department of Defense Memorandum for Correspondents, posted December 3, 1974, nearly three months after the September meeting in the Pentagon.

**Page 227**
"Sweden . . . promised to build Swedish *automobile* plants": *Manchester Guardian,* October 19, 1975.

**Page 227**
" 'He was very instrumental in convincing the consortium' ": Gordon interview.

**Page 227**
" 'Future funding is to be contingent' ": Conference committee report to accompany HR 16243, the Department of Defense appropriations bill for fiscal year 1975, p. 17.

**Page 227**
" 'This has made all the difference in the world' ": Transcript of Defense Department briefing by Malcolm Currie, the director of defense for research and engineering, May 8, 1975.

**Page 228**
"The Maremont Corporation, an American machine-gun manufacturer": Senator William Hathaway, testimony before Senate Armed Services Committee, July 28, 1976, part 6 of committee report, p. 48, and *Chicago Tribune,* June 16, 1975.

**Page 228**
" 'The competition . . . was intense' ": David Lewis, speaking to Downtown Rotary Club, of Atlanta, Georgia, March 22, 1976.

**Page 228**
" 'technology had won once again' ": *Flight International* (October 23, 1976), p. 1253.

**Page 230**
" 'They'll wreck the airplane' ": *The Wall Street Journal,* April 12, 1982.

**Page 231**
" 'There's no reason why you should continue' ": Gordon interview.

**Page 231**
" 'I think it's one of the great planes' ": *The Wall Street Journal,* April 12, 1982.

**Page 231**
" 'One cannot—and dare not—presume' ": Letter to the Editor by Alton G. Keel, Jr., then an assistant secretary of the air force, published *ibid.,* May 10, 1982.

**Page 231**
"an adversary aircraft": GD's 1984 Annual Report, p. 6.

**Page 232**
"unprecedented in-flight maneuvers": "AFTI/F-16's New Way to Fly," a press release issued by the Aeronautical Systems Division at Wright-Patterson Air Force Base, current as of May 1982, and *The New York Times,* December 7, 1982.

**Page 232**
"AFTI/F-16 isn't intended to become a production fighter": Author interviews with Calvin R. Jarvis, a NASA employee and deputy director of the AFTI/F-16 test program, and Dale Ford, GD site manager of AFTI/F-16 program, November 18, 1982.

**Page 232**
"the Air Force chose the McDonnell Douglas F-15E": *The New York Times,* February 25, 1984.

**Page 232**
" 'Rather than make a quantum leap in technology' ": Gordon interview.

**Page 232**
" 'We've got proven hydraulic pumps' ": Thomas interview.

**Page 233**
"The shirt-sleeved technicians": Author interview with Air Force Major Harry H. Heimple, director of AFTI/F-16 test program, November 18, 1982.

**Page 233**
" 'test pilots as fearless flying jocks' ": *The New York Times,* December 7, 1982.

**Page 233**
" 'It's no small trick to find a pilot' ": Thomas interview.

**Page 234**
" 'It's a bad idea to forget that airplanes can kill you' ": *The New York Times,* December 7, 1982.

**Page 235**
"impressive photos": *Aviation Week & Space Technology* (September 6, 1982), p. 52.

**Page 235**
" 'It was the cleanest separation' ": *GD World* (September 1982).

**Page 235**
"his engine was consuming too much fuel": *Ibid.* (January 19, 1981).

## Chapter Nine
## Tanks for Everything

**Page 239**
"Chrysler had watched its auto sales drop": Chrysler's 1981 Annual Report, p. 29.

**Page 239**
"By the spring of 1981 Iacocca had tapped $1.2 billion": Chrysler Corporation Proxy Statement, April 17, 1981, p. 22.

**Page 240**
"CDI earned about $81 million in pretax profits": Memorandum from Lachlan W. Seward, acting executive director of the Chrysler Corporation Loan Guarantee Board to members of the board, March 8, 1982, obtained by author under Freedom of Information Act.

**Page 240**
"The company modified another 1,610 tanks": *GD World* (February 1982).

**Page 240**
"ambulances, troop carriers, and swamp buggies": Michael Moritz and Barrett Seaman, *Going for Broke* (Garden City, N.Y.: Doubleday & Co., 1981), p. 46.

**Page 240**
" 'The people in "corporate" did not really understand' ": Author interview with John W. Day, executive vice-president of the Chrysler Corporation and former president of Chrysler Defense, Inc., July 11, 1983; hereafter referred to as Day interview. Day has since left the Chrysler Corporation.

**Page 241**
"He reached into his pocket": Moritz and Seaman, *op. cit.,* p. 98.

**Page 241**
"a DARCOM lawyer had assembled a reassuring answer": Memorandums from Burton M. Blair, command counsel of U.S. Army Matériel Development and Readiness Command, Alexandria, Virginia, to Delbert L. Spurlock, Jr., general counsel of U.S. Army, July 21 and August 5, 1981, obtained by author under Freedom of Information Act.

**Page 241**
"defense division as a distinct corporate entity": Chrysler Loan Guarantee Agreement, dated May 15, 1980, Article 6, Section 6.37.

**Page 241**
"Once the novation agreement had been signed": Novation agreement among U.S. government, Chrysler, and General Dynamics, signed February 19, 1982.

**Page 242**
"60 percent of GD's sales came from the government": Speech by David Lewis at business meeting sponsored by Tsai & Company brokerage firm, New York City, April 19, 1976.

**Page 242**

"government sales accounted for 84 percent": Securities and Exchange Commission Form 10-K, submitted by GD for year ending December 31, 1983, p. 8. The figure for 1984 was supplied by a GD spokesman.

**Page 242**

"he hated to part with Chrysler de México": Chrysler's 1981 Annual Report, p. 2.

**Page 242**

"Iacocca had pointed proudly to CDI's annual profits": *The Wall Street Journal,* February 1, 1982.

**Page 243**

" 'he visualizes himself a bit like General Patton' ": Day interview.

**Page 243**

"Actually he had come to ask Secretary Regan": *Ibid.*

**Page 244**

" 'Our sales went to hell' ": Lee Iacocca, testifying on Chrysler Loan Guarantee Act and status of U.S. automobile industry before Economic Stabilization Subcommittee of the House Banking, Finance, and Urban Affairs Committee, April 22, 1982, committee report, p. 51.

**Page 244**

"He had headed Chrysler's European automotive operations": Moritz and Seaman, *op. cit.,* p. 225.

**Page 244**

" 'My recommendation was to sell it' ": Day interview.

**Page 245**

"cooperative tank development program with West Germany": *International Defense Review* (December 1981), p. 1657.

**Page 245**

" 'missile-rich environment' ": Letter to the Editor of *The New York Times* by tank expert Steven Zaloga, January 12, 1983.

**Page 245**

" 'Its special armor' ": Malcolm W. Browne, "America's Mightiest Tank," *Discover* (June 1982), p. 21.

**Page 246**

" 'My God, I'm being set up' ": Author interview with Harry Moyer, mayor of Lima, Ohio, July 27, 1982; hereafter called Moyer interview.

**Page 247**

"home to several large corporate employers": Letter from Lima Mayor Harry Moyer to Representative Michael G. Oxley, reprinted in *Congressional Record*, March 22, 1982.

**Page 248**

"unencumbered access to cars, trucks, and railroads": U.S. Army fact sheet provided by Lima Army Modification Center, Lima, Ohio.

**Page 248**

" 'We got enough out of the President' ": Moyer interview.

**Page 248**

"misgivings about Chrysler's . . . quality control": Day interview.

**Page 249**

" 'teething pains uncovered in the trials' ": Analysis of M-1 tank program, published by DMS Inc., of Greenwich, Connecticut.

**Page 250**

" 'Whenever a new weapons system reaches the testing stage' ": Harold Brown, *Thinking About National Security* (Boulder, Colo.: Westview Press, 1983), p. 233.

**Page 250**

"at the suggestion of A. Ernest Fitzgerald": Author interview with Joseph Volz, Pentagon correspondent for the *New York Daily News,* June 3, 1983.

**Page 251**

" 'It was something the public could understand' ": Author interview with Dina Rasor, director of the Project on Military Procurement, July 22, 1982.

**Page 251**

"She supplied a group of reporters": Author interviews with Bill Lynch, Pentagon correspondent for CBS News (currently on a new assignment), and Roxanne Russell, a producer in the Washington bureau of CBS News, August 8, 1983.

**Page 251**

" 'People took that eighteen-billion-dollar number' ": Author interview with Major General Duard Ball, commander of Army Tank-Automotive Command, July 15, 1983; hereafter called Ball interview.

**Page 252**

"The procurement community uses four separate terms": The description of four distinct cost categories is drawn from Gordon interview.

**Page 253**

"He needed at least $150 million on hand": *The Wall Street Journal,* February 1, 1982.

**Page 254**

"turn their capital assets into cash": Lee Iacocca, testifying at oversight hearing on Chrysler Corporation loan guarantee, *loc. cit.,* p. 49.

**Page 254**

" 'He can go through a four-drawer file cabinet' ": Author interview with General John Guthrie (USA-Ret.), former commander of DARCOM, July 26, 1983.

**Page 254**

" 'I'm going to sell our defense business' ": Day interview.

**Page 254**

"M-1 tanks required extensive rework": Appendix D of Novation Agreement among General Dynamics, Chrysler, and U.S. Government, signed February 19, 1982, p. 2.

**Page 255**

" 'There was some thinking that this was a fire sale' ": *The Wall Street Journal,* February 22, 1982.

**Page 255**
" 'We didn't want the bidders' ": *Ibid.*

**Page 256**
"Five Year Defense Plan": The difference between the Carter and Reagan defense spending plans was based on long-range forecasts published in Defense Secretary Harold Brown's annual report to Congress, dated January 19, 1981, p. C-10, and Defense Secretary Caspar Weinberger's annual report, dated February 8, 1982, p. A-5.

**Page 256**
" 'We weren't looking for a lobbyist' ": Day interview.

**Page 257**
"Cyr pleaded guilty in July 1982": *The New York Times,* July 14, 1982, and September 30, 1982.

**Page 257**
" 'Boileau was only a figurehead' ": Veliotis interview.

**Page 258**
"Boileau listened to Chrysler's sales pitch": Day interview.

**Page 259**
"thirty-fifth-largest prime contractor": "100 Companies Receiving the Largest Dollar Volume of Prime Contract Awards in Fiscal Year 1981," Department of Defense, January 1982.

**Page 259**
"Army officials cited several conditions": Letter and accompanying appendices from Delbert L. Spurlock, Jr., general counsel of the Army, to John W. Day, executive vice-president of Chrysler Corporation, January 15, 1982, obtained by author under Freedom of Information Act.

**Page 260**
" 'the company possibly is overrating the risks' ": Memorandum for Record by Major General Oscar C. Decker, Jr., following meeting between GD representatives and tank command officials, January 7, 1982, obtained by author under Freedom of Information Act.

**Page 260**
"General Ball . . . was also impressed": Ball interview.

**Page 261**
"The two Army programs brought GD about $100 million": Analysis of General Dynamics Corporation by Andrew S. Adelson, of Sanford C. Bernstein & Co. stock brokerage firm, August 1981, p. 52.

**Page 261**
"gave GD a clean bill of health": Memorandum on General Dynamics's financial status prepared by Brigadier General Charles F. Drenz, deputy director of Defense Logistics Agency, for George E. Dausman, acting deputy assistant secretary of the army for acquisition, December 29, 1981, obtained by author under Freedom of Information Act.

**Page 261**
" 'The Defense Department worries' ": Lewis interview.

**Page 261**
" 'Chrysler was consumed with keeping Chrysler alive' ": Ball interview.

**Page 262**
" 'When you don't see quality come onto the floor' ": *Ibid.*

**Page 262**
" 'How can anyone expect to sell *our* contract' ": Day interview.

**Page 262**
"Chrysler was selling not only its Army contracts": *Ibid.*

**Page 263**
" 'I get a little ticked-off' ": Ball interview.

**Page 263**
"a large chunk of cash up front": Author interview with Brigadier General William Burdeshaw (USA-Ret.), defense industry consultant, May 13, 1983.

**Page 263**
" 'If the price is right' ": *The New York Times,* January 29, 1982.

**Page 263**
" 'You just cut enough hair, Dave' ": Day interview.

**Page 263**
"Douglas Fraser leaked word of the impending sale": *The New York Times,* February 17, 1982.

**Page 264**
"greeted sympathetically in investment circles": Author interview with Arvid Jouppi, auto industry analyst, July 11, 1983.

**Page 264**
" 'the military-industrial complex's supercontractor' ": *Chicago Sun-Times,* February 19, 1982.

**Page 264**
" 'the Pentagon as dependent upon General Dynamics' ": *The Wall Street Journal,* February 22, 1982.

**Page 265**
"came as welcome news to the UAW": Author interview with Edward Finn, international representative and negotiator with the UAW in Lima, Ohio, July 27, 1982.

**Page 265**
" 'We're paying for the automobile division' ": *Lima News,* February 17, 1982.

**Page 265**
" 'We're in a booming industry now with defense' ": *Ibid.,* June 23, 1982.

**Page 265**
"This 'get tough' memorandum was left": *Ibid.*

**Page 265**
"The union intercepted the memo": Author interview with Marc Stepp, a UAW vice-president, February 1, 1984.

**Page 265**
" 'David Lewis is no shrinking violet' ": Author interview with Wolfgang Demisch, defense industry analyst, July 21, 1982.

**Page 265**
"Signs quickly went up": Author interview with Major Richard A. Pienkos, of the Army's tank plant in Lima, Ohio, July 26, 1982.

**Page 266**
"a conservative, button-down image": Author interview with employees of Davis Plaza Motel, Lima, Ohio, July 25, 1982.

**Page 266**
"selling its AM General subsidiary to LTV": *The New York Times,* July 26, 1983.

**Page 267**
"Land Systems was turning a small profit": *Barron's,* February 7, 1983.

**Page 267**
"With Truxell in place, Boileau returned": *Aviation Week & Space Technology* (March 28, 1983).

**Pages 268–69**
" 'He is not a management-by-exception guy' ": *Business Week* (May 3, 1976), p. 88.

**Page 269**
" 'In government business' ": *Ibid.*

## Chapter Ten
## The Fraud Fighters

**Page 270**
"they would *not* seek indictments": *Hartford Courant,* January 6, 1982.

**Page 271**
" 'Justice Department is systematically closing down' ": Letter from Admiral Hyman G. Rickover to Attorney General William French Smith, dated January 13, 1982, published in Part IV of a series of reports on Admiral Rickover and the economics of defense policy by the Joint Economic Committee, p. 403.

**Page 271**
" 'finding individuals to hold accountable' ": *Ibid.,* p. 404.

**Page 272**
" 'He certainly got a lot more mileage out of it' ": Author interview with Captain Charles E. Masalin (USN-Ret.), March 28, 1984.

**Page 272**
" 'specific examples of apparent fraud' ": Letter from Rickover to Smith, *loc. cit.,* p. 403.

**Page 272**
"This selling process has often been a problem": *Defense Management Journal* (Fourth Quarter 1982), p. 44.

**Page 273**
" 'The opportunity is there to steal one percent' ": Author conversation with Joseph Sherick, then the assistant to the secretary of defense for review and oversight, while working as a consultant in Sherick's office in early 1982. Sherick is currently the Defense Department's Inspector General.

**Page 273**
"Government contract fraud . . . takes many forms": For an interesting look at the types of activities that can tip off Department of Defense investigators, see *Fraud Indicators Handbook,* published by the Air Force Audit, Inspection and Investigation Council, January 1980.

**Page 273**
"1,000 miles of substandard parachute cord": Department of Defense news release, No. 69-84, February 16, 1984, and *The Wall Street Journal,* January 17, 1983.

**Page 274**
" 'If we see evidence of an intent to defraud' ": Speech by Jo Ann Harris, then chief of the fraud section of the Justice Department's criminal division, to the public contracts section at the American Bar Association national convention in New Orleans, August 12, 1981.

**Page 274**
"an arsenal of legal weapons": James J. Graham, "Federal Criminal Statutory Structure," *Defense Procurement Enforcement* (New York: Law & Business, Inc., 1983), p. 49.

**Page 275**
"the boss is implicitly telling his subordinate": Author interview with Richard
Sauber, one of the principal Justice Department attorneys assigned full time
to the initial Electric Boat fraud investigation, October 21, 1982; hereafter
called Sauber interview. Without detailing what happened inside the grand
jury room during the Electric Boat probe, Sauber described how the Justice
Department carries out such a criminal investigation. He has since left the
Justice Department to practice law privately in Washington, D.C.

**Page 275**
"Their targets generally are chief executive officers": Paul Galvani, partner in
Ropes & Gray law firm, Boston, Massachusetts, in remarks to a seminar on
defense procurement enforcement, Crystal City, Virginia, May 18, 1983.

**Page 275**
"the long-standing indictments should be dismissed": *The Washington Post,*
  January 4, 1983.

**Page 276**
" 'I must have read the claim four hundred times' ": Sauber interview.

**Page 276**
"EB executives said their bid in 1973": Lewis interview.

**Page 277**
" 'we did not think we were buying in' ": *Ibid.*

**Page 278**
" 'The contemporary grand jury investigates' ": Marvin E. Frankel and Gary
P. Naftalis, *The Grand Jury: An Institution on Trial* (New York: Hill & Wang,
1975), p. 100.

**Page 278**
" 'Open and unlimited probing is possible' ": Leroy D. Clark, *The Grand Jury:
The Use and Abuse of Political Power* (New York: Quadrangle Books, 1975),
p. 46.

**Page 279**
" 'It scared hell out of me' ": Judah Best, Washington, D.C., attorney with
Steptoe & Johnson, at a seminar on defense procurement enforcement, *loc. cit.*

**Page 279**
"Reporters peppered Attorney General Bell": Transcript of press conference with Attorney General Griffin B. Bell, New Haven, Connecticut, April 20, 1978, pp. 8 and 9.

**Page 279**
"before a Hartford, Connecticut, grand jury": *The Wall Street Journal,* January 6, 1982.

**Page 281**
"it cooperated with the Hartford grand jury": Lewis interview.

**Page 281**
"Hoping for a breakthrough": Sauber interview.

**Page 282**
"they hadn't identified any star witness": *Ibid.*

**Page 282**
"FBI submitted a report to Justice": Testimony by Richard F. Kaufman, staff member on the Joint Economic Committee, testifying before its Subcommittee on International Trade, Finance, and Security Economics on allegations of wrongdoing in Navy shipbuilding, October 31, 1984, unpublished stenographic transcript of hearing, p. 12.

**Page 282**
" 'We weren't surprised and are pleased' ": *The Wall Street Journal,* January 6, 1982.

**Page 283**
" 'finding the so-called "smoking gun" ' ": Letter from Rickover to Smith, *loc. cit.,* p. 405.

**Page 283**
"These assertions were untrue": Sauber and three other sources who requested anonymity.

**Page 283**
"the department assigned only one full-time attorney": Kaufman testimony before Joint Economic Committee, *loc. cit.,* p. 15.

**Page 283**
"GD also obtained a copy of the prosecution brief": *The New York Times,*
March 22, 1985.

**Page 284**
" 'I was unhappy that the case was dropped' ": Sauber interview.

## Chapter Eleven
## "Taki"—Fugitive from Justice

**Page 285**
"a company that controlled six banks": *Forbes* (January 16, 1984), p. 33.

**Page 286**
"$1.35 million in illegal kickbacks": A seventeen-count indictment was filed
in United States District Court, Southern District of New York, September 6,
1983, against P. Takis Veliotis, James H. Gilliland, George G. Davis, and
Gerald E. Lee. All substantive allegations against Veliotis described in this
chapter are drawn from the forty-eight-page document signed by William M.
Tendy, Acting United States Attorney. In addition, articles on the indictment
were published in *The New York Times, The Wall Street Journal,* and *The
Washington Post,* September 7, 1983.

**Page 286**
" 'faster than a farmer can chop lettuce' ": *Business Week* (November 14,
1977).

**Page 286**
" 'A huge cloud which hung over the Thames River' ": Senator Abraham
Ribicoff, testifying before Senate Armed Services Committee on settlement of
GD ship claims, August 24, 1978, committee report, p. 4.

**Page 286**
"He pried more than $250 million": P. Takis Veliotis, testifying before Sea-
power and Strategic and Critical Materials Subcommittee of the House Armed
Services Committee, March 25, 1981, committee report, p. 384.

**Page 286**
" 'Electric Boat consistently beat the new schedules' ": *Ibid.,* p. 359.

**Page 287**
"carbon steel bar stock in the Navy's own shipyards": Robert Bush, a quality assurance official with the Naval Sea Systems Command, at a NAVSEA-Shipbuilders Council of America quality assurance convention in 1980, quoted by Veliotis, *ibid.,* p. 365.

**Pages 287–88**
"Electric Boat had to repair or replace": *Ibid.,* p. 366.

**Page 288**
" 'we will hold the Government liable' ": Unpublished letter from P. Takis Veliotis to Captain Joseph F. Yurso, the Navy's supervisor of shipbuilding at Electric Boat, dated September 15, 1980, obtained by author.

**Page 288**
" 'inaccuracies, innuendoes, and implied threats' ": Unpublished letter from Yurso to Veliotis, dated September 18, 1980, obtained by author.

**Page 288**
"employees the private shipbuilder should hire and fire": *The Wall Street Journal,* October 6, 1981.

**Page 288**
" 'I told Rickover to go to hell' ": *Ibid.*

**Page 289**
" 'I can pound harder on the desk than you' ": Transcript of television report entitled "Trident: Shadow of Death," broadcast November 12, 1981, on ABC-TV's *20/20* series, p. 4.

**Pages 289–90**
" 'SSBN 726 is the lead ship of a new class' ": Unpublished letter from P. Takis Veliotis to Vice Admiral Earl Fowler, commander of the Naval Sea Systems Command, dated November 13, 1980, obtained by author.

**Page 290**
" 'They clashed pretty hard' ": Lewis interview.

**Page 290**
" 'Electric Boat has no intention of being bludgeoned' ": Unpublished letter from Veliotis to Fowler, *loc. cit.*

**Page 290**

"paid him $180,000 in 1980": John Lehman's financial disclosure statement filed with the Office of Government Ethics within the Office of Personnel Management, dated January 26, 1981, p. 2.

**Page 290**

"sold his firm to a British businessman": The discussion of Lehman's potential conflict of interest was drawn from his financial disclosure statement, *The New York Times* on December 27, 1982, and additional articles in the *Chicago Tribune, The Wall Street Journal,* and *The Washington Post* on December 28, 1982.

**Page 291**

" 'If you have a "gridlock" situation' ": Navy Secretary John Lehman, testifying before Defense Subcommittee of the Senate Appropriations Committee, April 9, 1981, committee report, p. 27.

**Page 292**

" 'I could save him a consultant's fee' ": *The Wall Street Journal,* October 6, 1981.

**Page 292**

"left the impression that Electric Boat was totally inept": Senator Lowell Weicker, testifying before Defense Subcommittee of the Senate Appropriations Committee, April 9, 1981, committee report, p. 1.

**Page 292**

"Lehman invited David Lewis to Washington": Veliotis testimony, *ibid.,* p. 52.

**Page 293**

" 'I told him in words of one syllable' ": *Forbes* (May 11, 1981), p. 199.

**Page 293**

" 'by delivering six new 688 class submarines' ": Veliotis testimony, before House Seapower Subcommittee, *loc. cit.,* p. 393.

**Page 293**

" '23,600,000 pounds' ": *Ibid.,* p. 364.

**Page 294**
"internal estimates showed": *The Washington Post,* February 10, 1985.

**Page 294**
" 'to save the premium costs of commercial insurance' ": *Ibid.,* p. 376.

**Page 294**
" 'collision insurance on your new car' ": *Ibid.,* p. 377.

**Page 294**
" 'I was incredulous' ": Lewis interview.

**Page 294**
"the Navy had frequently settled insurance claims": Navy Secretary Lehman's written answer to a question posed by Senator Proxmire, part of hearing record of Defense Subcommittee of the Senate Appropriations Committee, April 9, 1981, committee report, p. 37.

**Page 295**
" 'It just didn't seem right to me' ": Lewis interview.

**Page 295**
"Avondale . . . was awarded about $300 million": Jacob Goodwin, *Defense Week* (April 6, 1981), p. 2.

**Page 295**
" 'an asset I couldn't throw out the window' ": Lewis interview.

**Page 295**
" 'I do not have a ballpark figure' ": Dialogue between Representative Charles F. Dougherty and P. Takis Veliotis during House Seapower Subcommittee hearing, *loc. cit.,* p. 415.

**Page 296**
" 'there will be an out-of-court settlement' ": Representative Dougherty, *loc. cit.,* p. 433.

**Page 296**
" 'This was a massive challenge to the Navy' ": Lewis interview.

**Page 296**

"Lewis took his case to Edwin Meese III": Lewis's meeting with Meese and his subsequent negotiations with Lehman and George Sawyer are drawn from excerpts of Veliotis's tape recordings, as reported in *The Washington Post,* February 10, 1985.

**Page 296**

" 'The Department of Defense will *not tolerate*' ": Navy Secretary John Lehman speaking at the National Press Club, August 19, 1981, quoted in Defense Department compilation, *Selected Statements,* August–December 1981.

**Page 297**

" 'You bet . . . we went around to Meese' ": Excerpts of a telephone conversation in August 1981, between David Lewis and Takis Veliotis, secretly recorded by Veliotis, were reported in *The Washington Post,* February 10, 1985. My account of the events discussed during that conversation was drawn from that article and the Lewis testimony.

**Page 298**

" 'What really scared us about this' ": Excerpts of another secretly recorded telephone conversation on October 7, 1981, between Lewis and Veliotis were reported in *The Washington Post* on September 26, 1984. My account of the Ashton incident was drawn from that article and the Lewis testimony.

**Page 299**

" 'We agonized at great length' ": Lewis interview.

**Page 299**

" 'I decided life was too short' ": *Ibid.*

**Page 300**

"remove the quarrelsome Veliotis from day-to-day operations": *The Wall Street Journal,* October 6, 1981.

**Page 300**

" 'Veliotis had just burned too many bridges' ": Lewis interview.

**Page 300**

" 'sometimes customers are more equal than suppliers' ": *Forbes* (January 16, 1984), p. 33.

**Page 301**

" 'We didn't trust him' ": *Newsweek* (February 20, 1984), p. 61.

**Page 301**

" 'There was an awareness that we had to do our part' ": Lewis interview.

**Page 301**

"few of his colleagues took such talk seriously": Author interview with Warren G. Sullivan, formerly corporate vice-president of General Dynamics for industrial relations, January 16, 1984.

**Page 301**

" 'I wanted to know if Lewis would be stepping down' ": Veliotis interview.

**Page 303**

"earning a salary of $150,000": *Forbes* (January 16, 1984), p. 33.

**Page 303**

"ninety years in prison and more than $150,000 in fines": *The New York Times,* September 7, 1983.

**Page 303**

" 'a horrifyingly, terribly disappointing thing' ": *Forbes* (January 16, 1984), p. 31.

**Page 303**

" 'He didn't need the money' ": *Ibid.,* p. 33.

**Page 303**

"Federal prosecutors contended": All allegations against Veliotis, Gilliland, Davis, and Lee described in this chapter were drawn directly from the government's indictment, *loc. cit.*

**Page 304**

"a small restaurant-refrigeration firm in Brooklyn": *Newsweek* (February 20, 1984).

**Page 304**

"Lewis sent a routine memo to Veliotis": The indictment cites on p. 35 a telecopier transmittal on March 22, 1978, of a memorandum from David

Lewis delegating authority to Veliotis and Gilliland to award subcontracts to IDT, a standard corporate practice.

**Page 305**
"Veliotis may have actually received more than $3 million": Federal prosecutors, who asked to remain anonymous, told the author that the Justice Department suspected that the total kickbacks to Veliotis exceeded $3 million.

**Page 305**
" 'Now that this has all come out' ": Lewis interview.

**Page 306**
"a Dublin judge had ordered him jailed for contempt": *The Wall Street Journal,* December 8, 1983.

**Page 306**
"fifteen counts he had faced were dropped": *The New York Times,* December 8, 1983.

**Page 306**
"Davis was convicted": *Ibid.,* August 2, 1984.

**Page 306**
" 'The company knew nothing' ": *The Washington Post,* February 12, 1984, p. G-6.

**Page 306**
"Lewis admitted having heard rumors of a kickback scheme": *Forbes* (January 16, 1984), p. 32.

**Page 307**
" 'did Mr. Davis ever give or transfer any sums of money' ": Excerpt of Veliotis's deposition in Frigitemp bankruptcy matter, given February 28, 1980, in Boston, quoted in indictment, *op. cit.,* pp. 46–47.

**Page 307**
" ' "Are you going to testify?" ' ": *Forbes* (January 16, 1984), p. 33.

**Page 307**
" 'That, of course, was a devastating blow' ": *Ibid.,* p. 33.

**Page 307**

"a handsome private house near the American Embassy": *Newsweek* (February 20, 1984), p. 61.

**Page 307**

" 'He may miss the 20-room mansion in Massachusetts' ": *Forbes* (January 16, 1984), p. 31.

**Page 308**

"it slapped a restraining order": Restraining order issued by U.S. District Court, Southern District of New York, September 8, 1983, Order 83 Cr. 551.

**Page 308**

"Veliotis, in turn, has sued GD": *The Washington Post,* February 12, 1984.

**Page 308**

" 'why General Dynamics should not have gotten one penny' ": *Ibid.,* January 17, 1984.

**Page 308**

"A spokesman . . . 'categorically denied' the allegations": *Ibid.*

**Page 309**

" 'the information may prove an embarrassment' ": *Ibid.,* February 9, 1984.

**Page 309**

"another grand jury investigation": *The New York Times,* August 2, 1984.

**Page 310**

"he was a member of the Hitler youth organization": Formal answer to author query provided by L. Emmett Holt III, assistant general manager, public affairs, at Electric Boat division of General Dynamics, April 13, 1984.

**Page 310**

"Their iron fence was dismantled": Author interview on July 28, 1983, with Frank Pleso, a project engineer who had worked under Fritz Tovar at GATX Corporation, before Tovar was hired by General Dynamics; hereafter called Pleso interview.

**Page 310**
"spent most of the war in German-occupied Holland": Pleso interview and formal answer supplied by Holt, of Electric Boat, *loc. cit.*

**Page 311**
"The U.S. government granted him American citizenship": Fritz Tovar's Petition for Naturalization, dated July 22, 1974, filed with the U.S. Department of Justice, Immigration and Naturalization Service, in Cleveland, Ohio, obtained by author under Freedom of Information Act.

**Page 311**
"he was granted a top secret security clearance": Author query answered by Holt, *loc. cit.*

**Page 311**
" 'He occasionally got upset with the TV show *Hogan's Heroes*' ": Author interview with George Gaston, a former assistant to Tovar when they both worked for the GATX Corporation, July 28, 1983.

**Page 311**
" 'They didn't let me see their shipyards' ": Veliotis, testifying before Defense Subcommittee, *loc. cit.,* p. 54.

**Page 312**
" 'on a daily basis' ": *The New York Times,* March 22, 1985.

**Page 314**
" 'the questioned items are probably allowable' ": *Ibid.,* March 26, 1985.

**Page 314**
"violated any conflict of interest laws": *The Washington Post,* March 26, 1985.

**Page 315**
" 'doesn't play it straight' ": *The New York Times,* March 22, 1985.

# Epilogue

**Page 318**
" 'We face a hostile ideology' ": Dwight Eisenhower's farewell speech as President of the United States, January 17, 1961.

**Page 318**
"29 percent of the federal budget": *Statistical Abstract of the United States,* U.S. Department of Commerce, Bureau of Census, September 1979, p. 364.

**Page 319**
" 'The future security of the nation' ": Memorandum for Directors and Chiefs of War Department, General and Special Staff Divisions and Bureaus, and Commanding Generals of the Major Commands, quoted in Seymour Melman, *Pentagon Capitalism* (New York: McGraw-Hill, 1970), p. 231.

**Page 320**
"This industry of some 25,000 companies": Calculations based on data from the Defense Department's Annual Report to Congress for Fiscal Year 1985, dated January 30, 1984, p. 280.

# Index

Aaron, David, 148
Abington Corporation, 290
Abrams, General Creighton, 243
Advanced Fighter Technology Integrator
(AFTI/F-16), 232
*Aerial Attack Study* (Boyd), 206
Aeronautical Systems Division, 206, 212
Aérospatiale, 165
Agee, William, 90*n.*
Air Force, U.S., 14, 93
   cruise missiles and, 168–70
      air-launched, *see* Air-launched cruise
      missile (ALCM)
      confrontation with the OSD over,
      179–81
      decoy, 169–70
      interservice rivalry and, *see*
         Interservice rivalry, over the cruise
         missile
      view of, 170, 179
   development of a new fighter and, 16,
      203, 209–14, 233–37
   F-16 and, *see* F-16 Fighting Falcon
      interservice rivalry over, *see*
         Interservice rivalry, over lightweight
         fighters
   institutional view of manned bombers,
      170, 174, 190
   Office of Special Investigations, 272
   Systems Command, 208, 212, 218
   Systems Program Office (SPO), 237
Air-launched cruise missile (ALCM),
   181–202
   advanced version of, 202
   advantages of, 190
   choice between Tomahawk and, 183–86
      Boeing's lobbying efforts and, 184–86
      Vladivostok summit and, 185–86
      *see also* Interservice rivalry, over the
         cruise missile
   commonality and, 181–82, 186–87
   competition between GD and Boeing
      over, 196–99
   OSD and, 181
   predecessor of, *see* Subsonic Armed
      Cruise Decoy (SCAD)
   use of previous work for, 182
Airmail, 52–57
Allied Corporation, 90*n.*
Altman, Roger, 255
Ambrose, James, 254, 259
American Institute of Aeronautics and
   Astronautics, 184

American Marietta Company, 90*n.*
American Motors Corporation, 266
AM General, 266
AMRAAM missile, 230
Anderson, Jack, 153
Anderson, Neal, 204
Antiballistic missile (ABM) treaty, 171
Applied Physics Laboratory of Johns
   Hopkins University, 163
Archbold, Dr. Richard, 71
*Argonaut I,* 40
Armed Services Board of Contract Appeal,
   147, 153
Army, U.S., 14, 70, 156, 228
   Air Corps, 59, 211
   Air Service, 52
      airmail flown by, 52–57
      contracts for aircraft, 57–60
   Army Tank-Automotive Command, 251,
      259–60
   Aviation Section, 50–52
   Criminal Investigation Command, 272
   M-1 tank and, *see* M-1 Abrams tank
   Matériel Development and Readiness
      Command (DARCOM), 241, 254,
      256–57, 262
   sale of CDI and, 241, 244, 254–57, 259,
      261–62
Arnold, Colonel Henry "Hap," 53, 211
Arthur Anderson & Company, 298, 299
Ashton, James E., 298–300
Aspin, Representative Les, 192
Associated Press, 59
Atlas space booster, 178
Atomic Energy Commission (AEC), 103,
   104
Auto industry, 239
*Aviation Week & Space Technology,* 180,
   235
Avco Lycoming, 249, 259, 262
Avondale Shipyards, 101, 105, 295


B-1 bomber, 172, 174
   Carter, ALCM, and cancellation of,
      190–96
   Reagan's revival of, 195
   SCAD decoy and, 170, 180
B-26 Martin Marauder, 90
B-52 Stratofortress, 168–70, 172, 196
   ALCM and, 190–93
   decoy missiles for, 169–70
Baker, George, 36–39